GETTING IT WRONG:
HOW CANADIANS FORGOT THEIR PAST AND
IMPERILLED CONFEDERATION

Archbishop Desmond Tutu, Chairman of South Africa's Truth and Reconciliation Commission, has said, 'If you don't have some accepted history, the chances are you will not gel as a community.' This provocative book explains how divergent views of Canada's past have sown dissension between Québécois and other Canadians.

Paul Romney reminds us that both French and English Canadians once regarded Confederation as a compact of provinces and peoples, designed to enable each partner to cultivate its own distinct society. With the rise of Canadian nationalism, English Canadians forsook this conception for a centralist myth, which alienated French Canadians by its celebration of nation building and exaltation of federal power. Romney explains how English Canada's forgetting of the original vision led to a 'historic blunder' – patriation of the Canadian constitution without Québec's consent.

Lively yet learned, *Getting It Wrong* speaks to Canada's present condition. By disclosing a lost middle ground between the Canadian nationalist and Québec nationalist visions of Canada's history, it offers us a new way to share our past and thus, our future.

PAUL ROMNEY has been writing Canadian history for twenty-five years. He has taught at the Center of Canadian Studies in the School of Advanced International Studies, Johns Hopkins University, and currently works as a freelance writer.

D1235422

PAUL ROMNEY

Getting It Wrong:
How Canadians Forgot
Their Past and
Imperilled Confederation

UNIVERSITY OF TORONTO PRESS
Toronto Buffalo London

© University of Toronto Press Incorporated 1999
Toronto Buffalo London

Printed in Canada

ISBN 0-8020-4267-8 (cloth)
ISBN 0-8020-8105-3 (paper)

Printed on acid-free paper

Canadian Cataloguing in Publication Data

Romney, Paul Martin, 1945–
 Getting it wrong : how Canadians forgot their past and imperilled
 Confederation

Includes bibliographical references and index.
 ISBN 0-8020-4267-8 (bound)   ISBN 0-8020-8105-3 (pbk.)

 1. Federal government – Canada.   2. Canada – Constitutional history.
 3. Canada – English-French relations.   4. Canada – Politics and
 government.   I. Title.

 FC98.R656 1999   971   C99-930782-7
 F1026.R67 1999

University of Toronto Press acknowledges the financial assistance to its
publishing program of the Canada Council for the Arts and the Ontario
Arts Council.

University of Toronto Press acknowledges the financial support for its
publishing activities of the Government of Canada through the Book
Publishing Industry Development Program (BPIDP).

Canadä

To Sharon and David

Contents

Acknowledgments

'If I have seen further,' wrote Isaac Newton, 'it is because I was standing on the shoulders of Giants.' Such an acknowledgment is obligatory in a book of this sort, where one is forced to dwell on the errors of earlier writers while taking their achievements for granted. Let me emphasize that disagreement does not signify disrespect. This book owes as much or more to what other historians have got right as to what they may have got wrong.

The book is about political ideas, and I am especially indebted to the work of three historians whose achievement and example permeate it far beyond anything that endnotes can register. I refer to the writing of J.M.S. Careless on Upper Canadian politics, S.F. Wise on Ontario's political culture, and Ramsay Cook on Canadian political ideas and constitutional history. Other writings that I have found especially useful include Carl Berger's *The Writing of Canadian History*, A.I. Silver's *The French-Canadian Idea of Confederation*, Robert Vipond's *Liberty and Community*, and Doug Owram's *The Government Generation*. In a class of its own is that powerhouse of historical scholarship, *The Dictionary of Canadian Biography*.

I owe a special debt of gratitude to Richard Risk for a decade and more of fascinating talk about the Canadian constitution and its scholars. Dick also criticized part of the manuscript. Others who graciously read part or all of it, charged with telling me where it didn't make sense or might be improved, are David Aylward, Patricia Bradbury, Jason Bruder, and Sharon Kingsland. None of them is to blame for its faults.

I gratefully acknowledge the award of a fellowship in support of this project by the (U.S.) National Endowment for the Humanities. The book also embodies research funded by the Social Sciences and Humanities

Research Council of Canada and by the Osgoode Society for Canadian Legal History. I am grateful, too, for the enthusiastic interest of the director, Charles Doran, and students of the Center of Canadian Studies at the Johns Hopkins University's School of Advanced International Studies. Teaching there enabled me to develop a perspective that has greatly enhanced the book.

In the end, though, I owe the most to Sharon, my wife, and David, my son.

GETTING IT WRONG

1

Introduction:
'The Hard Light of History'

I hope this book may help to form a basis for dialogue between French and English Canadians. That was not my intention in writing it. I set out to examine what was wrong with the account of Canadian history that I learned at the University of Toronto some twenty years ago. And that is what I've done. In the process, though, I realized that I was rediscovering a lost middle ground between French- and English-Canadian ideas of Canada. One of the things that bedevils relations between the two peoples is the discrepancy between what they each learn about the history of their country. But I had stumbled on an English-Canadian tradition of thought that bridged the gap – a way of thinking about Canada (or British North America, as it once was), and about the relations between its peoples, which fitted quite well with French-Canadian ideas. That tradition had later vanished from English-Canadian memory. This book describes it and explains how it came to be displaced by other ideas, which most French Canadians have found harder to stomach.

The francophones of Quebec have traditionally learned a history designed to inspire loyalty to their homeland. In Quebec alone, the story goes, their political strength has sufficed to defend the national language and identity, which elsewhere in North America has fallen victim to the dominant English-speaking culture. Only steadfast unity in the face of the anglophone threat has enabled them to preserve this space to call their own, and only such unity can preserve it in future. This essentially adversarial stance towards English-speaking North America lies at the root of modern Quebec separatism. In the past it encouraged French-Canadian nationalists to accept their homeland's incorporation in Canada, and in the British empire, as the lesser of two evils, the greater being absorption into the United States of America. They knew what had befallen the French of Louisiana and what was happening to their nearer kin in New England. Nowadays, political absorption into the United States is a remote possibility, and the chief threat to the national culture seems to come from the rest of Canada.[1]

There are three main reasons for this belief. One is the fate of French-speaking minorities in the rest of Canada. The old hostility of anglophone majorities is somewhat abated nowadays, but assimilation continues apace. A young Quebecer spoke to me recently of his qualms at hearing young Acadians, members of the largest francophone community outside Quebec, speaking English *to each other*. Such a spectacle gives baleful force to a second cause of Québécois apprehension: the steady decline of French-speaking Quebecers as a proportion of Canada's population.

What chiefly concerns me here, though, is a third obstacle to amity between French and English Canadians: a Canadian nationalism that many Québécois see as inherently dangerous to the survival of their culture. One variant of this nationalism refuses to distinguish francophones – at least as encountered outside Quebec – from the many immigrant communities that have so enriched Canadian life, particularly since the Second World War. Another variant acknowledges the special status of French Canadians as one of Canada's founding nations but shrinks from conceding any special status to Quebec as a historic French-Canadian homeland and the sole province with a francophone majority. Such attitudes offend against a deeply rooted Québécois belief: the idea that Confederation was and is 'a solemn pact between two nations,' which bears on Quebec's status within Confederation as well as on that of individual francophones within Canada. Those words appeared in 1991, in an official report of the Liberal Party of Quebec,[2] but the idea of a *pacte solennel* is much older than that: the term appears in a petition of 1823, more than forty years before Confederation.[3] There it refers to a supposed understanding dating from the British conquest of 1760, but the basic idea is the same. It is that of a solemn agreement establishing the terms on which the inhabitants of the former New France, and their descendants, were to live as a community now that the conquest obliged them to share their homeland with the British.

Since the 1930s, if not earlier, English Canadians have been consistently unwilling to accept this French-Canadian 'compact theory' of Confederation. They have had several reasons for their reluctance, some stronger than others. One is the theory's vagueness. It makes claims about the basis of English–French relations in Canada, and about Quebec's place in Confederation, that are quite unsupported by anything in the dominion's founding charter, the British North America Act of 1867, or in any other official document. Not only that, it has a distinctly opportunistic aspect. It typically pops up in response to political exigencies, its claims varying as occasion warrants and sometimes seeming to contradict each other.

Another problem is the relationship between this *national*, or *cultural*, or *racial* compact theory, as it has variously been called, and a variant that has nothing to do with English–French relations in themselves. This is the *provincial* compact theory, according to which the federal compact regulates relations not between English and French Canadians but between the provinces and the federal government. Quebec is a party to this compact, but only as one province among others. This theory looks reasonable, because Confederation was worked out in detail by conferences of British North American government leaders. It has developed its own contradictions in the course of time, however, and those inconsistencies have provided still more ammunition to Canadians who wished to deny that Confederation was a pact either of peoples or of provinces – at least in any sense that affected Canadian constitutional politics.

But why *have* some Canadians wished to deny it? In the case of the *national* compact theory, some have been motivated by their perception of French Canadians as 'foreign,' and by a consequent refusal to admit them as equal partners in the Canadian adventure. Others have failed to see how the concept of equal partnership could be reconciled with special privileges for a particular group or special status for a particular province. There is also the fear that special status for Quebec could weaken Canada and lead to Quebec's secession. Concern for Canadian unity has induced many people to reject the *provincial* compact theory too.

While the compact theory of Confederation has been rejected as illogical, internally inconsistent, and unhistorical, then, the impulse to condemn it has arisen from, or coexisted with, a commitment to a certain ideal of Canadian nationality. Like Quebec nationalism, this Canadian nationalism rests on a vision of history. The basic idea is that the Fathers of Confederation set out to found a great nation, with a strong central government having dominion from sea to sea and with provincial governments of subordinate stature, exercising merely municipal powers. Such a notion leaves scant room for the idea of local autonomy inherent in the provincial compact theory, or for that of special status for Quebec.

Thirty years ago, one commentator summed up the resulting alienation of French-speaking Quebecers as follows. 'Unable to convince their fellow countrymen that the Constitution is a compact, they have lost faith in it themselves; as a result, they no longer feel bound by it and regard nothing as settled.'[4]

This is where that lost middle ground between English- and French-Canadian ideas of Canada becomes relevant. I have discovered that the compact theory had English- as well as French-Canadian antecedents and that the Confederation settlement accommodated both ideas without contradiction. Both ideas sustained the late-nineteenth-century campaign for provincial rights, which was led not by a French Canadian but by the long-time premier of Ontario, Oliver Mowat. Subsequently, however, the compact theory was weakened in English-Canadian thought by the fading of the historical memory that had previously sustained it. The resulting void was filled by that centralist, nation-building idea of Confederation which still prevails in English-Canadian minds. In this book I explain how that happened and consider its consequences. In the process I try to sort out those compact-based claims which seem to me to be historically justified from those which do not.

As I said, Quebec nationalism and Canadian nationalism rest on mutually incompatible histories of Canada. Archbishop Desmond Tutu, chairman of South Africa's Truth and Reconciliation Commission, recently remarked on the effect of such discrepancies in his own country and others. 'If you don't have some accepted history the chances are you will not gel as a community. Look at Northern Ireland or Bosnia. They have different understandings of what took place, and they use them to blow up the resentments that the original events caused, or exposed.'[5] The archbishop's remark highlights two aspects of the problem. We learn to identify with our own community, and the values for which it claims to stand, partly by learning about its history. How can Canada gel as a community if French- and English-speakers learn incompatible histories of Canada, and in particular if one group's history tends to portray the other group as an adversary? But if in the past the two groups have indeed been adversaries, as in Ireland or South Africa, lasting reconciliation cannot occur without a shared understanding of the history of their relationship. Unfortunately, in such cases it is more usual for each group to cultivate a history that justifies its adversarial stance: in the case of the dominant group, a history that projects its values onto society as a whole; in the subordinate group, one that justifies a posture of defiance and rejection and perhaps sustains a claim to emancipation or secession.

There are crucial differences between the Canadian case and those of Ireland and South Africa. Francophones as individuals have always enjoyed civil equality with other Canadians, and as a community they have normally wielded substantial power in federal politics. This situation has muted the intensity of ethnic conflict as compared with South Africa or Ireland. In Canada at large, however, though not in their ancestral homeland, francophones have formed a political minority since 1840. Among English Canadians this has fostered a tendency to minimize the significance of the 'French fact,' and among French Canadians a predisposition to see themselves as a beleaguered garrison. Each group has told stories about the past that reinforced those attitudes, and so the problem of conflicting histories has arisen in Canada too.

This book explores some of the ways in which Canadians' sense of history has influenced their political behaviour and describes the efforts of some Canadians to shape their compatriots' sense of history for political ends. It focuses mainly on the lost tradition of English–Canadian thought that I mentioned at the outset, recounting its rise, its bearing on Confederation, and its displacement by the nationalist interpretation of their country's history that prevailed among English Canadians for most of the twentieth century. The compact theory of Confederation is a crucial part of that story, but not the whole story. The lost tradition arose out of a quarrel among Upper Canadians over the nature and meaning of their identity as British North Americans, and that quarrel persisted into the twentieth century, outliving both the lost tradition and the British empire. This is a story about the ways in which Canadians have thought about their country and about their relationships with the Americans and the British, as well as with each other.

No English Canadian did more to shape his compatriots' sense of their past than Donald Creighton. He was the foremost Canadian historian of his day and was acutely aware of the political significance of his work. In 1965, alarmed by the resurgence of controversy about the compact theory, he gave a talk entitled 'Confederation: The Use and Abuse of History.'[6] Quebec's 'quiet revolution' had given new force to demands for special status. According to Creighton, it was impossible to make such radical proposals without adopting an attitude towards the past. Revolutionaries, even quiet ones, needed to make up their minds about history. Was their revolution aimed at repudiating the past or restoring it? They could blacken the past as 'the bad old days,' from which society must strive to escape, or simply dismiss it as irrelevant to present problems. Or they could idealize it as a golden age, to which society must strive to return.

Creighton feared that Canadians were ill-equipped to respond to any such strategy. Colonies had no clear sense of an identity separate from that of the empire to which they belonged. As a result, they were apt to be ignorant of their own past and indifferent to it. Since achieving full political independence from Great Britain, Canadians had been growing more interested in their national history, but they were still ill-informed about it. Having no firm understanding of whence they had come, or of the aims and ideals that had guided them, they faced the future in confusion. Their ignorance left them susceptible to false prophets weaving specious stories about the past.

'Ignorance readily accepts myth and is vulnerable before propaganda,' warned Creighton. Yet there was no real reason for ignorance of Canada's past and the principles on which the nation had been founded. There was a large body of records on the making of Confederation, and until the 1960s there had never been any substantial doubt as to the founders' intentions. Creighton launched into a brief account of those intentions and explained why they still offered valuable guidance to Canadians in their current political predicament.

I'll be referring frequently to Creighton's views on Canadian history and politics, and those of like-minded Canadians, and I wish to start by drawing attention to the terms in which he framed his argument on this occasion in 1966. First, there is the notion that history can be 'used' and 'abused' for political ends. This idea did not originate with Creighton, of course; it was familiar to anyone who had read George Orwell's *Nineteen Eighty-four*, in which the hero earns his bad bread and worse tobacco by rewriting back numbers of *The Times* to match changes in the party line. Creighton himself cited Orwell's novel as an illustration of the terrible end to which the abuse of history could lead.

Creighton's unidentified targets must have been non-plussed at the idea that they were doing anything remotely similar to what Orwell described; but in fact Creighton's Canada was a world in which the past was being rejected, if not revised, in ways that smacked of censorship. The term 'Dominion' had been banished from the vocabulary of the federal government; the Royal Mail had turned into Canada Post; the armed forces were about to trade in their British-style uniforms and insignia for new ones on the American model; there was a new flag, which bore no trace of the Union Jack. This was a far cry from rewriting the past, but Creighton revered his country's British heritage, and this purging of its symbols from Canadians' daily consciousness may have reminded him of Orwell's Oceania. In 1966, as today, Canada had its own brand of political correctness.

In such a world, history had its uses. It could remind Canadians of the Fathers' intention to found a British nation overseas, and not only a nation but a British-style state, with power concentrated (wrote Creighton) in a single sovereign legislature. One could go on to explain why the Fathers' purposes and values were still relevant to Canada's present condition. But Creighton found himself confronted by revolutionaries who were not content to discard history as useless. These revolutionaries wanted to *abuse* history by twisting it into a 'myth,' which could serve as 'propaganda' for the radical changes they wished to make in Canada's constitution. Creighton undertook to expose the falsity of these fabrications by shining 'the hard light of history' on them, and he warned that 'History must be defended against attempts to abuse it in the cause of change; we should be constantly on our guard against theories which either dismiss the past or give it a drastically new interpretation.' It was here that he mentioned *Nineteen Eighty-four*.

So Creighton claimed to be engaged in a battle between truth and propaganda, between the 'hard light of history' and the wavering, delusive, will-o'-the-wisp illumination of myth. Not by a word did he concede that his adversaries might be honestly mistaken: they were not only wrong, but the worst of liars. This was his way with the dead as with the living. Look at his treatment of Oliver Mowat, a Father of Confederation who dared to disagree with Creighton's great hero Sir John A. Macdonald – and therefore with Creighton himself – about the object of the enterprise. In the late nineteenth century, Mowat had led the resistance to Macdonald's efforts to make the provinces constitutionally subordinate to the Dominion. Creighton denounced Mowat for deliberately repudiating principles that he had previously endorsed; he accused him of trying to cover his defection by falsifying the official record of the Quebec Conference of 1864, which he had attended with Macdonald as a member of the Upper Canadian delegation. Not only that, but Mowat was also guilty of physical incorrectness: 'a short, rotund person, with a bland, bespectacled countenance and a slightly sanctimonious expression.'[7] One is reminded of what Frank Underhill, a colleague and rival of Creighton's at the University of Toronto, said about Creighton's monumental biography of his hero: that the book would have been more impressive as history if it did not so often portray Macdonald's adversaries as not only intellectually deficient and morally delinquent but also physically repulsive.[8]

I mention this because I am going to show Creighton doing exactly what he accused his adversaries of doing in 1966. I am going to present him as a leading figure in an intellectual movement whose adherents zealously propagated a new idea of the history of Confederation in order to justify their 'revolutionary' political goals and made it their life's work to convince their fellow Canadians to join them in restoring an idealized past. Unlike Creighton, though, I will not be calling anyone a liar; and this will make my task more difficult. It is much easier to call someone a liar than to explain how an admittedly intelligent person, in reading a document or musing on a sequence of events, came to make an honest mistake. Rather than taking that easy route, I will be trying to show that my subjects' understanding of the past – even their memory of the past – may have been affected by their political preconceptions.

I was alerted to this possibility by my gradual discovery of a pervasive bias in the account of Canadian history that I learned as a student. Actually, I had run into that bias even before my student years. One of the first things I read on Canadian history was a dismissive account of William Lyon Mackenzie as mayor of Toronto.[9] The year was 1973. I was employed at the City of Toronto Archives and happened to be working with many of the records that Mackenzie's debunker had used. I found many mistakes in his article, but what made them interesting was the way they tended to make their subject look bad. Rightly or wrongly, I concluded that an intelligent person could not have been so consistently mistaken unless he had *expected* – perhaps even, in some sense, *wanted* – Mackenzie to look bad. I don't mean that he wanted to *make* Mackenzie look bad; I mean merely that he had conceived a dislike for him and jumped as a result to certain conclusions that the evidence, on close scrutiny, did not justify.

At any rate, Mackenzie's debunker was in good company. I soon realized that he had not conjured his prejudice (if that is what it was) out of thin air. There was, in the writing of Canadian history, a tradition of distaste for Mackenzie and his rebellion. The old standard work on Upper Canada, first published in 1927 but reprinted in 1963, dismissed the uprising as an anti-climax, an ill-advised diversion from the provincial Reformers' campaign for responsible government (i.e., government by ministers who belonged to the legislature and held office at the will of the elective chamber). The current authority, first published in 1963, trivialized the misdeeds of the infamous Family Compact, the colony's ruling elite, and presented the rebellion as the work of a handful of politically naive extremists.[10] Even as I watched, the tradition was maintained by two scholars of a younger generation. In 1985 they published a book on the rebellion in which they contended that it had done little or nothing 'to further meaningful political reform.'[11]

This prejudice against Mackenzie and his insurrection matched the derision then falling on his grandson William Lyon Mackenzie King. King's newly revealed taste for seances, and his belief that he was an instrument of divine providence, only intensified a disdain for him among intellectuals that was already widespread.[12] King had revered his grandfather's memory and fancied himself a radical reformer in the same mould, but this only earned him the scorn of scholars who dwelt on the laughable gap between his aspirations and his achievements – either the guy was a phoney or he was out to lunch. But in the last analysis, all this personal scorn served to justify a political grudge. In Creighton's words, King 'had systematically undermined Canada's connections with Britain; and, instead of strengthening her national self-sufficiency, he had simply replaced the broken imperial ties with infinitely stronger continental bonds, which had effectively shackled Canada to the United States.'[13] In this at least – in treason – he had succeeded where his grandfather had failed.

Anti-Americanism, then, was one aspect of the bias I discovered in contemporary writing about Canadian history. Another was centralism: the belief that the Fathers of Confederation had meant to award the lion's share of political power to Ottawa but had been thwarted by judicial misreading of the constitution. This slant was even older than the anti-Americanism, and it was shared by historians such as Arthur Lower and Frank Underhill, whose nationalism was more anti-British than anti-American.[14] Still, anti-Americanism and centralism went well together: Confederation had many causes, but a leading one was the desire to present a stronger front against American aggression – military or diplomatic – and to form a transcontinental nation, which could occupy the western hinterland of British North America before it fell, like Texas, to American penetration. The cultural insecurity of French Canadians had dictated a federal union, but to most British North Americans of the 1860s, warily eyeing a neighbour country torn by civil war, federalism was synonymous with political weakness. While federal, therefore, the union would have to be as centralized as possible. So the story went. To most if not all nationalists, the decentralization supposedly imposed by the courts was the great tragedy of Canadian history. But even writers who held that decentralization had been good for Canada admitted that the courts had reversed the founders' design.[15]

This brings us back to Creighton's other *bête noire*, Oliver Mowat; for if no Canadian had done more than Mackenzie King to subjugate Canada to the United States, none had done more than Mowat to weaken Ottawa's power over the provinces. In fact, I was to find that Mowat had done even more in that line than the most vehement centralist suspected. In modern writing, Mowat cut the same sort of figure as King: crafty, duplicitous, and unheroic; ostentatiously principled, yet ever ready to sacrifice a principle to political expediency. He had hefted a loyal musket in 1837, and no one could credibly call him pro-American, although some of his supporters were less easy to exonerate. Still, there could be no excuse for his relentless pursuit of provincial rights, with its damaging effects on Canadian unity. If not treasonous by design, he was fatally small-minded in his failure to embrace Macdonald's national dream.[16]

It was in thinking about the treatment meted out to Mowat that I came to realize how completely the bias that I had first suspected in one man's handling of Mackenzie pervaded English-Canadian writing on Canadian history. I had occasion to look into Mowat's campaign for provincial rights, and to my surprise I found that he and his supporters claimed to have been fighting for responsible government. No writing about provincial rights or responsible government had equipped me to understand this claim. It was well known that responsible government had prevailed in every mature colony of British North America by 1855. How on earth could Ontario Liberals pretend to be still struggling for it thirty years later?

As it happened, I had made one or two discoveries of my own about the campaign for responsible government, and these helped me to make sense of the Liberals' claim. As I thought about it, I realized that I had stumbled on an entirely different way of thinking about Canada and its history of which the entire canon of scholarly writing offered scarcely an inkling. It was not a new way of thinking about it; it was an old way, which had inspired Mowat and his supporters but had somehow vanished from the memory of Canadians, leaving them no way of understanding him. Why had it vanished? And why had no one rediscovered it before me? It was in pondering these questions that I first began to grasp how the account of Canadian history that I had absorbed as a student functioned as myth.

What exactly do I mean by 'myth'? Not quite what Creighton meant when he said that 'Ignorance readily accepts myth and is vulnerable before propaganda.' Creighton framed his argument crudely, as a clash between truth – 'the hard light of history' – and politically motivated untruth. I am not going to accuse anyone of lying, as I said – not any historian, at any rate. What I mean by myth is a story that embodies a certain idea of the order of things – the natural or the political order – and of our place in it as individuals and as members of a community. Who are we, and why are we here? These are questions we hunger to answer, as human beings and as communities of human beings. Myths impart identity and values; they encourage us to think of ourselves in a certain way and act accordingly. The Bible depicts the Creation as the work of a Supreme Being, inspiring us to think of ourselves as His creatures and obey what the book itself, or its accredited interpreters, present as His commandments. What Creighton called the hard light of history was a story of Canada's creation, which fostered a certain idea of what it meant to be Canadian and marked out a course of political action that he believed was enjoined by that identity. His purpose in telling it was to combat a different story of Canada's creation, one calculated to promote a different course.

According to this view, a myth is not necessarily a story that is untrue. But it is unlikely to meet a historian's standard of objective truth because the story-teller's objectivity is compromised by an ulterior motive. There are such things as historical truth and falsehood, and I don't mean that it is either impossible or unprofessional for a historian to warn the public that a false or inaccurate account of the past is being spread for political purposes. In this case, however, Creighton's own account of Confederation was mythic in just the way he alleged of his opponents' account. He had perhaps done more research on Confederation than any historian before or since; but his account of it was biased by his nationalist ideals.

The clue to Creighton's bias lies not in his efforts to draw a political lesson from his understanding of the past so much as in his invoking the 'hard light of history' and warning of the need to defend Canadian history against attempts to abuse it for political reasons. Such language suggests a clash between absolute truth and absolute error. It is better

suited to divine revelation than to the provisional and tentative perceptions of past reality to which the historian can aspire. Historians can
hardly talk in such absolute terms even in *dating* events that were witnessed by millions. Canadians speak of an event that they call the Second World War or (in the Americanized argot of the media) World War
Two, which lasted from 1939 to 1945, but a recent book on Chinese history sees that war already raging in 1937,[17] while Russians are more
likely to speak of the Great Patriotic War of 1941–5. When it comes to
interpreting events, things get even more confused. Canadians and
Americans both think they won the War of 1812, in which they fought
each other; and French and English Canadians (as I said) have often had
very different perceptions of Canadian history.

And Creighton isn't even discussing an *event*; he is talking about certain people's declared or supposed *intentions*. To be sure, to him those
intentions were as certain a reality as death and taxes: 'With the utmost
clarity and precision, in speech after speech and resolution after resolution, the Fathers set out their purpose of establishing a great transcontinental nation in the form of a constitutional monarchy under the British
Crown. Constitutional monarchy meant, of course, parliamentary sovereignty – the concentration of legislative power in a single sovereign legislature; and, if they could have had their way, most Canadians ... would
have preferred to see all the British North American Provinces joined in
a legislative union under one common parliament' (as opposed to a federal union).[18]

We will see that the intentions of the Fathers of Confederation, and
the meaning of their speeches and resolutions, were less clear and pre-
cise than Creighton believed, and I will suggest that his explanation of
them reflected the faith of the true believer rather than the reasoned
conclusion of the scholar. For now I simply point out that his certainty
about what 'most Canadians' would have preferred is a case in point.
There was no election or plebiscite or referendum on the subject; in
those days there were no public opinion polls. Just how could he say
without qualification what most Canadians would have preferred? It is
a statement of faith masquerading as a conclusion of scholarship.

I don't want to dwell on Creighton too much. Myths are not generally
the work of single authors, though a myth may originate in a single
mouth. They pass down from generation to generation, each generation
adapting and embellishing the story to conform to its own sense of what
must have taken place. Sometimes two stories, quite distinct in origin,
combine to form a single myth. From time to time, some person or

group comes up with a variant of the myth that seems more convincing than the existing one, partly because it conforms better to the experience and perceptions of the audience – it 'makes better sense.' Such persons are honoured as prophets by believers and may be vilified in equal measure by unbelievers. Creighton's revisioning of Canadian history made a powerful contribution to the shaping of the myth, and it earned him much more honour than contumely. But the myth neither originated nor ended with him.

As it stood some twenty years ago, the story recounted the political history of Canada as an epic clash of two opposing principles – a 'Conservative tradition' and a 'Reform' or 'Liberal tradition.' The former was the principle of loyalty to traditional values, of national unity, of resistance to American domination. It was imagined as running from the United Empire Loyalists, through John A. Macdonald, to John Diefenbaker, then the latest Conservative prime minister. By establishing a new community in the northern wilderness, the Loyalists had bravely set bounds to the anarchic republicanism that had driven them from their old homes. By his promotion of Confederation, the Canadian Pacific Railway, and the 'National Policy' of industrial tariff protection, Macdonald had carried the resistance to American expansionism to its highest flight. In the changed world of the 1950s, Diefenbaker's efforts to save some freedom of action for Canada stood in noble contrast to the weak-spirited policies of his Liberal opponents.[19]

The rival principle was the negation of these virtues: it was the tradition of the rebel Mackenzie, of Oliver Mowat, of Mackenzie King, and of those lesser masters in treachery who, having toppled Diefenbaker, had gone on to wipe out the most cherished symbols of Canada's past. Liberals had been lukewarm towards the CPR and hostile to the National Policy. In the nineteenth century, some had been pro-American to the point of advocating annexation to the United States. The voters had turned that down, and it had taken King to find a better way. The very name Liberal imparted a taint; for 'Canadian conservatism,' with its exaltation of social stability and group identity, was imagined as standing in valiant, if doomed, opposition to 'American liberalism' – the atomistic, materialistic, invasive ideology of U.S. imperialism. The tranquil virtues of Peace, Order, and Good Government confronted the hustling, selfish individualism of Life, Liberty, and the Pursuit of Happiness.

Such was the myth in broad outline. Not everyone bought the whole package, but it set the terms of discussion. Sceptics might pick holes in it, but there was no alternative on offer: no equally sweeping and credible explanation of Canada's past, no equally compelling account of its identity and destiny. Dissent was trapped within the confines of the myth – it was limited to details.

Why was this story so compelling? First of all, much of it was true – it offered an explanation of Canada that rested on a solid basis of fact. Canada owed its existence to people who, for one reason or another, had opted out of being Americans. Canadians had spent a good deal of money and effort, and shed a quantity of blood, to avoid becoming Americans. Some Canadians, however, were less zealous in this enterprise than others, and such reprobates were to be found clustered along the line of political descent that led from William Lyon Mackenzie to his grandson. The Reform-Liberal tradition *had* included a pro-American element. Liberals *had* been hostile towards the CPR and the National Policy. Liberal governments *had* presided over the country's progressive absorption into the American empire.

The story seemed to make sense of the present as well as the past. To many Canadians, the swaggering, bullying, self-regarding demeanour of the United States in the era of the Vietnam War – the racism, riots, and assassinations – bestowed high credit on the idea that the business of being Canadian was that of being something better than American. It shed lustre on certain supposedly un-American values and institutions, which were celebrated as hallmarks of the Canadian political culture: international peacekeeping, public ownership of industries and natural resources, public broadcasting, public health insurance. These things verified the myth, and the myth verified them.

Some of these practices were associated with provincial government. To the intellectuals who chiefly cherished the myth, though, the ideal of positive government was indelibly identified with Ottawa's supremacy over the provinces. It had been so since the 1930s, when the Great Depression had underlined the importance of nation-wide economic and social regulation, but the identification had even older roots in the idea that one of Ottawa's chief tasks was the defence of minorities – in effect, francophone minorities – against provincial oppression. These centralists also valued the myth because it discredited the principle of provincial rights. Macdonald's centralism was exalted into the founders' common purpose, and Mowat was disdained for resisting it.

As I said, a myth need not be untrue, but it is unlikely to be the whole truth, because it is shaped by the impulse to instil values and identity.

That impulse was especially prominent in the way the story treated Mowat, which is why that part of it alerted me to its mythic character. It was evident throughout, though. The heroic Conservative tradition was worked out in loving detail and the rival tradition neglected, its exponents figuring mainly as foils to the champions of Canadian destiny. There was little interest in engaging with them on their own terms: apparently their record of weakness and perfidy repelled closer scrutiny. The very power of the myth closed off avenues of inquiry that might call it into question.

But how did the myth – this story that was true but not the whole truth – arise in the first place? Why were some aspects of Canada's past incorporated into the story while others were discarded and forgotten? That is the story I aim to tell in this book. It is an important one – important for the light it sheds on Canada's current plight. Many things have shaped Quebec's relations with the rest of Canada, but the centralist myth is one of the most powerful. The belief that the Fathers of Confederation, including those from Quebec, had meant to create a highly centralized union was pitted against Québécois aspirations for greater autonomy within Confederation. Those aspirations, in so far as they were founded on an idea of Canadian history that differed from the centralist myth, were denounced as deluded and baseless. And there came a day, in 1981, when the centralist myth influenced a judicial decision that was crucial to Canada's future. If English Canadians had remembered the ideal of Confederation that inspired Oliver Mowat's resistance to the centralizing policies of John A. Macdonald, the Supreme Court of Canada might not have decided that the constitution could be patriated without Quebec's consent.

This, then, is the story of how Canadians forgot a crucial aspect of their past and, in doing so, imperilled their country. The first half of the book traces the origins and growth of the forgotten vision of Canada; the second half explains how it came to be forgotten and why it eluded rediscovery. We begin chapter 2 with Oliver Mowat, at a turning-point in his career, speaking to the voters of the Ontario riding of North Oxford about the history of their province and the decades of heroic struggle that at last, in 1867, had culminated in the attainment of self-government – or at least the prospect thereof. I point out the crucial differences between Mowat's view of the past and the story told in modern history books and lecture halls, and I show that each version of the past embodies a myth of Canada's founding. Chapters 3 to 5 outline the events that engendered Mowat's vision – the Reform interpretation of Upper Canadian history, so to speak.

Part II presents Canada's founding in a light that exalts the power and status of the provinces far beyond the trivial measure admitted by Donald Creighton and his contemporaries. In the Reform interpretation, Confederation figured as a second great struggle for responsible government, Mowat's campaign for provincial autonomy being the third. Chapter 6 recounts the origin of the Reform idea of Confederation, as Reformers applied their ideal of local autonomy to their community's predicament within the united province of Canada in the 1850s. Chapter 7 describes how the Reformers' commitment to local autonomy influenced the Confederation settlement, and chapter 8 shows how it informed Ontario's campaign for provincial rights. Chapter 9 wraps up the argument by telling how the Reformers' quest for local autonomy led them to a rapport, founded on a shared understanding of Confederation, with their old *bête noire*, French-Canadian clericalism.

In parts III and IV I try to explain how the Reform vision dissipated and the effects of its disappearance. How does one explain the fact that people *stopped* thinking in a certain way? In chapters 10 and 11 we will see men advancing political views consistent with the Reform vision but failing to invoke history effectively in their support, while others – the originators of the centralist myth – boldly do so to discredit those views. I point out the differences between this centralist history and the Reform interpretation. Chapters 12 and 13 sketch the changing circumstances – economic, political, sociological, demographic – that killed off the Reform tradition and buried it ever deeper beneath the soil of oblivion. The resulting rift between French- and English-Canadian understandings of Canada widened as Quebec nationalism entered a new, assertive phase with the Quiet Revolution while anglophones groped for a new, non-British national identity that could hold fast against the threat of American domination. Chapters 14 and 15 relate that phase of the story; chapter 16 carries it to a climax with the election of a separatist government in Quebec in 1976 and the patriation controversy of 1980–2.

The rest is not yet history; but I offer this book in the hope that history can help us to understand it as it happens and thereby respond more effectually to the exigencies of the present day.

Part One

1820–1850:
Reformers and Responsible Government

2

Reform versus Loyalism: Two Canadian Myths

On a snowy day in November 1872, an unusual by-election took place at Woodstock, in southwestern Ontario. Both of the candidates were Reformers (Liberals), and both were members of the government. Oliver Mowat, the attorney general and premier, had resigned as a judge of the Ontario Court of Chancery only five weeks earlier to take political office. He needed a seat in the legislature. Archibald McKellar was minister of public works and agriculture. He had been leader of the Opposition from 1867 to 1870, when Edward Blake took over, and but for Mowat's intervention might well have succeeded Blake as premier. He was a member of the legislature already.[1]

Why then was McKellar running against Mowat? Was he an embittered loser, intent on harassing his victorious rival? Not at all. Within two years, Mowat's government would introduce the secret ballot in provincial elections, but in 1872 things were still being done in the old way. On election day candidates were nominated and seconded at the hustings, often a wooden platform specially erected at some central place in the constituency. The candidates would then make their pitch to the assembled voters, before the latter, in more or less disorderly fashion, made their way one by one onto the hustings to declare their votes to the returning officer. North Oxford was a strong Reform riding – just the place for a Reform minister needing to get into the legislature. Unfortunately, it was so strongly Reform that the Conservatives had not bothered to nominate a candidate; Mowat was in danger of being elected by acclamation. Nothing wrong with that, except that it would rob him of the opportunity to address the voters beforehand. That was why McKellar was nominated. He had travelled to Woodstock to show his support, as the senior member of the Reform caucus, for the new premier. Who better to run against Mowat for a few minutes while the latter got going on his election speech?

I am not sure why Mowat had to speak *before* being elected, instead of waiting to make a 'victory speech' after the return. Perhaps it had to do with the way by which Mowat had come into the province's top political job. He had been appointed by the lieutenant-governor on the recommendation of three leading Reformers: the retiring premier, Edward Blake, the provincial treasurer, Alexander Mackenzie, and George Brown, proprietor of the Toronto *Globe* and still the most influential Reformer of all. Blake and Mackenzie were members of the Canadian Parliament too, and a new Ontario law forbade simultaneous membership of Parliament and the provincial legislature. Both men had opted for Ottawa – where, in a year's time, Mackenzie would take office as prime minister. In Toronto, the Reformers had overthrown the government of John Sandfield Macdonald less than a year earlier, but by a majority of only one on a vote of confidence. With such a precarious hold on power, they needed the most prestigious and effective leader they could find. Stalwart trooper though he was, McKellar did not fill the bill any better than he had in 1870. As a Father of Confederation, as a judge, as Brown's loyal lieutenant in the political struggles that had resulted in Confederation, and as a practical politician of genius, Mowat did.[2]

But his elevation to the premiership was conspicuously lacking in any tincture of popular approval. He had not been elected to lead the Ontario Reformers; he had not won the premiership as an acknowledged party leader at a general election; he was not even a member of the legislature. Unanimous election by a strongly Reform constituency was the nearest thing to a popular crowning that could be laid on at short notice, but the premier must be heard first – heard making his first political speech since his appointment to the bench in 1864.

Mowat's opening remarks make it clear that this was the nature of the occasion.[3] North Oxford, he said, had long been known among Reformers as the banner constituency of Upper Canada. The invitation to stand there told him that its electors still remembered the part he had played in their battles and those of their country. It was of the utmost importance that someone in his position should have the support of such a constituency – one composed of electors whose hearts were full of Reform principles, one that would never tolerate a representative who went against Reform principles. Such a constituency gave courage to the heart and strength to the arm of its representative; it emboldened him in hours of depression and difficulty; it gave him moral power (he said) in discharging the duties of his office.

This was trite stuff, but such words are not necessarily meaningless. Mowat's remarks defined the occasion as a moment of spiritual communion between the newly appointed premier and the people to whose service he had been called. On this truly auspicious day, what was his message to the people, reported in the *Globe* in four long columns of tiny print? Surprisingly, perhaps, much of it was a history lesson – a recapitulation of the political history of Upper Canada. In it we can discern the outline of an almost forgotten vision of Canadian history – one that pitted a virtuous people against a venal elite and saw Confederation as a phase in that struggle.

He began by reminding the electors of some earlier Oxford County representatives. Sir Francis Hincks had led them in the struggle for responsible government and had risen to become co-premier of United Canada, the province formed by the union of Upper and Lower Canada in 1841, but then he had taken up views that they considered incompatible with Reform principles, and they had parted company with him. (Cheers.) Then had come the Hon. William McDougall. (Laughter.) McDougall had once been a leader of the radical 'Clear Grit' Reformers. More recently both he and Hincks had served in John A. Macdonald's Conservative federal cabinet. Mowat, however, recalled those not-so-distant days when McDougall and he had fought side by side for Reform, and he voiced his regret that McDougall was not there today. Last, to cheers and applause, Mowat mentioned George Brown. By his splendid abilities, powerful oratory, indomitable energy, and noble patriotism, Brown had made himself a name 'that would live in the history of our Province as long as our Province had a history.' (Cheers.)[4]

Such names, said Mowat, must remind old Reformers of the long struggle for Reform principles. He proceeded himself to remind old and young alike. First he recalled the time when the affairs of Upper Canada had not been in the hands of the people but had been rather in those of an oppressive oligarchy, the Family Compact, and its minions – a time when the people's representatives had had no control over the public administration and expenditure. This was a state of things to which no people could tamely submit and at the same time be free, and it might be said that it would have justified the rebellion of any people. From this careful allusion to the uprising of 1837, Mowat moved on to the union of Upper and Lower Canada in 1841, and the declaration of the legislative assembly that same year that the people (as he put it) should thenceforth enjoy all the advantages of responsible government. With that, 'one of the great reforms for which the Reform party had been for years contending was at last accomplished.' But jubilation was premature, because of the interpretation that a new governor general, Lord Metcalfe, had put on the assembly's words. Several years were to pass before responsible government was finally secured.

Was exultation then at last in order? Alas, there was no reform in which the people could rest content. They must ever be standing on the watch, in order that reforms once achieved – liberty once gained – might be made secure. From the domination of the Family Compact, Upper Canada had passed under that of Lower Canada, and it had been necessary to make another stand. The great power of the Lower Canadian members in the legislature – a result of their always voting as a bloc – had resulted in extravagant expenditure on that section of the united province and constant interference in the affairs of Upper Canada against the will of a majority of its representatives. This evil was aggravated by a provision of the Act of Union that gave each section an equal number of seats, although Upper Canada had the larger population.

So began the campaign for representation by population – 'rep by pop' – indelibly associated with the name of George Brown. In 1858 Brown had come to office, only to see another governor general, Sir Edmund Head, thwart his bid for power by refusing to dissolve the legislature and call a general election. The struggle had gone on, and Canadian politics had fallen into such a state of deadlock that great constitutional reforms were unavoidable. Representation by population must be instituted, and each section put in sole charge of its local affairs. In 1864 Brown had again taken office, this time in coalition with John A. Macdonald, and their collaboration had resulted in Confederation.

Confederation. It was impossible to overestimate its importance. It had given the Reformers everything for which they had been struggling up to that time: representation by population in Canadian affairs and self-government in local affairs. There was still a Canadian government, but now it was confined to matters of common interest. Ontarians' money (said Mowat) could no longer be taken for the benefit of Lower Canada; their school system could never again be modified without their consent. But Confederation had done more than this. Loyal men as they all were (there were no female voters in those days), they had feared that, if they continued as separate provinces, they might be absorbed into the great American republic. Confederation was an important step towards rendering that event very distant or, rather, wholly impossible. (Hear, hear.) He hoped that it had made it wholly impossible. He saw no reason why this nation in the north, a free Russia in British America, should not be strong enough to hold its own against all the nations of the world, while still cordially acknowledging the supremacy of the imperial Parliament; a nation not independent of every other but still forming part, and desiring ever to form part, of that loved land from which we had sprung, whose language we spoke, whose institutions we had adopted or imitated, whose glorious history was our own ...

The history lesson was over, but the lessons of history remained. The people must be ever standing on the watch. The glorious promise of Confederation could be achieved only if the governments of Canada and Ontario were in trustworthy hands. Mowat launched into an attack on the late John Sandfield Macdonald and his provincial government. Sandfield Macdonald's had definitely not been trustworthy hands. Though a professed Reformer, he had opposed both 'rep by pop' and the Brownite policy of converting United Canada into a federal union. He had collaborated with John A. Macdonald against Brown's supporters in the simultaneous Dominion and provincial elections that followed Confederation in 1867 and had led a 'non-party' government, mainly with Conservative support, until its defeat in 1871.[5]

The events in Mowat's story have become standard items in many a textbook, and his history of Canada may read like a bland and familiar sketch of thirty years of politics. That is just what you might expect. 'Bland' has become one of the stock epithets applied to Mowat (along with 'conservative,' which allows historians to dwell on the paradox of the Liberal who was more conservative than his Conservative rivals).[6] But to his younger contemporary, the historian John Charles Dent, the premier was an 'advanced Liberal' who did not believe that the time had come for putting all his theories into practice. George Ross, a long-time cabinet colleague who later became premier himself, fused the two perspectives: 'Naturally conservative, when the psychological moment arrived, however, he would cast his idols to the moles and bats and lead a procession of the most advanced radicals with all the enthusiasm of a new convert.'[7]

If Mowat was bland, he was bland to a purpose, and his bland summary of Canadian political history, delivered at his coronation on that snowy day in Woodstock in 1872, was in fact the expression of a radically dissenting, if not subversive, view of the past. If this is not

immediately apparent, there are two reasons, in addition to the bland-
ness of Mowat's exposition. One reason is that the historical vision he
voiced that day has long since disappeared from our collective memory.
The other is that its distinctiveness is evident less in what Mowat said
than in what he did not say.

As I said, most of Mowat's story is perfectly familiar to modern ears.
Historians still tell of how the rebellions gave rise to Lord Durham's
appointment as governor general and in due course to his famous report
recommending that Upper and Lower Canada be reunited under a
single government responsible to the provincial legislature. Union followed in short order, and in 1841 Robert Baldwin, the leader of the
Upper Canadian Reformers, moved a series of resolutions in the legislature designed to confirm that responsible government, as the Reformers
understood it, now prevailed in Canada. Baldwin withdrew his resolutions in favour of a set preferred by the government, but only on the
understanding that these bore substantially the same meaning as his
own.[8]

The next year the Reformers came to power in alliance with the
French-Canadian bloc led by Louis-Hippolyte LaFontaine, but in 1843
they resigned after quarrelling with a new governor general, Sir Charles
(later Lord) Metcalfe, over the meaning of responsible government. Metcalfe was upheld by the British government, and the Reformers were
badly defeated in the general election of 1844. Despite the success of
LaFontaine and his followers in Lower Canada, the allies remained in
opposition for more than three years. They resumed office only after a
sweeping victory in the general election of 1847–8. Meanwhile Britain
had come to accept the allies' conception of responsible government,
and that system came into effect in all the North American colonies
within a few years.

Then came six rather turbulent years of Reform government, first
(until 1851) under LaFontaine and Baldwin and then under Francis
Hincks and Augustin-Norbert Morin. The turmoil arose partly from
conservative resentment of the new state of affairs: Montreal and Toronto saw furious rioting in 1849, in which Orangemen played a leading
part. More important from the Reform point of view, though, was a
resurgence of the radical populism that had fuelled the Upper Canadian
rebellion. Many Reformers, especially those of the western peninsula
lying between Lakes Erie and Huron, disliked the costly and centralized
administrative structure that United Canada had inherited from the old

oligarchic provinces. To them, responsible government was no bargain in itself: they also wanted a cheaper, decentralized system, the filling of local offices by election rather than appointment, and an end to the professional monopolies enjoyed by the province's lawyers and doctors.

When these changes did not materialize, they turned from their new leaders to older ones. William Lyon Mackenzie was quickly elected to the legislature after returning in 1849 from twelve years' exile; his collaborator in rebellion, the veteran Reformer John Rolph, was elected in 1851 and went straight into the cabinet. In 1851, too, Mackenzie's move to abolish the Upper Canadian Court of Chancery received overwhelming support from the Upper Canadian members, and the government defeated it only with Lower Canadian support. It was an early instance of what Mowat was to call domination by Lower Canada. Robert Baldwin treated the result as a vote of no confidence and resigned from the government, but later ministers would not quit so readily.

By 1854 most of the Reform leaders had concluded that, with responsible government accomplished, they had more in common with their old Tory foes than with their own fractious followers. The French-Canadian majority came to a similar conclusion, and a political realignment took place. Most of Hincks's collaborators combined with the Upper Canadian Tories to form the Liberal Conservative party, of which John A. Macdonald, a canny lawyer-politician from Kingston, quickly established himself as leader. They and their *bleu* allies were to govern United Canada for the next eight years.

In Upper Canada the mantle of opposition was donned by the radical 'Clear Grit' Reformers and a few others, who, for one reason or another, had been at odds with the Reform establishment or could not stomach the alliance with the old Tory enemy. One of these was John Sandfield Macdonald, solicitor general for Canada West (Upper Canada's official name under the union) under LaFontaine and Baldwin, who felt that Hincks had given him less than his due. Another was George Brown of the *Globe*, a crusading journalist who had assailed Hincks's ministry for its corruption and reluctance to carry out certain elements of the Reform program. Brown had no sympathy for the Clear Grits' quasi-republicanism, but his attitudes were more to the liking of these western radicals than those of Sandfield Macdonald, a Catholic from the eastern tip of Upper Canada. Brown's polemical talents, and his control of the leading Reform newspaper, enabled him to rally the decapitated party on the platform of representation by population.

In 1858 the government resigned after losing a vote in the assembly on the 'seat of government' question: the problem of where to establish the capital of United Canada. (Since the Montreal riots in 1849, this had been alternating every four years between Toronto and Quebec City.) Brown accepted Sir Edmund Head's invitation to form a government, but the new ministry was defeated within a day, and Head refused to dissolve the legislature at its request. It was obliged to resign within two days of taking office, and the Conservatives were back in power. The débâcle threatened Brown's leadership of the Reform party and gave force to radical demands for a dissolution of the union, but in 1859 the party staged a grand convention. Brown managed to persuade the delegates to reject separatism in favour of a combination of 'rep by pop' and federalism: the conversion of the legislative union of 1841 into a federation.

Brown's new platform paid dividends at the election of 1861, but Brown himself lost his seat. It was Sandfield Macdonald who was called on to form a ministry when the Conservatives were defeated in the legislature in 1862. Sandfield was as hostile to federalism as to 'rep by pop,' but these eastern foibles, and perhaps his Catholicism, helped him in his dealings with francophone politicians, most of whom loathed the Brownite constitutional agenda. The middle ground was untenable, however; Upper Canada was so hot for 'rep by pop,' and French Canada so hostile to it, that the status quo was indefensible. By 1864 John A. Macdonald and his *bleu* allies were forced to accept federation as inevitable. There followed the 'Great Coalition' of 1864–5 and the beginning of the process that was to result in Confederation.

Such, in brief, is the textbook political history of United Canada. At first glance, I suggested, there is little to choose between this account and Mowat's. In fact, though, there is a critical difference between the two. We have been taught to think of the introduction of responsible government in the 1840s as a major step towards political freedom. The old system of authoritarian rule was superseded, and the colonial governments at last were made accountable to the people as represented in the legislature. In Mowat's account, however, responsible government is a big flop. Its ostensible advent in 1841 is exposed as a delusion by the intransigence of Sir Charles Metcalfe; its apparent triumph later in the decade merely replaces the domination of the Family Compact with that of Lower Canada. Then comes the débâcle of Brown's two-day government, followed by years more of political struggle. Only with Confederation does Upper Canada at last attain true political liberty – or, at any rate, the prospect of liberty for a vigilant people.

What is the cause of this gap between Mowat's understanding of Upper Canadian history and our own? The simple answer is that we don't today think about responsible government in terms of *Upper* Canadian history at all. We have 'nationalized' it into a *Canadian* matter – the advent of internal self-government throughout the North American colonies at mid-century. We also tend to think of it as an abstract or technical question concerning the constitutional relationship between the British government and the colonies. We are still influenced by those earlier historians who celebrated colonial self-government as Canada's special contribution to the evolution of British political liberty. As a result, although we are aware of the increasing unpopularity of the union of 1841 in Upper Canada, we blame it on 'sectional grievances' and put it in a different box from the struggle for responsible government. We ascribe it to anti-Catholicism, Francophobia, and the program of populists and radicals to whom responsible government was 'not enough.'

That is how we have been taught to think about it. But Mowat spoke for people to whom the campaign for responsible government was not a 'Canadian' matter at all, and certainly not an abstract question. They thought of themselves as belonging to a political community called *Upper* Canada, and what they wanted was self-government for Upper Canada. Whatever they thought at first, they soon concluded that the coming of responsible government to United Canada had not brought self-government to their community. The domination of the Family Compact and its British backers had merely given way to the domination of Lower Canada. That was one reason – though not the only one – why to them responsible government was not 'enough.'

This Upper Canadian viewpoint also explains two other striking features of Mowat's history: the lack of any direct reference either to the union of 1841 or to the party-political realignment of 1854–7. Both events are as crucial to Mowat's story as to our modern one, but their meaning is different from that which they bear in current textbook history, and they go by a different name. From a 'Canadian' perspective, the union figures in some sense as a first step towards the larger union of 1867, which we call Confederation. As for the political realignment, this was the origin of both the Conservative and the Liberal parties (because of their Clear Grit ancestry, Liberals have been known as 'Grits' ever since), and it paved the way for John A. Macdonald's thirty-five-year career as a party leader. Both, then, are major events in Canadian political history. But from Mowat's Upper Canadian point of view, they both mean one thing only: domination by Lower Canada. And so he goes straight from the rebellions to the first false triumph of responsible government in 1841 without even noticing the union, and he mentions no specific event between the second false dawn in 1848 and Brown's two-day premiership ten years later.

The result is a startling inversion of the familiar story. For English-speaking Canadians today, their country's history is largely an account of the formation of a distinctly un-American English-speaking society in North America, a great nation stretching from sea to sea. From this perspective, Upper Canada appears first and foremost as a rampart of embattled loyalism, beset by American military power and weakened within by a horde of less-than-loyal American settlers. It figures, secondly, as a seedbed of responsible government, but here too the emphasis falls on the invention of a British-style solution to the problem of colonial self-government in preference to the American remedies favoured by the radicals of the 1830s and their Clear Grit successors. In both respects the story is one of resistance to, or rejection of, Americanism and its domestic advocates.

In Mowat's story, by contrast, the cardinal theme of Upper Canadian history is that of a struggle for liberty – the unceasing struggle of the Upper Canadian people, politically incarnated in the Reform party. The anti-American theme runs a poor second, entering only in his acknowledgment of a secondary benefit of Confederation; nation-building comes last and least. The chief importance of Confederation lies in the belated prospect of self-government for Upper Canada. There is still a common government, as under the union, but now it is confined to matters of common interest and its legislature is based on representation by population. In Mowat's story, moreover, there is no hint of subversion from within – not in the cause of Americanization, at any rate. Even the rebellion is justified as a righteous resistance to despotic and unaccountable government. Treason lurks not on the left, so to speak, but on the right. Where, in the standard story, a loyal garrison 'stands on guard' (in the words of the national anthem) against the American menace, in Mowat's, 'the people must ever be standing on the watch' against oppression and betrayal from above.

Mowat did not dwell on the sordid details – it would not have been fitting for the new premier of Ontario to do so at his coronation – but he did not need to do so. All was implicit in the story he told and the names he mentioned. If the grand story of Upper Canadian history was that of the Reformers' struggle for liberty, then their opponents must have been tyrants or friends to tyranny. If the Reformers' cause was that of the people, then their opponents must have been – must still be – enemies of the people. The stigma applied not only to the Tories (a vile name to Reformers, no less applicable to John A. Macdonald and his followers than to the old Family Compact) but to those false friends of the people who had abandoned the struggle in progress, justifying their apostasy with fraudulent claims of victory. The Hincksites in 1855, and the likes of William McDougall and John Sandfield Macdonald a decade later, had tried to vindicate their desertion of Reform by asserting that the battle for Reform was won. The Hincksites had been proved wrong, and the promise of Confederation must also prove fraudulent unless the people remained vigilant.

Obviously, Mowat's story is self-serving. As he presents it, history itself testifies to the legitimacy of the Reform party and its right to govern Ontario; history itself discredits its opponents. Donald Creighton might well have accused him of distorting the history of Upper Canada into a myth, which could serve as propaganda for the radical changes he wished to make in Canada's constitution.[9] And Creighton would have been right, up to a point. Mowat's history of Upper Canada is mythic in its ordering of the facts, in its emphasis on certain events and its neglect of others, and in its political purpose.

It is not, however, more obviously mythic than the textbook history to which I have juxtaposed it. There is no objective standard that makes the conventional emphases any more 'real' or 'true' than Mowat's. The structure of both stories is essentially the same: in one story the Canadian people struggle to preserve their autonomy against an alien aggressor – the Americans; in the other, the *Upper* Canadian people struggle to assert their autonomy against an alien oppressor – first the British, then the French of Lower Canada. In each case, the alien foe is aided by domestic traitors. The difference is a matter of perspective: Canadian versus Upper Canadian.

To label Mowat's myth 'Upper Canadian,' however, and its opposite 'Canadian' is to miss what made Mowat's myth so appealing to his audience as an explanation of their collective identity and destiny. His story recounted the fortunes not of the Upper Canadian community but of the Upper Canadian *people*. These are first seen groaning under the domination not of Lower Canada but of the Family Compact, an oligarchic elite. From this point of view, what distinguishes Mowat's 'Upper Canadian' myth is its populist character. By the same token, the 'Canadian' myth bears more than a passing resemblance to that Loyalist myth which sustained the political pretensions of the Upper Canadian oligarchy.

Writers on the Loyalist myth, in both its central Canadian and its Maritime variant, have stressed its elitism.[10] The myth exaggerated the social status of the Loyalist refugees, depicting them as an upper class in exile, when in reality most of them were ordinary farmers. On this basis it made 'loyalism' into a creed that preferred an orderly, hierarchical society to the anarchic democracy that supposedly typified American republicanism. The rejection of republicanism became an excuse for the authoritarian political system that prevailed before the advent of responsible government. Afterwards it justified that centralization which – as Creighton rightly contended[11] – was an essential feature of monarchical government in the British style, as opposed to the devolved and elective government favoured by populists. In short, the Loyalist myth traces a line from the Loyalists to that 'peace, order, and good government' which the Parliament of Canada is supposed to provide under the terms of the British North America Act.

Mowat's history embodies a populist counterpart to this Loyalist myth. It expresses the worldview of those whom conservatives wanted to keep in order. Against an idea of the Upper Canadian community that exalts members of the elite as leaders in the fight against Americanism and republicanism, it poses an alternative conception, which degrades the elite as despotic itself and allied to alien despotism. It is the myth underlying that much-misunderstood feature of nineteenth-century political life, the Upper Canadian Reform tradition. The origins of this populist myth have long remained hidden in those much-written-of, yet still mysterious years before the Rebellion, when Upper Canadian politics first took shape.

3

Strangers in Their Own Land

I'm suggesting that the Loyalist and Reform ideas of Upper Canada were myths, each based on a biased account of the province's history and each reflecting the outlook of a group that saw the other in some sense as alien. The alienation dominated politics in the 1820s and resulted in part from conflicting material interests. Hard up and chronically indebted, the farmers of early Upper Canada bargained at a disadvantage with the merchants who were their economic lifeline to the outside world, and there was no bargaining over the fees they had to pay for government services. Most officials, from the lieutenant-governor down, drew much or all of their official income from such fees.

Superimposed on these economic frictions were cultural ones. Differences of manners and values (to say nothing of accent) divided even leading Loyalists from the British officials who crossed the ocean with Lieutenant-Governor John Graves Simcoe to run the new colony. Loyalists soon began to resent the carpetbaggers who governed them, took their money for doing so, and despised them into the bargain. In 1807 a Loyalist MPP, David McGregor Rogers, complained that the chief government offices were habitually filled by British nominees who knew nothing of the American population and viewed it with contempt. A lesser official himself, Rogers dared to suggest that a similar sense of alienation from colonial officialdom had helped to provoke the American Revolution. A year later another critic, writing under the pen-name 'A Loyalist,' complained of 'upstart office-hunting hypocrites' of unproven loyalty, who identified themselves with the Loyalist tradition and condemned any complaint against their administration as disloyal.[1]

The two grievances were not identical. Rogers lamented the exclusion of 'Americans' from higher office in favour of 'Europeans'; 'A Loyalist' deplored the tendency of the official elite as a whole, Loyalist and European, to pervert the Loyalist tradition to its own ends, superseding the original test of Loyalist descent by a new, false standard of loyalty to the colonial regime. But both critics were talking about *alienation* – the alienation of the community by its governors. Both claimed to speak for the community against an administrative elite that they saw as alien, and both were reacting to an emerging political snobbery that distinguished between a loyal, 'British' elite and a disloyal, 'American' populace.

The War of 1812 strengthened these trends. On one hand, what seemed a miraculous deliverance from invasion confirmed the Loyalist idea of special destiny and of Upper Canada as a special Loyalist homeland. It also allowed the official elite to admit to its charmed circle anyone, Loyalist or not, whom it valued for his distinguished service in the hour of trial. On the other hand, the treasonable or seditious acts of some colonists and the frank neutrality of others confirmed the government's worst fears about the American majority.

By 1812 two-thirds or more of the population consisted of Americans who had been drawn to Upper Canada not by love for monarchical government or British liberty but by the abundance of good, cheap land. Governor Simcoe had encouraged such immigration in order to stimulate the economy; later officials had condoned it, grateful for its stimulating effect on their fees. The policy assumed that Americans could still be British subjects, since only the king's subjects could own land and take part in politics, as these immigrants did from the start. After the war, however, such immigration began to seem more dangerous than beneficial, and officials in Britain and Upper Canada began to question the immigrants' nationality. The legal controversy lasted for years and culminated in the hottest political quarrel the colony had yet seen. The so-called alien question turned the pre-war antagonism between the American farmers and the administrative elite into a lasting feature of Upper Canadian political culture.

I have written about the alien question in detail elsewhere and won't repeat myself here.[2] What matters is that British subjects could not legally renounce their allegiance to the Crown and that at the time of American independence neither the Crown nor Parliament had done anything that expressly relieved Americans of their allegiance. Indeed, in 1790 Parliament had passed a law to encourage Americans to settle in the remaining North American colonies, a measure that made no sense if Americans had irretrievably lost their old allegiance. Legally speaking, then, British-born or naturalized inhabitants of the Thirteen Colonies could be supposed to have remained British subjects even after becoming U.S. citizens, unless the very fact of American independence had irrevocably alienated them. In hindsight it seems only common sense to suppose that independence, generally speaking, had done just that, but it was only the War of 1812 that got most British officials thinking along those lines, and it was not until 1824 that a British court decided the matter. By then, thousands of Americans had settled in Upper Canada and begun to exercise all the rights and privileges of British subjects.

It was in 1821 that people in high places suddenly began insisting that the immigrants and their children were aliens, with no political rights and no title to the farms on which they had expended long years of labour and much hard-earned cash. Naturally, this caused alarm. The problem was nothing that legislation could not fix, and in the end it was fixed; but only after whipping provincial politics to unprecedented heights of acrimony. First the British government declined to act until the courts had had their say; then the colonial secretary (the British minister responsible for the colonies) refused to legislate in Britain, throwing the responsibility on the provincial legislature.

Unfortunately, naturalizing aliens was something that colonial legislatures could not do; but the provincial attorney general, John Beverley Robinson,[3] unaccountably failed to remind the minister of that fact when they discussed the matter in London in 1825. Instead he went home and drafted a bill so vaguely worded that, even if valid, it could easily be read as securing only the immigrants' property rights while leaving the immigrants themselves disenfranchised. Robinson assured the house of assembly that the bill conferred both political and property rights and that, even if it were technically invalid, the colonial secretary would hardly reject a bill he himself had sanctioned; but the opposition suspected a plot. It defeated Robinson's measure and, defying the recent English legal judgment, passed a bill declaring that the endangered settlers always had been British subjects and were so still. Justifying this action, an opposition journalist alluded ominously to the fate of the Israelites in Egypt, first invited to settle, then stripped of their rights and enslaved.[4]

After this fiasco, the British Parliament passed a law empowering the provincial legislature to deal with the matter; but the quarrel continued. The British government tried to dictate the terms of the legislation, insisting that it should benefit only persons who took a special oath of allegiance and had their names registered. The provincial opposition objected both to the dictation and to the registers, which looked suspiciously like proscription lists. The provincial authorities bullied the assembly into passing the bill by harping on the danger of inaction, but outraged opponents dispatched a mass petition to Britain, where a new government had just taken office, and managed to have the measure disallowed. Furious at this rebuff from the mother country, the provincial government gave up in disgust and allowed the opposition to draft and carry its own bill. So, in 1828, the alien question was settled after seven years' controversy.

The alien question is important to our story not only for its legacy of lasting political bitterness but for the terms in which the question was debated. From the start it was a quarrel about history and identity, about the nature of the Upper Canadian community and its relations with the mother country. What was Upper Canada? Who were Upper Canadians? And did Upper Canada belong primarily to its inhabitants or to its British suzerain? It was by raising these themes that the alien question fostered the development of the conflicting myths at the foundation of the politics of nineteenth-century Ontario.

The debate was shaped by the refusal of the provincial elite to discriminate between Americans in general and those who had moved to Upper Canada. Even if Americans in general had lost their British allegiance, one could still rescue the immigrants from the looming threat of disenfranchisement and expropriation by distinguishing them as a special case. This was only fair. Governor Simcoe himself had invited the immigrants to settle on the strength of the British statute of 1790, and by the early 1820s they had been accepted as British subjects for thirty years. You could argue that, in moving to British territory, they had marked themselves out from other Americans by making a positive choice for British allegiance. But the elite dismissed all these considerations, often with arguments so flimsy that they added insult to injury.

Spokesmen for the elite did what people often do when they cite historical facts to prove a point – they distorted the facts by ignoring their context. One Loyalist MPP suggested that the British statute of 1790 might have been meant to attract tenant farmers or artisans rather than freeholders.[5] In view of the scanty population of the territories in question, Upper Canada in particular, this proposition was nonsense: the statute could have been meant only to encourage the immigration of persons to settle as freehold farmers on land granted by the crown. Likewise, a report of the legislative council (the upper house of the provincial legislature, whose members were appointed by the government, like those of today's Canadian Senate) quoted Simcoe's land-granting proclamation of February 1792 in order to show that it contained 'not a word, which, either directly or indirectly, invites any person not attached to the unity of the empire and to the supremacy of the British parliament.'[6] This was quite true: the proclamation said nothing about politics. It was addressed 'to such as are desirous to settle on the Lands of the Crown in the Province of Upper Canada,' and all it did was set out the land-granting regulations. But Simcoe had sent a copy to the British consul-general in Philadelphia for the information of Americans wishing to settle in the province.[7]

An order of Simcoe's dating from 1794 was similarly abused. It directed 'that no settlers are to be admitted but those whose loyalty, industry, and morals shall appear to entitle them to His Majesty's bounty.' Attorney General Robinson insisted that the criterion was loyalty to the crown, but in fact it was nothing of the sort. The order discriminated against individuals who had proven themselves disloyal *to the United States of America* by taking part in a recent uprising in western Pennsylvania, the so-called Whiskey Rebellion. As far as Simcoe was concerned, when it came to emigrating to Upper Canada, only good republicans need apply![8] Thirty years later, Robinson could not accept that meaning.

The immigrants and their supporters were also outraged by their opponents' insistence on preferring British authority to Upper Canadian. It was, of course, a British authority – the court decision of 1824 – that finally brought the matter to a head, but even before then leading Loyalists were quite ready to play the imperial trump. Over the years, for instance, the provincial legislature had passed four laws that treated the American settlers as British subjects. As late as 1814, it had enacted that immigrants who had voluntarily returned to the United States since the outbreak of war, or who did so in future, were to be considered as 'Aliens born and incapable of holding lands within this Province.' Such a law was pointless if they were aliens already, as Attorney General Robinson well knew, because he had drafted it. Now, however, Robinson tried to deny the implications of his own measure by citing certain British trade legislation that discriminated against persons domiciled in the United States. The American-born MPP John Willson rebuked him for according higher authority to British administrative practice than to provincial statute. When someone pointed out that British customs officials treated Americans as aliens, Willson denied that they would so treat an American who had lived seven years in Upper Canada and taken the oath of allegiance.[9]

Willson was rather conservative in his politics and had been impeccably loyal during the war. He and Americans like him deeply resented their opponents' refusal to distinguish them from the invading enemy. 'Who are those persons to be styled Aliens?' asked one MPP. 'Surely not those who have brought Upper-Canada to display its value to the Imperial Government by bringing the wilderness to blossom as the rose; and certainly it could not be those or the sons of those who in danger, rushed to our standard and repelled the Invaders from our shores.'[10] Some Loyalists, however, would not except even those immigrants who had served in the militia. 'It is admitted that, although some of them left the country, others remained and served under our colours; but was this the effect of principle, loyalty, or of circumstances?' So asked an anonymous correspondent in the *Kingston Chronicle*. 'Could they have retained their property, and act otherwise? Could they have remained in the country, and act otherwise? Could they avoid fighting when drawn up in line with British soldiers, and the loyal tories of the old school?'[11]

Such reasoning left no room at all for the immigrants to be loyal – no room for them to belong – no room for them in Upper Canada. The guests had outstayed their welcome and were threatening to take over the farm. 'Shall the guest, who is admitted to the feast prescribe the dishes, to which he has not contributed? Shall we, who have sought for ourselves through wildernesses, with the greatest difficulties and exertions, a new home, after having lost all which we once considered our patrimony, yield up to interlopers an equal claim with ourselves to the highest offices in our Government?' So asked another writer to the *Chronicle*.[12] The legislative council denounced the idea that the immigrants were British subjects as one that 'virtually places traitors to the king's government, the destroyers of our parents and friends during the American revolution, upon an equal footing with ourselves.'[13] Such presumption could not be tolerated. And why not? In the words of Christopher Hagerman, a Loyalist MPP who was to reach the heights as attorney general and as judge of the Court of King's Bench, 'This province could no longer be considered a safe retreat for the loyal people who left that country [i.e., the United States], and came here for asylum, if they allowed them to be followed by the very men who had committed treason, and destroyed the constitution.'[14]

These statements illustrate the preconceptions that the provincial elite brought to the quarrel over Upper Canadian history. The American settlers appealed to the experience and practice of thirty years as they and their parents had lived it. They had been invited to settle the province; they had acquired land and political rights. That history, however, was fundamentally at odds with a cherished tenet of Loyalism: the idea of Upper Canada as a Loyalist patrimony, a special gift of the Crown in recompense for their sufferings in the cause of imperial unity. How could the province also belong to the immigrants? It could not; and evidence that seemed to favour the immigrants' claim must be susceptible to some other interpretation. Some of the efforts of Attorney General Robinson and his friends to impose such an interpretation may seem strained to the point of dishonesty, but they were rooted in a sort of idealism, based on certain long-held ideas about Upper Canadian history.

In fact, the same idealism actuated Robinson and company both as Loyalists and as lawyers. As early as 1818, Robinson had written that unless Americans were aliens, English law entailed the 'monstrous absurdity' that 'they may become in 1815 under the sanction and protection of our laws the legal proprietors of our soil, which in 1814 they invaded in open war, without incurring the guilt of treason.'[15] The law cannot carry conviction as an instrument of social regulation if seems to result in monstrous absurdities, and the courts may legitimately shape it to avoid that effect. In this instance, however, the obvious way to do so was to treat the immigrants as a special case; and that would be a violation of the Loyalist vision of Upper Canada, a vision validated and intensified by the recent war. Robinson and company could not shape the law in order to confirm the immigrants' claim to British allegiance because they were under a compulsion to reshape history in order to deny that claim. Later we will run into other lawyers reshaping history to suit their preconceptions. (Some may say we already have. Oliver Mowat, whose account of Upper Canadian history we reviewed in the last chapter, was a lawyer.)

The immigrants might well have accused their adversaries, as Donald Creighton was to accuse his 140 years later, of distorting history into a myth, which could serve as propaganda for the radical changes they wished to make in society. Certainly Robinson and company had a radical end in view: no less than the transformation of Upper Canada from an American to a British community. The plan was wide-ranging, including assisted immigration from Britain and the founding of King's College, the ancestor of the University of Toronto.

The modern city of Peterborough, Ontario, originated in 1825 as the centre of a large-scale planting of Irish settlers, who were helped to emigrate in pursuit of a policy of de-Americanizing the population. The town was named after the attorney general's brother, Peter Robinson, who managed the project.[16] King's College was established in 1827 in York (Toronto) in accordance with a recommendation of the province's executive council (the governor's advisory council) in its report on the alien question. The council advised that a university connected with the Church of England 'would tend to establish a most affectionate connection between this Colony and the Parent State and ... from its natural relation with an increasing Clergy, would gradually infuse into the whole population a tone and feeling entirely English, and by a judicious selection of Elementary Books issuing from its Press, render it certain, that the first feelings, sentiments and opinions of the Youth should be British.'[17] Not just the university but its press twinkled in their mind's eye. How could these visionaries refrain from prescribing the history that such textbooks should impart to their tender readers? Their success in doing so can be seen in almost every twentieth-century account of the controversy – not only those published by the University of Toronto Press.

In the short term, though, the attempt to brand the immigrants as aliens backfired. In forcing them to spell out their claim to membership of the community, it strengthened their sense of identity as Upper Canadians, for their claim was rooted in Upper Canadian history. This nascent Upper Canadian nationalism was populist and exclusive, and what it shut out was the provincial elite. This sort of populism is common among farming populations governed by an elite whose wealth and manners mark off its members from the mass of the people. Such elites may have originated as conquerors; they may speak a different language from the people. In Upper Canada, we have already heard an echo of such culture-based class consciousness in the complaint of the Loyalist David MacGregor Rogers about condescending 'Europeans.'

Robinson and his leading collaborators in the alien controversy were also Loyalists, but they did not, as Rogers did, identify themselves with the 'Americans' without distinguishing between Loyalists and later arrivals. On the contrary, the essence of their policy was to identify themselves with the 'Europeans' in order to brand the great majority of the 'Americans' as aliens. This posture was reflected in their strategy, which was to overrule Upper Canadian history – to deny the authority of shared experience – by invoking British authority.

The result was ironic. Spurred by loyalty and ambition to identify themselves with the imperial ruler rather than with the people they governed as imperial agents, Robinson and his friends stigmatized themselves as aliens in the eyes of those whom they sought to stigmatize as aliens. Thus were born the conflicting myths I mentioned in chapter 2: the Loyalist myth of alien subversion and the populist myth of alien oppression.

The alien question ended in a triumph for the opposition and a humiliation for the government. The general election of 1828 produced the most radical House in the history of Upper Canada. Attorney General Robinson gratefully quit electoral politics to become chief justice. For a moment it seemed that a new leaf had been turned in provincial politics. But the American immigrants could not feel secure. For years they had lived under a shadow. They had heard the government zealously propagating a new-fangled legal doctrine that threatened to rob them of land and political liberty. Their alarm had been increased by Robinson's equivocal naturalization bill of 1825. Insults had been offered, and menaces uttered. And even as they celebrated their victory, a flood of British immigration threatened to make them a minority in the land, the prospect of losing which had stirred them to call it their own.

4

A Federal Constitution:
Reformers and the Empire

The myths of alien oppression and alien subversion were to affect provincial politics long after the rapid evolution of a colonial frontier society had reduced the alien question to a vague memory. They were absorbed into the ideologies of Reform and Toryism, respectively, whose endless conflict informed Oliver Mowat's account of Upper Canadian history. As Mowat's narrative shows, though, the event that would be remembered as the source of that political divide was not the alien question itself but the constitutional struggle it engendered: the struggle for responsible government.

Today the story of that struggle no longer thrills Canadian hearts as it did once, but to earlier generations the winning of self-government within the British empire was their country's chief claim to glory, and in remembering it they fused several distinct campaigns for colonial autonomy into one grand national struggle. Ironically, in doing so they forgot how large a part the goal of local self-government had played in their country's founding – in Confederation. In this chapter we see how the alien question begot the struggle for responsible government, and we rediscover the long-lost ideas that inspired Ontarians like Mowat to equate their campaign for provincial rights within Confederation with their forebears' struggle for responsible government. It will appear that the compact theory of Confederation and the principle of provincial sovereignty grew in the very soil that nourished the demand for responsible government – a federal conception of the British empire.

The alien question was of vital concern to the mass of the population. The house of assembly wrangled over it year after year. Tempers flared, and the government and its supporters were goaded into acts of petty vengeance against individuals. Several notorious incidents occurred in 1826, in the six months following the defeat of John Beverley Robinson's naturalization bill. Two MPPs were victimized for their outspoken support of the American settlers: Charles Fothergill lost his job as king's printer, and Captain John Matthews nearly lost his military pension.[1]

Two incidents in June 1826 included the biggest scandal of the time: the wrecking of William Lyon Mackenzie's printing-shop 'by Officers of the Provincial Government of Upper Canada and Law Students of the Attorney and Solicitor General,' as Mackenzie pointedly put it in the title of his pamphlet on the outrage.[2] A few days later George Rolph, brother of the leading Reform politician John Rolph, was tarred and feathered by men who seized him at midnight at his home near Hamilton. Again the miscreants were current and future officers of government. One was sheriff of the Gore District and also a magistrate. His accomplices included another magistrate, a future prime minister of United Canada (Sir Allan MacNab), and a future mayor of Toronto.[3]

These incidents may not seem to amount to much, but they revealed in the government and its supporters a persecuting spirit and a contempt for the rule of law. The attacks on Mackenzie and George Rolph also highlighted something else: a systemic weakness in the administration of justice. In Britain prosecutions for serious crimes were normally instituted by private individuals and conducted by counsel hired by the prosecutor. In Upper Canada, by contrast, such prosecutions were invariably conducted by the attorney general or the solicitor general, who received a fee from the government for each case. In view of the vengeful spirit prevailing in government, how could Mackenzie and Rolph rely on public officials, one of them (Robinson) the government's chief spokesman in the house of assembly, to prosecute their attackers? In Mackenzie's case the problem was aggravated by the personal tie between the officials and several of the rioters.

At this point the nascent Reform opposition had a stroke of luck: John Walpole Willis arrived from Britain to fill a vacancy on the Court of King's Bench. The provincial elite – the Family Compact, as it was becoming known – had come to think of such offices as their own. It resented the appointment, and Willis added insult to injury by refusing to see provincial politics through its eyes. His court provided the ideal forum for the Reformers' attack on the administration of justice. The leading Reform politicians at the time were the Irishman William Baldwin and his son Robert, the Englishman John Rolph, and two

Americans, Marshall Bidwell and his father, Barnabas. All lawyers, they were well equipped to exploit Willis's attitude.

The journalist Francis Collins had acted closely with John Rolph and the Baldwins, and Attorney General Robinson had instituted several proceedings against him for criminal libel. Once in court, in March 1828, Collins launched a bitter attack on the attorney general for prosecuting him while allowing Mackenzie's assailants to escape criminal sanctions. Helped by Willis, he forced Robinson first to make a detailed defence of the government monopoly of criminal prosecutions and then to prosecute Mackenzie's attackers.

For Robinson it was a moment of humiliation to compare with the defeat of his naturalization bill some two years previously, but his revenge was swift. Shortly afterwards, prompted by John Rolph and the Baldwins, Willis declared that the Court of King's Bench could not legally sit unless all the judges were present. Since the chief justice was absent on leave, Willis refused to take part in the proceedings of the court. Lieutenant-Governor Sir Peregrine Maitland, advised by Robinson, at once suspended Willis from the bench. Then, that autumn, Robinson successfully prosecuted Collins for a libel on him. His fellow-Loyalist Christopher Hagerman, sitting as a temporary replacement for Willis, imposed a sentence that the law officers of the Crown in Britain would later (too late for Collins) condemn for its harshness.[4]

To the Reform leaders, the suspension of Willis was the last straw. Miraculously, the lottery of colonial patronage had brought to the province a judge willing to take a stand against political abuses, and look what had happened. Still, things had taken a hopeful turn in London. The British government's disallowance of its predecessor's naturalization bill in the summer of 1828 was followed by the publication of a House of Commons select committee report highly critical of the governance of both Canadas.[5] Together with the dispatch of Willis to Upper Canada, such doings seemed to the Reform leaders to augur a liberal spirit in the British government and a new attentiveness to colonial grievances.

In the summer of 1828, the Reformers responded to Willis's suspension by mounting a campaign in support of a comprehensive petition of grievances. The petition asked for several changes in the provincial constitution, including an elected legislative council and, as in Britain, a judiciary independent of the executive. And in order to make the executive accountable to public opinion, the petition asked that it be made responsible, as in Britain, to the elective legislature. So it was that the demand for responsible government first appeared in the platform of the Upper Canadian Reformers.[6]

By 'responsible government' I mean a system whereby the royal power is exercised not by the monarch but by a committee of politicians, the cabinet, which includes the heads of the great departments of state. Though appointed by the monarch, whose ministers they are, they hold power only as long as they can command a majority in the elected legislature.

In the traditional story, responsible government figures as the goal of 'moderate' Reformers led by William Baldwin and his son Robert, while 'radical' Reformers such as Mackenzie preferred American forms of representative government, such as an elective upper chamber. Profiting from the disgrace that the rebellion of 1837 brought on the radicals and the Family Compact alike, the Baldwins pressed their idea on the receptive Lord Durham during and after his visit to Toronto in 1838. Durham bestowed on the idea a respectability that gave new life to the decimated Reform party. For several years during the 1840s, the Baldwin-led Reformers and their French-Canadian allies held steadfast against the disapproval of British statesmen less liberal than Durham, until circumstances and the justice of their cause gave them the victory.

This story is true as far as it goes, but it contains two biases that severely distort our understanding of the Reform tradition and its place in Canadian history. One is the way in which it severs responsible government, the constitutional principle, from the sense of common cause that inspired many of those who upheld the principle. It neglects to ask: responsible government for whom? It simply assumes that the system achieved in the 1840s satisfied the Reformers' dreams of being masters in their own house. This ignores the fact that, in 1840, the British Parliament had combined Upper and Lower Canada into a single Province of Canada, leaving Upper Canadians sharing a house with many more strangers than felt comfortable. The troubles that arose from the union are consigned to a separate locker labelled 'sectional tensions,' the sections being the two parts of United Canada.

As we saw, Oliver Mowat made no such distinction between the successive phases of the struggle for responsible government. His story recognized the sense of common identity that fuelled Reform politics, an identity forged on the anvil of Upper Canadian history. He realized that many Reformers were indifferent to responsible government as an abstract principle: what they wanted was self-government for Upper

Canada. In his story, therefore, the coming of responsible government to United Canada merely inaugurated the next stage in the struggle: that of resistance to domination by Lower Canada. So it was that, to Mowat, the fight for responsible government did not end in the 1840s.

The second flaw in the conventional story arises from the idea that responsible government, as a 'British' remedy for the misrule of the provincial oligarchy, was a more 'moderate' reform than the 'American' remedies proposed by 'radicals.' To be sure, it entailed a less sweeping reorganization of the constitution than the reforms pushed by William Lyon Mackenzie, but that did not make its political consequences less radical. Power concentrated in the hands of an unaccountable executive is one thing; the same power subject to the control of a legislative assembly elected mainly by rural smallholders is quite another. That was one reason why the founders of the United States of America had adopted a written constitution, which limited the legislative power.

Of course, written constitution or no, the United States in the 1830s and 1840s, the high tide of Jacksonian democracy, was hardly a conservative backwater. That had little to do with the nature of American political institutions, however. The high tide of Jacksonian democracy was also the flood-tide of American expansion across the Appalachians along a front stretching from Wisconsin to Texas, and soon enough from the Oregon Territory to California. The radicalism of that era was an effect of the rapid advance of the frontier of settlement. Forty or fifty years later, things had settled down a bit in the United States, and the British monarchy stood on the verge of its own era of mass democracy. When that happened, conservative British intellectuals such as A.V. Dicey and James Bryce would envy the republic and its written constitution as a model of conservative stability.[7]

Mid-nineteenth-century Canada did not undergo the sort of expansion that fuelled Jacksonian democracy, but Upper Canada in particular was being rapidly settled and the Clear Grit radicals might have been hard to check but for the union of 1841, which allowed Upper Canadian conservatives to call on Lower Canadian aid in the legislature. (That, of course, was one reason why so many Reformers were disappointed with responsible government under the union.) Fifty years later, though, the Torontonian Goldwin Smith would compare Canadian with American institutions to the latter's advantage, much as his friends Dicey and Bryce compared British with American institutions. In 1891 he would characterize both Canada and the United States as countries 'where tradition has no force and every one goes to the full length of his tether,' but he would contend that the American constitution provided a shorter tether. The British doctrine of parliamentary sovereignty, as instituted in Canada, permitted a provincial legislature to enact the most momentous change in anything connected with civil rights or property. Responsible government allowed it to do so without any risk of executive veto, even in provinces with a single-chamber legislature, where there was no chance of veto or revision by a senatorial upper house.[8]

In short, to Goldwin Smith in 1891 Canada's monarchical institutions would seem nothing but a fig leaf for the Dominion's rampant democracy; and this was after decades of heavy British immigration and the founding of several universities that, though unconnected with the Church of England, might have been expected to impart something of that 'English tone' which the executive council of Upper Canada, in its report of 1826, had hoped to acquire by the foundation of King's College. So much for the notion that responsible government was a more 'moderate' reform than the American-style institutions favoured by Upper Canadian radicals!

But quite apart from its impact on colonial politics, there is another reason why responsible government was not a 'moderate' demand. This concerns Upper Canada's place in the British empire. Here, too, the British doctrine of parliamentary sovereignty lay at the heart of the matter; but in this case what mattered was the sovereignty of the British Parliament, as established by the Glorious Revolution of 1688 and the ousting of King James II. The revolution had subordinated the independent political power of the monarchy to that of Parliament, and British politicians had persuaded themselves that their new power extended to the king's dominions overseas, though these had legislatures of their own.

It was on this basis that Parliament presumed to tax the American colonies after the Seven Years' War. Although colonial indignation soon compelled it to repeal the levies, Parliament had affirmed its right to impose such taxes in the Declaratory Act of 1765. Thirteen years later, in an effort to conciliate the rebellious colonies, it had renounced that claim with respect to British North America, except for duties imposed for the regulation of navigation and commerce. This renunciation was applied to Upper and Lower Canada by the Constitutional Act of 1791, the British statute that served as the constitution of both colonies; but Parliament's general claim to sovereignty throughout the empire, including the Canadas, persisted.

The point is this: responsible government was inseparable from political sovereignty. The lieutenant-governor of Upper Canada was a British official, and his government an instrument of imperial sovereignty. How could it possibly be subject to the control of the provincial legislature? The idea went against the maxim that no man can serve two masters.

Canadian historians have not overlooked this problem, but most have misunderstood it. They have seen the campaign for responsible government chiefly as a struggle against domestic oppression – the despotism of the Family Compact in Upper Canada and similar oligarchies in other colonies. Their account of relations with the 'mother country' has been too much influenced by certain rather complacent ideas about Canada's political development – in particular, the idea that Canada achieved self-government, unlike the United States, without anything so uncouth as a revolution, and that it did so because its political leaders formed the ingenious idea of simply operating the British constitution in Canada as it was operated in Britain. The British balked at first (so the story goes) but were ultimately brought round to the idea by its sheer moderate reasonableness.

This story makes the Baldwins look like clever employees pertinaciously urging a neat technical innovation on a sceptical boss. The image hardly does justice to the temerity of those Reformers who first advocated responsible government in the 1820s. Since it entailed Westminster's renunciation of a part of its claimed sovereignty, one might better liken them to peasants brazenly suggesting that their lord share his wealth. But even this comparison does not fully capture their radicalism, for the Baldwins' demand for responsible government was based on an outright rejection of the imperial claim of overriding sovereignty. These peasants contended that the wealth in question was by right not the lord's but theirs.

You can see this attitude in William Baldwin's response to the Union Bill controversy. The bill was introduced at Westminster in 1822 through the influence of Lower Canadian capitalists, anglophones whose interests and ambitions were frustrated by francophone control of the house of assembly. In order to reduce the French party's power, the bill proposed to reverse the Constitutional Act of 1791 by reuniting Upper and Lower Canada into a single province, with a single legislature, in which Upper Canadians would be hugely over-represented. It also provided a high property qualification for membership of the legislature and banned the use of French there.[9]

This story is rightly recognized as an important chapter in the history of Lower Canada. It was in fact a Lower Canadian counterpart to the alien question: an attempt by the provincial elite to mobilize British power against what the elite saw as a hostile alien majority. As such it figures as a leading episode in the age-old history of racial conflict in Canada between 'French' and 'English.' It figures much less prominently in Upper Canadian history, because it does not fit the primary theme of that story: the growing resistance to oligarchic oppression that led to responsible government.[10] Whether writing about Upper or Lower Canada, though, historians have said little or nothing about the controversy as an episode in the history of the campaign for responsible government. This is because they have seen that campaign primarily as a struggle against local elites. But responsible government also touched the relationship between the colonies and the British government, and the controversy of 1822–3 forms a chapter of that story too.

The Union Bill was conceived as an exercise of overriding imperial power: it was introduced into the British Parliament without reference to public opinion in either colony. It has never occurred to historians to question the British government's right to do this, any more than the government itself questioned it. But William Baldwin absolutely and repeatedly denied Westminster's right to repeal the Constitutional Act before obtaining the consent of the people of both colonies. The act was a grant of legislative institutions to both peoples by the imperial sovereign, the King-in-Parliament. It was the very foundation of the political community in both provinces. To Baldwin, that made it an 'indefeasible' constitution. Parliament had no right to repeal it with respect to either colony, or even to alter it significantly, without the consent of the people, as expressed in a 'solemn enactment' of the provincial legislature. If Parliament could do so, that could mean only that the province had no constitution, its legislature no rights or privileges, and its people no security in their political rights.[11]

Baldwin's argument rested on an idea long central to British political thought – that society rested on a compact between the ruler and his subjects. In his view, the Constitutional Act was binding on the imperial sovereign just as an English king's summoning of the first Parliament back in the supposedly immemorial past had been binding on that king and his successors. In giving his subjects a share in the making of laws, the king had shared his sovereignty with them. Once he had done so, the King-in-Parliament was sovereign in the realm. The king alone, no longer sovereign, could not alter the gift, or take back what he had given, without his subjects' consent. Likewise, by passing the Constitutional Act, the imperial sovereign – the British King-in-Parliament – had given the people of Upper Canada a share in the sovereignty of Upper Canada, and the deed was unalterable and irrevocable. If Westminster passed the Union Bill without the consent of the peoples affected by it, it would be committing an illegal and unconstitutional act.

Anything that Dr Baldwin may have left unsaid during the controversy was plainly stated by him and his son Robert on an equally important occasion five years later. It was at a public meeting called at York, in the summer of 1828, to arrange for sending to London the people's petition for political reform, including responsible government. Dr Baldwin was in the chair. The meeting proceeded in the usual fashion, passing a series of resolutions. One of them, moved by Robert Baldwin, included a statement so important that I must quote it in full. It said:

We hold it as a principle never to be abandoned that our Constitutional Act as passed by the Parliament of Great Britain and as accepted and acted upon by us, is in fact a treaty between the Mother Country and us, her children of this Colony, pointing out and regulating the mode in which we shall exercise those *rights which, independent of that act, belong to us as British subjects*, and which, therefore, neither the Parliament of the Mother Country, nor any power upon earth could legally or constitutionally withhold from us; and that thus that act, being in fact a treaty, can only be abrogated or altered by the consent of both parties to it, that is to say, the Mother Country and the Colony.[12]

Like Dr Baldwin in 1823, this resolution declared boldly that Westminster had no right to alter the Constitutional Act unilaterally. This time, though, two things were stated which Baldwin (so far as we know) had not said. First of all, despite its form as an act of Parliament, the Constitutional Act was 'in fact' a treaty between two parties – the mother country and the colony. Secondly, Parliament had not created the rights that the colonists enjoyed under the act. The act merely established the forms under which the colonists were to exercise rights that inhered in them as British subjects, and 'which, therefore, neither the Parliament of the Mother Country, nor any other power upon earth could legally or constitutionally withhold from us.'

In the old days, when the constitution of Canada was known as the British North America Act,[13] writers sometimes liked to compare its flat, ponderous complexity with the ringing phrases of the American Declaration of Independence and the elegant economy of the United States constitution. They would use the comparison as evidence of the prag-matic, unheroic, impoverished, unemancipated – in a word, *colonial* – nature of the Canadian political culture as compared to the American. To my mind, here, in 1828, is a statement with something of the rhetori-cal bravura of the Declaration. It doesn't say the same things. It doesn't say that all men are created equal; nor does it proclaim full indepen-dence from Britain. But it does warn Parliament quite plainly not to meddle with the provincial constitution. In doing so it asserts the sover-eignty of the Upper Canadian people.

The Baldwins were not the only Upper Canadians to think like this about the Constitutional Act. In 1822 there appeared a book called *A Statistical Account of Upper Canada*. Its author was Robert Gourlay, a Scottish would-be immigrant to Upper Canada who had tried to whip up public opinion against the provincial oligarchy and got himself deported for his pains. Gourlay's book included some 'Sketches' of the province written some five years earlier by 'An Inhabitant.' The 'Sketches' are pretty bland, but their account of the province's constitu-tion includes one pregnant sentence: 'Upper Canada derives her consti-tution from acts of the British Parliament, which are of the nature of a legislative charter, and may be considered as amounting to a *solemn compact* between the parent kingdom and the province, establishing the form of provincial government.'[14]

'An Inhabitant' is thought to have been the Reform politician Barna-bas Bidwell. Bidwell had pursued a flourishing career in the United States, first as a congressman and then as attorney general of Massachu-setts, and had had every prospect of appointment to the Supreme Court of the United States until 1810, when suddenly he fled to Upper Canada under suspicion of having embezzled public funds. It was his election to the provincial legislature in 1821 that had first brought the alien question to public notice, since his enemies had cited nationality as well as moral turpitude as reasons for expelling him from the house of assembly.

Though barred from legal practice in Upper Canada, Bidwell had helped Gourlay to defeat two charges of seditious libel brought against the agitator by the provincial government. During the 1820s – now barred from the legislature as well as the law – he remained influential in Reform politics, operating through his son Marshall, a leading MPP from 1824 on. Barnabas is also a leading candidate for the authorship of another anonymous publication, the fullest statement we have of the 'compact theory' of the Constitutional Act. It is the so-called Letter on

Responsible Government, a document of unique importance in the complex and fascinating history of Canadian constitutional thought.[15]

The Letter appeared in the *Upper Canada Herald*, a Kingston newspaper, in October 1829, over the pen-name 'X.'[16] It gave a brief but exact account of the practice of responsible government, which it identified as part of the British constitution and proposed to introduce in Upper Canada. Like the British government, it suggested, the provincial government should be run by heads of department who belonged to both the executive council (the governor's advisory council) and the legislature. One of these officials should be prime minister, and they should all resign their offices in a body when they could no longer command the confidence of a majority of the house of assembly.

In the 1920s, when the document first came to light, scholars were not sure when the demand for responsible government had first entered the program of the Upper Canadian opposition. Some thought it dated back to the time of Judge Robert Thorpe, who had arrived from Britain in 1805, got himself elected to the house of assembly (colonial judges could do this), and whipped up a storm of grievance against the merchant and administrative elite until suspended early in 1807 by the newly arrived governor Francis Gore. Other scholars held that responsible government had not been a feature of the British constitution before the passage of the great parliamentary Reform Act of 1832. It could hardly have been part of a colonial political program before then.

So the Letter of 1829 showed that the theory and practice of responsible government was known in Upper Canada at least a decade before Lord Durham's report recommended its implementation in British North America.[17] But it set another puzzle. 'X' did not present the proposal as his own idea. He ascribed it to an anonymous treatise that he claimed to have found on the provincial constitution. This treatise was written under the pen name 'Canadiensis,' he said, and dated probably from the time of Judge Thorpe. Ever since the letter was discovered, historians have wondered whether Canadiensis and his treatise had an existence outside X's mind and, if so, whether the document had been penned as far back as 1806.[18]

This does not concern me. I don't care whether Canadiensis and his treatise were real or merely figments of X's imagination, or whether the arguments in the epistle originated in 1806, 1829, or any time between. For simplicity's sake, I write as though author and treatise were real, for the ideas ascribed to them are crucial. What interests me, though, is less the proposal for colonial responsible government than the reasoning behind it. Canadiensis, like the Baldwins, linked responsible government to an outright rejection of British legislative sovereignty. Like the Baldwins, he regarded the Constitutional Act as a treaty between the colony and the mother country, designed to establish the mode in which the colonists were to exercise their inherent rights as British subjects. Together with the Baldwins' scattered statements, the treatise shows that the movement for responsible government was rooted in a deliberate rejection of the orthodox British doctrine of imperial legislative supremacy.

Once the source of their vision becomes clear, its radicalism is less surprising. The Baldwins were Irish, and Dr Baldwin's father had been active as a journalist in the great patriotic movement of the 1780s. Irish patriots, like American ones, had resented Parliament's claim to legislative sovereignty over their country. The Declaratory Act of 1765, by which Parliament had asserted its claim to legislate for British North America, had a precedent in the Declaratory Act of 1719, which asserted the same claim over Ireland. In 1782, inspired by the American Revolution, an Irish mass movement forced Parliament to pass an Act of Renunciation formally relinquishing that claim. With this renunciation, and the repeal of certain ancient constraints on the legislative power of the Irish Parliament, the Irish patriots re-established their country as a separate kingdom, united with the British empire through the person of the monarch but governed by an executive responsible to the Irish Parliament.[19]

In a sense, then, the very demand for responsible government was an Irish idea; but Ireland was something of a special case. Unlike Ireland, Upper Canada was not a kingdom but a province created by the British king and Parliament. In order to defy Parliament's right to legislate for the province it had created, the Upper Canadian Reformers had to resort to American doctrines. There were a batch of these, which colonial patriots of the 1770s had relied on in their quarrel with Parliament. One doctrine declared that British subjects, on settling in the king's dominions overseas, carried with them certain fundamental rights. These were part and parcel of the ancient common law of England, as declared in statutes ranging from Magna Carta in the early thirteenth century to the Bill of Rights of 1690. Another doctrine held that the power of Parliament to legislate for the colonies was confined by binding custom to the subjects of trade and defence. A third, the doctrine of irrevocable surrender, stated that once the laws of England had been introduced into a colony, the monarch could not change them 'without Parliament.' Colonial patriots understood 'Parliament' in this context to mean the colonial legislatures ('Colonial Parliaments,' as Canadiensis called them).[20]

Here Barnabas Bidwell may well have made a contribution. The Yankee democrat was old enough to have seen American patriots invoke these doctrines against Parliament. John Willson, the American, and Dr Baldwin, the Irishman, both invoked the 'doctrine of irrevocable surrender' in the Union Bill debate of 1823.[21] They may have raised it of their own accord, or they may have been briefed by Bidwell. They must have been in touch with Bidwell during the previous session of the legislature, when they were leading supporters of his claim to sit in the house of assembly, but Bidwell's case must have brought the doctrine of irrevocable surrender to mind in any case. It so happens that the doctrine was derived from the very same early seventeenth-century legal judgment, known as *Calvin's Case*, that underpinned Bidwell's claim to British allegiance.

Either Baldwin or Bidwell could have penned the Letter on Responsible Government. To Lieutenant-Governor Francis Gore, back in 1807, the young Dr Baldwin's ties to the circle of Judge Thorpe were sufficient to brand him as 'an Irishman, ready to join any party to make confusion.'[22] X, as we saw, identified Canadiensis with the Thorpe circle, and some scholars have tentatively ascribed the letter to 'the Baldwin circle'; but it could just as well have been Bidwell's work.[23] It hardly matters, really. The Irish and American patriots of the 1770s and 1780s had shared many beliefs, and in 1829 the Baldwins and the Bidwells were close allies in the cause of responsible government.

What does matter is that the language of both Canadiensis and the Baldwins is saturated with the same unorthodox colonial doctrines. Canadiensis, for instance, echoed the 'doctrine of binding custom' by declaring that Parliament could legislate for the colonies only in regard to trade (including navigation and commerce) and defence. The idea of the Constitutional Act as a treaty, establishing the forms according to which the colonists are to exercise rights that already belong to them as British subjects – rights that no power on earth could rightfully withhold from them – also reflects the influence of these doctrines. X alluded to them in his introduction to the treatise, tracing Canadiensis's ideas back to Magna Carta and the Bill of Rights.

In short, the case for responsible government, whether presented by X or by the Baldwins, ultimately relied on the language of uncompromising opposition to imperial legislative sovereignty. It was the language of the two great foes of the unity of the British empire – American and Irish patriotism.

This is a crucial discovery, because it points to a link between the campaign for responsible government before 1850 and that for provincial rights within Confederation. To Canadiensis and the Baldwins, the keynote of the imperial constitution was equality – the equality of the mother country and the colonies. Colonies did not exist for the benefit of the mother country alone but for the benefit of both, wrote Canadiensis. The government of the empire was vested not in the British Parliament alone, but in that body 'conjointly' with the 'Colonial Parliaments.' Just as the Baldwins maintained that Westminster had no right to alter the Upper Canadian constitution without the consent of the colonial legislature, so Canadiensis generalized that it could not alter even the imperial constitution without the consent of all the colonial legislatures.

To these colonial patriots, the equality of mother country and colony entailed a division of legislative power between the British and colonial parliaments, the lion's share going to the latter. Self-government being the first principle of every free constitution, declared Canadiensis, nothing short of absolute necessity could justify the violation of that principle. Since Upper Canadians were represented in their own parliament, not at Westminster, it followed 'that in the former must be vested *the powers of Government generally*, and in the latter only those *special powers of Government* which for the preservation of the *safety* and *integrity* of the Empire *at large*, it is absolutely necessary to have lodged in the hands of *one body only* for the whole Empire.' This imperial sphere of competence boiled down to military defence and the regulation of commerce and navigation, the two subjects recognized in the 'doctrine of binding custom.' Robert Baldwin expressed very similar views.[24]

This account of the imperial constitution bears a startling resemblance to Oliver Mowat's idea of the Canadian constitution half a century later. Just as Canadiensis saw colonial legislatures as sovereign bodies, essentially equal to the British Parliament, so Mowat insisted on the sovereignty of the provincial legislatures and their equality to the Parliament of Canada. Canadiensis's idea that the empire is governed 'conjointly' by the British and colonial parliaments matches Mowat's insistence that the provinces possessed coordinate status with Ottawa in the governance of Canada. Canadiensis's division of legislative powers into a broad colonial sphere and a restricted imperial sphere foreshadows the conception of the division of powers between Ottawa and the provinces that Mowat was to urge on the Judicial Committee of the Privy Council, the highest tribunal of the empire, with such success in the 1880s and 1890s.

Most important of all, the idea of the Constitutional Act as a treaty or compact, and the belief that the imperial constitution can be altered only with the consent of all the colonies, prefigure the theoretical basis of Mowat's campaign for provincial rights – the compact theory of Confederation. I said at the start that the compact theory had antecedents in English-Canadian as well as French-Canadian political thought. Now I have revealed those antecedents in contemporary allusions to the Constitutional Act as a treaty or solemn compact – counterparts to the French-Canadian idea of the act as a *pacte solennel*. The next chapter explains how the Reformers pursued the goal of local self-government by dissembling their unorthodoxy and how their doing so helped to obscure the connection between responsible government, Confederation, and provincial rights.

5

Myths of Responsible Government

How did Canadians lose sight of the thread linking responsible government with Confederation and provincial rights? Part of the explanation, in my view, is that the Reformers of the 1830s and 1840s misled them. Advocates of responsible government had to overcome two ideological obstacles. One was the political ascendancy of Loyalism in Upper Canada, the other the doctrine of Westminster's legislative sovereignty. As long as the demand for responsible government was tied to a frank insistence on colonial sovereignty, it was difficult, if not impossible, to reconcile it with either the political or the legal doctrine. It seemed disloyal from both standpoints. There seemed to be no difference between responsible government and independence.

In the 1830s, British immigration aggravated these ideological handicaps. The campaign for responsible government merged from the political struggles of the 1820s, but Upper Canada was more and more becoming home to individuals who had no memory of those struggles. Most of the newcomers were antagonistic to the cause, partly from British patriotism and partly from hostility to the American settlers who held the ground that they, the newcomers, had come to occupy. Upper Canadian conservatives exploited that antagonism to turn them against Reform. I mentioned in chapter 3 how the Family Compact saw British immigration as their best chance of overcoming the American majority. At first its hopes looked justified.

To surmount these obstacles and reduce the risk of antagonizing British politicians, the champions of responsible government began in the 1830s to accentuate certain aspects of their ideology and play down others. They masked its unorthodox inspiration and its challenge to British legislative sovereignty. They dwelt on their esteem for British parliamentary institutions and their grievances against the Family Compact. Since responsible government was a British principle, they managed by the 1840s to assimilate their colonial heresies to the imperial orthodoxy. But they did so by means that blinded historians to the very aspects of their creed that led later generations of Reformers first to accept Confederation and then to defend provincial rights.

Of course, the Reformers' propaganda had an element of truth, or it could not have served their purpose. Unlike American Whigs of the 1760s and 1770s, the Reformers did not usually find themselves going head to head with the imperial authorities. Their immediate enemy was the Family Compact, and the British government normally figured in their rhetoric as a benign but ill-informed ruler, misled by governors who had fallen under the influence of the oligarchy. To later generations, the favourable British response to some of the Reformers' complaints confirmed this view of things. While the provincial government, insecure amid a Yankee horde, was trying to quell the growing discontent in Upper Canada, British conservatives were fighting demands for reform 'at home.' British and colonial reformers found common ground in their struggle against British and colonial reaction, and the British government came under pressure to disavow the excesses of its colonial servants.[1]

As a result, the Reformers enjoyed some dramatic successes in their appeals to Whitehall and Westminster. One was their challenge to the naturalization bill of 1827. Six years later William Lyon Mackenzie matched that triumph by getting Henry Boulton and Christopher Hagerman, respectively attorney general and solicitor general for Upper Canada, fired for their part in his expulsion and subsequent exclusion from the house of assembly. In between came lesser but still significant victories. The newspaperman Francis Collins's sentence for libelling John Beverley Robinson was partially remitted, and the legislative council was pressed into repealing the notorious Sedition Act, which had been used to banish the Scottish agitator Robert Gourlay from the colony.[2] These events lent a certain credibility to the idea that the British government sympathized with the people of Upper Canada and deplored the excesses of the colonial government.

British developments also helped to legitimize the demand for responsible government. One thing at least is sure about the mysterious Letter on Responsible Government: it shows that the principle was recognized in Britain in the 1820s and that Upper Canadian Reformers knew this. Organized political opposition within the House of Commons had become an accepted feature of British politics, and the opposition was seen as an alternative ministry, available to the monarch should his current ministers be politically incapable of carrying on the government. The phrase 'His Majesty's Opposition,' coined in 1826 as a facetious play on the term 'His Majesty's Government,' epitomized this development. The quip made a sensation, and John Rolph almost certainly heard of it when he arrived in England a few weeks later to lobby on the alien question. Rolph peppered his letters to the Colonial Office with references to the 'Provincial ministry' and 'His Majesty's Provincial Cabinet,' and when he returned to Canada he began using the same language in the assembly. In 1828, replying to a proposal by Dr William Baldwin to form a 'cabinet' of leading opposition MPPs to concert their tactics at the coming session of the legislature, he termed himself 'one of his Majesty's faithful opposition.' For his part Baldwin emphasized the Britishness of colonial responsible government in a letter explaining the petition of 1828 to the Duke of Wellington, newly appointed prime minister.[3]

These political and constitutional developments, and the relatively good grace with which the British finally accepted colonial self-government, made it easy for historians to accept the notion that the great enemy of Upper Canadian liberty was the Family Compact, not the British government. But that is not how leading Reformers saw it at the time – and I mean Rolph and the Baldwins, not just populists such as Mackenzie. The hopes aroused by the liberalization of 1827 and 1828 did not last long.

In truth, the oligarchy was the creature of the British government – its Frankenstein's monster, if you like – and Whitehall policy-makers were by no means ready to destroy it. The provincial constitution – the Constitutional Act of 1791 – had been framed by men intent on avoiding the mistakes they thought had led to the revolt of the Thirteen Colonies. The conventional wisdom of 1791 stated that the old colonial constitutions had been too democratic. They had contained no effective counterweight to the power of the representative assemblies, and these, as a result, had come into direct conflict with the crown. The keynote of the British constitution was aristocracy, and the new colonial constitutions were to conform more closely to the British model. In Upper Canada, the aristocratic provisions of the Constitutional Act – notably the appointed legislative council – were supplemented by an elitist, English-style legal system, which was foisted on the house of assembly by the prestige of Lieutenant-Governor John Graves Simcoe and his advisers. These institutions became the seats of oligarchic power.[4]

In January 1829, the assembly passed a vote of no confidence in the provincial 'ministry.' According to the principle of responsible government, this action should have obliged the governor to replace his advisers with new ones who commanded the confidence of the house. But the Duke of Wellington – the fourth prime minister in eighteen months – was now in power in Britain at the head of a government pledged to hold the fort against parliamentary reform. In May, when Parliament debated the Upper Canadian reform petition, Wellington and various other statesmen dismissed the demand for responsible government as inconsistent with the overriding sovereignty of Parliament and unsuited to Upper Canada's precarious position next to the United States.

Then, in July, a batch of new appointments revealed the futility of hoping for any change in the conduct of provincial affairs. John Beverley Robinson became chief justice. His successor as attorney general was the equally unpopular solicitor general, Henry John Boulton. Boulton's own successor was Christopher Hagerman, the Loyalist lawyer, whose performance as a temporary substitute for the suspended Judge Willis on the Court of King's Bench had made him an object of hatred and derision in opposition circles. To round off the affront to Reform sensibilities, another leading light of the Family Compact was to be Willis's permanent replacement.[5]

The Letter on Responsible Government reflected the Reformers' disillusionment. The Letter's bearing on current affairs was plain, but the mysterious X bitterly insisted that it had no relevance at all – that had been demonstrated once and for all by 'the Great Captain of the age' (Wellington) in his comments on the petition for responsible government. No, these 'principles of liberty,' this compendium of 'what were once *supposed to have been* our rights,' held no interest whatever for the politician. They were relics of the past, 'delusions' springing from such discredited sources as Magna Carta and the Bill of Rights. X was moved to publish a digest of them (he wrote) only in order to preserve them 'for the future antiquarians of our country to dispute upon.'[6] Where X was bitterly satirical, John Rolph was plain bitter. 'When I see the disposal of the principal revenues of the country assumed by the executive, and the wishes and feelings of the people so continually despised, I am really disheartened,' he told Dr Baldwin. 'I can see nothing in a country so governed to be morally or politically envied. It differs in but few particulars from a government by the sword.'[7]

If Rolph thought this way in 1829, it is no wonder that he joined William Lyon Mackenzie's rebellion eight years later. The rebuff of 1829 could be explained by the rise of a reactionary Tory ministry to power in London. But it was a Whig government, which had recently imposed parliamentary reform on a protesting king and House of Lords, that late in 1835 was to make the most disastrous appointment of all: that of Sir Francis Bond Head as governor. As the nominee of a reforming ministry, Head was hailed by some Reformers as the harbinger of responsible government, and on his arrival he dramatically confirmed these expectations by appointing Rolph and Robert Baldwin to the executive council. Reformers in the council: what next! But it was all a delusion. A few weeks later, the council resigned en bloc to protest against Head's refusal to consult it in making appointments. When the house of assembly supported the retiring councillors, Head dissolved the legislature and mounted a demagogic election campaign, in which he denounced the Reformers as republicans and traitors. Mackenzie, Marshall Bidwell, and other leading Reformers lost their seats, and the opposition was routed.

Historians have long ascribed the Tory triumph of 1836 to the mass of new voters who had emigrated from Britain since the mid-1820s. It showed that the Family Compact had been justified in hoping that loyal folk from 'home' would politically neutralize the Yankees. There is much truth in this, but other explanations made more sense to the Reformers. They blamed Head's unprecedented and unconstitutional rabble-rousing. They pointed bitterly to the work of one group of newcomers in particular: Irish immigrants, members of the Orange Order, who had sabotaged the electoral process in several ridings by beating and bullying Reformers. To the victims of this violence, the new assembly was illegitimate from the moment of its election, and it soon disgraced itself by another breach of constitutional propriety. The death of William IV was known to be imminent. According to the constitution, a general election should follow this event. The Tories' popularity was already waning, and a new election would give the Reformers a chance to recoup their fortunes. To avoid this, the legislature passed a statute abolishing this requirement.[8]

Such actions allowed William Lyon Mackenzie and his supporters to justify the rebellion of 1837 as a rising against an unconstitutional and oppressive colonial regime and an imperial suzerain besmirched by its rogue governor. Actually, the colonial secretary, Lord Glenelg, was vexed by Head's divisive policies and had ordered him to appoint Bidwell to the Court of King's Bench. By the time of the rebellion, Glenelg had already moved to dismiss Head for disobeying that order.[9] But the rebels had no way of knowing this and no reason to expect it.

In truth, the policy of the British government from 1827 on was not so much liberal as wavering. The Reformers owed their success at the Colonial Office in 1827 and 1833 to one man, Lord Goderich, and both times he soon left office owing to the vagaries of British politics. The brief political thaw of 1827–8 had ended in a Tory reaction, as Wellington rallied the party against parliamentary reform. In 1834 it was the same again. The Tories returned to office, after four years in opposition, when William IV seized an opportunity to dismiss the Whig ministers who had forced reform on him. They did not last long, because the voters preferred the Whigs, but meanwhile Christopher Hagerman had successfully lobbied to be restored to his office as solicitor general of Upper Canada. A new attorney general had already been appointed, but Henry Boulton received the chief justiceship of Newfoundland as a consolation. Then came the Head fiasco and its traumatic sequel.

Even after the rebellions, when the Earl of Durham, home from his brief tour as governor general of Canada, spoke out in favour of responsible government, his less radical colleagues in the Whig government dismissed the idea. They included the colonial secretary, Lord John Russell. In 1842 the governor general of United Canada, Sir Charles Bagot, reluctantly yielded to the principle of responsible government by appointing a ministry led by Robert Baldwin and Louis-Hippolyte LaFontaine, but his action was condemned by the British government, which had again fallen to the Tories (or Conservatives, as they now called themselves). The Conservatives upheld Bagot's successor, Sir Charles Metcalfe, in his rejection of the Baldwinite conception of responsible government, and colonial self-rule was finally assured only in 1846, when the Whigs returned to power.[10]

Of course, British dithering was not the Reformers' only problem. Upper Canadians kept voting against them. Many such electors were newcomers from Britain, and British immigration was a persistent handicap for the Reformers for the rest of the century. Newcomers did not share in the history of struggle that animated the Reform tradition. After 1867, when that tradition found expression in the defence of 'Ontario's rights' against Ottawa, there was no reason for them to identify with 'Ontario' rather than 'Canada.' The story of the Reform tradition is one of continuing creative adaptation to the problem of British political ascendancy and immigration. That process began with the Baldwins themselves.

In the 1830s and 1840s, at any rate, British immigration presented

Reformers with an opportunity as well as an obstacle. For one thing, the idea of reform was becoming fashionable in Britain itself, though bitterly resisted by conservatives: in 1836 most Upper Canadian voters had accepted Sir Francis Head's equation of responsible government with 'republicanism,' but in British politics the principle was becoming more and more firmly established. For another, British newcomers to Upper Canada were hardly less hostile to the Family Compact than to the Reformers. Even before the rebellion there was talk in the newspapers of a 'British party' as a third force in provincial politics. Scarcely had Mackenzie, disguised as a woman, scuttled across the U.S. border than the spokesmen of this new force began to condemn oligarchic misrule as the true cause of the rebellion.[11] Herein lay the Reformers' chance. If only they could dress up colonial responsible government as a British principle rather than as a grab for sovereign power, as a monarchical rather than a republican solution to the colony's problems, as a remedy for domestic tyranny rather than a threat to imperial unity, they might be able to convince Whig ministers and British immigrants alike. This was to be Robert Baldwin's great achievement.

For a long time Baldwin's historical reputation was that of an earnest plodder, whose career was dignified mainly by the tenacious pursuit of his and his father's great ideal. Some writers, though, have detected hidden passion in the very intensity of his devotion to that idea, and we now know too of the bizarre will that directed an incision like a Caesarean section to be made on his corpse in final atonement for his wife's death from that operation.[12] Passion there assuredly was. But what nobody has noticed is the sheer cleverness of his argument for responsible government, as presented to the colonial secretary, Lord Glenelg, in London in 1836. No doubt other Reformers influenced his thinking – his father, for one, and maybe John Rolph. But Robert Baldwin's name stands alone on the wiliest paper we possess from any Reformer before Mowat.

Baldwin's problem in 1836 was to prevent his heterodox proposal from being dismissed out of hand on doctrinal grounds, and his trick was to shift the debate from the ground of principle to that of practical politics. Whether colonists had a *right* to responsible government was irrelevant, he told Glenelg in London; the only question worth discussing was whether it was *advisable*. On this basis he dismissed the 'astute reasonings' and 'fine distinctions' that might be urged against it. 'Plain common sense' dictated that members of the colonial parliament must have the same influence on the provincial government as members of the British Parliament exercised over that of the mother country. The only alternative was 'a Government of the sword,' and Britain could hardly desire that.

With similar deftness, Baldwin presented responsible government to Glenelg as both the most moderate reform and the only one drastic enough to work. It was moderate because it amounted 'merely to the application of an English principle to the constitution as it stands.' This made it preferable to 'the more violent measure of a legislative change in the Charter,' such as making the upper chamber elective. But he also praised its efficacy. Reformers railed against the legislative council as an insuperable obstacle to popular legislation, but the council presented such an obstacle because it was controlled by the same people who ran the government. Make the council elective, as many Reformers wanted, and you would merely set it too, like the assembly, at loggerheads with the executive. Only responsible government could produce harmony between the executive and the people's representatives.[13]

Baldwin was telling the British that the structure they had devised in 1791 to restrain colonial democracy no longer worked. He took care to sugar the pill, though. He assured Glenelg that responsible government involved no weakening of the paramount authority of the mother country. Colonial legislation would still be subject to British veto, whether wielded by the governor in the colony or by the Privy Council at Whitehall. Nor would the new principle alter the governor's constitutional responsibility to the British government. But could that paramountcy be more than nominal? Could the British government effectively check a colonial legislature that enjoyed all the attributes of sovereignty in the colony's internal affairs? Baldwin ignored these questions. What mattered was the fact that the colony could be governed only with the consent of colonial public opinion. Self-government was the English 'genius,' he told Durham in 1838, and responsible government was the only way to avert a second and worse rebellion. When push came to shove, the only effective ties between Britain and Upper Canada were those not of law but of sentiment. If, under responsible government, the people still found themselves misgoverned, they would have only themselves to blame and not, as now, the British.[14]

Baldwin's arguments found a ready audience in 'Radical Jack' Durham, but not all of Durham's colleagues were so easily convinced: as I noted earlier, the colonial secretary, Lord John Russell, persisted in rejecting the proposal on account of its theoretical inconsistency. He did, however, instruct Durham's successor, Poulett Thomson (Lord Sydenham), to govern as far as possible in harmony with public opinion.[15] Owing to this ambiguity, the government of United Canada was set up on a somewhat uncertain basis. It was run by department heads, who made up the executive council and sat in the legislature. They looked, therefore, like British cabinet ministers. But to whom were they responsible: the people's representatives or some British official? It was important to clarify the situation, or at least to turn the confusion to the Reformers' advantage.

Baldwin's 'sovereignty by stealth' tactics were well suited to this contingency. In September 1841 he introduced in the legislature a set of resolutions affirming that responsible government now prevailed in Canada. He did not fight for their adoption, though, but accepted a set of government amendments as having 'substantially the same' meaning as his own. Afterwards the Reformers claimed that the ministry, on that occasion, had solemnly admitted the fact of responsible government, and the Reformers' appointment to office a year later by Sir Charles Bagot only strengthened the claim. When Bagot's successor, Sir Charles Metcalfe, tried to turn the tide in 1843 by dismissing the Baldwin–LaFontaine cabinet despite its legislative majority, the Reformers could argue that he was acting against both the theory and the practice of the constitution. Metcalfe prevailed in the short term, because his supporters won the general election of 1844. This was a 'loyalty election' reminiscent of 1836, and the Upper Canadian conservatives gained enough seats to offset the success of LaFontaine's party in Lower Canada. At the next election, though, the Reform alliance triumphed throughout United Canada. Baldwin and LaFontaine returned to power, and the matter was decided once and for all.[16]

In a sense Baldwin's responsible government resolutions of 1841 were an updated version of that 'irrevocable surrender' which two decades earlier had underpinned his father's compact theory of the Constitutional Act. They even retained something of the old Yankee and Irish lilt. One of them described the provincial legislature as possessing the power to legislate 'upon all matters which do not, on the ground of absolute necessity, constitutionally belong to the jurisdiction of the Imperial Parliament, as the paramount authority of the Empire.' These words differed little from those of Canadiensis, who confined imperial legislative sovereignty to 'those special powers of government which ... it is absolutely necessary to have lodged in the hands of one body only for the whole Empire.'[17]

Baldwin sounded the same theme at a grand dinner in Toronto during the general election campaign of 1844, when he proclaimed 'the first principle of British Liberty – the right, the inalienable right, of being concerned through our representatives in the government of ourselves.'[18] Theoretically speaking, he explained, this principle gave Canadians just the same authority over the government of the empire as their fellow-subjects in Britain. In practice the British Parliament was paramount, but only from geographical necessity and a regard for the safety of the empire as a whole. Outside Britain its powers were limited to matters of common concern – matters of 'peace or war, of trade and commerce, or the like.' The constitutional rights of colonists as British subjects required that all other matters be handled by the colonial governments, and they necessitated the establishment of responsible government in Canada.

While Robert Baldwin continued to proclaim the old verities, however, a rather different sort of politician took the lead in propounding new ones. This was Baldwin's cousin and fellow-minister, Robert Baldwin Sullivan, a pragmatist with a special interest in modernizing the government. Sullivan had broken with his kinsman in 1836 by joining the executive council after Baldwin resigned over the principle of responsible government. His abilities had enabled him to dominate the council and had won him the approbation of Lord Sydenham, Lord Durham's successor as governor general of Canada, who carried out the union of 1841. Sydenham appointed Sullivan to the first cabinet of United Canada.[19] In that capacity Sullivan, with his fellow ministers, paved the way for the Reformers' accession to office by warning Sir Charles Bagot that the 'responsible government' resolutions of 1841 would oblige them to resign if they lost a vote of confidence. Bagot avoided a crisis by appointing several Reform ministers while retaining Sullivan and two others from his old cabinet.[20] After that, Sullivan embraced the principle of responsible government, and in the 'Metcalfe election' of 1844 he became the Reformers' chief propagandist; but he was too modern and pragmatic to bang the drum for any idea so exotic as the ancient indefeasible rights of British subjects.

In any case, it was unwise for the Reformers to put all their eggs in that basket. As I said, the constitutional crisis of 1844 was a replay of the Upper Canadian crisis of 1836: both had been precipitated by the governor's insistence on making official appointments without consulting his executive council. Accordingly, Sullivan pitched his argument to that part of the Upper Canadian electorate which had supported the government in 1836 and 1841 – the voters who had rejected the Reformers when they quarrelled with Sir Francis Head over responsible government and had rejected the Tories when they quarrelled with Lord Sydenham over the union. This time they might well support Metcalfe unless they could be persuaded that the governor general had acted unconstitutionally. In the summer of 1844 Egerton Ryerson, the influential Methodist minister, wooed this element of the electorate with a series of open letters defending Metcalfe. Sullivan replied with a set of *Letters on Responsible Government*, published under the pen-name 'Legion.'

Sullivan's *Letters* was a classic of Baldwinite propaganda. Like Robert Baldwin in 1836, he spurned theory in favour of pragmatism and emphasized the loyal Britishness of colonial responsible government and its champions. One need only look at the United States, he wrote, to see how political theories could impart a dangerous rigidity to a constitution. South of the border liberty was surrounded by a palisade of words and enactments, under cover of which it was assailed almost as often as it was defended. British liberties, by contrast, relied not on theories written into law but on unwritten conventions, flexible enough to be adjusted to every exigency as it arose.[21]

It was certainly not on theoretical grounds that Sullivan asserted the colonists' right to responsible government. Far from it: he claimed it rather as part and parcel of the modern British constitution, and as the only alternative to that un-British abomination, government by the sword. Besides, it had been conceded as a practical matter by Lord John Russell in his instructions to Lord Sydenham, and formally by Sydenham's government in the 'responsible government' resolutions of 1841 – 'the *constitution* of 1841,' Sullivan pointedly called them at the Reformers' election-eve dinner in 1844, speaking with special authority as a former member of Sydenham's government.[22] There was, he concluded, no point in discussing whether the Canadian claim to responsible government rested on the inalienable and inherent right of British subjects or on concession by the British government. 'We have it, in fact, both ways theoretically,' he wrote, 'and have only to insist on our rights, whether inherent or conceded, to have it practically.'[23]

So Sullivan, like his cousin, treated the resolutions of 1841 as a formal surrender of authority by the crown, but in doing so he contrived to assimilate the idea to the modern British constitutionalism of binding practice. British responsible government was a matter not of *law* but of *convention*. The monarch's powers remained legally intact but by custom were wielded by ministers responsible to Parliament. This arrangement made it possible to hold someone other than the monarch legally liable for the abuse of those powers, thereby affording a way of checking the government without destabilizing the state.

The system of political accountability that we call responsible government was an extension of this legal responsibility. Under the old system, the only way of ousting a minister against the king's will was the legal process of impeachment by the House of Commons and trial by the House of Lords. As we see today in the United States, that process was all too vulnerable to abuse for political ends. The new system required both individual ministers and the government as a whole to resign their offices if they could not command the confidence of a majority of the Commons. In that way the government was kept reasonably responsive to public opinion without placing the king's ministers in legal jeopardy.

The achievement of Robert Baldwin and his collaborators, Sullivan among them, in the 1840s was that of setting the government of Canada on the same constitutional footing as that of the mother country. By playing down the challenge that responsible government posed to the sovereignty of the British Parliament, by stressing its Britishness and its importance as a remedy for domestic misrule, they paved the way for its acceptance as a constitutional convention that outweighed formal legality.

I said at the start of the chapter that the Baldwinites had achieved responsible government by means that blinded later generations to the underlying unorthodoxy of their creed. In a sense the principle itself had that tendency: by subordinating law to convention, it diverted attention from the Reformers' challenge to the legal supremacy of the British Parliament. But there was more to it than that. In assimilating their colonial constitutionalism to the British orthodoxy, the Baldwinites infused the Canadian political culture with the myth that validated that orthodoxy: the myth we know today as the Whig interpretation of history. As applied to Upper Canadian history, that myth tended to highlight the Reformers' resistance to colonial misrule rather than their challenge to imperial sovereignty and, in general, to stress constitutional issues rather than the tension between Upper Canadian and British identities.

The Whig myth presented British history in terms of the gradual victory of parliamentary government over absolute monarchy. Famous episodes in that story included the signing of Magna Carta in 1215, the summoning of the first Parliament later in the thirteenth century, and the Glorious Revolution of 1688, which decisively subjected the royal power to the control of Parliament. This story was the common heritage of British Whiggism, both at home and overseas – even the Americans had objected only to certain modern corruptions, such as Parliament's claim to have inherited the king's powers over the colonies; but there was one crucial difference between the metropolitan and colonial traditions. The British battle for liberty had been fought against arbitrary government pure and simple: the story contained nothing about a struggle against imperial oppression. That idea was the grand myth of the American Revolution and of the Irish struggle for self-government, and it had flowed from these sources into the Upper Canadian Reform tradition. By playing down these anti-imperialist elements of the Reform ideology and emphasizing the struggle against domestic tyranny, the Baldwinites promoted the ascendancy of the metropolitan version of the Whig myth over the colonial version.

This substitution coloured later perceptions of Upper Canadian history, inducing historians to portray the campaign as a reaction to oligarchic misrule within the colony rather than a struggle against imperial power. The responsible government petition of 1828 was stuffed with complaints against the provincial authorities. It was natural for historians, seeing this, to link the movement to popular resentment of the Family Compact: why should they think otherwise, when Reformers from Robert Baldwin onward had insisted on it? They did not notice that in 1828 the Reformers were also smarting under one act of coercion that could not be included in a petition for relief from colonial misrule, for the culprit was not the colonial but the British government. That was the British attempt in 1827 to dictate the terms of a provincial naturalization act.

The alien question was in fact tailor-made to stimulate a desire for local autonomy. I described in chapter 3 how it set up a conflict between imperial and Upper Canadian authority. First the American settlers were told that thirty years of Upper Canadian history, including several provincial statutes, counted for nothing against British trade legislation regarding U.S. residents. Then they had to swallow the political reality that their history did indeed count for nothing against an English judicial decision concerning an American who had never set foot in the province. By its very nature the controversy made them think of themselves as Upper Canadians and of their province as a distinct political community within the empire, with its own unique history. This new-found sense of belonging focused on the house of assembly, where year by year they and their champions fought a desperate rearguard action against disenfranchisement.

Such were the obvious consequences of the alien question, but it also had a deeper effect. To the American settlers and their sympathizers, the threat of legal disenfranchisement only accentuated a discrimination that was part and parcel of provincial life, afflicting even Reformers whose allegiance was not in question. This condition was inherent in the colony's constitution. Local government was controlled by magistrates appointed by the provincial government at York. These officials were unaccountable to the neighbours whose lives they regulated as judges and administrators. The popular representative body, the house of assembly, was hobbled by the legislative council, which in most things was just a tool of the executive. The government itself was run by administrators who owed their places to the British government. Living under such a regime, Upper Canadians might well perceive their entire community as wrongfully disenfranchised by the British doctrine of overriding imperial sovereignty and by the political power that enforced that doctrine.

Tactical prudence and daily slights might direct popular resentment towards the Family Compact, but Reformers could never forget that the oligarchy owed its power to British (that is, for many Reformers, to alien) support. That perception would carry over into the era of responsible government and would then receive less inhibited expression, for the new oppressor of the 1850s could claim none of the charisma that attached to the imperial overlord; indeed, the more patriotic the mid-nineteenth-century Englishman, the more likely he was to be an anti-Catholic francophobe. And so 'the domination of the Family Compact' would give way, in Oliver Mowat's story, to 'the domination of Lower Canada,' and the struggle for Upper Canadian autonomy would go on. Authoritarian, unaccountable government by elites whose power derived from a distant capital; mutual alienation and unappeasable distrust between rulers and ruled: from these symmetries between the experience of Upper Canadians in their local communities, on the one hand, and that of the Upper Canadian community as a whole on the other, sprang the movement whose arduous history Mowat recited in his speech at Woodstock in 1872 – a movement devoted to realizing, against all odds, self-government for Upper Canada.

The dogged, defiant righteousness of that movement was personified by Robert Baldwin, who resigned political office three times between

1836 and 1843 in pursuit of his 'one idea.' The attorney general's official letterbook for the 1840s contains seventeen form letters dating from Baldwin's tenure of office in 1842–3. One is entitled 'Reply to Unsolicited Advice from Political Supporters.' They must not think that their advice is unwanted or disregarded, it says, just because Baldwin is too busy to reply in person. 'On the contrary, I feel the responsibility of my position too sensibly not to be glad of information & Counsel from any quarter. And when it comes from my political friends [& more particularly when from those who stood firm by us in the hour of our political prostration when our opponents fancied they had their feet upon our necks & could keep them there for ever] it is to me be assured ever doubly welcome.'[24]

The bracketed insert is an indispensable acknowledgment of comradeship, to be included only in letters to veterans of the campaign for responsible government. It is passion reduced to an incantation or formula, but the note of grim defiance is unmistakable. It announces the emergence of what was to become a mythic tradition of struggle: a tradition to which Oliver Mowat was to pay homage thirty years later in his tribute to the constancy of the Reformers of North Oxford. In part II of this book, we see how that sense of tradition sustained the Reformers of Upper Canada, first in their campaign to reform United Canada and then in their defence of provincial rights within Confederation.

Part Two

1850–1890:
The Confederation Compact

6

'One Great Confederation'

The Reform party that campaigned in the late 1850s and early 1860s to reform United Canada was much altered from that which had struggled for responsible government in the 1840s. From 1848 to 1854, the party and its Lower Canadian allies governed the province, first under Robert Baldwin and Louis-Hippolyte LaFontaine and then, from 1851 on, under Francis Hincks and Augustin-Norbert Morin. Almost from the start, the exercise of political power opened a rift between the party leaders and many of their followers. Baldwin's social conservatism annoyed not only the party's populist wing but many of its business supporters, including Hincks. Meanwhile the Tories, alienated by Britain's endorsement of responsible government, embarrassed him by proposing or supporting measures that they would previously have condemned as disloyal and republican: notably, the conversion of the legislative council – the upper house of the provincial legislature – into an elected body.

It was one such episode, in 1851, that drove Baldwin to resign his office. Upper Canadian conservatives supported a radical motion to abolish the Upper Canadian Court of Chancery, a crucial part of a legal system that Baldwin cherished. The government defeated this measure only with the aid of Lower Canadian votes. Baldwin, supported by only a handful of MPPs from his own province, decided to treat the vote as an expression of no confidence in him as attorney general. Ironically, the resolution to abolish the court was moved by William Lyon Mackenzie, the rebel leader of 1837, whom Baldwin had allowed to return to Canada in 1849 after a decade's exile in the United States. Mackenzie had quickly been elected to the legislature – testimony to the enduring strength of the Clear Grits, as the Reform party's populist wing was coming to be known.

The party's dissolution continued under Hincks. The new Upper Canadian leader had actually lived in Montreal since 1844 and was closely involved with Montreal business circles. In ecclesiastical policy, the growing conservatism of his French-Canadian allies (now called *bleus* to distinguish them from the more liberal *rouge* minority) prevented Hincks from gratifying the fervent anti-clericalism of many Reformers by decisively separating church and state. These issues, and the increasing aura of financial corruption which surrounded his ministry, alienated George Brown, the assertive Scot whose Toronto *Globe* had rapidly become the biggest newspaper in Canada. In 1854 Hincks and his circle of business-oriented Reformers decided that they had more in common with the old Tories than with most of their own party. Taking their *bleu* allies with them, they combined with the Tories. The new bedfellows called themselves the Liberal Conservative party, but in the minds of their deserted comrades the Hincksites became, and their new friends remained, Tories.

For three years George Brown applied the leverage provided by his newspaper, with its daily and weekly editions, to the task of reviving the Reform party. His paper and the slogan of resistance to Lower Canadian domination gave him a substantial advantage over his main rival, John Sandfield Macdonald of Glengarry. Both as an easterner, from the part of Upper Canada that was nearest to Montreal, and as a Catholic, Sandfield Macdonald was ill-fitted to appeal to the prejudices that animated most Reformers. In 1857, at a small organizational convention in Toronto, Brown presided over the formation of the Reform Alliance. This body united the Clear Grits, who were strongest in the western peninsula of Upper Canada, with other Reformers who shared the Grits' loathing of Tory corruption and Lower Canadian domination but not their fondness for American-style political institutions.[1]

The Alliance's great goal was parliamentary representation by population. This meant reforming the constitution of United Canada so that Upper and Lower Canada no longer had equal numbers of seats. The British government had provided this equality in the Act of Union in order to allay the fears of Upper Canadian conservatives such as John Beverley Robinson, who feared that the Upper Canadian Reformers would combine with the French party to dominate the legislative assembly.[2] At that time Lower Canada had the larger population, and the effect of the measure was to limit the power of the French party. By

1851, however, Upper Canada's population outnumbered that of the lower province, and the census of 1861 was bound to show a still greater disparity. A measure designed to weaken the French Canadians when they were suspected of revolutionary sentiments now helped the *bleus* to impose their conservative values on Upper Canada. It was their votes that defeated William Lyon Mackenzie's proposal of 1851 to abolish the Upper Canadian Court of Chancery. Four years later, it was their votes that set up separate public schools for Upper Canada's Roman Catholics in heinous breach of the principle of separation of church and state.

For a year and more after its founding convention, things went brilliantly for the Reform Alliance. In the general election at the end of 1857, the Liberal-Conservative party, handicapped by a serious business depression, lost several seats. Now led by John A. Macdonald, it clung to power through its coalition with the *bleus*, but in the parliamentary session that began in February 1858 the coalition's majority steadily eroded. At the end of July the government decided to resign, if only to demonstrate that no other combination could hope to govern the province. In conformity with British constitutional practice, the governor general, Sir Edmund Walker Head, invited George Brown, as the leading opposition politician in the legislature, to try to form a ministry.

How could Brown hope to govern? He did not enjoy unanimous support even among the Reformers – Sandfield Macdonald had stood ostentatiously aloof from the Alliance, although his brother Donald deterred him from accepting an invitation from John A. Macdonald, early in 1858, to join the Conservative government.[3] More seriously, Brown's vehement opposition to the domination of Lower Canada was a grave handicap in attracting Lower Canadian support. Even if he surmounted that obstacle, the Lower Canadian liberals, the *rouges*, were heavily outnumbered by the *bleus* in the legislature. Brown was well aware of all this, of course, as was his *rouge* counterpart, Antoine-Aimé Dorion. Still, they decided that they could settle their differences, although they had no time just then to work out the details. If defeated in the legislative assembly, they counted on the governor general to dissolve the legislature and let them take their program to the people at a general election.

The outgoing ministers' gamble seemed to have failed. Despite the odds, the Liberals had managed to put together a cabinet; and who could tell how a new government, with a fresh plan for solving the province's constitutional problems, might fare at the polls? But the Conservatives had a crucial ally in Sir Edmund Head. The governor general

had had to invite Brown to form a government, but he disliked the belli-
cose Reformer personally as well as politically. He now let Brown and
Dorion know repeatedly and emphatically that, should they be defeated
in the assembly, they could *not* count on him to dissolve the legislature
so soon after the last election – this even though such a defeat was virtually assured, even under the best of circumstances. In those days members of the assembly, on being appointed to office, were under a
constitutional obligation to resign their seats and stand for re-election.
This would rob the new government, in any early confrontation in the
house, of a dozen indispensable votes. It looked as if Head, disagreeably
surprised by Brown's success in forming a ministry, was trying to deter
the pugnacious Reformer from accepting the invitation that he had been
constitutionally obliged to tender him.

The confrontation was played out to its bitter end. Brown's government was sworn in at noon and defeated at midnight. The next day,
Brown requested a dissolution and was refused. The governor general
justified his decision in a long memorandum, but the Liberal leaders
had ample reason to feel ill-used. Sir Edmund Head would have earned
his billing, along with Governor General Metcalfe, in Oliver Mowat's
saga of the tribulations of the Upper Canadian Reformers even if he had
not lent himself to the charade that followed.

The Conservative ministers, recalled to office after a few days in
opposition, had no wish to resign their seats as their rivals had done.
But the rule that obliged newly appointed ministers to do so was inflex-
ible – or was it? A year earlier, a law had been passed exempting any
official who was appointed to a new office within a month of resigning
his old one. The act was meant to make it possible to shuffle ministers
without the ministers concerned having to fight by-elections. It was not
meant to allow whole new governments to take office without doing so;
but the act did not expressly forbid this, because no one had dreamed
that it could happen. (Governments usually last longer than a month!)
In a manoeuvre as ingenious as it was discreditable, Governor General
Head swore John A. Macdonald and his colleagues late one evening to
the faithful performance of offices that they had no intention of per-
forming. Next morning they resigned their new offices and resumed
those that they had quit a few days earlier. And so the term 'double
shuffle' entered the lexicon of Canadian history.[4]

Unfairly perhaps, the Liberals suffered worse from this political binge
than their rivals. Many of Brown's and Dorion's supporters had been as
surprised at their sudden amour as their opponents were. Had they

abandoned their principles out of lust for office? Eyebrows were raised; explanations had to be made. The Upper Canadian leaders were all re-elected comfortably enough, as were all but one of their Lower Canadian colleagues, but relations between the two groups cooled noticeably as sectional issues intervened to pull them apart. In particular, representation by population threatened to lose as many votes for the *rouges* in Lower Canada as it won for the Reformers in Upper Canada. Apart from that, Head's blatant favouritism and the double shuffle shook Brown's faith not just in the British commitment to responsible government but in responsible government itself. Thirty years before Goldwin Smith, Brown found himself wondering whether Canadian politicians were genteel enough to operate a system that left vast discretionary power in the hands of the executive. For much of 1859 he let his radical columnist George Sheppard dilate unchecked on the virtues of a written constitution and the total separation of the executive and legislative powers – both American institutions – and on another Grit favourite, dissolution of the union between Upper and Lower Canada.

By autumn, however, Brown had recovered his optimism. His change of mood was linked to his sudden embrace of a new policy: federation. First mooted in 1856 by Dorion, it was the ideal way to enjoy simultaneously the advantages of union and dissolution. If Upper and Lower Canada had separate governments for local affairs, while a federal authority dealt with matters of common interest, then Upper Canada would no longer suffer domination by Lower Canada, yet Lower Canada would have no reason to fear the reverse. With their special laws and institutions thus safeguarded, French Canadians need not fear the consequences of representation by population in the federal legislature. They might even accept Canada's absorption of the vast open spaces of the Hudson's Bay Company's fur-trading empire north and west of Lake Superior, a prospect that they now disliked for fear that it would increase the imbalance of population between east and west. And Upper Canada would not be politically cut off from the Atlantic seaboard, as it would if the union were dissolved completely. Brown muzzled Sheppard and called a convention for November 1859 to set the Reform Alliance firmly on the right track.[5]

There was one thing on which they were all agreed, Brown told the 500-plus delegates after two days of fervid debate. It was time for a change – a constitutional reform that would put an end to those strifes of race and creed that *almost* threatened Canada with civil war. Several speakers made some such strident allusion, more or less carefully qualified, to the plight of their homeland. Brown himself spoke of 'fighting the battles of Upper Canada' and 'under the banner of Upper Canada.' The Clear Grit journalist William McDougall, who was now on Brown's payroll at the *Globe*, bitterly recalled how eagerly the French Canadians had embraced the Reformers in 1841; 'but no sooner did we get for them the rights they required, than they put us under their heels.' 'Sooner than see our country enslaved by Lower Canadians or any others, we would spill our blood,' proclaimed another delegate to cheers before going on to observe that, luckily, there was no need of that. A fourth spoke of being 'trodden in the mire by the Lower Canadians.'[6]

Every mind was on the country's present plight. Little was said about the past. But early in the proceedings the MPP for South Ontario, a prominent Toronto lawyer, offered a historical perspective that placed the present fight in the Reform tradition of struggle for self-government. Oliver Mowat's theme was 'foreign domination,' the 'baneful domination we are now suffering from Lower Canada,' which he compared unfavourably with an earlier phase of his homeland's existence. Before responsible government, he recalled, the country had been under a regime that no free people ought to endure. He did not sympathize (he said) with those who had tried to alter it by rebellion. Still, the situation must have been truly deplorable for Lord Sydenham to say that, had he lived under that regime, he would not have fought for it.

But if things had been bad under the Family Compact, were they not now worse? Then, after all, it was an English-Canadian influence that prevailed. Then their oppressors had been men who lived among them, spoke their language, and read their newspapers. Now they were ruled by men of another language, another race, another country. If rebellion had been justified under the old regime – not that he agreed that it was – what were they to say of their current plight? Mowat left the question hanging and went on to talk about the peaceful, constitutional remedy that was so fortunately available to them: federation.

Mowat's speech sparked off other xenophobic remarks, most notably from a delegate who referred repeatedly to 'Frenchmen' and compared the *bleu* leader, George-Étienne Cartier, to another 'little Frenchman,' Napoleon Bonaparte. But Ebenezer Bodwell of Oxford County stressed another point. Speakers were placing undue emphasis on the domination of the French, he protested. The blame ought to be attached to those Upper Canadian politicians who had bartered away their country's interests. Moving the first of the resolutions crafted by Brown's hand-picked committee of party stalwarts – a resolution stating the convention's discontent with the existing union of the Canadas – Bodwell said that the union was unsatisfactory because it had enabled certain Upper Canadians, by pandering to the Lower Canadian majority, to rule Upper Canada contrary to the interests of the people. It was not the French who were to blame for this, he declared, but the truancy of the 'Britishers.'[7]

Bodwell's rebuke to Mowat was purely rhetorical. Both sides of the question needed airing: there was no Tory villainy unless there was Lower Canadian tyranny, and the worse the tyranny the worse the villainy. What could be worse villainy in a Britisher than to deliver up his fellow-subjects to a French tyranny? Said the *Globe*: 'There is no creature more despicable than the Western Canadian who at this moment aids the [Roman Catholic] hierarchy and dominant clique of Lower Canada to fasten upon our necks the French yoke.'[8]

The most important thing about Mowat's speech was not its vilification of the Lower Canadians but its comparison between the 1850s and the 1830s. Upper Canadians were again (or still) an oppressed people, and the Reform party was the vanguard of popular resistance. In this way Mowat identified the Reformers with the great fight for responsible government at a time when many Reformers were denouncing that system as a failure.

The most vehement denigrator of responsible government was James Lesslie, the veteran Reformer who had backed William Lyon Mackenzie in many a sally against Tory tyranny. Lesslie recalled his own role in the struggle for what he called the 'grand panacea,' but only to assert with greater authority that the cure had not worked. Responsible government was a vain attempt to graft onto the province institutions foreign to the character and circumstances of the people. It worked well enough in Britain, where life and property were much more secure, and the administration of justice much purer, than they were in the United States. In Upper Canada, though, responsible government had only perpetuated the tyranny of a minority. He personally would prefer to live under the Tsar of Russia, because he would prefer one tyrant to many.[9]

No other speaker quite matched Lesslie for hyperbole, but many demanded that responsible government be ditched in favour of a written constitution and a directly elected executive. To judge by the *Globe*'s report of the convention, only one delegate spoke up for responsible government, and that was at a very late stage, when delegates had started to call impatiently for George Brown to wrap up the debate.

Only then did Abner Hurd, a grain merchant from Ontario County, make the obvious argument that responsible government might work perfectly well if only the union with Lower Canada were dissolved. Picking up on Lesslie's admission that the system worked well in Britain, he observed that life and property were much more secure in Canada too than in the United States. He saw this as a strong argument for sticking to British institutions.[10]

It shows the complexity of the debate that, on the main issue, Hurd and Lesslie were in agreement. Both men favoured a total dissolution of the union rather than the partial disruption that federation would entail. It was on this ground that the main challenge to Brown took place, led by his own employee, George Sheppard. Sheppard was a talented journalist, whose career was to peak in seventeen years' service (1863–80) as political correspondent and (briefly) editor of the *New York Times*. He had decided to stay silent at the convention, fearing that his well-known pro-Americanism would be a liability to his cause, but when he saw the federationists running away with the prize he stepped in to lead a charge in favour of total dissolution.[11]

Sheppard took aim at the rank-and-file Reformer's traditional hostility towards government. Brown and his supporters maintained that federation would mean cheap government. The local governments at least might be built on the American model, with a directly elected executive completely removed from the legislature. Brown was not so sure about the general government, but the main thing (he said) was to give it as little to do as possible. It would have a few clearly defined tasks: it would administer and liquidate the public debt amassed by United Canada; it would run the post office; it would regulate navigation on the Great Lakes and the St Lawrence River; it would enact common criminal and commercial codes for the federated provinces. And such as it was, it would be organized on the basis of representation by population. Lower Canadians could not object once their local concerns had been committed to exclusively local control.[12]

The total dissolutionists, including Sheppard, wondered about all this. They were not convinced that replacing one government by three would make for cheapness, and they doubted that Lower Canadians would go so easily for 'rep by pop.' Sheppard's superior grasp of political science and history allowed him to play effectively on these doubts. Federal government was inapplicable to a colony, he said. The general government would have little to do, because most of what such authorities did belonged in Canada's case to the British government. Yet it would entail all the expense of a viceregal court. 'Are you prepared to create local governments, and then to create a central legislature, a central executive, with a vice-roy at the top – all to transact the business of a Province?'

Worse still, the federal legislature would have to be bicameral, for pure rep by pop was inappropriate to a federal system. In the United States, for example, rep by pop in the House of Representatives was balanced by the states' equality in the Senate. Such an expensive government was quite unsuited to Canada's simple needs. But there was more to fear than extravagance. Central bodies had an inherent tendency to acquire increased power. (Sheppard, alone of the delegates, seems to have used the word 'central.') In the United States, the Federalists' ambitions had obliged their opponents to organize nationally in defence of states' rights. Presciently, Sheppard warned that federation would set off a similar struggle in Canada.[13]

Sheppard argued well, and his intervention was the more effective because the convention was overloaded with delegates from the western peninsula, where total dissolution was popular. Unfortunately, that policy was quite unacceptable to most Upper Canadians from the Kingston area and points east. Their regional economy was too dependent on the St Lawrence River for them to share the westerners' happiness with the alternative line of maritime communication via New York City. They needed some arrangement that would guarantee free trade with Lower Canada and free navigation of the St Lawrence. Several delegates rose to warn the convention that, if it went for total dissolution, it would split the party and destroy its majority in Upper Canada.[14]

At this crisis in the debate William McDougall rose to present a compromise in the interest of party unity. He had long viewed the union of the Canadas as a mistake, he said. It must be dissolved. But two decades of union had created two or three matters of common concern, which would still need attention after the dissolution. Sheppard was right to deny that these common interests justified the erection of a cumbersome federal apparatus, but the convention had not been called to enter on the minutiae of constitution-making. Referring to the resolution that called for two local governments, with a general government to regulate matters of common concern, McDougall proposed to substitute for the phrase 'a general government' the words 'some joint authority.' Not only did this sound less imposing, but it had the sanction of prior imperial usage. When Lord Durham had been sent out as governor general in

1838, noted McDougall, he had been instructed to look into the possible erection of 'some joint Legislative authority' to manage the common interests of Upper and Lower Canada.[15]

Both Brown and Sheppard accepted McDougall's compromise, and the convention ended on the desired note of unanimity. Historians have accused Brown of sharp practice, because the *Globe* at once began to trumpet the decision as a victory for federation and Sheppard found himself barred from writing about the alternatives.[16] Brown had assured the delegates that they were not there to make a final commitment and would have ample opportunity to continue the debate. Sheppard's gagging was not quite in the spirit of that assurance, to be sure. But that does not mean that Brown secured unanimity by affecting to make a political concession on which he immediately reneged.

McDougall had presented his proposal as an alternative to the cumbersome and extravagant federal structure that Sheppard pictured. But the federationists themselves did not propose an expansive central government. Brown rammed the point home in a powerful closing speech, in which he asserted that the 'general government' as he conceived it was identical to McDougall's 'joint authority.' He announced his willingness to accept McDougall's formula as the basis for an honourable compromise, in that it sought to confine the scope of the federal government within the narrowest limit. He appealed to the total dissolutionists to join him on this ground for the sake of unanimity.

Brown's appeal was not a major political concession. If anything, it was an invitation to his opponents to abandon their position in return for an assurance that the general government would be the minimal organization that he depicted. Sheppard virtually acknowledged as much in withdrawing his own amendment. He and his supporters did not like McDougall's formula, he said, but they were willing to 'surrender their particular proposition' rather than risk a charge of 'stupid obstinacy' by sticking to their guns at the expense of unanimity.

The fact is that the Brownites had the better of the argument. Everyone wanted to throw off the domination of Lower Canada – the only question was how best to do it. Federation would cure the disease, asserted Brown, who could turn a metaphor as well as the next man. Total dissolution might look better in theory, but it would not sell east of Cobourg. Would the dissolutionists let the disease persist rather than accept any remedy but their own? Brown dramatized the contrast between the ideal and the practical by picturing James Lesslie enjoying his hard-earned wealth in comfortable retirement, refusing all appeals to help the Reformers by running for office, while the legislative caucus was slogging it out daily in the political arena. Lesslie was ready to commit the convention to dissolution – but was he ready to quit his snug country retreat and fight for it on the field of battle?[17]

While debate centred on the idea of Canadian federation, several delegates spoke in favour of a different sort of union: a grand confederation incorporating all the territories of British North America in a transcontinental union. This was in fact the policy of the governing coalition. The railway baron Alexander Galt, an independent MPP, had introduced resolutions in its favour in 1858. A few weeks later, after their short holiday from office, the Conservative leaders invited him to join the government, and Galt accepted on condition that they adopt his policy. They did so partly because of its impracticality, which was exposed when the idea was put to the Maritime provinces and greeted with universal indifference. Galt's policy committed the government to precisely nothing. The Reform convention recognized its pie-in-the-sky character by unanimously resolving that it offered no practical solution to the present crisis.[18]

Still, the idea drew favourable comment at the convention from supporters of both federation and total dissolution. 'While other nations are seeking unity; while the Italians are fighting for it, and the Germans sighing for it – why should we not seek the formation of a national feeling in this part of British America, which must eventually take its stand among the nations of the earth?' So asked George Wilkes, who favoured Canadian federation as the first step towards the founding of a nation stretching from the eastern to the western sea. Even George Sheppard, while condemning federation as unsuitable to a mere colony like United Canada, declared himself willing to accept it as a step towards 'nationality' – but in that case, let it be a federation of all the provinces. Another delegate, a dissolutionist like Sheppard, also favoured a wider federation once the Red River Colony, the Métis settlement west of Lake Superior, had been annexed. This speaker envisaged a union so colossal that Lower Canada could not dominate it, yet would 'have her rights.'[19]

Such declarations opened the way for an appeal to the dissolutionists to accept Canadian federation as a first step towards 'nationality.' 'I for one have no hesitation in saying that such is its tendency,' averred David Christie, George Brown's old schoolmate from Edinburgh, who was a leading Clear Grit and a member of the legislative council. Every true patriot must believe that one day 'this great British North American continent' must be a separate nation. According to Skeffington Connor, MPP for South Oxford, there was not a man who did not hope that the British provinces would one day become a great and mighty people. 'I do place the question on the ground of nationality,' affirmed George Brown in his closing address to the convention. 'I do hope there is not one Canadian in this assembly who does not look forward with high hope to the day when these northern countries shall stand out among the nations of the world as one great confederation.'[20]

Obviously, some of this talk was tactics – Brown had been conspicuously cool towards the idea in his earlier speech. Still, even in Brown's mouth it was not necessarily insincere: perhaps it was his initial restraint that was tactical, a matter of waiting to see the mood of the convention. British North American union had been a recurrent theme in colonial discourse since the 1750s. Its appeal transcended party lines. In Upper Canada alone, John Beverley Robinson and John Strachan, the chief ideologues of the Family Compact, had written favourably about it, but so also had two such different Reformers as William Lyon Mackenzie and Charles Fothergill.[21] Now, thirty years later, the Liberal-Conservatives were at least nominally committed to it, but it appealed to a wide range of Reformers too. Though now a federationist, as a Clear Grit MPP David Christie had regularly voted for Mackenzie's resolutions in favour of dissolution. George Wilkes had created a brief fuss by asserting, in answer to Mowat's disparaging allusion, that the rebellion had indeed been justified. (Another delegate demurred to loud cheers, reported the *Globe*, and Wilkes was allowed to atone at the close of the convention by leading three cheers for the Queen.) Connor, by contrast, was an Irish lawyer of Baldwinite stamp, as moderate a Reformer as you could find in the 1850s.[22]

So a hankering after a national sovereignty that was not just Upper Canadian but British North American was to be found in every corner of the party (and had its detractors in every corner too). But no one suggested that national sovereignty was worth having at the price of continued submission to the domination of Lower Canada. No one argued that a wider union need not be federal. It was at most a better route to liberation, though unfortunately one that was not immediately attainable. But liberation – autonomy for Upper Canada – remained the *sine qua non*. That was what the convention was about.

7

Confederation: The Untold Story

In 1859 Upper Canadian Reformers embraced the idea of Canadian federation, somewhat gingerly, as a way of securing the autonomy which they had expected from responsible government but which the union of 1841 had denied them. Some of them also expressed enthusiasm for a broader scheme, which George Brown called *con*federation: the political union of British North America as a whole. But no one advocated confederation as a substitute for Upper Canadian autonomy; no one argued that local autonomy was worth sacrificing to achieve the wider union.

This fact is important because, less than five years later, both Canadian federation and British North American confederation suddenly entered the realm of political reality. In June 1864 Brown and George Cartier, leader of the *bleus*, agreed to pursue federation. At once John A. Macdonald scrambled aboard the bandwagon and reached for the reins, committing himself to federation as long as the others would pursue its implementation within a wider union if possible. In September 1864, at Charlottetown, the Canadian leaders persuaded their counterparts in the Maritime colonies to consider such a union, and a month later they all worked it out in detail in conference at Quebec. Not all the colonies pursued the scheme to its conclusion, but in 1867 a British statute, the British North America Act, 'federally united' the colonies of Canada, New Brunswick, and Nova Scotia. As part of that scheme, Canada was divided into two provinces, Ontario and Quebec, corresponding to Upper and Lower Canada (they could not keep their old names, since Canada was to be the name of the union as a whole). So it was that, five years after that, in his speech at Woodstock to the voters of North Oxford, Oliver Mowat could hail Canadian confederation as the long-delayed realization of Upper Canada's aspirations to self-government.

It is crucial to remember that Confederation originated in an agreement to federalize United Canada, because the implications of its origin
have too often been forgotten. Historians have seen Confederation as the
fruition of a succession of proposals for British North American union
dating back to the eighteenth century, ignoring the feature that distinguished this particular scheme: its origin in the need to gratify the yearning of French Canadians and Upper Canadians alike to be masters in their
own house. English-Canadian writers in particular treated Confederation as essentially an exercise in nation-building. They degraded the federal structure of the new union into a secondary feature, designed chiefly
to accommodate the cultural peculiarity of French Canadians; but they
asserted that Canadian federalism was meant to be much more centralized than the classic model, as epitomized by the United States.[1]

In this chapter I redress this old-established and largely unrecognized
tendency to exaggerate the nation-building aspect of Confederation. In
considering the founders' expressions of centralizing zeal, I pay closer
attention than previous writers to the historical context that evoked
their words. I also challenge a story that has long been fundamental to
the centralist idea of Canada: the notion that the Quebec conference
decided to reverse the American pattern of federalism by assigning
what is called the residuary legislative power to the 'general' (i.e., federal) government rather than to the 'local' (provincial) governments.
The chapter closes with a look at the Upper Canadian Reformers' assessment of what had been achieved, expressed at a party convention in
Toronto in June 1867.

Without doubt the Quebec scheme was far more centralized than the
federation the Reformers had discussed in 1859. The federal legislature
received much more power than the bare minimum that the convention
had been willing to concede, including several powers lacked by the
U.S. Congress. The Quebec conference also departed from the American
pattern in another way that defeated the assumptions of 1859: it refused
to assign the residuary power to the local governments. The U.S. constitution defined the powers of Congress only, leaving the residue of
legislative power to the states. This arrangement was generally taken
as evidence that the individual states had retained their original
sovereignty and were therefore constitutionally superior to the federal
government. Under the Quebec scheme, by that measure, the local governments would *not* outrank the general.

In the executive sphere, too, the Quebec resolutions gave the general government important powers lacked by its American counterpart. The governor general (acting through his ministers, of course) was empowered to appoint all judges above the rank of magistrate and given sole charge of the colonial militia, the equivalent of the state-controlled National Guard in the United States. Not only that, he would wield over the provinces certain powers until then exercised in London. He could disallow provincial legislation within a year of its enactment. He would also appoint the provincial lieutenant-governors, who could themselves veto legislation at the time of enactment or reserve it for review by the general government. These powers appeared to give the general government the same pre-eminence within Confederation as the British government enjoyed within the empire.

Such provisions created the appearance of a dominant central power, and that impression was enhanced by the frankness with which advocates of confederation celebrated the nation-building aspect of the enterprise. They proclaimed their intention to found a new nationality, which would turn British North Americans into something more than mere 'colonists.' Instead of being half a dozen inconsiderable colonies, said George Brown, they would rise at once to the position of a great and powerful state. John Hamilton Gray of Prince Edward Island foretold the day when they would take their places among the first nations of the world. D'Arcy McGee dreamed famously of an end to hyphenated Canadianism, of a day when 'Canadians' pure and simple formed 'one great nationality, bound, like the shield of Achilles, by the blue rim of the ocean.' John A. Macdonald, George Cartier, Charles Tupper, and Alexander Galt spoke to similarly exalted effect.[2]

Besides these paeans to wider union, there were many testimonies to the Fathers' centralizing intent. With civil war raging in the United States, the promoters of Confederation took care to assure British Americans that the proposed constitution was free of the flaws that seemed to have contributed to the American débâcle. Macdonald declared that the Quebec resolutions encompassed 'a powerful Central Government, a powerful Central Legislature, and a decentralized system of minor legislatures for local purposes,' giving the former 'all the great subjects of legislation ... all the powers which are incident to sovereignty.' A clamour of voices belittled the proposed local governments as subordinate, minor, inferior, and municipal. The powers of the federal government would in reality be unlimited, objected Louis-August Olivier of Montreal. Provincial parliaments would be left to legislate on dog taxes and the running at large of swine, grumbled Prince Edward Islander George

Coles. Most telling was the testimony of Antoine-Aimé Dorion, the *rouge* leader who had joined George Brown to form the abortive Liberal ministry of 1858. At that time, he said, he (Dorion) had advocated 'a real confederation, giving the largest powers to the local governments, and merely a delegated authority to the General Government.' The present proposal reversed that arrangement, as well as reaching beyond the province of Canada – a scheme that he had always opposed.[3]

While Dorion clung to his earlier views, those of Brown, his former ally, seemed to have changed dramatically. Even before the preliminary conference at Charlottetown in September 1864 – even before talk had finally turned from Canadian federation to British North American *con*federation – Brown's newspaper was announcing that the 'sovereign' power, including the legislative residue, would be vested in the general government, while the local governments would wield only 'definite and expressly delegated' authority. According to the *Globe*, the Americans had got it the wrong way round when they made their federal government the creature or delegate of the states. In the Canadian federation, the local governments would be subordinate to the general, much like municipalities vis-à-vis the provinces. 'Almost all the important subjects of legislation' would belong to the federal government. The local governments should be constructed on the simplest and cheapest model, as befitted their modest status.[4]

At Quebec, Brown himself pressed this last idea on an unreceptive conference. The local governments, he said, 'should not be expensive, and should not take up political matters.' He wanted the local executive and legislature to be directly elected for a term of three years. The legislature should consist of a single chamber and should exercise its authority subject to a lieutenant-governor appointed by the general government. When other delegates balked at this proposal, he reminded them how trivial were the matters that they had agreed at Charlottetown to leave to the local governments.[5]

To the centralist scholars of the 1920s and 1930s, all these voices from the 1860s proved that the Fathers had intended to create a dominant federal government. Some historians came to hear something else in them as well. Brown's words in particular, supplemented by those of future prime minister Alexander Mackenzie, were evidence that the Upper Canadian Reformers had subscribed fully to the centralist scheme and that their subsequent championing of provincial rights was a renegade act. True, there were no self-incriminating statements from Oliver Mowat, who had become a judge right after the Quebec conference and played no part in the ensuing controversy, but silence did not exempt him from blame. In an influential work on the provincial-rights controversy, one of Donald Creighton's students would argue that Mowat's failure to contradict his colleagues invited 'at least a presumption' that he acquiesced in their views, even if privately he disagreed with them. This argument prepared the ground for Creighton himself to arraign Mowat as a liar and traitor – fit companion in this for the Liberal Lucifer, Mackenzie King.[6]

But was Brown really quite the centralizer in 1864 that modern historians have supposed? When you look at what he said in the light of the Upper Canadian Reform tradition, or in the immediate context in which he said it, some of it appears less centralist than first appears. Take his zest for the nation-building aspect of Confederation. There had been a lot of talk about British American 'nationality' at the 1859 convention, and Brown had contributed his share. The mere fact that he talked up the same line after the Quebec conference does not make him any more of a centralist then than five years earlier.

Nor does his and the *Globe*'s tendency to compare the local governments to municipalities in itself contradict his earlier position. To twentieth-century writers it signified that the local governments were to be inferior and even trivial, and some of his contemporaries made the same assumption. That is what the municipal analogy meant to them. But that is not necessarily what it meant to Upper Canadian Reformers. To Reformers, municipal government was the best sort, because it meant local control. One of the first big measures of the LaFontaine–Baldwin government was the Municipal Corporations Act of 1849, which set up a completely elective system of local government in Upper Canada right down to the township and village level. The success of this system influenced Reform thinking on the subject of federation.

Listen again, then, to Mr Nickerson of Norfolk County, who was so ready in 1859 to spill his blood to resist enslavement by Lower Canada: 'He approved of Federation. They had that principle already in their township and county municipalities, and had it not wrought most admirably and successfully? (Hear, hear.) ... The two provinces would have their own Legislatures to transact their own local business, and there would be a general body to transact *any little business of a general nature,* affecting the whole Federation.'[7] To Reformers like Nickerson, speaking of the new local governments as municipal was by no means to belittle them. If anything, it was to emphasize their efficacy as organs of local autonomy.

Unlike Nickerson (and Brown himself) in 1859, however, five years later Brown and his paper apparently *did* use the municipal example to belittle the new local governments, not merely to explain them. Like municipalities, the local governments would be 'subordinate.' Their powers would be 'delegated.' Their jurisdiction would be 'insignificant.' Yes, Brown and the *Globe* said all that. But why did they say it, and what else did they say? In order to understand what they meant, we need to consider their words in a wider context.

Brown was a leading member of the coalition formed in June 1864 to pursue the policy of Canadian federation. For two years, the province had had a weak government committed to a last effort to make the constitution of 1840 work properly. Its western leader was John Sandfield Macdonald, Brown's main rival for the Reform leadership. Brown and his closest friends stood aloof, promising only provisional support and watching carefully, although William McDougall broke ranks and asserted his independence by joining the cabinet. Sandfield Macdonald's eastern counterpart was Louis-Victor Sicotte, a moderate whose position between George Cartier's *bleus* and Antoine Dorion's *rouges* sometimes earned him the epithet *mauve*. Sicotte boosted his strength in Lower Canada by persuading Dorion to join the government.

This arrangement crumbled within a year. Dorion quit over fiscal policy; Upper Canadian Reformers were offended by the passage of a bill to strengthen the Roman Catholic separate schools, despite the opposition of most Upper Canadian members. Sandfield Macdonald was forced to dump Sicotte in favour of Dorion as his eastern co-premier and to take Mowat into the cabinet as a guarantee of his future adherence to Reform principles. The new government went to the polls in July 1863, but the election only sharpened sectional tensions, since the Reformers won a big majority and the *rouges* suffered an equally sweeping defeat. The government succumbed to a vote of confidence as soon as it met the new legislature, in March 1864. The Conservatives resumed office, only to be defeated in their turn three months later. Canadian politics was deadlocked, at least in the short run, since a new election offered little likelihood of any fundamental change of forces. Not only that, but with politics so polarized, and Upper Canada continuing to gain in population on the lower province, representation by population began to seem inevitable. Suddenly federation – Brown's favourite policy since 1859 – seemed to offer the only alternative.

Seemed so to Cartier at any rate; to John A. Macdonald perhaps it was less promising. A master coalition-builder, he needed more room to manoeuvre than a polarized politics afforded. So far the constitution of 1840 had served him well. If it must be changed, he preferred to widen the field of play by bringing in the other British American colonies. This had, after all, been his party's policy since 1858, though less (as we saw) because Canadian Conservatives liked the idea than because it offered an imposing, but satisfactorily impracticable alternative to Dorion's policy of federalizing United Canada. Now it seemed more feasible, and Brown thought it a fine idea as long as the new arrangement provided genuine autonomy for Upper Canada and representation by population in the federal legislature. The result was the Great Coalition – a government led by Cartier, Brown, and Macdonald under the nominal premiership of a *bleu* elder statesman, Sir Étienne-Paschal Taché.[8]

In the early weeks of the Great Coalition, the chief opponents of its policy in Upper Canada were people who feared that federal government must be weak government. Naturally, the *Globe* tried to reassure them by emphasizing those aspects of the scheme that made for a strong central authority. Even then, though, it took pains to assure its readers that the local governments would enjoy genuine autonomy. The general government would be sovereign, in the sense that it would possess the residuary legislative power and the local governments only specified powers; but this federal sovereignty would not mean very much in practice. It was largely a formal device, designed to establish the point that the federation was indissoluble: reversing the American model would quash any idea that member governments could opt out when they felt like it. Sovereignty need not give the general government a very wide range of duties and would not give it the slightest power to interfere with local functions.[9]

The *Globe* had to amplify these assurances at the end of August. Lower Canadians had been keeping an eye on the only paper owned by a minister. They did not have a comprehensive system of local government as Upper Canada did, and to them the municipal analogy did indeed signify triviality and weakness. The succession of editorials harping on the strength of the central government, and describing the local powers as *delegated*, made them fear that federation would pose a threat to French Canada. The *Globe* told them not to worry. The local governments would not be subject to the general government in the way that municipalities were subject to the province that created them. No: their authority would derive from the British Crown and Parliament,

and 'Congress' (the general legislature) would have no power to interfere with it. 'Such legislation would be beyond the control of the central
power, set apart from it, untouchable by it.'

We must remember that the point of federation was to depoliticize the
contentious issues that had led to sectional deadlock in United Canada.
The *Globe* maintained that this could be done just as effectively by allo-
cating specific powers to the local governments as by awarding them
the residuary power, with its connotations of sovereignty. When the
paper spoke of *delegated* powers, it meant law-making powers that were
expressly defined rather than residuary. It did not mean that those powers would be granted to the local legislatures by the general legislature,
which could therefore resume them as it saw fit.

So federal 'sovereignty' would not in itself pose a threat to provincial
autonomy. Having established that, the *Globe* went on to argue that
what really mattered was the actual distribution of power. 'The real sovereignty under a federal form of government rests with the body which
has the largest share of power ... The central power might be nominally
supreme, but yet it might delegate to the local bodies such extensive
jurisdiction as to deprive itself of all weight in the country.' The crucial
thing was to write a constitution that gave the local legislatures ample
power and confined the federal authority – call it sovereign or not – to
matters of general interest.[10]

Well! Haven't we just caught the *Globe* with its foot in its mouth? Less
than three weeks later, after Charlottetown, Brown's paper was report-
ing that almost all the important subjects of legislation would be allotted
to the general government. At Quebec, as we saw, Brown himself would
press for simple local governments on the ground that the powers pro-
visionally assigned to them at Charlottetown were insignificant. On top
of that, as summer turned to autumn, the scope of local autonomy
appeared to be shrinking in other ways. The *Globe* began talking about a
lieutenant-governor – possibly one appointed by the central government – armed with a veto over local legislation.[11] After the Quebec conference, there was also the federal disallowance power to explain away.
It is easy to understand why French-speaking critics in particular condemned the Quebec scheme as a legislative union in all but name.[12]

Clearly Brown believed that the federal government would be the leading political forum after Confederation. The strategy in 1864 was to
identify certain thorny questions and localize them, thereby relieving
the polarization that had deadlocked union politics. But this does not

mean that the local legislatures were not to enjoy genuine autonomy. Far from it: local autonomy was essential to the goal of sanitizing Canadian politics. More important, though, it was implicit in the founders' decision to base Confederation on the constitution of the British empire. Even in the 1820s, before the advent of responsible government, William and Robert Baldwin and the Letter on Responsible Government had insisted on the sovereignty of the colonial legislature as a matter of inherent right. With the maturing of the colonial system in British North America, local autonomy had become a political reality. Whatever they had once been, the governor's authority to reserve or veto colonial legislation, and the imperial government's authority to disallow it, had shrunk to the merest contingent power, to be wielded only in the last resort.

Robert Baldwin Sullivan had tried to define the limits of responsible government in 1844. The governor general, he suggested, would be justified in ignoring his ministers if they advised him to appoint a rebel in arms to command the militia. Obviously, this was an extreme contingency and a very unlikely one. Such an example implied that, short of such extremity, the governor was obliged to act on his ministers' advice and correspondingly to give his assent to the acts of his legislature. One of the Reformers' complaints against Governor General Metcalfe in 1844 concerned his decision to reserve for imperial review a government bill, duly passed by the legislature, that banned secret societies such as the Orange Order. Metcalfe's action was incontestably *legal* – the Act of Union vested that power in his office – but the Reformers condemned it as a breach of the conventions of responsible government. Accordingly, the great symbol of the final triumph of responsible government in Canada was the refusal of a later governor, Lord Elgin, to reserve another controversial measure, the Lower Canada Rebellion Losses Act of 1849, which entitled victims of military action during the rebellion to compensation.[13]

This brings us to Donald Creighton's accusation that Oliver Mowat lied about the Quebec agreement, for the charge relates in part to the issue of federal control of provincial legislation. One of the leading episodes in the provincial-rights controversy was Ottawa's repeated disallowance between 1881 and 1885 of an Ontario measure called the Rivers and Streams Act. This and similar episodes persuaded Mowat and other provincial premiers that the federal veto should be abolished. In a newspaper interview in 1887, Mowat recalled the discussion of the disallowance proposal at Quebec. Delegates had granted the power because some of them feared that the federal government would be too weak without it. It was generally understood, though, that the power would be subject to the same constitutional constraints as the imperial veto.[14]

The record of the Quebec conference contains not a word to contradict Mowat's statement, and the resolutions, if anything, confirm it. The fiftieth declares that any bill of the general Parliament may be reserved 'in the usual manner' for imperial review and that local bills may be reserved 'in like manner' for review by the federal government. The next resolution states that bills of the general Parliament shall be subject to disallowance by Her Majesty like those of the existing colonies and that local bills shall be subject 'in like manner' to disallowance by the governor general. Nor was this mere verbiage. So clearly was it understood that the two powers were to be analogous that A.-A. Dorion made a point of criticizing the assumption. Unlike the British government, he argued, the proposed federal government would be embroiled in colonial party politics and would inevitably succumb to the temptation to use the veto for party-political purposes. The controversy over the Rivers and Streams Act proved his criticism to be prescient; but the criticism itself only confirms what Mowat said later about the founders' conception of the veto.[15]

Twentieth-century centralists were well aware that Confederation was based on the imperial constitution, but they invariably saw this as evidence of the founders' intention to set up a dominant central government. They knew about the advent of responsible government, and they all thought it a good thing; but for some reason, when they came to think about Confederation, they forgot about it. In Creighton's story, for instance, British Americans, anxious to avoid the fatal flaws of American federalism, found the answer in 'another rather informal federal system, with which they were all perfectly familiar and which they infinitely preferred to the American. This was, of course, the Old Colonial System of the second British Empire, with its sovereign Imperial Parliament and its dependent colonial legislatures.' Yet by Creighton's own account, some fifty pages earlier, the Old Colonial System had expired in the 1840s, when the British government conceded responsible government to the North American colonies.[16] Why should the Fathers of Confederation have had that obsolete system in mind in designing the Canadian constitution, rather than the new system with which they were in fact 'all perfectly familiar' in 1864? Creighton did not even consider the question.

For the Upper Canadian Reformers at least, we need only read the

Globe to prove Creighton wrong. In an editorial entitled 'English Ideas of Federation,' it cited the British empire as an example of the way in which local self-government could render the central power stronger, not weaker – only it was the *new* imperial system that showed this, not Creighton's Old Colonial System. So long as the British colonies were governed from Downing Street, declared the *Globe*, 'they were always discontented, and complaints were constant, sometimes ending in rebellion, and always injurious to the authority of the parent State. When local self-government was granted all this ceased, and the colonies are now more loyal to the mother country than the mother country is loyal to the colonies.'[17]

This article is especially pertinent, because it was written to reassure people who feared that federal union must be weaker than legislative union. It did not propose to resolve that difficulty by putting the local governments under the political constraints of the Old Colonial System. It proposed to do so by granting them the freedoms of the new system. Accordingly, the *Globe* dismissed the idea that the Quebec scheme was a legislative union in disguise: the conference had done too much to preserve the autonomy of the provinces, and given the local legislatures too much real power, for that charge to hold. The *Globe*'s argument conformed to Brown's own remarks at Quebec, where he insisted that the specified local powers were ample to maintain local autonomy.[18]

Certainly disallowance made no difference. The *Globe* compared it not to the imperial veto but to something still less threatening: the Crown's power in Britain to refuse assent to bills passed by Parliament. That power, though still existing in law, had atrophied long since. According to the *Globe*, the central government's veto would no more destroy the federal character of the constitution than the defunct royal veto could destroy the 'popular' character of the British constitution. It had been created to guard against the chance that local legislatures might abuse their autonomy by passing laws that were unjust to local minorities, but the federal government would not dare to exercise it unless the local government were clearly in the wrong. Any indiscretion in its use would probably cause an outcry that would sweep it into oblivion.[19]

It looks then as though Brown and his supporters were not quite the zealous centralists in 1864 that some twentieth-century writers made them out to be. They did intend to make the federal government stronger than its American counterpart seemed to be. And they did hope to lay the basis of a new nationality – even Mowat, in one of his few recorded remarks at Quebec, approved of that idea.[20] But they did not

mean to subject the local governments to a dominating federal overlord-
ship or to award them merely municipal powers and status. Their first
priority was to relieve Upper Canada of the 'baneful domination'
(Mowat's words in 1859) of Lower Canada. In fact, the whole confederation movement sprang from Brown's timely proposal, in March 1864, to
resolve United Canada's political deadlock by moving towards a federal
union. He consented to pursue a wider union, or *con*federation, only on
condition that, if it did not happen, Canadian federation would proceed
regardless. But even if the wider project did go ahead, experience convinced the Reformers that it could succeed only if based on a genuine
local autonomy, designed to remove vexatious local issues from the
sphere of 'national' politics.

To Reformers in particular, the *new* imperial system offered a promising model for the new nationality. It had made a reality of the ideal of
local self-government that had inspired them since the 1820s. It also presented a spectacle of multinational cohesion that the Old Colonial System, with its political constraints and restrictive trade regulations, never
had. Looking back, we may well think that that cohesion owed less to
the structure of the imperial constitution than to the massive flow of
British population and investment to the North American colonies after
1850. Still, in the 1860s that constitutional machinery seemed an effective means of combining local autonomy with the minimum of political
cohesion required to dissuade the member provinces from thinking that
they had joined a club that they could leave whenever they liked. The
federal appointment of lieutenant-governors, the formal powers of that
office, the federal power of disallowance – these were not instruments of
federal dominance but symbols of the new national unity.

The same is true of the residuary legislative power. When Reformers
such as Brown proposed to define the local powers and leave the
remainder to the central legislature, they did not mean to create a powerful engine of federal legislative domination. On the contrary, their
intention was to shore up the new federal power, lest it be too feeble, by
investing it with a symbolic sovereignty. The *Globe* said repeatedly that,
in terms of actual power, it did not matter whether you specified the
powers of the local government or those of the general government.
Local autonomy would be guaranteed by the amplitude of the authority
assigned to the local governments and by the fact that it was conferred
by the British Parliament.

Besides, the Fathers of Confederation did not assign the residue to

Ottawa after all. True, it is generally accepted that they reversed the American pattern by assigning the residuary power to the federal instead of the local governments and that they did so in order to create a highly centralized federation, in which the central government would predominate. The evidence seems strong. The Canadian government was committed to that plan from the start. Both John A. Macdonald and the *Globe* advocated it strongly. It may actually have been adopted at the Charlottetown conference, although the only people who said so were those who favoured the plan. At Quebec, when certain delegates denied that the question had been settled at Charlottetown and insisted on reopening it in any case, their bid to allocate the residue to the local governments was defeated. And in 1872 one of the delegates, John Hamilton Gray of New Brunswick, published a book in which he stated that the conference had reversed the American scheme.[21]

When, therefore, Donald Creighton stated that the Fathers of Confederation had 'unanimously resolved that general or residuary powers were to lie, not with the local, but with the general legislature,'[22] he was stating common knowledge. *But common knowledge was incorrect – the Fathers had done nothing of the sort.* Instead, having unanimously declined to assign the residue to the local governments, they had split it in two. They had devised a list of itemized powers for each government and rounded off each list with a catch-all category. That for the 'General Parliament' stated: 'And *Generally* respecting all matters of a general character, not especially and exclusively reserved for the Local Governments and Legislatures.' And that for the 'Local Legislatures' stated: 'And *generally* all matters of a private or local nature, not assigned to the General Parliament.'[23] In short, 'general' powers were assigned to *both* legislatures.

John A. Macdonald claimed nothing more when he explained the Quebec resolutions to the provincial legislative assembly at the opening of its debate on the subject in February 1865. At one point he declared: 'We have expressly declared that all subjects of general interest not distinctly and exclusively conferred upon the local governments and local legislatures, shall be conferred upon the General Government and Legislature.' Later he quoted that declaration verbatim, as I have above. Both times he presented this arrangement as the delegates' answer to what they had perceived as the great weakness of the American system. He never claimed that they had assigned the residue to the general legislature. Neither did Charles Tupper, premier of Nova Scotia. Presenting the Quebec scheme to the house of assembly, Tupper explained that it remedied the weakness of the American system by defining the powers of both the general and the local legislatures rather than those of the former alone. He did not even mention what it did about the residue.[24]

In the course of the Canadian debate on confederation, where these details were discussed more thoroughly than in the other provinces, two MPPs asserted that the Quebec scheme reversed the American pattern, but this was just one of many misconceptions that found expression in the legislature.[25] Most Canadian politicians regarded the American system as flawed in that the states had bestowed specific powers on Congress, reserving the residue for themselves. That arrangement had fostered ideas of state sovereignty, including the notion that individual states could nullify federal laws within their territory or even secede from the union. It was natural to see a reversal of the American pattern in the arrangement devised at Quebec to avoid this error. If there was anything more than this to Gray's statement in 1872, it may have been an urge to believe that the position that he himself had advocated at Quebec had prevailed.

In 1872, though, Gray, like later generations, was seeing the Quebec Resolutions through the prism of the British North America (BNA) Act. The circumstances under which this momentous document was drafted, early in 1867, are still unclear, but they bear the marks of a determined effort on the part of British officials to overbear the colonial will and centralize the scheme of confederation. Drafting was delayed for nearly two years by opposition to the Quebec scheme in the Maritime provinces. Newfoundland and Prince Edward Island stayed out, and it was only in December 1866 that plenipotentiaries from Nova Scotia and New Brunswick met a Canadian delegation in London to work out a revision of the scheme, on the basis of which their provinces might join the impending Canadian federation. The London resolutions retained the division of the legislative residue as agreed at Quebec, and the conference inserted that arrangement in its draft bill based on the resolutions. Then the British got into the act. In the first parliamentary draft of the confederation bill the local residuary power disappeared, while the federal residue was moved to the head of the section dealing with the powers of the federal parliament and presented in the terms with which we are familiar from the final act. It invested parliament with the power to make laws for the 'peace, order, and good government' of the 'United Colony' in relation to all matters not exclusively confided to the local legislatures and went on to enumerate certain federal powers 'for greater Certainty, but not so as to restrict the Generality of the foregoing Terms of this section.' The local residue gave way to a clause referring to matters that the general parliament might from time to time, as it saw fit, transfer to the local jurisdiction.[26]

It was Creighton's guess that these changes reflected the influence of the governor general, Lord Monck, and the Colonial Office ministers, all of whom shared Macdonald's centralizing zeal. If so, they had a field day: this draft also designated the local heads of government as 'super-intendents' instead of lieutenant-governors. School districts have super-intendents: this was municipalization with a vengeance. In a lyrical account of these proceedings, Creighton described how the North American delegates, when they met to discuss the British draft, grate-fully accepted the new, improved federal residuary clause but felt obliged to reject the superintendents, 'perhaps with some regret.' I won-der how much regret Hector-Louis Langevin felt: his letters from Lon-don complain of having to watch Macdonald like a hawk in order to stop him from using his rapport with the British to make centralizing changes on the sly. Creighton makes no mention of this, although he does report Langevin's departure on a pious pilgrimage to Rome.[27]

Nor does Creighton mention the local residuary clause. Of course, he never admitted its existence. But to those who do notice its presence in the Quebec and London resolutions, its vicissitudes in those early weeks of 1867 are a matter of great interest. As draft succeeded draft, it flickered like a candle in a draft. The second official draft omitted both the original clause and its substitute. The third restored it. The fourth replaced it again with the substitute. Only with the final bill, which duly became law as the BNA Act, did it finally reclaim its place in the scheme as 'generally all matters of a merely local or private nature in the province.'[28]

In its final form, the BNA Act granted the Canadian Parliament the power to make laws for the 'peace, order, and good government of Can-ada' in relation to everything not confided to the local legislatures. This made it possible to say not only that the residuary power had been vested in the federal government but that the federal power was *wholly* residuary – it comprised everything that was not specifically allotted to the provinces. Twentieth-century nationalists were to make much of this arrangement, as we shall see in chapter 11. But there is a huge difference between a power that comprises everything but certain exceptions (the specified powers of the local legislatures) and one that excludes not only those powers but an extra, indefinite category consisting of everything else that is 'local' rather than 'general.' In the first case, a judge would have to look at the defined local powers and decide if a disputed subject belongs there or in the federal residue. In the second case, even if a subject did not come within the defined local powers, he might have to make a judgment as to its nature. He might have to decide whether, under the circumstances, it is essentially 'general' or 'local.'

It is impossible to make a judgment of that sort without considering the question of local autonomy. Twentieth-century critics were to blast the Judicial Committee of the Privy Council for taking account of provincial autonomy in their decisions,[29] but it is hard to see that the committee was wrong in principle to do so. The Fathers of Confederation had imposed the task on it by establishing indefinite categories of 'general' and 'local' legislative powers.[30] More than that: by basing the Canadian constitution on the imperial model, they hinted at a broad conception of local autonomy, much like that enjoyed by the self-governing colonies. Whatever else the Quebec resolutions, the London resolutions, and the BNA Act may say, they certainly make no mention of the Old Colonial System, which Donald Creighton said was the basis for Confederation.

Oliver Mowat's greatest contribution to the shaping of Canada lay in his steering the Judicial Committee towards this genuinely federal view of Confederation. He may have done so for good or for ill, but his doing so was no betrayal of any commitment made by him and his political associates at Confederation. George Brown and his supporters never endorsed any other view of Confederation than was contained in the Quebec resolutions; neither did the legislature of United Canada approve anything else.

In June 1867, six hundred Upper Canadian Reformers met in convention in Toronto. The event was billed as a reprise of what the circular of invitation called 'the great Convention of 1859.' The circular recalled how 570 prominent and influential men, from all sections of Upper Canada, had then reached conclusions that had changed the course of Upper Canadian history. Their proposals for constitutional reform had at last been implemented with the almost unanimous assent (it said) of the people of Canada, Nova Scotia, and New Brunswick.

One purpose of the new gathering was to celebrate that great victory; another was to prepare to exploit it. The Dominion of Canada would come into being on July the first, and federal and provincial elections must soon be held. Reformers must now achieve the political reforms for which constitutional reform had been merely a prerequisite. That depended on victory at the polls. A convention would help to reconcile Reformers who might have become temporarily estranged during the arduous struggle for the new constitution. It would breathe new vigour into the Reform cause.[31]

Victory had taken its toll. By arousing and channelling discontent with the constitution of 1840, the Reform party under George Brown had launched the political process that had culminated in Confederation; but it was the Conservatives who stood to benefit from it. As in 1859, the Reformers were in disarray. The worst damage had been sustained at the start. The pursuit of federation in 1864 had estranged them from their Lower Canadian allies under Dorion. Brown and two colleagues (Mowat and McDougall), obliged to enter into coalition with the Conservatives as the price of reform, had had to do so as three liberals in a cabinet of twelve. To a man of Brown's nice conscience, political cohabitation with John A. Macdonald was a purgatory, and by the end of 1865 he had had enough. Confederation was assured by then, despite the defection of Prince Edward Island and Newfoundland and continuing opposition in Nova Scotia and New Brunswick. Brown quarrelled with Alexander Galt over what he saw as Galt's bungling of tariff reciprocity negotiations with the United States. Outvoted on the issue in cabinet, Brown resigned.

Another Reformer replaced him, and the coalition continued. But the following summer Brown took umbrage at Galt's budget, which he thought favoured Montreal financial interests and penalized those of Toronto and western Upper Canada. When he tried to whip up opposition in the legislature, he found himself deserted by almost the entire Reform caucus, with McDougall in the lead. Brown devoted himself to personal affairs, responding coolly when Lord Monck suggested that he take part in the Canadian delegation to the London conference. As a result, by 1867 many Upper Canadians were tending to associate Confederation with John A. Macdonald and the Conservatives, rather than with Brown and the Reformers. That tendency could only be strengthened by Macdonald's appointment as prime minister of the Dominion – an appointment earned by his congeniality to British officials but officially ascribed to his seniority as an executive councillor.[32]

For Brown and his supporters, Confederation promised a new beginning. Under the BNA Act, Ontario's local affairs would be a matter for Ontarians alone. At Ottawa, thanks to the principle of representation by population, the province would supply eighty-two MPs out of 181, with the prospect of a still larger share after the next census. But the party must be united and the voters reminded of what it stood for. The problem was no longer the caucus as a whole: after its initial repudiation of Brown over the budget, most of its members had returned to the fold. But Macdonald had cleverly moved to perpetuate Reform divisions by proposing to continue the coalition. He had secured the adherence of the three Upper Canadian Reform ministers by appointing them to the federal cabinet. One leading purpose of the Reform convention was to discredit and isolate the renegades.

The convention was boosted by the failure of the renegades' preemptive strike. The three Reform ministers called a meeting of Reform legislators in Toronto. Few attended, and only three MPPs and a clutch of legislative councillors were willing to remain in coalition. Brown and company improved on this advantage by nominating William Patrick to the chair of the convention. Patrick, a businessman and Methodist lay preacher, presented himself as 'a Reformer of the old stamp.' As a Baldwinite he had supported the Liberal Conservative coalition of 1854, but after a year or two he had quit in disgust. More recently, he had been associated with John Sandfield Macdonald, and earlier in 1867 he had been mentioned in the press as a possible supporter of John A.'s coalition.[33]

Patrick symbolized the futility of the coalitionist cause by his very presence, and he could speak with authority on the 'immorality' of coalitions and the virtue and necessity of political parties. He also symbolized the continuity of Reform politics. Though long a resident of Prescott, on the St Lawrence River, he had grown up in Toronto when it was still a town called Muddy York and had been related by marriage to Thomas Morrison, a leading collaborator of William Lyon Mackenzie's. He commenced his duties as chairman by reminiscing about the York election of 1828, when Dr Morrison had stood against John Beverley Robinson with the backing of Robert Baldwin and R.B. Sullivan. He recalled 'young Sullivan' running to and fro in his shirtsleeves at the hustings, marshalling support for the Reform candidate. By the end of his speech, few in the audience could doubt that the true Reform tradition reposed with them that day in the Toronto Music Hall.[34]

Led by Patrick, a series of speakers descanted on the themes announced in the circular of invitation. They celebrated Confederation as a triumph for the principles of 1859. The BNA Act contained defects, to be sure – the Senate was non-elective, for instance, and the House of Commons subject to re-election only at five-year intervals. Nevertheless, the act had delivered the two essential requirements: representation by population and local control of local affairs. Only by abandoning coalition and returning to party politics, however, could Upper Canadians reap the benefits.

Two features of the discussion were especially portentous. First of all, Confederation was celebrated almost entirely as a realization of Upper Canadian autonomy.[35] One resolution looked forward to transcontinental expansion, but on the whole there was less grand talk about transcontinental nationality now than in 1859, when it had seemed only a distant prospect. This was natural, since most Reformers had embraced Confederation chiefly as a means to ending the union with Lower Canada, but it foreshadowed the zeal with which Reformers would defend Ontario's autonomy within the new union. The second portent was the delegates' attitude to the man who was to be their great enemy in the struggle for provincial rights, John A. Macdonald. In 1859, speakers had flayed Tories in general for subjugating the province to the Lower Canadian yoke, but they had not named names. This time they singled out Macdonald.

Brown led the way. He did not try to hide his chagrin at the prospect that his great enemy, the chief agent of Lower Canadian domination, might receive credit for the victory, and reap the fruits of the victory, for which Reformers had sacrificed so much. The gangling Scot spoke feelingly of the 'degradation' of being obliged, as the price of Upper Canadian liberty, to enter into coalition in 1864. No men had ever entered government with such sore hearts as he and Mowat on that occasion, and the day he got out of that business was the happiest of his life. After such sacrifices, and such a victory, were they now to 'make terms with the enemy'? Were they to 'renew the hateful compact' and make Macdonald prime minister?[36]

The prospect of Macdonald as prime minister coloured the delegates' hostility to coalition. Coalition was bad in any case, because a strong, watchful opposition was essential to good government, and corruption flourished in its absence. But coalition with Macdonald was like supping with the devil, and coalition under Macdonald's leadership was worse still. Alexander Mackenzie recalled that he had opposed coalition in 1864 as 'an extremely dangerous experiment,' fearing that some Reformers would end up 'not merely coalesced but fused with the Tories.' His fears had been justified, but he had been outvoted in caucus by those who felt that Macdonald was so treacherous that he must be watched from inside the cabinet. Then, however, Macdonald had not been prime minister. At first Sir Étienne Taché had headed the government. On his death, Brown had vetoed Macdonald's succession (as well as that of Cartier, the *bleu* leader) and secured the appointment of a lesser *bleu*, Sir Narcisse Belleau. Mackenzie contrasted Brown's principled defence of Reform interests in 1864 and 1865 with the craven alacrity with which McDougall and his fellow-renegades were now reaching for office under the arch-enemy of Reform.[37]

Macdonald was the enemy: the enemy of Reform, the enemy of the people – perhaps something worse. William McDougall's plight reminded one delegate of a picture of a simple young man who had just been checkmated in a chess game with the great enemy of mankind. The speaker laughingly denied any intention of comparing Macdonald to the enemy of mankind or McDougall to a simple young man, but he believed that the latter had sold himself for $8,000 a year. This was the only explicit reference to Satan, but several speakers depicted Macdonald as a figure of diabolical cunning. One spoke of William Howland, another Reform collaborator, as an honest man who had got caught in one of Macdonald's 'clever political tricks.' The collaborators were bewitched, suggested Brown; Macdonald, a very 'astute' man and a skilled manipulator, had thrown 'the glamour' over their eyes. Even the one delegate to speak up for coalition appealed to these fears. They were told, he noted, that Macdonald was crafty and cunning and that he had kept up the coalition in order to split the Reformers. Why play into his hands, then? Why meet cunning with foolishness?[38]

The temper of the meeting was thrown into sharp relief by the speeches of Howland and McDougall. They attended only after receiving special invitations by a vote of the convention. Howland's speech was conciliatory and McDougall's combative, but they conveyed the same message. There was nothing wrong with coalition in a good cause. They had agreed to enter the federal cabinet out of consideration for the four Maritime members, all Reformers, who would otherwise be outnumbered by Tories. With the Maritimers, the Upper Canadian collaborators would make seven Reformers in a cabinet of thirteen. This would prevent Macdonald from using the patronage of the Intercolonial Railway, which the BNA Act required to be built between Halifax and Quebec, to establish a Conservative hegemony.

Such were their excuses, but what really mattered was the challenge they posed to their fellow-Reformers' deepest convictions. Howland chided the delegates for thinking only of Upper Canada and not of their fellow-colonists, particularly the Maritime Reformers. When invited to join the federal cabinet, said McDougall, they had felt bound to look at the question 'not only from a party point of view, but from an Upper Canada and also a British North American point of view.' He flouted the Reformers' propensity to identify Upper Canada with themselves: Upper Canadians as a whole, Tories as well as Reformers, had been disadvantaged by the constitution of 1840. Not only that, but Tories as well as Reformers had worked and taken risks for Confederation. In a deliberate rebuff to Brown's claims to the chief credit for the achievement, he paid pointed tribute to Macdonald's hard and devoted labour for the cause.[39]

These were fighting words. To dispute the identity of Upper Canada and Reform was to challenge the Reformers' self-conception as the people's champions against Tory oppression. To say that Tories and Reformers alike had suffered under the old constitution was to scorn the belief that Tories had used it to rule Upper Canada against the wishes of the people. To offer Macdonald even qualified praise was to prove that you had sold out to a man who was the people's enemy, if not the enemy of mankind. Maybe McDougall had forgotten how to talk to Reformers, but more probably he didn't care. His reputation within the party had never recovered from his accepting office under Sandfield Macdonald in 1862. He was really addressing himself to the electors, not the convention.

At any rate, inside the Music Hall his words fell on deaf ears. Brown jeered at the notion that a seven-to-six majority (even if all seven were Reformers, which he doubted) could stop an astute operator like Macdonald, armed with prime ministerial powers and the patronage of the Intercolonial, from having his way in cabinet. And what was to happen at the provincial elections? Were Reformers to surrender Ontario to the Tories for the sake of having McDougall and company in cabinet in Ottawa for a few weeks, until Macdonald should choose to dismiss them? Seconding his leader, Alexander Mackenzie tarred the Maritime Reformers with the collaborationist brush. They would have done better to work with Reformers in Upper and Lower Canada to install a Reform government in Ottawa. They should certainly not have accepted office without consulting their Canadian counterparts, especially in a cabinet that excluded Dorion and the *rouges*. (Here he eulogized the *rouge* leader.) And what had the people of Upper Canada done, that they should be sacrificed at the shrine of the Maritime so-called Reformers?[40]

Refusing to be sacrificed, the convention rejected coalition all but unanimously. Led by Brown, the Reformers bid vigorously for the fruits of Confederation at the federal and provincial elections. The Reform vote split sufficiently to give Macdonald a majority of federal seats in Ontario as well as power in Ottawa, while his provincial collaborator Sandfield Macdonald was able to form a coalition ministry in Toronto. In 1871, however, Sandfield Macdonald would be ousted, and two years later Alexander Mackenzie would replace John A. Macdonald as prime minister of Canada.

8

Je me souviens: The Great Fight for Responsible Government, Part III

We have returned to our starting-point: to Oliver Mowat speaking to the electors of North Oxford on a snowy November day in 1872. Now we know why he talked about Confederation as he did that day in the rural county town of Woodstock. To Reformers, Confederation meant self-government for Upper Canada or it meant nothing. They had been campaigning for self-government since the 1820s, and at last they had it. The wounds of 1867 were healed; the party was whole again. Not only that: it was in power.

By November 1872, when Mowat became premier of Ontario, the Reformers had spent remarkably little time in power. There was the year of office so abruptly terminated in November 1843 by the quarrel with Sir Charles Metcalfe. There was the period from 1848 to 1854, which had begun with such promise only to end in disappointment and betrayal – the defection of the Hincksites. There were two unsatisfactory years from 1862 to 1864 under the traitor Sandfield Macdonald. But now Clear Grit Brownites held the reins in Upper Canada: first, for a year, Edward Blake and Alexander Mackenzie together, and now Mowat. It was the dawn of a new era.

This time Reformers were not to be disappointed. Mowat gave them the principled, economical government they craved. He won a clear majority in 1875 and a larger one four years later. When he went to the polls for the third time, in February 1883, his party had won seven out of eight recent provincial by-elections.[1] But in 1883, Ontario Reformers had more on their mind than the minutiae of provincial government.

Mackenzie and Blake had quit provincial for federal politics in 1872 under favourable auspices. The Conservatives under John A. Macdonald (there was no pretence of coalition this time) had won re-election in

August, but the Liberals had scored majorities in Ontario and the Maritimes. The government's overall majority was decent, but hardly massive. Then, in April 1873, the Pacific Scandal erupted. It appeared that Macdonald and Cartier had taken huge sums for election expenses from a syndicate that was negotiating with the government for a contract to build the projected Pacific railway. The scandal ballooned over the summer. When Macdonald met Parliament in the autumn, his majority evaporated and he was forced to resign. Mackenzie took over as prime minister and went to the people. In January 1874 the Liberals won a huge majority, including sixty-six out of eighty-eight seats in Ontario.[2]

But five years is a long time in politics, and in September 1878 Macdonald came back. Mackenzie lacked Mowat's deft political touch, and the affairs of a transcontinental dominion were harder to manage than those of its wealthiest province. What really holed the Liberal boat, though, were the economy and the liquor question. Mackenzie's ministry had the bad luck to coincide with a long and deep slump in international trade. The Conservatives campaigned in 1878 on a so-called National Policy of industrial tariff protection, well aware that the protracted depression had made voters receptive to the idea.[3] As resolute free traders, Mackenzie's Liberals could not compete with the protectionist cry.

Doctrine was their downfall in the liquor question too. The Scott Act of 1878 introduced prohibition in any city or county where a majority voted for it in a referendum. It pleased the rapidly growing minority of temperance zealots but outraged the powerful liquor lobby – particularly tavernkeepers, who tended to be figures of influence in the circles to which they dispensed hospitality. Musing on the folly of the Scott Act some thirty years later, Sir Richard Cartwright, Mackenzie's finance minister, recalled that there had then been some five or six thousand licensees in Ontario, each of whom 'personally controlled' quite a number of votes.[4] These were significant numbers in the small electorate of 1878. Most licensees were Conservative to start with, no doubt, but when it came to prohibition none can have been Liberal. And that was just Ontario.

Anyway, there was a Conservative landslide to match the Liberal avalanche of 1874. Like William Gladstone's Liberal government in 1874 in Britain, which had rashly introduced restricted hours for public houses, Mackenzie's was 'borne down in a torrent of gin and beer.' Macdonald resumed the prime ministership, sixty-three years old and powerfully aware of the need to strike while the iron was hot. His return set the stage for a new struggle for provincial autonomy. Soon Reformers would summon Upper Canadians to a third great campaign to secure their rights as a people.

Twentieth-century nationalists tended to be preoccupied with the division of legislative power, and especially with the fate of that contentious residuary power. During the era of the provincial-rights controversy, however, the division of powers was only one concern of the warring parties, and the residuary power only a minor issue. Ontario Reformers were mainly concerned to fend off what they saw as Macdonald's assaults on provincial sovereignty.

Of course, guarding the bounds of the provincial legislative domain formed part of this project. The 1870s and 1880s saw the first judicial efforts to give exact meaning to the division of powers in the BNA Act. Some early decisions, especially in the newly formed Supreme Court of Canada, tended to treat the provinces as inferior jurisdictions and define their powers in a rather niggardly fashion. Confronted by this bias in the Supreme Court, Mowat took pains to educate the Judicial Committee of the Privy Council in the principles underlying the division of powers. This was less a matter of details than of making sure that British judges took the provincial domain as seriously as the federal. He had to make them understand that the provinces were not subordinate to the Dominion but its sovereign equals.[5]

Decades of centralist criticism have accustomed us to think of the Privy Council as the champion of provincial autonomy. Because of this, it is hard to imagine what Mowat was up against in those early years. British officials had little understanding of federalism and less sympathy for it. We have seen how they colluded with Macdonald at the London conference to centralize the proposed confederation beyond the Fathers' intentions. They were very reluctant to accept that lieutenant-governors appointed by Ottawa could be representatives of the Crown in the same immediate fashion as lieutenant-governors appointed in London. They refused to admit that such officials could exercise the prerogative powers of the Crown – powers symbolic of sovereignty.[6] Mowat fought long and hard to establish in law that the lieutenant-governors could do such things as appoint queen's counsel, pardon convicts, and receive escheated estates (i.e., estates resumed by the Crown when the proprietor died intestate and without heirs). These were matters of little practical significance, but they were vital as symbols of the provinces' sovereign status and constitutional equality to the Dominion.

In dealing with the Privy Council, Mowat also suffered the handicap that cases could originate in other provinces and involve private parties. The federal cause might gain an edge because of inept presentation of the provincialist position. Mowat was always playing catch-up. Although he won 'on the merits,' as lawyers say, his eventual victory owed much to strategic ingenuity and deft opportunism.[7] But at least the division of powers and prerogative rights were issues in which the wording of the BNA Act gave hope of success in the courts. Mowat had no such hope in the quarrel over the Rivers and Streams Act, the controversy that really brought the issue of provincial rights home to Ontario voters. As he told the *Globe* in 1887, the federal government was entitled in law to disallow whatever provincial legislation it chose. If ever the Privy Council were called on to judge the issue, that was what the Judicial Committee would say.[8]

The row over Macdonald's disallowance of the Rivers and Streams Act originated in a quarrel between lumbermen in Lanark County. Peter McLaren had spent decades and a fortune improving the headwaters of the Mississippi River, a stream in eastern Ontario, in order to float timber down to his lumber mill at the village of Carleton Place. He had built slides to pass the rapids and dams to control the water flow, and in order to build them he had bought land at strategic points athwart the waters.

The trouble began in the late 1870s, when a rival concern also wished to float logs down to Carleton Place. A statute of 1849 had established a general right to float logs regardless of the rights of riparian landowners. A judicial decision of 1863 had limited this right to streams that were floatable only in their natural state. Where floatability depended on building slides and other aids, the owner of such improvements was entitled to reasonable compensation for their use. It looks as though McLaren's rivals disagreed with his idea of reasonable compensation and decided to take a stand on the proposition that the 1863 judgment was mistaken. If the statute meant exactly what it said, they could use McLaren's facilities without paying a penny. Not only that, but his dams were an illegal obstruction to their lawful use of the waters. Boyd, Caldwell and Co. broke a couple – once on a Sunday, when McLaren had withdrawn his guards in the belief that the enemy would not profane the Sabbath. McLaren went to court for an injunction forbidding his rivals to use or damage his property.

In 1881 Mowat's government responded to this dispute by carrying the Rivers and Streams Act. The statute declared a general right to float logs and empowered the government to establish tolls for the use of private improvements. It may have borne hard on McLaren, who claimed that Boyd, Caldwell could not use his improvements without seriously hindering his own use of them, but in general it was a reasonable solution to the conflict. It promoted an economically valuable use of provincial watercourses while providing compensation for proprietors who, if the judgment of 1863 was mistaken, had not previously been entitled to it. But McLaren was not just a lumberman – he was a Conservative MP from eastern Ontario and as such had the ear of John A. Macdonald. Not only that, but his opponents were Reformers. (Perhaps that was why he thought they would not profane the Sabbath.) He petitioned the federal government to disallow the act, and Macdonald obliged.[9]

Mowat was incensed. At the moment the Rivers and Streams Act was disallowed, he was in London to superintend the defence of another Ontario statute – a measure establishing fair conditions for fire insurance policies. Several insurance companies had challenged it as an infringement of Ottawa's right to regulate trade and commerce. They had lost in every Canadian court, even the Supreme Court, and had tried to buy off their opponent in order to make an unopposed appeal to the Privy Council. Mowat foiled that scheme by underwriting their opponent's legal costs. Then he sailed off to London to make sure that this case at least did not fail for want of provincial vigilance.[10]

To Mowat, thus engaged, disallowance of the Rivers and Streams Act came as an unexpected and outrageous assault on provincial autonomy. It was quite inconsistent with the understanding at Quebec in 1864 that the federal power of disallowance was analogous to the imperial. The act was within the provinces' power to regulate property rights. The British government did not disallow valid colonial legislation, even when it was arguably detrimental to imperial interests – it had not vetoed the National Policy, for instance, although the Canadian tariff worked against British exports to Canada. By that standard, disallowance of the Rivers and Streams Act was an unconstitutional violation of the provinces' right to self-government.

Not only that – it flouted Macdonald's own standards. Soon after Confederation, he had set guidelines that limited the veto to legislation which was beyond the provinces' powers under the BNA Act, or conflicted with valid federal legislation, or affected the interests of the Dominion as a whole. In 1871 he had affirmed these principles in refusing to veto a New Brunswick statute that abolished public funding of sectarian schools. Roman Catholics had attacked the act as a breach of minority rights that were guaranteed by the BNA Act, but Macdonald had left that question to the courts. The provinces were entitled to legislate on education, and he had refused to disallow the act on the ground of possible injustice to minorities.[11]

The Schools Act injured thousands, especially among New Brunswick's large French-speaking minority. If Macdonald would not disallow that, what excuse could he offer for vetoing a measure that at worst, it seemed, harmed only one man and may in fact have done him good? Apart from that, Macdonald had flouted convention by not consulting the Ontario government beforehand. His guidelines of 1868 stated that legislation should not be disallowed until the provincial government had had a chance to justify it or the legislature a chance to remove the taint, if possible, by amending it. This procedure had invariably been followed until the Rivers and Streams Act was struck down.

From the start, therefore, Ontario Reformers condemned disallowance of the Rivers and Streams Act as a betrayal of the Confederation compact and its promise of local self-government. They made an impressive case, grounded partly on a reading of the Confederation Debates of 1865 but mainly relying on two authorities. One was Alpheus Todd, a Canadian whose treatise on the British constitution had won him an international reputation. In his new book on the British colonies, Todd declared that the Canadian provinces had brought their constitutional rights intact into Confederation. Their right to self-government was no less than Canada's right to self-government within the empire. Each provincial legislature was equal, within its own domain, to the Canadian and even the Imperial Parliament. The Crown's right to interfere with provincial legislation was 'a reserve right ... under exceptional and indefinable circumstances and as a last resort.' The Reformers reinforced Todd's authority with an appeal to that of Sir John Macdonald. They frequently cited Macdonald's disallowance guidelines of 1868. They threw in his face his words in the Confederation Debates, when he had stated that the relationship of the general to the local governments would be identical to that of the imperial government to the colonies.[12]

Undoubtedly, then, Macdonald had violated the Confederation compact – but why? The *Globe* now recalled Dorion's warning in 1865, so little heeded by Upper Canadian Reformers at the time, that the federal government would be tempted to disallow provincial legislation at the behest of local supporters. Who was more likely to do so than Macdonald, with his unconcealed contempt for the ideal of local autonomy?

Harking back to the history of the Confederation movement, Mowat recalled that the Reformers had consistently demanded the largest possible powers for the provinces. Macdonald, by contrast, had preferred a legislative union – and by his own admission still did.[13]

Such wanton disregard of constitutional propriety, in such a bad cause, had to be resisted if provincial autonomy were not to become meaningless; but it could not be resisted in the courts. Mowat was in the same predicament as the Reformers of the 1840s as they struggled to realize a legally unenforceable right to colonial responsible government. They had succeeded by mobilizing public opinion; he must do likewise. But here he shared another handicap with his predecessors. Reform politics was rooted in collective memories that many voters, especially newcomers, did not share. And while British immigrants of the 1830s and 1840s might have sympathized with the idea that their new North American home should enjoy autonomy in its domestic affairs, later ones had no particular reason to identify themselves with Oliver Mowat's Ontario as against Sir John Macdonald's Canada.

Yet the attempt must be made. The Reformers re-enacted the Rivers and Streams Bill and made it a major issue in the federal election of 1882, along with a bread-and-butter concern: Ontario's claim to a vast, timber-rich swath of the Hudson Bay watershed, bounded on the north by the English and Albany rivers and stretching westward almost to Lake Winnipeg.

Ontario's territorial claim arose from Canada's assumption of sovereignty over the Hudson's Bay Company's old fur-trading domain in 1869. Canada's northern and western boundaries had never been exactly defined, and the historical record afforded ground for opposing claims. The Quebec Act of 1774 had set the western boundary at a line drawn due north from the confluence of the Ohio and Mississippi rivers (the American Mississippi, of course) and the northern boundary at the height of land separating the Hudson Bay and Great Lakes watersheds. Other evidence pointed to the wider boundaries claimed by Ontario. With economic exploitation and settlement now in prospect, it became important to fix the line. If the disputed territory belonged to Ontario, the province would own its natural resources and control their exploitation; if not, Ottawa would. The decision was of interest not only to the governments directly concerned but to other provinces, which might look jealously at the further aggrandizement of Canada's wealthiest and most populous province.

Even friendly governments found it hard to settle the question. John A. and Sandfield Macdonald could not agree. The Mackenzie and Mowat governments appointed arbitrators but did not press them to a conclusion – not, at any rate, until Mowat began to worry about Mackenzie's electoral prospects in 1878. The board awarded the territory to Ontario only a month before the election, and then Macdonald, restored to power, refused to implement the award. In 1880 he disallowed a provincial act to establish civil government in the territory; a year later he carried an act of Parliament annexing the western portion to Manitoba. By the Manitoba Act (the federal statute of 1870 that had established the province), the federal government had retained ownership and control of that province's natural resources. Macdonald's ploy, therefore, brought another government into play against Ontario at little or no cost to Ottawa.[14]

Evidently Macdonald was as determined to deny his native province its territorial as its constitutional rights; and in this case too, Reformers were in no doubt as to his motives. To be sure, Mowat pretended to be puzzled by the prime minister's perversity. 'I cannot account for it except that there is a little hostility somewhere against this Province as a Province. Is it on the part of Upper Canadian Ministers in the Government? Have they this bitter feeling to us? If not, then they are bowing their neck to this hostility in others ... There is hostility somewhere, and those who ought to stand up for Ontario are not doing so.'[15]

What Mowat hinted at the *Globe* stated bluntly. Macdonald had abandoned any pretence of impartiality between provinces and now relied on the same combination that had sustained him in the bad old days. He looked for his main force to Quebec and hoped by bribery and political arts to augment his *bleu* battalions with enough MPs from other provinces to give him a working majority. 'Quebec has not merely been treated with effusive deference by the Dominion Government, but her Tories have had the gratification of seeing Sir John at their dictation override the self-governing rights of Ontario, and attempt to cheat this Province of a vast and valuable territory.' Cartier had promised his followers that they should rule Confederation, and with Macdonald's aid that promise was now being fulfilled with a vengeance. This was happening not only because Macdonald could not resist his domineering allies, though – it also manifested his own malignance towards his native province. Upper Canada had never been more than temporarily amenable to his wiles, and even his electoral triumph in 1878 had been marred by personal defeat in his old riding of Kingston. 'By giving the reins to the Bleus he punishes Ontario frowardness in a very practical and no doubt, to him, highly satisfactory way.'[16]

So there it was. Confederation, which Mowat had celebrated as recently as 1879 for putting an end to 'French Tory rule' in Upper Canada's affairs,[17] had proved to be a snare and a delusion. 'The evil we supposed had been corrected by the Confederate Act is still rife, and we are no more free than before – as much under the heel of others as when this complaint was first made' – so the premier told the party convention that assembled in Toronto at the beginning of 1883.[18] Reformers must gird their loins and fight for responsible government once more.

The convention of 1883 was, to use a modern phrase, the mother of all conventions. The previous autumn the Tories had made a respectable showing in Toronto's Shaftesbury Hall. The Reformers scheduled their event for the same venue, but so many delegates flocked to the leader's call that it had to be shifted to the Pavilion Music Hall, a three-storey edifice of iron and glass that graced the Horticultural Gardens at Carlton and Jarvis Streets. Even this much larger building was packed to the roof, and simultaneous meetings had to be held there and in Shaftesbury Hall, the leading speakers shuttling between the two. The combined attendance was well over six thousand. The applause must have been deafening.[19]

And to go by the *Toronto Mail*, the stench must have been appalling. 'There is no doubt at all that the managers of the Grit convention have appealed very strongly to their peculiar constituency of delegates' – so sniffed the Tory organ in language redolent of City's age-old contempt for Country. 'Cheap railway fares, board at half price, whiskey and cigars at the expense of the combined License Commissioners, and the promise of a "cordial" welcome at "the station" – such a feast of Reason and flow of Soul – such a combination of free lecture and free lunch never yet tempted the imagination of a somewhat dull-witted mob of semi-civilized partisans. All that was needed was a promise to throw in some old clothes and a few spelling books, a ration of cut-plug, the promise of a bath, and a copy of the *Globe*'s Christmas illustrated paper, and the rush would have been tremendous.'[20] At the Horticultural Pavilion, speakers used the *Mail*'s insults to fire up the delegates, whose opinion of themselves was very different. Colin Macdougall, a veteran of conventions dating back to the 1850s, hailed them as a gathering of earnest, intellectual men, capable of discussing the burning question of the hour. A party election pamphlet saluted an assembly of 'more than six thousand of the best men in the Province.'[21]

The delegates needed inflaming. With the economy restored to some semblance of health, even many Liberals were inclined to thank Macdonald's National Policy. In the summer's federal election, the Conservatives had not repeated their success of 1878, when they had won sixty-three Ontario seats out of eighty-eight. Still, they had taken half the vote, which a blatant gerrymander translated into a handsome majority of seats. During the campaign, moreover, Macdonald had threatened to demolish a pillar of Mowat's political system – the provincial liquor-licence commissioners. In September he had disallowed the Rivers and Streams Act for the second time. Soon afterwards, buoyed up perhaps by the federal poll, the provincial Conservatives abandoned their previous support of Mowat in the territorial dispute.[22] The enemy was massing; the lines were drawn. It was imperative, said Mowat, that the coming provincial election return a government that would defend Ontario's rights in the legislature, the law courts, and the court of public opinion.

The tocsin of war, as Colin Macdougall called it, resounded through the Horticultural Pavilion from beginning to end. The veteran conventioneer summoned his audience to stand up for rights that their predecessors had won on many a hard-fought field. In a formal address to the leader, the convention hailed Mowat as one who had stood in the front rank of those earlier battles. George Ross, soon to become Ontario's minister of education, compared the present struggle for provincial rights with the American Civil War. Ross can hardly have meant to identify the provincial cause with that of the slave-owning Southern secessionists. Probably he was echoing exchanges that had rung through the legislature a year earlier. William Ralph Meredith, leader of the provincial opposition, had inveighed against the 'almost treasonable' language of the Reform press – language 'provocative of civil war' – and Mowat had marked his words as a revelation of Macdonald's intentions should Ontario continue to insist on its rights.[23]

Macdonald was the real enemy – no one doubted that. Veteran Reformer Joseph Rymal decried the prime minister as a man who had not lived in Ontario for many years and bore a grudge against his native province. Of course, Ottawa lies on the Ontario bank of the river, but no doubt Rymal was thinking of the capital's proximity to Quebec and the city of Montreal. Perhaps, too, his error reflected some lurking sense of Macdonald as the fallen Lucifer, plotting revenge against Heaven from his fastness on the Quebec border. It certainly drew attention to the enmity of Quebec. John Charlton, MP, spoke bluntly of 'the sworn and mortal enemies of this Province – the Bleus of Quebec.' He told a story of two Yankees and an Irishman, in which Macdonald figured as 'his Satanic majesty.'[24]

Rymal was a famous wit among Reformers, and the *Globe* judged Charlton's speech droll too. Mowat too got a laugh while explaining how Macdonald's offer to refer the territorial dispute to the Privy Council was really a trick designed to produce indefinite delay. 'It is said that Sir John Macdonald is a pretty astute man, and I have no doubt he is, but I felt that ... it was my duty to take care that the great man did not get the better of me in this matter. (Cheers and laughter.) If I had at once blindly consented to the proposal without any conditions ... I would have allowed myself to be caught by Sir John Macdonald. (Laughter.) He has not caught me yet, and I don't think he will. (Applause.)'[25]

So the Reformers laughed; but Mowat left them in no doubt that they were laughing at danger. The impending election was no ordinary contest between a provincial government and its local opposition. The Ontario Conservatives were mere lackeys of the prime minister, who told them what to think – when to change their minds – when to say yes and when no: 'Anything he desires they are ready to do.' The real enemy was Macdonald himself. 'We have to contend with his power and influence; we have to contend also with his patronage, contractors, and all their money; we have to contend with the cry that the N.P. [National Policy] is in danger ... and we have to contend with the cry that we are disloyal to Confederation ... Ontario has all these things against her, but I believe she will be equal to the task of defeating all.'

In the hour of peril, speakers appealed to the electors' patriotism as 'citizens of Ontario,' 'citizens of this free Province.' Alderman Peter Ryan of Toronto scouted the Tory claim that the territorial quarrel was merely a bread-and-butter issue. On the contrary, it involved 'the autonomy of our Province and the rights of our people.' To defend those rights was a matter of patriotism and a duty owed to future generations of Ontarians. In order to summon the present generation to that duty, Reformers invoked the inspiring example of past generations. Colin Macdougall spoke of 'a party with grand traditions, and one which had secured the rights of the people of this Province.' If Reformers submitted to Macdonald's dictation, said Joseph Rymal, they would prove themselves unworthy scions of noble sires. Several speakers praised Confederation as a fulfilment of the promise of 1859. The task at hand was to make sure that the old battles would never have to be fought over again.

An election pamphlet, issued shortly after the convention, epitomized this appeal to history by tying the impending contest firmly to the Reform tradition of struggle for local liberty. It hearkened back to the first party convention of 1844, when Robert Baldwin had boldly demanded full self-government in domestic affairs. Quoting Lord Durham on the undesirability of British interference with colonial legislation on local matters, it applied the same principle to federal–provincial relations. The future of Confederation depended on maintaining the rights of self-government so boldly maintained by the convention of forty years earlier. 'Are the men of Ontario now less faithful in devotion to liberty than their fathers were? Or may Sir John Macdonald succeed where Sir Charles Metcalfe failed? The vote of next election day will answer. The duty of the hour is the duty of standing by ourselves.'[26]

The Reformers' majority – a comfortable twenty-eight seats in 1879 – fell to fifteen. John Beverley Robinson, lieutenant-governor of Ontario and son of the old chief justice, told Mowat that it had been a mistake to campaign against Ottawa rather than on the government's record. Looking back in old age, George Ross thought just the opposite – that Mowat's stand for Ontario's rights had won him his majority.[27] In a sense, it makes no difference. The Reformers won just the same slender plurality of votes over the Conservatives as in 1875 and 1879: a paltry one per cent. In an election fought on the cry *la patrie en danger*, nearly half the voters had found other things more compelling. It was a bad omen for traditional Reform politics. And Ontario was only just embarking on an era of rapid urbanization and rural depopulation that would hit the Reformers where it hurt.

In the long run, these social and demographic changes would help undo the Reform tradition; but Ontario still had more than twenty years of Reform government ahead of it, and in 1883 it was easy to blame the close shave on other things. The *Globe* described how land grants, grants of Dominion timber lands, grants of Ontario disputed territory, promises of contracts and offices, vast sums of money, in fact the whole power and resources of the Dominion machine had been quietly brought to bear. 'The Custom house was deliberately turned into a political engine, and from actual experience many merchants know how unscrupulously this power can be used by the present government.

Hordes of emissaries from the central power were dispersed throughout the country. The whole force of Tory members and Senators, no matter from what Province, officials, judges, prospective judges and others were let loose upon us. Confidential agents went about from one place to another distributing the corruption fund.'[28] And still virtue had won the day. And now victory – victory on all fronts – was near in the struggle for Ontario's rights.

In 1882 the Privy Council had shocked defenders of provincial rights by its decision in *Russell v. The Queen*, a challenge to the Scott Act, the federal prohibition statute of 1878. The Judicial Committee upheld the act in terms that seemed to imply that the Canadian Parliament could legislate for the peace, order, and good government of Canada pretty much as it pleased, notwithstanding the limits to that power in the BNA Act. Macdonald saw this decision as a means to a cherished political goal.

Ontario's liquor-licensing system rested on a small army of paid inspectors, who were always available to electioneer for the Reform party, while Conservative victuallers felt compelled to lie low in order to protect their licenses. In 1883, Macdonald set up a national system, which would supersede all provincial regulations and enable Ottawa to replace Liberal inspectors with Conservatives. That November, however, in a case called *Hodge v. the Queen,* the Privy Council delivered a double blow to Macdonald's ambitions by affirming the validity of Ontario's licensing law. The decision cast doubt on the validity of the McCarthy Act (the federal licensing law, so called after the MP who had carried it through the Commons), forcing Macdonald to refer it to the courts. It also went a long way towards declaring that the provincial governments were constitutionally equal to the Dominion government, not subordinate to it as partisans of federal power maintained.

In 1884 the Supreme Court of Canada struck down the McCarthy Act; a year later the Privy Council concurred. In 1885 too, the Privy Council confirmed the legal assumptions underlying the Rivers and Streams Act, which by then had been disallowed for the third time and enacted for the fourth. It held that the Canadian statute of 1849 had indeed established a general right to use private stream improvements for the floating of timber. What Macdonald had impeached as an atrocious interference with the rights of property turned out to be a boon to the proprietors concerned, who would otherwise have had no right to charge for the use of their facilities.

Mowat defended Ontario's territorial rights with equal success. In the spring of 1883, he sent a large force of constables into the disputed northern territory in order to enforce the authority of 'the Queen in right of Ontario' against that of 'the Queen in right of Manitoba.' The western province had less at stake than Ontario, since it could not benefit from the territory's natural resources, and Mowat's escalation of the struggle soon persuaded Manitoba to refer the quarrel to the Privy Council on terms acceptable to Ontario. In the summer of 1884, the Judicial Committee affirmed that the disputed territory belonged to Ontario. Macdonald still refused to ratify the award, claiming that it gave the province only the territory but conferred no right to the natural resources, but in 1888 the Privy Council declared that these too were Ontario's. Only then did the perplexed prime minister finally give up the struggle.[29] 'What luck Mowat has had with the PC,' he exclaimed to a friend;[30] but luck had little to do with it. Mowat owed his legal victories, like his political ones, to hard work, tactical guile, strategic vision, and a good case.

One September day in 1884, Oliver Mowat passed into Canada across the Clifton Suspension Bridge at Niagara Falls, en route from the capital of the empire, where he had successfully defended Ontario's claim to the disputed territory before the Privy Council. A great concourse of patriots had gathered to cheer home the man the *Globe* hailed as Ontario's Champion. Illuminations at the Falls proclaimed 'Ontario's Champion, Welcome' and 'See the Conquering Hero Comes.'[31]

Addressing the throng outside the city hall, Mowat spoke of fighting the Battle of Ontario. Far smaller parcels of territory had often been the subject of long and bloody and expensive wars. 'Had it been some foreign foes that endeavoured to deprive us of our territory, you[r] young men and middle-aged men would have sprung to arms to defend their country, and your old men would have mourned that their age prevented them from joining them.' The year 1884 was the official centenary of the Loyalist settlement of Upper Canada, and Mowat lauded the glorious ancestors who had fought against the dismemberment of the empire and then, having sacrificed their all to what they believed to be duty, had come to make their homes in the wilderness on the western bank of the Niagara River. He had no need to state plainly – only the dullest listener could fail to feel it – how his own successful defence of the northern territory had re-enacted the Loyalists' defence of their homeland against the invaders of 1812–14.

As Mowat and his escort advanced in procession from the railway station to the town hall, the very skies enacted the beloved country's passage from darkness into light. 'The rain had threatened and a few drops had actually fallen, but before the Town Hall was reached it was manifest that the storm had blown over and that the weather would not be a bar to open air speaking.' So it was the next day, when the premier and his party, accompanied by an escort that swelled at every station, made what *Globe* headlines called a Triumphal Progress from the Falls to Toronto for The Grandest Reception Ever Tendered a Canadian Public Man. 'The morning broke fair, but it was not long before the sky was overcast, and the outlook was unpleasant, not to say discouraging.' At Hamilton, as the premier responded to admirers in his usual cordial style, some heavy drops fell, and it seemed almost certain that a day's rain would sadly interfere with the rejoicing. But, as if in sudden acquiescence with the hearty wishes of so many, the rain ceased in a moment, and from then on the day grew brighter and brighter. Except for the dust that for some reason seemed to blow in greater volumes than usual, the Thousands of Voters in Procession who escorted the premier from Toronto's Union Station to the Queen's Park had nothing to complain of.[32]

It was a procession of banner-waving contingents from every part of old Ontario, with several bands. No gaudy uniform was required to add to the grandeur of the spectacle, opined the *Globe*, for no uniform could have added dignity to the faces, stamped with the impress of honesty and intelligence, which passed in review. At the Park the advance guard halted opposite the pedestal of George Brown's monument, where the Hon. Oliver Mowat received and acknowledged Greetings from the Sons of Ontario – a vast throng amounting, together with what daughters of Ontario may have braved the crush, to an estimated fifty thousand. In the evening there was a banquet at a Granite Rink Crowded to Overflowing. The feast featured another Great Speech by the Hero of the Hour, with Addresses by Other Eminent Liberals for dessert.

Soon afterwards, similar triumphs were enacted in the towns of Woodstock and Barrie. Such was the Reform party of Ontario at the height of its last glory.

9

Peoples and Pacts

In the 1880s the bedrock of Reform politics was still those rural communities, mainly of American and Scottish stock, that had powered the movement fifty years earlier. The Americans were mainly Methodists, the Scots mainly Free Kirk Presbyterians. Though settled throughout Ontario, they were thickest in the country between Lakes Huron and Erie. 'The Peninsula must not get hold of the ship,' wrote John A. Macdonald anxiously in 1856. 'It is occupied by Yankees and Covenanters, in fact the most yeasty and unsafe of populations.'[1]

Writing of the Peninsula community in which he grew up between the world wars, the economist John Kenneth Galbraith reports that most of 'the Scotch' voted much as they went to church – as a recurrent act of obeisance to the faith of their fathers and grandparents. And most of them voted Liberal.[2] Galbraith's Scotch were recognizably from the same mould as the rustics the *Mail* sniffed at in 1883 (he even echoes the *Mail*'s comments on their hygiene), and what went for the Covenanters went for the Yankees too. By and large they were men of narrow horizons, who gave their political bibles – chiefly William Lyon Mackenzie's *Colonial Advocate* in the 1820s and 1830s, and later George Brown's *Globe* – much the same credence as they gave the Good Book itself.

To metropolitan observers, the quality of their political belief was bizarre. 'It is astonishing with what tenacity a Canadian farmer adheres to his party Shibboleth,' exclaimed Goldwin Smith in 1891. His friend James Bryce reported that 'in Canada ideas are not needed to make parties, for these can live by heredity and ... by memories of past combats.'[3] One can see why outsiders might say such things, yet there is condescension as well as alienation in both men's words. What Smith called shibboleths were values cherished by generations of Reformers: responsible government; local autonomy; a spare, efficient administration; the separation of church and state. Where Bryce failed to discern ideas there flourished a worldview fashioned by generations of living – the collective experience that Reformers knew as the history of Upper Canada.

Perhaps Reformers couched their politics in what sounds like an old-fashioned language; but if they still responded to the causes that had brought Reform politics into being in the 1820s, was it because they were fixated on past combats or because those combats were not past but still present? To Reformers of the 1880s, the political universe was still recognizably that of their fathers and grandfathers. Their province was still oppressed by Tory agents of an outside power. In spirit, if nothing else, Macdonald's Tories were lineal descendants of the Family Compact, and his assault on local liberties was an attempt to reimpose oligarchic centralism. The new oligarchs were the barons and baronets of capitalism: privileged monopolists such as the Canadian Pacific Railway and the manufacturers who sought to avoid competition by means of tariff protection. Like the old oligarchy, they imposed themselves on the people by pandering to the immigrant Irish, Catholic and Orange, and by kowtowing to outside power – no longer the imperial power, as of old, but French-speaking clericalism and the money barons of Montreal.[4] This Reform anti-elitism confronted a matching continuity in Tory rhetoric. As long as Reformers adopted a posture of resistance to political injustice, their opponents remained ready to brand them as disloyal to monarch and empire. Like the struggle to win responsible government for Upper Canada, this went on longer than historians have suspected.

So far in this book I have described how these opposing attitudes came into being and how the clash of interests and ideas in Upper Canada gave rise to two political traditions – a Reform tradition based on a myth of alien oppression, and a Tory tradition based on a myth of alien subversion. I have traced the former through three generations. Now I want to see how that tradition, rooted in the colonial struggles of an earlier era, adapted itself to the rapidly changing milieu of the later nineteenth century. By the late 1880s Ontario Reformers were cooperating with the 'alien oppressor,' the much-vilified French of Quebec, to resist the centralizing policies of John A. Macdonald. Crucial to that alliance was a shared vision of Confederation as an interprovincial compact. I explain the underlying logic of that idea, so passionately denied in the Canadian nationalist thought of the twentieth century.

The historian David Mills identifies the idea of loyalty as the main ideological focus of Upper Canadian politics before 1850. Drawing on the idea of Upper Canada's providential mission to uphold British values in North America, the administrative elite tried to equate loyalty with an unswerving attachment to the existing political order and thereby discredit any concerted opposition to that order as infidelity to the mother country. Gradually, Upper Canadian Reformers managed to establish British constitutional practice as the standard of political propriety. They succeeded in legitimizing outspoken criticism of the status quo, the formation of an organized political opposition, and finally responsible government. Conservatives fought a rearguard action, trying at every stage to limit the field of legitimate political activity and aspiration. By 1850, however, a consensus had arisen that identified loyalty with devotion to the British empire and British political values.[5]

According to Mills, this consensus lasted until the 1880s, when a loss of confidence in Canada's economic and political viability prompted many intellectuals and politicians to champion radical solutions to their country's plight. The Liberals' federal election platform of 1891, with its advocacy of unrestricted commercial reciprocity with the United States, was a moderate expression of this trend. More advanced thinkers, some identified with the Liberal party, dreamed of complete independence from Britain or even political union with the United States. Faced with this loss of faith in the imperial tie, devotees of the British connection responded, like their predecessors fifty years earlier, by raising the disloyalty cry against the renegades.[6]

Like most writers on Canadian history, Mills places too much stress on the advent of responsible government. His supposed forty-year hiatus has no reality; as long as Reformers stood up for local autonomy against central power, they found themselves beset by charges of disloyalty.[7] 'At every succeeding Parliamentary, and indeed at many of the municipal elections, Reformers are insulted by having their loyalty called in question, and the epithet Rebel flung in their teeth.' So complained the *Brockville Recorder*, edited by the veteran Reformer David Wylie, in 1864.[8] Even if Confederation provided temporary relief, the provincial-rights controversy brought a return to basics. 'Who Are the Rebels?' seethed the *Globe* in 1882. 'If the Ontario Government secures the rights of this Province by the only means available, viz., by keeping possession of rights hitherto exercised, and taking possession of rights withheld – that, we are told, will be rebellion! If Manitoba defends her right to charter railways, that also will be rebellion! The true rebel is the Minister who violates the Constitution in the hope that those wronged will not use against his usurpation weapons not provided by the Constitution.'[9]

The *Globe*'s words confirm Mills's central thesis on the loyalty issue. Confronted with the demand for unquestioning loyalty to the existing regime, Reformers lofted a competing standard of loyalty: that of faithful adherence to the British constitution, with its cherished safeguards for political dissent. This strategy was epitomized in the motto that had adorned the *Globe*'s masthead since its founding in 1844: 'The subject who is truly loyal to the Chief Magistrate will neither advise nor submit to arbitrary measures.' This was the famous dictum of Junius, an anonymous critic of King George III's government in the 1760s. Mowat adapted Junius by asserting that the subject who was truly loyal would not submit to wrong by encroachment but, like the Liberal party, would insist on his just rights. Mowat was as much attached to Confederation as anybody; but if the BNA Act was to be interpreted as the Tories wished, and if Ontarians could maintain Confederation only by giving up half their province, then Confederation must go.[10]

Needless to say, such a slogan did not enhance the Reformers' reputation for loyalty in Conservative circles, but Mowat and his supporters had a ready reply. *They* were loyal to Confederation, Alderman Peter Ryan of Toronto told the convention of 1883 – its enemies were those who sought to insert the thin end of the wedge of centralization. Reformers were fighting not just for Ontario but for provincial rights from Halifax to the Pacific Ocean – thus George Ross, before going on to compare the struggle with the American Civil War. In its ceremonial address to Mowat, the convention averred that his resistance to Ottawa's encroachments on provincial rights would not weaken but strengthen Confederation.[11]

Reformers thought it mighty unfair that they should constantly have to defend their loyalty against the accusations of men who in 1849 (the *Brockville Recorder* recalled) had threatened annexation to the United States because their party had been driven from power. The *Recorder* was referring to an embarrassing episode in the past of certain leading Conservatives. Incensed by Britain's dismantling of the Old Colonial System and concession of colonial responsible government, and demoralized by three years of deep commercial depression, members of Montreal's Tory business elite had been goaded into championing political union with the United States as the only means of economic survival.[12]

But Upper Canadian memory reached back further, to 1833, when Lord Goderich had dismissed Attorney General Boulton and Solicitor

General Hagerman for their part in William Lyon Mackenzie's repeated expulsions from the house of assembly. In his *Story of the Upper Canadian Rebellion*, published in 1885, the Liberal historian John Charles Dent recalled with gleeful horror how the *Courier of Upper Canada*, the Family Compact's pet newspaper, had asserted that even loyal colonists were beginning to ponder some new state of political existence. 'Some new state of political existence!' exulted Dent. 'This was a pretty strong suggestion of rebellion! And it emanated from the organ of those in whose mouths the word "loyalty" was ever present; whose "loyalty" had for years been vaunted from every hustings, and who, so long as the tide ran in their favour, had preached doctrines worthy of the middle ages about submission to the higher powers.'[13] It was an axiom of Reform politics that Tory loyalty was something that existed to a purpose and could be counted on only so long as the tide ran in the Tories' favour.[14] And had not Conservative governments introduced those Yankee abominations – an elective upper chamber and directly elected mayors?[15]

But Reformers had only themselves to blame if the epithet 'rebel' was flung in their face whenever opportunity offered. Whatever Conservatives may have said in moments of disaffection, they had never resisted the government with 'weapons not provided by the Constitution,' as the *Globe* put it, and they did not boast of their indiscretions afterwards.

The rebellion of 1837 was a twofold embarrassment to the Reform party: not only did it freeze Reformers for posterity in a posture of disloyalty towards Queen and empire, but Reformers disagreed about it among themselves. In chapter 6, we saw the fuss resulting from Mowat's disapproving reference to it at the convention of 1859.[16] Twenty-five years later Mowat had to cope with a similar spat within his own caucus. In March 1885 a Conservative member moved in the legislature that the government should 'make some suitable recognition to the volunteers of 1837–1838 ... for the valuable services they rendered in defence of their country.' Several Reformers rose to the bait, even while suspecting that the motion was designed to allow the opposition 'to wave the flag of loyalty.' One member wondered whether the resolution referred to those who had trampled on the constitution or those 'true patriots' who had risen against the Family Compact in defence of the constitution. But two or three Reformers had themselves taken up arms in support of the government, or their fathers had, and some of them spoke in favour of the resolution.[17]

Mowat had to step carefully. As a Reformer, it was one of his assets that he had grown up a Conservative in Kingston, 'the very hotbed of Conservatism' as he put it on one occasion, and had turned to Reform only in his thirties out of disgust at the tone of Conservative politics under Macdonald.[18] This allowed him to cite his own youthful errors and subsequent enlightenment as a lesson to other young Conservatives. And as a teenager in 1837 he had hefted a musket for Queen and country, although he did not number that among his errors. At a suitable stage in the debate he moved an amendment 'cordially recognizing the loyalty and services' of those, like himself, who had responded to the call of the 'lawfully constituted authorities' but also acknowledging the services of the Reformers of that period, whose efforts had secured for Canadians the blessings of responsible government. George Ross tacked on another amendment, which sententiously acknowledged the services of those who had rallied to resist the Fenian invaders of 1866. Even with this garnish the amendment passed by only four votes. Four Reformers opposed it, and the *Toronto Mail* accused Mowat of moving a vote of thanks to the rebels.[19]

But why bring up the rebellion at all? In 1885, of course, the Conservatives did so, but in 1859 it was Mowat who had raised this perilous topic, and there is also that circumspect reference in his speech to the electors of North Oxford in 1872.[20] Well, then: for one thing, many Reformers considered the rebellion a great, if not exactly glorious, moment in their history. In 1859 William Lyon Mackenzie was still living in Toronto, having returned from exile a decade earlier. Though recently retired from the legislature, he had demonstrated his enduring appeal by winning four successive elections in Haldimand County between 1850 and 1857 – the first of them against that rising Reform politician, George Brown.

A quarter-century later, Mowat could find evidence of the living importance of the rebellion in the *Parliamentary Guide*, where the MPP for Hamilton boasted of his kinship with David Gibson, a Reform MPP 'who was prominently associated with W. Lyon Mackenzie in the troubles of 1837.' John Morison Gibson was no wild-eyed rustic but a lieutenant-colonel of militia and prize-winning marksman, who had represented Canada in several British tournaments. He had also won prizes as an undergraduate and law student at the University of Toronto.[21] He would wind up his political career as attorney general for Ontario in George Ross's Liberal government (1899–1905) before becoming Sir John, lieutenant-governor of Ontario and first president of the Canadian Red Cross.

Some Reformers, then, sympathized with the rebels of 1837 more than Mowat had done at the time or was prepared to admit twenty or fifty years later. But all Reformers had to come to terms with the rebellion, because there were always Conservatives willing to hurl it in their faces. Mowat's allusions were contributions to a collective project: that of putting the best possible light on an armed uprising against Queen Victoria. And not only that but a bungled rising, which had deteriorated into a series of border raids featuring American marauders.

Reformers could not regret that the rebellion had failed. The radical tenor of Mackenzie's politics on the eve of the rising was too well known for them to deny that success would have meant an end to monarchy and the British connection, if not annexation to the United States. How, then, to justify the event? Blame it on the Family Compact and – more daringly – on 'Downing-street rule.' Upper Canadians, some of them indisputably conservative in their politics, had been publicly blaming the oligarchy for the rebellion within weeks of the uprising.[22] The Reform myth went further, ascribing it not merely to oligarchic misrule but to the lack of responsible government.

From there it was easy to match Loyalist mythmakers by finding victory in defeat. Where the Loyalist myth followed its heroes and heroines through the darkness of exile to the consolations of a new and better land, Reformers had made a similar passage through 'the hour of our political prostration, when our opponents fancied they had their feet upon our necks and could keep them there for ever' (Robert Baldwin's words in 1842).[23] Rebellion had contributed to the triumph of Reform by opening British eyes to the iniquity of Compact rule and hastening the advent of changes that might or might not have come in the course of time. Britain's repudiation of the Old Colonial System permitted liberals, without unduly offending imperialist sensibilities, to contrast the bad old days of Downing Street rule with the new era of enlightened governance.

This view of the rebellion, long in the crafting, received quasi-academic sanction with the appearance of Dent's *Story of the Upper Canadian Rebellion* in 1885, but Dent had too sharp an eye for discomfiting detail to make the ideal propagandist, and he condemned Mackenzie as a self-centred bungler. However, a short commentary in the *Globe*, published as a semi-centennial commemoration in December 1887,[24] wraps up the Reform myth neatly for us. It portrays the rebellion as a rising against a system of 'baneful domination' (the phrase occurs twice in a passage excerpted from Mackenzie's newspaper the *Constitution*) and in favour of Canadian independence, and it describes the rebels' constitution as one framed with a view to securing the broadest liberty, equality of rights, and freedom of speech and of the press.

It was no mere discontent of the rabble, no infection of Anarchic poison, no quarrel begotten of creed, or race, or class prejudice which had thus thrown all Canada into a ferment. The people who were thus calmly preparing to resort to the last argument of the oppressed were among the best, most intelligent, and most upright to be found in the land. They were the real Canadian citizens as distinguished from the official and office-seeking classes, the hangers-on of the oligarchy, or so-called Family Compact, which had long ruled with a high hand and unmercifully fleeced the country, and the Orange and other high Tory factions, who asked nothing better than to accept their law and their gospel, yes, and even their right to breath[e] and earn their bread, at the hands of aristocratic British Lords.

Having thus distinguished virtuous rebellion then from vicious rebellion now in the usual way of those who have risen to power with the help of the sword, the writer posed a question that he might already seem to have answered: was the resort to arms justifiable? It all depended, came the judicious reply: 'In the eyes of the ultra-loyalists, who abounded in those days and of whom not a few specimens may even yet be found in Canada, who deem it the bounden duty and the highest honor of a colonist to bow to any behests or impositions of Royalty or its representative, nothing could justify rebellion ... In the view of men who respect themselves, who mean and dare to be free, the question assumes a different aspect. The grievances, oppressions and petty tyrannies partly described [earlier] were such as no true Briton, and no Canadian worthy of his heritage, would long submit to.'

Had all constitutional means of relief been tried and exhausted? That was the crucial point. 'It must be confessed the situation was far from hopeful ... Through many long years constitutional methods had been pretty thoroughly tried. Some progress had been made, some reforms promised, but then had come [Lieutenant-Governor] Francis Bond Head and despair.' The uprising was rash and foredoomed; it had been disastrous in some of its consequences – especially the 'cool-blooded murder,' under forms of law, of some of the bravest and noblest of the patriots. But had it been an utter and disastrous failure? Not at all. Constitutional freedom and self-government might have come without it, or they might not. 'The habit of submission to absolutism once ingrained, soon becomes inveterate in a people. The power of absolute rule once successfully established, is seldom voluntarily handed over by a Government. Certainly the rebellion of 1837 hastened the period of Canadian emancipation by a quarter of a century. It is always so. The cause of freedom must have its martyrs. It is easy to talk of constitutional means of redress, but the roots of constitutionalism have generally, even in British soil, been planted by insurrection and watered with patriotic blood.' The truth of this could be seen in 1887, not only in Ireland but in the Canadian Northwest, with its two Métis rebellions.

'Nothing less than the crack of rifles or the boom of cannon seems able to attract the attention of the average Tory Government to the wrongs of the people, or to startle them into questioning their own divine right to despotic rule.' The conclusion took its point from the incumbency of Conservative governments at Downing Street and on Parliament Hill. Reformers tended to identify with the British Liberals and their leader, William Gladstone, who had recently established a nearly democratic franchise and committed themselves to Home Rule for Ireland. These policies had affronted mid-Victorian liberals such as A.V. Dicey, Goldwin Smith's friend, who had gone over to the Conservative party. The bulk of the old Whig aristocracy went with them, making the Conservatives pre-eminently the party of 'aristocratic British lords.' It was no great stretch to depict Macdonald's party as the colonial counterpart of blue-blooded British Toryism. It was the party of big business, of Ontario's old Anglican upper class, of loud-mouthed loyalism.

The *Globe* commentary is remarkable for its strong feel for the temper and dynamics of the early Reform movement, and also for its forthright anti-imperialism at a time when (as we will see in chapter 12) Canadian loyalism was reaching new heights of imperialist ardour. It shows that the Reform tradition was still in touch with its historical roots and still had fire in its belly. But the *Globe*'s other semi-centennial observance spoke with Reform's conciliatory voice: the voice that reached out to all Canadians of goodwill and true British feeling. The paper had first published 'Old Limpy: A Tale of 1837' in 1869 and now reprinted it 'by urgent request'; but the reason for the request is hard to imagine, for the author's narrative and dialogue are as lame as his hero. (The author was Archibald Riddell, a Toronto medical practitioner and sometime city coroner.[25])

'Old Limpy' nicely illustrates the Reformers' efforts to assimilate the rebellion into their history. It tells of a farming family victimized by neighbours who covet their land. The paterfamilias is murdered by his grasping neighbours at the second attempt, and his son wreaks a drawn-out revenge on the culprits before fleeing to Texas. The setting is the countryside north of Toronto, from which William Lyon Mackenzie drew most of his political support and ultimately the few hundred foot-soldiers of his rebel army, and the story is interesting chiefly for its author's use of the politics of the 1830s as a backdrop for his narrative, and in particular for his acknowledgment of the existence at that time of decent 'Conservatives.'

The culprits are *not* decent Conservatives: they are an English family, 'distant and haughty in their manner; there was no friendship about them; and they kept aloof from all the neighbors and particularly shunned our family,' although they were civil and obliging enough at 'bees' and funerals. Their paterfamilias is 'one of those loud-tongued loyalists, who succeed by their noise and impudence in making themselves prominent.' When sent to jail for attempting his neighbour's murder, he obtains early release by vaunting his loyalty in a petition to the lieutenant-governor. The petition is supported by prominent local Conservatives, it being a time when 'every Conservative vote was wanting.' All this is as you might expect. But the local 'squire,' though a Conservative, is a quiet and obliging neighbour. Not only that: Old Limpy, an Irish Protestant who had fought under Wellington in the Peninsular War before sustaining at Waterloo the wound that earns him his nickname, is himself a resolute Conservative. He votes against Mackenzie even at the height of the latter's popularity – the years 1832–4, when Mackenzie was repeatedly expelled from the house of assembly and as often re-elected.

In different ways, both the commentary and the story served to clothe the rebellion with respectability. The commentary did so by depicting it as the irrepressible response of British souls to despotism, and the story, by distinguishing between good and bad Conservatives – between the 'thousands of really good, loyal men in the country' and those whose strident loyalism was merely a cover for self-seeking and wrongdoing. The rebels' target had been only the latter: a venal oligarchy and its minions. The former counted as part of the Upper Canadian people, who suffered under oligarchic oppression and rejoiced in its demise. Thus the story renewed for the 1860s – and the 1880s – the vision of Upper Canada that had underpinned the Reform tradition since its genesis in the days of the alien question. In contrast to the Tory vision of Ontario as a loyal garrison beset by danger without and within, Reformers beheld a people struggling for liberty against an oppressive oligarchy.

But a host of British settlers had arrived since the 1820s. How could a political tradition born in the trauma of the alien question appeal to these newcomers, in whose eyes the Yankees then threatened with disfranchisement were aliens indeed? As early as the 1830s, Reformers had found it necessary to adapt their language to British ears. Now fifty years had passed. What was it that allowed the Reform tradition to survive and flourish in 1887?

One thing was the way it fitted so nicely with the ascendant values of the mid-nineteenth century. This was the age of the great liberal challenge to vested privilege of every sort. Reform's hostility to the Family Compact, French-Canadian clericalism, the Canadian Pacific Railway and the National Policy made it the foe of aristocracy and monopoly; it made it the champion of political liberty, the rule of law, and the separation of church and state. It helped, too, that after 1850 the baneful domination of the mother country gave way to that of Lower Canada. The change coincided with the rise of Napoleon III in France and with the Roman Catholic division of England into territorial dioceses for the first time since the Reformation. 'Papal aggression' and the rise of a second Napoleonic empire tilted British patriotism even further than usual towards anti-Catholicism and Francophobia.

As a Scottish Presbyterian who had arrived in Canada only in the 1840s, George Brown shared these prejudices. They helped him build a bridge even to the Orange Order, a heavy trader in loud-tongued loyalism: that was what got Brown elected in 1859 as MPP for 'Tory-on-toe.'[26] The bridge was shaky, and Brown lost his seat at the next election; but the Conservatives had lost their monopoly of the Orange vote, and British immigrants of less florid hue were more lastingly receptive to Reform's message.

Mowat, a cannier politician than Brown, went one better than his mentor. Confederation had cured the complaint that made even Orangemen vote Reform – the imposition by Lower Canadian votes of laws benefiting papists in Upper Canada. Even as his supporters continued to rail against French-Canadian clericalism, Mowat exploited the slackening of animosity at home to build bridges to the mainly Irish Catholics of Ontario. Reformers spoke feelingly of Ireland's pain and began to campaign for provincial autonomy under the slogan of 'Home Rule for Ontario.' Edward Blake, son of an Irish-born Baldwinite of the 1840s, quit Canadian politics in 1892, after eight years (1879–87) as Liberal leader at Ottawa, to become an Irish Nationalist MP at Westminster.

And when the provincial Conservatives, in despair of winning power, started trying to outdo the Reformers in religious and racial intolerance, Mowat seized the chance to make friends among the province's newest immigrants: the rapidly growing French-Canadian population of eastern Ontario.[27]

These feats of domestic alliance-building paved the way for a correspondingly bold policy in external affairs: combination with the enemy. In 1887 five of the seven provincial premiers met at Quebec to voice their discontent with the state of Confederation. Only British Columbia and Prince Edward Island – two Tory pocket boroughs – were unrepresented. John Norquay, a more independent Conservative, arrived from Winnipeg, along with Liberal premiers from Toronto, Fredericton, and Halifax. They came at the bidding of Honoré Mercier, recently elected to office at the head of his new Parti national.[28]

Until 1886 the Conservatives had ruled the roost in Quebec. Macdonald had won a majority of Quebec seats at every general election except that of 1874, when, mired by the Pacific Scandal, his party took only thirty-two seats out of sixty-five. The Quebec Conservatives had won every provincial general election since 1867. Then came the conviction of Louis Riel for high treason. Quebec's French-language newspapers had taught their readers to identify with this symbol of the French fact in Canada's new North-West. Québécois sympathy for the Métis leader had grown because of his long persecution at the hands of Ontario's militant Protestantism; but John A. Macdonald vowed to hang him 'though every dog in Quebec should bark in his favour.' A year later Mercier swept to victory in Quebec at the head of a party – a Parti national – designed for voters who were disgusted with Conservatives and Liberals alike.[29]

The conference that Mercier hosted at Quebec in 1887 dealt with two subjects: finance and the constitution. The financial issue was the size of the subsidies that Ottawa paid the provinces under the BNA Act: except for Mowat, all the premiers wanted more. What brought the Ontarian to the table was the prospect of a common front against Macdonald's centralism. Historians have tended to treat this as a secondary concern for the other participants, but Mowat was by no means the only premier with a constitutional grievance. Norquay, the Conservative from Manitoba, resented Ottawa's disallowance of thirteen provincial railway charters in order to preserve the CPR's monopoly on the prairies. Mercier had no such specific complaint but was deeply concerned by the question of Quebec's place within Confederation.[30]

What then can have induced centralist historians to play down Quebec's constitutional concerns at that time? Perhaps the answer relates to Quebec's special interest in federal as opposed to legislative union. According to the centralist story, Canada adopted a federal constitution, although most people disliked the idea, in order to accommodate the French fact. This makes Quebec's early attitude towards Macdonald's constitutional policies a touchstone of their legitimacy. If Quebec approved of his administration of the settlement of 1867 – an arrangement shaped above all by the need to please Quebec – it stands to reason that his policies were consistent with the spirit of 1867 and that the complaints of the Ontario Reformers were baseless. True, during the twentieth century Québécois sensibilities were to be the great stumbling-block to constitutional reform; but as long as that obstinacy can be explained as a response to events that were exogenous to the constitution (English-speaking colonization of the west; a series of blows to minority rights there and in Ontario; controversies over military conscription in both world wars), it poses no challenge to the idea of Confederation as an exercise in centralization.

The Conservative record of electoral success in Quebec, and the Ontario Reformers' portrayal of the 'Quebec Tories' as enemies of provincial rights, make it easy to conclude that Quebec approved of Macdonald's policies. But look deeper, and you find something else. Even while sustaining Macdonald in power in Ottawa, francophone Conservatives had been far from happy with his centralizing bent. As early as April 1869 Sir Narcisse Belleau, last prime minister of United Canada and first lieutenant-governor of Quebec, had accused the federal government of grasping for legislative power at the provinces' expense. In 1872 a *bleu* newspaper had reminded its readers that their leaders had touted Confederation as a means to autonomy for Quebec. To be *bleu*, it had concluded, meant supporting provincial rights and opposing centralization. In 1881 the Conservative government of Quebec had intervened on Ontario's side before the Supreme Court of Canada in one of Mowat's early constitutional battles, the *Escheats Case*.[31]

Then, if not earlier, Mowat must have realized that Quebec Tories did not necessarily like Macdonald's approach to the constitution. Soon he might have noticed something else. In 1884, at the height of Mowat's confrontation with Macdonald, the Québécois constitutional expert Thomas-Jean-Jacques Loranger published in English the first of his *Letters* on the BNA Act. Loranger had represented Quebec in the *Escheats Case*, and his first *Letter* was partly a reprise of his argument before the

Supreme Court. Now, however, it appeared with an emotional preface, which placed the campaign for provincial rights in the context of his people's historic struggle for survival.

According to Loranger, the fundamental reality of Confederation was a 'rivalry of races,' and beneath the federative provisions of the BNA Act lurked the spectre of legislative union. Macdonald's centralizing policies – particularly the McCarthy Act, his assault on Mowat's liquor-licensing system – amounted to the recrudescence of the anti-French policies of 1822 and 1840: of the Union Bill and the Act of Union. The Supreme Court backed Macdonald, and only the Privy Council stood between French Canada and peril. Perhaps that peril was only a spot on the horizon – he, Loranger, would love to be exposed as a false alarmist. But if the danger was real, he wished to be the sentinel whose challenge resounded throughout the national camp, calling its defenders to arms. *Si vis pacem, para bellum*, he concluded: If you would have peace, prepare for war![32]

Here certainly was something to give a noticing man pause. At the very moment when Mowat and his Reformers were attacking Macdonald's policies as a manifestation of baneful *bleu* domination, the *bleu* Loranger was denouncing those same policies as a threat to French Canada's survival. With the rise to power of Mercier, an avowed follower of Loranger's constitutional ideas,[33] the way was open for a rapprochement that must have been Macdonald's worst nightmare.

Mowat and Mercier could come together in 1887 because they both spoke for communities that twenty years earlier had wanted the same thing out of Confederation. Most Reformers had desired autonomy for Upper Canada, and most French-speaking Lower Canadians had sought autonomy for Lower Canada. French-Canadian politicians had been unanimous in making national survival their first priority and in thinking that it depended on preserving their political power within the British empire. Some had touted the Quebec scheme as a means to such automony; others had opposed it as a trap leading to legislative union. All were agreed, though, that a genuine and inviolable autonomy was crucial.[34]

So Mowat and Mercier were united on the need to defend provincial autonomy. Not only that: they were at one in believing that the 1867 settlement guaranteed it. Both men knew that Canada had been created by the founding provinces. Confederation had emerged from an intercolonial agreement to form a federal government and devolve part of the provincial powers on it while retaining the sovereignty that was inherent in internally self-governing colonies of the British empire. The imperial government was represented in Canada not by the governor general alone but by the governor general for federal purposes and the lieutenant-governors for provincial purposes. This fact symbolized the essential equality of the two orders of government.[35]

In Mowat's case, this view of Confederation reflected his personal experience as a member of the Great Coalition of 1864 and a participant in the Quebec conference. He well remembered the circumstances that had brought his party into coalition with the detested Macdonald and had prompted the coalition government to approach the Atlantic provinces. He knew too that the Quebec conference had refused to distribute the legislative power in any way that, however symbolically, would make one order of government supreme and the other subordinate. Mercier, his junior by twenty years, was more than old enough to recall the promises of provincial sovereignty that Cartier and other *bleus*, anxious to overcome *rouge* reservations, had descried in the Quebec resolutions.

But there was more to it than that. Each man's view of his province's status within Confederation reflected a tradition of thought regarding his community's status within the British empire. The Reform tradition, as we have seen, was rooted in an essentially federal vision of the empire, in which the imperial government was no better than first among equals; and I have pointed out the startling resemblance between the imperial constitution as described in the Letter on Responsible Government and Mowat's reading of the BNA Act half a century later. Among other things, early Reformers had advanced a 'compact theory' of the Constitutional Act of 1791 that strongly resembled the later compact theory of Confederation. As I also noted, French Canadians had their own 'compact theory of the Constitutional Act.'

In view of its importance to the patriation controversy of 1980–2, it is noteworthy that this French-Canadian theory was evoked by the same traumatic event that had prompted William Baldwin's first statement of it in Upper Canada: the Union Bill controversy of 1822. Confronted by a proposed imperial measure that would have destroyed the constitution of Lower Canada, French Canadians had denounced it as both unconstitutional and illegal. To them the Constitutional Act was a *pacte solennel*, by which the imperial government had given French Canadians a legal and permanent guarantee of the preservation of their liberty, property, and dearest rights. If London could abrogate that pact without even consulting them, they would be left with no real security for what remained of their rights. These could be wiped out in the same fashion at any moment, and in any case they would lie at the mercy of an illegally constituted legislature (that of united Canada) unsympathetic to French-Canadian interests, feelings, and welfare.[36]

So the Lower Canadian Patriotes, like the Baldwins, saw the Constitutional Act as a pact or treaty, not only constitutionally but legally binding on the imperial Parliament. The two ideas differed in one important respect, however. The Baldwinite treaty was derived from the common-law rights of British subjects and applied to Upper Canadians as a whole. The Patriote pact was derived from international law and originated in promises supposedly made by an imperial conqueror to a conquered people. Its first expression was the 'capitulations' of Quebec and Montreal – the stipulations under which those cities had surrendered to the conqueror – and it had been successively confirmed and extended by the Quebec Act of 1774 and the Constitutional Act. As the Patriotes understood it, this *pacte solennel* guaranteed the survival of their ancient culture – their language, laws, customs, and religion. It did not benefit all Lower Canadians, only those who called themselves *Canadiens*.

How could the Constitutional Act work as a 'permanent legal guarantee' of the French-Canadian culture? Obviously the crucial feature was the formation of a French-dominated legislative assembly: if the Lower Canadian constitution could not be amended without the consent of the legislature, this gave the Canadiens a veto over such change. But you could see much more than this in the act. It had created not merely the Lower Canadian legislature but Lower Canada itself. Together with the Quebec Act, it could be seen as creating a country belonging especially to its French-speaking inhabitants. After all, had it not been passed partly to create Upper Canada as a country belonging especially to its English-speaking inhabitants?

Here was a striking parallel between Patriote ideas and Upper Canadian Loyalism. Seeing Upper Canada as an imperial reward for past sufferings and present exertions in the cause of imperial unity, leading Loyalists had envisaged themselves as the colony's natural rulers. They resented it when carpetbaggers such as Judge Willis in 1827 turned up from Britain to fill offices that they believed were rightfully theirs. Leading Patriotes came to see things in a similar light. One of the Ninety-Two Resolutions – their radical program of 1834 – cited the Quebec Act as authority for denouncing the preponderance of British Canadians in public office as 'contrary to the engagements of the British Parliament, and to the rights guaranteed to His Majesty's Canadian [i.e., *Canadien*] subjects, on the faith of the national honour of England, and on that of capitulations and treaties.' Neither had the interlopers any right to subvert Lower Canada's peculiar laws and institutions, whether by mendacious appeals to London or any other means. No one had forced them to settle in Canada. They had come of their own free will. If they wanted to stay, they should accept the state of affairs that the Quebec Act had acknowledged and affirmed as the law of the land.[37]

These similarities between Patriote and Loyalist attitudes are striking, but they were not politically important. That is because the ultimate Loyalist posture was one of dutiful submission to, and identification with, imperial power. The Loyalist tradition was one of resistance to rebellion, not to oppression. Loyalism might permit its devotees to imagine a compact between themselves and the mother country, but it did not authorize any attempt to enforce that compact in defiance of the imperial will. What brought Mowat and Mercier together in the 1880s, apart from their immediate political ends, was each man's status as the representative of a compact-based tradition of resistance to the centre in the interest of local autonomy.

All this talk of compacts may seem fanciful. Certainly no British statesman ever wrote or said anything that could rationally be understood as preferring French Canadians to other British subjects in the province of Quebec, or subsequently in Lower Canada. The Quebec Act in no sense expressed an arrangement that had been negotiated between the British government and delegates of the Canadiens; nor were the provisions of the Constitutional Act negotiated by British and colonial representatives, either Upper or Lower Canadian. Literally speaking, then, neither the Quebec Act nor the Constitutional Act were compacts, and the notion that they were seems to be open to the same objections as were long ago made against the compact theory of Confederation. It seems to be a figment of the imagination, without foundation in either law or history. And in a sense it was; yet it was none the less a valid conception of the relationship between Britain and the Canadian colonies. It was so because it expressed a fundamental principle of civil society: the rule of law.

When you think about it, all law has a contractual aspect. The reason is that we live our lives within the framework of law and cannot make sensible choices without some assurance that that framework will not be casually disrupted. The principle of the rule of law recognizes that need.

It has several aspects, but two are especially relevant to the present discussion. One is the requirement for due process in legislation and adjudication. This condition subjects the making, interpretation and enforcement of laws to elaborate procedures designed to give a fair hearing to every party or interest. Secondly, legislation damaging to vested interests, as they are called, should be undertaken reluctantly and only to meet an overriding public need, and should grant reasonable compensation to the affected interests. That was why the Ontario Rivers and Streams Act entitled people such as Peter McLaren to collect tolls for the use of their timber-slides. McLaren had invested large sums on the basis of a judicial declaration that the law was such-and-such. Mowat's government did not believe that judgment to be correct; but even so, in writing a law that negated that judgment, it provided that owners of log-floating improvements should be entitled to compensation for their use by others.[38]

If such care must be taken in altering ordinary laws, how much greater is the need for caution in the amendment of fundamental laws, which establish the very framework of government. For this reason, many governments are based on constitutional charters with special amending procedures. British constitutionalism relied instead on what may be called a culture of restraint in the exercise of political power. The ideology of the rule of law was itself one expression of that culture, since it frowned on whimsical or arbitrary legislation. Another was the system of unwritten conventions that was the essence of the British constitution. But it is one thing to leave a country's constitution at the mercy of its own legislature, in which some at least of its people are represented, as in Britain, and quite another to place it at the disposal of another legislature. As both Upper and Lower Canadians protested in 1823, if the British Parliament could repeal the Constitutional Act without the consent of those affected by it, they had no constitution at all, and no security in their rights.

Upper Canadian Reformers were well aware that the Constitutional Act had not emerged from negotiations between colonists and the British government; indeed, they did not call it a treaty as such. Barnabas Bidwell wrote that the provincial constitution 'may be considered as amounting to' a solemn compact between the parent kingdom and the province. The Baldwins proclaimed it 'a principle never to be forgotten' that the act was 'in fact' (i.e., in effect) a treaty. In the Letter on Responsible Government, Canadiensis did not *call* the act a treaty: he 'treated' it as one.[39] This conception did not depend on its being a product of negotiations; it was inherent in its being a constitution. The act was 'in fact a treaty' because by its very nature it was not amendable without the consent of those whose constitution it was.

When Reformers spoke of a compact or treaty, they meant it metaphorically; and they were using a metaphor that was central to British political though. English Whig constitutionalism rested on the notion that constitutional government, and even society itself, were contractual in nature. In England, constitutional government had developed over the centuries out of a series of concessions extracted from the Crown and enshrined in custom. The idea that the resulting political order was based on a compact or contract served to convey the notion that it was permanent, not subject to revision at the Crown's whim.

Unlike the Upper Canadian compact theory, the Canadien *pacte solennel* was rooted in actual negotiations: the capitulations of Quebec and Montreal and the Treaty of Paris of 1763. This notion suited the Canadiens' political needs by enabling them to represent the treaty as one between themselves and the British rather than between 'Lower Canadians' and the British. But even the latter conception would have allowed them to argue, as they did during the Union Bill controversy, that the act could not properly be amended without the consent of the provincial legislature.

The BNA Act was just as much a constitutional act as the Constitutional Act and therefore just as much a compact – perhaps even more so, since it really was the outcome of negotiations between the parties governed by it. And like the Constitutional Act, the Confederation compact was a treaty that Upper Canadians could imagine as one between their province and other polities and that French Canadians could imagine as one between themselves and the English. That is because the BNA Act did for Quebec what the Constitutional Act had done for Upper Canada: it gave each province its own government in order to establish the cultural autonomy of a minority.

A Québécois in fact could see the BNA Act as both sorts of compact at once. In arguing that the provinces had retained their autonomy in entering into Confederation, the Quebec jurist Loranger explicitly invoked the idea of a compact of cultures: 'Why should the province of Quebec, for example, have, on an inauspicious day, with utter want of thought, abandoned its rights the most sacred, guaranteed by treaties and preserved by secular contests, and sacrificed its language, its institutions and its laws, to enter into an insane union, which, contracted under these conditions, would have been the cause of its national and political annihilation? *And why should the other provinces, any more than Quebec, have consented to lose their national existence and consummate this political suicide?'*[40] Why indeed, when, for the two largest provinces at least, the achievement of a secure 'national' autonomy had been the main object of the enterprise?

Loranger's words are significant in two ways. First of all, they explain why provincial consent to constitutional amendment remained as essential after as before Confederation, even though the BNA Act had set up a government that represented all Canadians. Secondly, Loranger's support for the idea of a provincial compact has been seen as weakening the validity of the cultural-compact theory. The latter is ascribed to the French-Canadian nationalist Henri Bourassa, who saw the Confederation compact as a guarantee of francophone rights throughout Canada, not just in Quebec. Since Bourassa did not advance this proposition until the 1890s, the theory is thereby severed not only from its pre-Confederation roots but even from Confederation itself. It appears as a coinage of a later generation, estranged by the asperities of intercultural relations in the aftermath of Louis Riel's execution. But Loranger's reference here to treaties, and the ominous allusions in his preface to the Union Bill of 1822 and the Union Act of 1840, clearly place his compact theory of Confederation in the Lower Canadian tradition stemming from the idea of the *pacte solennel*. The real difference between him and Bourassa is that he did not try to extend the cultural compact beyond the borders of Quebec.[41]

Loranger was a leading politician of the Confederation era and the leading French-Canadian jurist of his time. His defence of provincial autonomy and the compact theory provides strong authority for the provincialist position. But sixty years later a constitutional authority of a later generation would see things differently. If the provinces had wished to preserve their autonomy, F.R. Scott would write in 1943, they would never have entered Confederation at all.[42]

Part Three

1890–1940:
Forgetting the Compact

10

Amending the Constitution

In September 1930, the premier of Ontario, G. Howard Ferguson, wrote urgently to his fellow-Conservative R.B. Bennett, newly appointed prime minister of Canada. Four years earlier, the British government had formally recognized the constitutional independence of His Majesty's self-governing dominions. A committee of experts had been formed to frame legislation giving the force of law to that independence. In 1929 the committee reported in terms that aroused Ferguson's alarm. It recommended, among other things, repealing a British statute of 1865, the Colonial Laws Validity Act, which barred colonial legislatures from passing any law that conflicted with any British statute. But the committee spoke only of freeing the dominion parliaments from its constraints. The matter of freeing Australian state and Canadian provincial legislatures was left open.

To liberate the Parliament of Canada and not the provincial legislatures might have major consequences for the Canadian constitution. One of the pillars of provincial autonomy under the BNA Act was the Privy Council's recognition in 1883 in *Hodge v. the Queen*[1] – the case in which it had validated Oliver Mowat's liquor-licensing system – that the legislative powers of Ottawa and the provinces were identical in nature. If Ottawa alone were freed from the constraints of the Colonial Laws Validity Act, this fundamental proposition would cease to be true. Not only that: there would be no legal barrier to protect the provinces should some latter-day John A. Macdonald aspire to convert Canada into a legislative union. No Canadian who valued provincial autonomy could accept this in 1930 any more than Mowat and Loranger fifty years earlier. Ferguson protested vigorously against any action that might compromise 'the Provincial Treaty,' as he called it, until the provinces had had a chance to consider the matter.

Ferguson took the same ground as his nineteenth-century predecessors. The BNA Act was usually spoken of as the Compact of Confederation, he reminded Bennett. This expression recognized that the act was a transcript of the Quebec resolutions, themselves in essence a treaty between the founding provinces. Briefly Ferguson rehearsed the story of Canada's founding, recalling that even Macdonald, an advocate of powerful central government, had acknowledged the importance of establishing an inviolable local autonomy. In the legislature, Macdonald and Cartier had both presented the scheme as a treaty, which must be rejected or swallowed whole. Cartier had promised that it would be presented to the British in that light and that Canadian delegates would accept no scheme of union that was not based on the resolutions.

Moving on, the premier mentioned two crucial Privy Council judgments in order to illustrate the breadth of the provinces' power and their standing vis-à-vis the federal government. One was *Hodge v. the Queen*, the other the so-called *Maritime Bank Case* of 1892, which had affirmed that the purpose of the BNA Act was not to subordinate the provincial governments to a central authority, but to create a federal government in which the provinces should all be represented, while individually retaining their independence and autonomy. This decision had formally recognized what Mowat had been asserting for twenty years: that the imperial sovereign formed part of the provincial as well as the Dominion government and that the two orders of government were therefore essentially equal.

Unfortunately, there was a wee problem. The British Parliament had substantively amended the BNA Act five times since 1867, but the provinces had been consulted only once. In Ferguson's view, these precedents had undermined the provinces' constitutional right to be consulted before the act was amended. As a result, in 1924, the Canadian government had not bothered to consult the provinces before proposing to ask the British Parliament for a law confirming Canada's power to enact extraterritorial legislation (that is, laws affecting Canadian individuals and organizations outside the country). This power was a key incident of full national sovereignty, and the proposed amendment would mark a significant change in the Dominion's constitutional status; yet the federal minister of justice had rejected the provinces' claim to be consulted.

Ferguson had vigorously rebutted the minister's position, opposing as a threat to national unity any extension of Ottawa's powers without the consent of the provinces. Now, in 1930, the Ontario premier beat the unity drum again. As applied to Canada, the proposals of the imperial committee were likely to be a source of friction and weakness. Nothing should be done to disturb the constitution before a proper amending procedure was worked out. Ontario should accept no formula that did not acknowledge the right of all the provinces to be consulted and become parties to the decision.[2]

So it was that the problem of how to amend the constitution emerged as a leading topic of political debate. This chapter explains why the constitution could be seen as an interprovincial compact, why politicians sometimes found difficulty in applying that notion, and the solution they found to that difficulty when the Liberals under Sir Wilfrid Laurier took over in Ottawa. It then describes how new views of Canada and her place in the British empire arose to challenge that consensus, leading to the establishment of a new orthodoxy based on a distinctly biased recall of the history of Canada's founding. The derision that greeted Howard Ferguson's appeal to the compact theory in 1930 set the tone for the next half-century.

All this talk in the 1920s about amending the constitution was an effect of the First World War. The clash of empires had weakened and impoverished the mother country, but it had evoked an impressive display of national might from her self-governing dominions. The Anzacs at Gallipoli, the Canadians at Vimy – after that, things could never be as they had been. The legislation that alarmed Howard Ferguson in 1930 would be enacted a year later as the Statute of Westminster, a historic proclamation of the full national independence of the dominions; but that was just the legal implementation of a political reality. And underlying all for Canadians was an issue that was to throb for two generations: the incongruity and embarrassment of an independent Canada's having to ask another country to amend its constitution.

One problem was figuring out a better way. A debate in the House of Commons in 1925 exposed the breadth of the gulf to be bridged. The debate was initiated by W.F. Maclean, veteran nationalist MP and sometime editor of the Toronto *World*, who had been kicked out of the Conservative caucus in 1905 and had sat ever since as a self-styled 'independent Conservative.' Maclean wanted the Parliament of Canada to have absolute authority to amend every aspect of the BNA Act but those guaranteeing the rights of minorities. The labour member from

Winnipeg, J.S. Woodsworth, would accept this proposal only if such amendments were made with the prior consent of the provinces. In short, parliamentary opinion ran the gamut from an extreme provincialism to a centralism verging on legislative union. And that was just among those who were willing to talk about patriating the constitution. Most members – probably most Canadians – were happy enough with the status quo.[3]

So much for relations between Canada and the United Kingdom; but what about those between Ottawa and the provinces? Why was Ferguson so skittish about reforming the constitution? Reading his letter and memo to Bennett, you might think that the provinces were as hard beset in 1930 as fifty years earlier, when Mowat and Grit Ontario, almost unaided, had fought off an insurgent centralism. But if one thing was generally agreed in the 1920s, it was that the BNA Act, as the product of an interprovincial compact, could not be altered in any fundamental way without the agreement of the participants. That, however, left many issues unresolved.

Part of the problem was the multi-dimensional complexity of the compact. As implemented in 1867, it had bound four provinces (from 1864 on, Lower and Upper Canada had been represented in the negotiations as separate units); but presumably the five newer provinces had acquired all the privileges of membership. Ernest Lapointe, the minister of justice, said so in the House of Commons in 1925, but it is significant that he needed to do so. Lapointe had posed a hypothetical question as to whether the Parliament of Canada was entitled, without provincial consent, to ask the British Parliament to transfer provincial powers to Ottawa. Thomas Crerar, former leader of the western-based Progressive party, interjected (sarcastically, perhaps) that it need consult only the four founding provinces. Lapointe replied that the provinces were all equal in this regard.[4]

And what about the United Kingdom – still, to many Canadians, the mother country? Canadians tended not to think of the compact as embracing the United Kingdom. It is always tricky to explain why people *don't* think things, but I suspect that it was because Britain's role in the founding of Canada was different from that of the provinces. The British government had approved of British North American union; it had exerted influence on New Brunswick and Nova Scotia when they showed signs of rejecting the scheme; it had tried to impose greater centralization than the Quebec and London resolutions contemplated. But it had not taken the initiative in promoting Confederation, and it had not taken a leading role in designing it. Confederation was presented to British North Americans in the years 1864 to 1867 as a work of their own making, and it lived on as such in Canadian memory.

And of course it *was* their own work in a way that was not true of any earlier constitution. Responsible government had changed the rules of the game. The British might cajole, they might warn, and they might exert covert influence, but they could no longer take the sort of initiative, and exert the sort of pressure, that they had employed in imposing the union of 1840. And as the years passed, and Canada became more powerful and more independent, British authority waned further. The great point that Baldwinites and Patriots had wanted to establish in the 1820s by calling the Constitutional Act of 1791 a treaty – the principle that Britain could not impose constitutional change on the colonies against their will – was taken for granted in Canada a century later. There was no need to invoke a compact against British dictation; nor had there been since 1867.

However, the British were still part of the problem that the compact theory was designed to meet. What mattered was their attitude towards Ottawa and the provinces. Their sympathy with Macdonald's centralism persisted after 1867. They balked at recognizing the provincial governments as Ottawa's equal, refusing, for instance, to allow lieutenant-governors to receive a twenty-one-gun salute on ceremonial occasions as the Queen's representative. That was reserved for the governor general. When Macdonald asked the British government in 1871 if lieutenant-governors were entitled to exercise the royal prerogative by creating queen's counsel, its legal advisers answered 'no': only the governor general could do so. This was typical of the British tendency to exalt Ottawa at the provinces' expense. Oliver Mowat dismissed the law officers' opinion – what did British lawyers know about federalism? – but it took him twenty years to establish his point in the face of British indifference. The British tendency to treat Ottawa as the only government that counted makes Mowat's success before the Judicial Committee of the Privy Council, a tribunal of British judges, the more remarkable.[5]

When it came to implementing Confederation, the British soon showed themselves ready to give the Dominion government a long rein despite provincial objections. In 1867 the voters of Nova Scotia resoundingly repudiated the government that had taken them into Confederation. The new ministry tried to get the British government to allow the province to secede, pointing out that the electors had only now had a chance to vote on the issue. But in Whitehall this argument ran into a blank wall of imperial apathy; the British simply refused to become involved. If Nova Scotia had a grievance, the province should take it up with Ottawa.

Thus fortified, Macdonald managed to placate the Bluenose anti-confederationists by offering Nova Scotia a special subsidy on top of that which Ottawa paid to all the provinces under the BNA Act. It was this deal that evoked the first statement of the compact theory of Confederation. Ontario Reformers attacked the settlement as a breach of the Confederation compact and denied Ottawa's right to take such action without the consent of all the provinces. The British law officers rebuffed this objection with an opinion that Ottawa was legally empowered to take such action; but the premier of Ontario, John A.'s ally Sandfield Macdonald, could not prevent the provincial legislature from calling on the British to amend the BNA Act to prevent such abuse of Ottawa's legal powers in future. The British government refused, on the ground that Ottawa's legal powers were themselves part of the terms of confederation, to which Ontario, along with the other provinces, had agreed.

While giving aggrieved provinces the cold shoulder, the British gladly embraced Dominion requests for constitutional changes. In fact, they were willing to act at the mere request of the federal government, unsupported even by an address of the Parliament of Canada. In 1871 Liberals challenged the validity of the Manitoba Act, the federal statute establishing that province. The resulting uncertainty obliged the Dominion government to ask for British legislation confirming the act's validity. Macdonald's government approached the British without consulting Parliament, and only a vigorous protest by the opposition persuaded him and the British to wait for a supporting address from the Parliament at Ottawa. A few years later it was the Liberals who sinned. In 1875 Alexander Mackenzie's government asked the British to legislate so that Parliament could authorize parliamentary committees to examine sworn witnesses. The Liberals rightly argued that this was a very different thing from setting up provinces, but even so they felt embarrassed. Though a purely technical matter, it still meant amending the BNA Act, and Mackenzie had to admit that the government should have obtained parliamentary sanction for the desired change.[6]

These early controversies reveal the many-sidedness of the Confederation compact and the complexity and uncertainty entailed in amending it. The BNA Act was a multifarious document. It abolished United Canada and set up governments for Quebec and Ontario; it established a federal government; it defined the provincial constitutions to some extent, although mostly it left them unchanged; it defined the relationship between the provinces and the new federal government; and it defined that between the new confederation and the imperial government. As a legal instrument, it could be amended only by the British Parliament. As a constitution it had various functions, and there was no logical reason why the same sort of colonial input should be required for amending all of them. But, apart from a clause empowering provincial legislatures to amend their own constitutions, the act was silent on how to proceed in any of these different cases.

One might assume that fundamental changes in Confederation would require the consent of each party to the compact; but what about changes in the federal government of the sort that the provinces might enact for themselves? The Dominion was a powerful and autonomous entity – not only equal to the provinces, constitutionally speaking, but arguably first among equals. Although the Parliament of Canada could not enact such changes itself, that did not mean that it needed provincial consent before asking Westminster to enact them. But what were the limits to Ottawa's unilateral action, and how should it proceed on such occasions? Opinions varied.

No one denied Parliament's right to seek the power to take sworn testimony in committee or even the immensely greater power entailed in establishing provincial governments in the vast western territories acquired in 1869. What worried some Canadians in these early years was Parliament's capacity to alter the terms of the founding compact by exercising its ordinary legislative powers. At issue in 1868 and 1869 was Ottawa's use of its taxing and spending power to pay Nova Scotia a subsidy beyond that to which all the provinces were entitled under the BNA Act. In 1870, criticism focused on the provision of the Manitoba Act that gave the new province more MPs than its population entitled it to. The BNA Act laid down certain rules of parliamentary representation, but Ottawa had been able to contravene those rules in exercising its power to establish new provinces in the North-West Territories.

Underlying these quarrels were two important constitutional issues. One was the extent of the Dominion's autonomy vis-à-vis the provinces; the other was that staple of British and Canadian constitutionalism – the force of constitutional convention. Take special terms for Nova Scotia. As a matter of law, Ottawa could spend its money that way as well as any other. But was that expenditure a proper exercise of autonomous power by a government founded to deal with issues of common concern to the provinces? Or did it effect so great a change in the founding compact that Ottawa's *legal* powers should yield to the provinces' *constitutional* right to be party to such changes? Ontario Grits might have seen things differently had they been in power at Ottawa; but they had been asserting the superiority of convention to law ever since the 1840s, and that is how they responded in 1868.

These early controversies raised a disturbing doubt: could British officials, including the Judicial Committee of the Privy Council, the final arbiter of the constitution, be trusted to treat the BNA Act as a constitution? Increasingly the evidence suggested that they could not. Special terms for Nova Scotia were an early warning: in upholding them on the ground that they came within the legislative powers of the Dominion, the British law officers simply ignored the possibility that those powers were subject to constitutional constraints. The law officers' opinion on the creation of QCs was another omen. Then, in 1882, the Privy Council decision in *Russell v. The Queen* set the alarm bells ringing.[7]

Things looked worse for provincial rights because the Supreme Court of Canada had turned out to be unreliable. Even the original bench, selected by the Liberal minister of justice Edward Blake in 1875, proved insensitive to the limits on Ottawa's legislative power. Subsequent nominees were even more so. When the issue of queen's counsel came before the court in 1879, several judges showed even less respect for the provinces than the British law officers eight years earlier. The suit originated in Nova Scotia, and, as in *Russell* three years later, incompetent presentation of the provincial case influenced the result. In 1880 the court did give Mowat a landmark victory in the fire insurance case mentioned in chapter 8 (a decision affirmed by the Privy Council). In 1881, though, it found against Ontario in the *Escheats Case*.[8] Now, in *Russell*, the Privy Council too had failed the cause of provincial rights.

Russell, however, turned out to be the high-water mark of judicial centralism. Macdonald had overreached himself with the McCarthy Act; not even his old friend John Wellington Gwynne, the most centralist judge on the Supreme Court, would accept it. The Privy Council upheld Mowat's liquor-licensing system in *Hodge v. The Queen* and reversed the Supreme Court in the *Escheats Case*. In a series of judicial reference cases, Mowat convinced the courts to acknowledge the provinces' constitutional equality to Ottawa and to respect provincial autonomy in construing the division of legislative power. Even the *Maritime Bank Case*, which Howard Ferguson cited together with *Hodge*, was really Mowat's victory:

although it originated in New Brunswick, that province was represented before the Privy Council by Richard Burdon Haldane, a British barrister who had been on retainer to the province of Ontario since 1884.[9]

Then, in 1896, five years after Macdonald's death, the Liberals at last returned to power at Ottawa, and Mowat resigned as premier of Ontario to become minister of justice under Wilfrid Laurier. His long struggle to persuade British and Canadian courts, and Canadian politicians, to treat the BNA Act as a constitution rather than an ordinary statute had ended in victory. Macdonald's abuse of the federal veto during the 1880s, and the courts' early insensitivity to the federal character of the constitution, had induced the interprovincial conference at Quebec in 1887 to adopt a wish-list of reforms to the BNA Act, including abolition of the veto. With the Liberals now in power at Ottawa, amending the BNA Act no longer seemed necessary.

The triumph of provincial rights, and Laurier's fifteen years in office, allowed a constitutionalist consensus to form on the question of amending the BNA Act. It became generally accepted that the Parliament of Canada could legitimately seek to amend some provisions without consulting the provinces, while other changes required provincial consent. Sir George Ross, Liberal premier of Ontario from 1899 to 1905 and subsequently a senator, stated the position as he understood it in a book published in 1914. Since the BNA Act expressed an interprovincial compact, he wrote, it could not, technically speaking, be amended in any respect without provincial consent. As long as the amendment did not prejudice any provincial rights or privileges under the constitution, however, the provinces would have no reason for complaint if Ottawa acted without them.[10]

Such was the position on the eve of the First World War; but the war changed everything. I mentioned earlier how it filled many English Canadians with a stronger sense of national destiny and compelled the British to recognize the self-governing dominions as fully independent actors in international affairs. It also imbued federal bureaucrats with a taste for the expansive exercise of power. Parliament had met the emergency by passing the War Measures Act, which gave Ottawa wide powers to act by executive proclamation in the national interest. It had enacted other laws regulating public life to a degree previously unknown. Provincial affairs seemed trivial by comparison, and at one point the local governments even confronted an attempt by Ottawa to prohibit their borrowing in the world's money markets. When peace returned, the Dominion gladly withdrew from many shared-cost social programs initiated during the war, but it maintained the wartime income tax in order to finance the war debt and competed stubbornly for constitutional primacy in economic regulation.

Premier Ferguson's attitude towards Ottawa in 1930 was coloured by two disputes in particular: one over the regulation of insurance companies and the other over water-power rights on navigable rivers. It is no coincidence that insurance companies and rivers had also been the object of major disputes during the 1880s, for both were very important to the Canadian economy. In the matter of insurance companies, large amounts of revenue were at stake. The quarrel over water rights was fuelled by Ontario Hydro's predictions of a severe shortage of electric power to fuel the province's burgeoning industrial sector. And in Ferguson's mind, both disputes were sparked by federal invasions of established provincial rights. Like Reformers of the 1880s, he impeached Ottawa's position on water-power rights as a breach of the Confederation compact and the thin end of the wedge of legislative union. In the insurance controversy he was especially annoyed by Ottawa's refusal to bow to the courts. Three times between 1916 and 1931 the Privy Council struck down federal attempts to control the insurance business, and still federal officials persisted in their efforts.[11]

With such attitudes on display in Ottawa, and a fashion for outspoken nationalism prevailing among the English-speaking intelligentsia (several of whose leading figures were themselves rising members of the Ottawa establishment),[12] Ferguson found Britain's resolve to abdicate its residual authority over the self-governing dominions profoundly alarming. Federal political leaders, Liberal and Conservative, continued to pay lip-service to the compact theory of Confederation and to Ross's dictum giving the provincial governments a decisive voice on amendments to the BNA Act that affected provincial powers. In the Commons in 1925, both Lapointe and Arthur Meighen, leader of the Opposition, did so.[13] But in the new state of affairs, was that enough? With federal officials grasping for power even against the decisions of the courts, could Ottawa be trusted with the vast accession of new power entailed in extraterritorial authority unless the provincial governments had a say in amending the BNA Act as a whole, not just the parts specifically relating to provincial powers? So it was that Ferguson, returning to the broader conception of the compact theory asserted by the Grits against John A. Macdonald, invoked it to justify the provinces' interest in the transfer of extraterritorial authority to Ottawa.

In any case, there were voices in the land that denied any validity to the compact theory at all, and these were especially prominent in the ranks of the Liberal party. One was John Wesley Dafoe, influential editor of the *Manitoba Free Press*. Dafoe mocked the compact theory as a hallucination, lacking any sanction in law, in practice, or in the intentions of the Fathers of Confederation as revealed by contemporary documents. One could search from cover to cover the fat volume in which the Confederation debates were enshrined without finding a shred of evidence to support it. Another scoffer, thirty years younger than Dafoe, was Norman Rogers, private secretary to Prime Minister Mackenzie King. Rogers scorned the theory when Ferguson invoked it at the interprovincial conference of 1927. Four years later, now a professor of political science at Queen's University, he reacted to Ferguson's memo of 1930 with an onslaught that was to make the theory an object of derision for generations.[14]

According to Rogers, the theory was nonsense from beginning to end. Problems arose the moment you tried to identify the parties to the supposed compact. Was the Dominion a party? It had not even existed before the passing of the BNA Act. What about Ontario and Quebec? They were not distinct provinces until 1867, although Upper and Lower Canada had been separately represented at the Quebec and London conferences. British Columbia and Prince Edward Island had joined Confederation by agreement with Ottawa; they had made no compact with the other provinces. And the three prairie provinces had been created by the Parliament of Canada.[15]

All this presented no obstacle to proponents of the compact theory, as Rogers admitted. In their eyes the provinces were all equal, and the latecomers and new creations possessed exactly the same rights as the original partners. But to Rogers the very notion that the Dominion had been founded by provincial compact was absurd. It would scarcely deserve serious consideration but for all those speeches in which Macdonald, Cartier, Brown, and other leading men of the day had referred to the outcome of the Quebec and London conferences as a treaty. All those solemn assertions by men involved in negotiating Confederation, and in securing its endorsement by the Canadian and imperial legislatures – Rogers bent his mind to explaining how they did not, could not, mean what Ferguson and other supporters of the compact theory took them to mean.

Why not? Well, for one thing, British colonies had not possessed the legal power to conclude political or commercial agreements between themselves or with foreign countries, and the imperial Parliament had passed no law authorizing the North American colonies to do so on this occasion. From this legal argument Rogers passed on to the history of Confederation. The legislature of United Canada had endorsed the Quebec resolutions, but those of New Brunswick and Nova Scotia had never done so. They had merely authorized their governments to appoint delegates to arrange a union with Canada and each other on such terms as would secure the just rights and interests of their own province. These arrangements had been negotiated at the London conference of 1866, whereupon the delegates had immediately joined the imperial government in drafting the BNA Act.

From these facts Rogers drew a string of devastating conclusions. Neither the people nor the legislatures of British North America had consented to the terms of union worked out at London and embodied in the founding statute. Their representatives had attended the London conference merely in an advisory capacity, to assist the imperial authorities in drawing up an act of union, not in any sense as delegates authorized to work out a treaty between their respective colonies. Not only that, but the London resolutions had differed substantially from Quebec resolutions of 1864. This meant that the Quebec scheme – the only interprovincial agreement to have been ratified by any colonial legislature – had not formed the basis of Confederation at all. The theory that traced Confederation back to a so-called compact concluded at Quebec was devoid of constitutional or historical substance. There was nothing in the entire process to support the contention that amendments to the BNA Act should require provincial consent.

What then could explain the frequent use of the word 'treaty' by leading members of the Quebec conference? Rogers noted that the usage was confined to Canadian participants; it did not occur among Maritimers. From this he concluded that Canadian ministers had used the word as a tactical ploy, in order to deter the legislature from trying to amend the proposed scheme. They had not meant to suggest that the agreement was a compact in any formal sense.[16] Certainly, they had said nothing to sustain Ferguson's claim that the BNA Act could not properly be amended without the consent of the provinces. Ferguson was quite right about all those times the act had been amended without provincial input, but he had no good reason to complain about it.

In view of the immediate and enduring influence of Rogers's critique, it is remarkable how flimsy some of his objections were, particularly from a historical angle. First, and most important, he quite overlooked the political and constitutional realities of the 1860s. By then, as we have seen, the British claim to legislate for the colonies at will had become subject to powerful constitutional constraints. These made it quite reasonable to envisage the BNA Act as merely a retrospective endorsement by the British of a compact concluded by the colonies affected by it. Whether the colonies possessed the *legal* capacity to conclude agreements with each other was irrelevant.

It was also irrelevant that the legislatures of Nova Brunswick and Nova Scotia had not ratified the London resolutions. Rogers, a Nova Scotian himself, made much of the fact that both legislatures had rejected the idea that the London agreement should be referred back to them for ratification.[17] This fact was indeed significant, but he completely misunderstood its meaning. He saw it as evidence for the legalistic proposition that the London conference had gathered merely to advise and assist the imperial authorities and that the London resolutions could not be viewed as a treaty of union. Its actual import was quite different: it meant that both legislatures had invested their representatives at the London conference with full power to commit their provinces to any terms. The two legislatures did not need to endorse the London agreement after the fact because they had done so in advance.

Besides, the way in which the Maritimes joined Confederation, and the failure of Maritime politicians to speak of the Quebec resolutions as a treaty, were secondary matters. Like most English Canadians of his generation, Rogers overlooked the crucial fact that Confederation had sprung from an agreement by the representatives of Upper and Lower Canada to convert United Canada into a federal union. The Upper Canadian Reformers were interested in westward, not eastward expansion. They had agreed to pursue union with the Atlantic provinces only on condition that, if it came to nothing, the federation of United Canada would go ahead regardless.[18] Most French Canadians were even more indifferent to the prospect of wider union: they accepted Confederation, not as a first step towards a transcontinental Canadian empire, but as the closest they could get to national independence without having to fight the redcoats again.[19]

Seen in this light, the Quebec resolutions stood unimpeached as terms of a federal compact – or *treaty*, as Canadian politicians freely called it – between the two sections of United Canada, endorsed by a majority of MPPs from both sections. Other provinces had subsequently become parties to the compact in one way or another, some (New Brunswick and Nova Scotia) before it became law in 1867, and the rest later. How they did so was irrelevant to the integrity of the original compact. It was also irrelevant to their status as parties to the compact. That status was of necessity identical to that of the two founding members.

All this and more could have been said to refute Rogers, but none of it was. His paper, several times reprinted,[20] quickly became the definitive statement of a new orthodoxy. And throughout the length and breadth of English-speaking Canada, answer came there none. The only efforts to defend the compact theory against Rogers's onslaught were written by Québécois and published only in French.[21]

11

Centralist Revolution

Norman Rogers's assault on the compact theory was part of a broader campaign of constitutional criticism by English-Canadian intellectuals. Their main target was the Judicial Committee of the Privy Council, which they charged with misinterpreting the division of legislative powers between Ottawa and the provinces in sections 91 and 92 of the BNA Act. Their campaign gathered force throughout the 1930s and, like their attack on the compact theory, went virtually unopposed in English-speaking Canada. Based on a biased history, it quickly eclipsed not just the authority but even the memory of that earlier understanding of the division of powers which Oliver Mowat had worked so long and hard to establish.[1] People forgot what responsible government meant to the Canadian constitution; they forgot what the Fathers of Confederation had meant by sharing the residuary legislative power between Ottawa and the provinces. A mythic history flourished, which told of the Fathers' centralizing intentions and the malicious or besotted undermining of those intentions by a panel of British judges.

This chapter describes how that myth arose. It looks first at the argument over the division of powers in the late nineteenth century, and then at the uproar that arose in the 1920s and 1930s over the Privy Council's handling of the Dominion residuary power. After observing the way in which partisans of central power used historical evidence to justify their conception of the residuary power, it tests their approach and arguments by two different comparisons. First, it presents the views of two English Canadians who dissented from the new centralist orthodoxy. These two men discussed the constitution in very different terms, but they shared one remarkable attribute. Then it considers the ways in which twentieth-century centralists differed from their nineteenth-century predecessors – men who had witnessed and taken part in the founding of the Dominion. The mythic character of twentieth-century centralism appears in the value-laden biases that these comparisons disclose.

Section 91 of the BNA Act authorized the Canadian Parliament to make laws for the peace, order, and good government of Canada in relation to all matters not coming within the 'Classes of Subjects' reserved to the provincial legislatures in section 92. Then, 'for greater Certainty, but not so as to restrict the Generality of the foregoing Terms of this Section,' it declared that, 'notwithstanding anything in this Act,' Parliament's authority extended to all matters coming within certain classes of sub-jects (basically those assigned to the general legislature in the Quebec and London resolutions), which it proceeded to itemize. That list, how-ever, merely illustrated the scope of Parliament's power, which was defined as a whole by the opening declaration that Parliament could make laws in relation to all matters not reserved to the provinces. In this way, section 91 realized the founders' intention that Parliament should possess a residuary legislative power. Instead of being confined to spe-cific subjects, as the U.S. Congress was, it should be able to make laws on all matters of a general character not specifically reserved to the local legislatures.

This division of powers raised two primary questions of interpreta-tion. One concerned the relationship between the Dominion powers itemized in section 91 and the provincial powers in section 92. In a few early cases, the statement that Parliament might legislate on its listed subject-matters 'notwithstanding anything in this Act' misled Canadian courts to conclude that it might make laws on any matter that might conceivably come within those subjects. The *Insurance Case* of 1881 was so important because it enabled Oliver Mowat to correct this misconcep-tion. He pointed out that the 'notwithstanding' proviso was itself quali-fied by the declaration that it was not to restrict the foregoing terms of the section. It did not, then, license Parliament to legislate on matters coming within subjects reserved to the provinces in section 92. The pro-vincial subject-matters had priority over the Dominion's. On this basis Mowat persuaded the Privy Council to uphold his fire insurance statute as a valid exercise of the provinces' power to make laws on property and civil rights rather than disqualifying it as an intrusion on Ottawa's power to regulate trade and commerce.[2]

The second major problem of interpretation was how to decide whether or not an act of Parliament, though it did not come within Ottawa's listed powers, was yet valid as an exercise of its residuary power. It became politically important as a result of the Privy Council's decision in *Russell v. The Queen* (1882), which upheld the Scott Act, Ottawa's local prohibition law. As I mentioned earlier, that decision was framed in terms which seemed to imply that the Parliament of Canada could pass pretty much what laws it liked on the mere assumption that the peace, order, and good government of Canada was at stake. This alarmed supporters of provincial autonomy, because it seemed to nullify one of the basic understandings of Confederation: that the federal and provincial jurisdictions were mutually exclusive, and that there were, therefore, certain matters on which Ottawa simply could not legislate.[3]

Here too Mowat played a crucial role in rectifying the problem. He saved Ontario's liquor-licensing system in *Hodge v. The Queen* (1883) and led the attack on the national system that the McCarthy Act set up on the basis of *Russell's* construction of the Dominion legislative power. Invalidation of the McCarthy Act relieved the pressure on provincial autonomy but did not solve the problem entirely. The *McCarthy Act Case* was a so-called judicial reference, in which one or more governments would ask a court for an opinion on a constitutional problem, and in such cases a court did not have to give its reasons in writing. Mowat still had to get the Privy Council to codify the division of powers.

His scheme took years to implement, because the liquor trade – the subject of all three leading cases – was a powerful and popular concern, though beset by a rising tide of militant prohibitionism, and he also had to wait for legislation requiring written explanations in judicial reference cases. In 1890, however, he took the crucial step by carrying a local prohibition statute essentially similar to the Scott Act. This obliged the courts either to reject his measure or to explain why both Ottawa and the province could pass laws to prohibit the trade but only the provinces could regulate it by licensing. The result was Lord Watson's famous *Prohibition* judgment of 1896. As the supreme judicial tribunal of the empire, the Privy Council could not lightly reverse its own decisions, but Watson did all he could to limit the scope of *Russell.*[4] The resulting decision influenced adjudication of the division of powers into the mid-twentieth-century.

It did so in two main respects. Firstly, it laid down a standard for valid application of the federal residuary power to matters that were normally provincial. Watson acknowledged that some such matters might attain such dimensions as to affect the Dominion at large and so justify action by Parliament. But great caution must be exercised in deciding whether or not a matter had become so important as to justify federal intervention. To leave it to Ottawa's discretion, he warned, would practically destroy the autonomy of the provinces. The Scott Act must be assumed to have passed this test, but that did not mean that Ontario's local-option law was either invalid or ineffectual. The federal law must prevail wherever the two came into conflict, but the Ontario law could operate wherever the Scott Act had not been implemented by local referendum.

The second way in which Watson influenced subsequent adjudication was by upholding the Scott Act as valid residuary legislation but not as a proper use of Ottawa's power to regulate trade and commerce. In *City of Fredericton v. The Queen* (1879), the Supreme Court had upheld the Scott Act as a regulation of trade and commerce, and the *Insurance Case* was in part an attempt by Mowat to block that path. Watson's decision in 1896 followed the *Insurance Case* in subordinating the trade and commerce power to the provincial power to legislate on property and civil rights. One Supreme Court judge, John Wellington Gwynne, who had upheld the trade and commerce power in both *Fredericton* and the *Insurance Case*, approached the *Prohibition Reference* as a last chance to give that power, and the Dominion legislative jurisdiction as a whole, the priority he thought they deserved. 'If ever it should be reversed,' he wrote of *Fredericton*, 'it will in my opinion be a matter of deep regret, as defeating the plain intent of the framers of our constitution and imperilling the success of the scheme of confederation.'[5] But Watson did not heed him, and the Privy Council's debasement of the trade and commerce power would rank second only to its degradation of the Dominion residuary power in the twentieth-century centralists' inventory of grievances.

The spark that ignited the centralist revolution was the Privy Council's disqualification in 1926 of a Dominion statute, the Industrial Disputes Investigation Act of 1907. Known as the Lemieux Act, after the minister responsible for its enactment, it was in reality the brainchild of Mackenzie King, then deputy minister of labour. Its object was to prevent labour disputes from stopping production or service in any mine or public utility, and it did so by prohibiting any strike or lockout until the dispute had first been referred to a board of conciliation.[6] Ontario courts upheld the act when it was first challenged in 1923, but the Privy Council rejected it on appeal as legislation affecting the civil rights of employers and employees, a matter of provincial rather than national concern.[7]

In defending the Lemieux Act, counsel invoked the precedent of *Russell v. The Queen*. That decision certainly afforded scope for the act, but the most senior and influential figure on the panel that considered the legislation was an admirer of Lord Watson and the way he had cut *Russell* down to size in the *Prohibition Reference*. He was R.B. Haldane, who had represented Ontario before the Privy Council in the *McCarthy Act* and *Prohibition Cases* among others. Now Viscount Haldane, a veteran Liberal statesman and recently lord chancellor in Britain's first Labour government, he commented forcefully on the weakness of *Russell* and its inconsistency with later decisions on licensing and prohibition. Parliament, he declared, could use its residuary power only in cases arising out of some extraordinary peril to the national life of Canada, such as the recent world war. *Russell* could be justified only on the assumption that in 1882 the evil of intemperance had presented so grave a menace to the life of the nation that Parliament had had to intervene to avert disaster. An epidemic of pestilence might conceivably have been regarded as analogous. The Lemieux Act did not meet that standard of national need.

Haldane's judgment did little, if any, lasting damage to the Dominion's role in industrial arbitration, but it caused a stir by its narrow conception of Ottawa's residuary power. The remarks about *Russell* were especially controversial. Nothing could be more absurd than to suppose that the Scott Act had been passed to meet some national emergency, and Haldane may well have made the suggestion only as an ironic comment on the shortcomings of *Russell*. To Canadian centralists, however, his remarks were simply dotty and quickly became a byword for judicial imbecility. 'By a great effort of pure reason, entirely unhampered by even the thought of historical research, he announced that the Canada Temperance Act (the Scott Act) must have been passed in a period of transcontinental intoxication, of acute, all-Canadian alcoholism, of Dominion-wide moral collapse through drink.' Thus Donald Creighton; but he was not alone.[8]

It was a McGill University law professor, Herbert Smith, who in 1926 launched the first general attack on Haldane's judgment.[9] Smith accused Haldane of standing the constitution on its head. He referred back to the Quebec and London resolutions and to the determination of John A. Macdonald and other Fathers of Confederation not to confine the general legislature to specific subjects of legislation. In their anxiety to avoid this cardinal error of American constitution-making, they had awarded the federal Parliament the power to make laws respecting 'all *matters of a general character,* not specially and exclusively reserved for the local government and Legislatures.' Smith could not believe that such sweeping words were meant to give authority only in cases of war or similar extraordinary emergency, and he backed up his contention with ample quotation from Macdonald and the British ministers responsible for the BNA Act. His conclusion was simple. No contemporary, whether friend or foe of the proposed confederation, had seemed to doubt that the Quebec agreement empowered the Dominion Parliament to make whatever laws it thought necessary for the general interest of Canada.

Smith praised *Russell v. The Queen* for taking this view of Parliament's powers but did not quite condemn Lord Watson for setting limits to them. He was in fact rather equivocal on the matter. Encroachment on the 'sound and lucid doctrine' of *Russell* had begun long ago, he said, quoting Watson's judgment in the *Prohibition Case* as evidence. He granted, though, that Watson's 'test of jurisdiction' was true to the intentions of the statesmen of 1867. It drew a line between matters that were merely local and provincial and those which had ceased to be so and become legitimate objects of Ottawa's concern. The notion that Parliament could deal with 'provincial' matters only in emergencies of the magnitude of war and pestilence was one that had seen the light only in three recent judgments of Haldane's, that on the Lemieux Act being the last and most infamous.

So Smith drew a sharp line between Watson's formula and Haldane's; and in fact the Lemieux Act of 1907 was a perfect justification for that distinction. It had originally been passed to deal with a protracted dispute in the coal mines of southern Alberta, which threatened, as winter approached, to produce widespread hardship and possible mortality beyond the bounds of that province. In fact, Ottawa had been stirred into action by an appeal from the premier of Saskatchewan.[10] It was therefore a textbook case of an emergency that fell short of war or pestilence but transcended provincial bounds and threatened civil calamity on a significant scale.

To be fair to Haldane, however, the act contained no words limiting its effect to such cases. This omission mattered because, in the last quarter of the nineteenth century, a doctrine had taken hold that barred judges from pondering the historical context of an enactment as an aid to its interpretation. In imagining the sort of emergency that might justify federal action, Haldane was probably influenced by Ottawa's wartime assumption of sweeping powers under the War Measures Act of

1914; at any rate, his two earlier judgments that Smith censured both concerned laws relating to that emergency. Had the Lemieux Act contained words that indicated its origin in, and applicability to, the sort of emergency with which it was designed to deal, those words might have prompted Haldane to interpret Ottawa's powers more expansively. As it was, Haldane confronted a case in which Dominion legislation on a 'provincial' matter had been applied to an industrial dispute purely local in scope.[11]

Smith, an Englishman, made his later career in Britain, but he passed on the torch to a disciple, F.R. Scott.[12] During his decades on McGill's law faculty, Frank Scott published a succession of comments on the constitution, including several general discussions of the division of powers. Another influential early critic of the Privy Council was W.P.M. Kennedy, a law professor at the University of Toronto. Kennedy's attitude is the more striking because he had first studied the BNA Act under the guidance of A.H.F. Lefroy, the leading constitutional scholar of the early twentieth century.[13] In his own book on the constitution, published in 1922, Kennedy wrote complacently of the Privy Council's role in 'gradually bringing to light the essentially federal nature of the Canadian constitution.' Seven years later, though, he put out an article that mocked Haldane's 'emergency' doctrine and lamented the Judicial Committee's descent from the pristine wisdom of *Russell*. Like Scott's, his comments on the Privy Council grew sharper with time.[14]

To be fair, in the matter of the residuary power the surviving record of past political battles set a trap for the unwary. I described in chapter 7 how John A. Macdonald and his Colonial Office collaborators, in trying to centralize Confederation during the drafting of the BNA Act, had wiped out the symmetry between the general and local residuary powers as stated in the Quebec and London resolutions.[15] By empowering Ottawa to make laws for the peace, order, and good government of Canada in all things not assigned to the exclusive authority of the provinces, the phrasing of section 91 made it easy to talk as though the Fathers had simply inverted the American distribution of powers. This misconception was made easier by the reticence of Hewitt Bernard, secretary to the Quebec conference and Macdonald's brother-in-law-to-be. In his meagre record of the debates, silence fell once the delegates had rejected the American model. He withheld the slightest summary of whatever they said about their eventual compromise, with its division of the residue into local and general components.

Under such influences, writers had got into the habit, long before the centralist revolution, of describing the Canadian system as an inversion of the American. Even A.H.F. Lefroy declared, in a popular reference work, that 'Canada's arrangement is in this respect the exact converse of that of the United States.' But Lefroy went on, three pages later, to notice the provincial residuary power and the limits it posed to the federal power, and elsewhere he was more careful in describing the division of powers.[16] Others ignored the provincial residue entirely. Zebulon Lash and George M. Wrong both did so in a public lecture series at the University of Toronto in 1917. Lash was a leading business lawyer with a background in constitutional litigation; in 1883, as deputy minister of justice, he had represented Ottawa before the Privy Council in the *Escheats Case*. Wrong, a historian, was son-in-law to Edward Blake, the Liberal leader at Ottawa at the height of the provincial rights controversy.[17] Both men should have known better.

No doubt it was such gaffes that prompted W.P.M. Kennedy, in his book on the constitution, to write in 1922 of the need 'to get the so-called "residuary power" of the dominion free from the rather vague conceptions which have passed into currency.'[18] He pointed out that the federal residue was curtailed by its provincial counterpart and could be exercised only when the interests of Canada as a whole were clearly involved. But it was not only the vagueness of which Kennedy complained that led to the final apotheosis of Parliament's power. The Privy Council's early critics – Kennedy himself, Herbert Smith, and Frank Scott – continued to weave the provincial residue into their analysis.[19] In his paper of 1931, Scott actually quoted the relevant resolutions of the Quebec conference in support of his contention that the delegates had intended to divide the legislative power into two spheres: general and local. Even in the most radical phase of his constitutional thinking he rarely went beyond the perfectly accurate claim that the founders had awarded Ottawa 'general powers of legislation.'[20]

But with the erection of *Russell* as the standard of correctness in interpreting the division of powers, the provincial residuary power lost its old meaning. If Parliament might legislate for the peace, order, and good government of Canada as it saw fit, then the provincial residue by definition set no bounds to Parliament's power. Centralists lost sight of the fact that the two residues were complementary, and that the Fathers of Confederation had meant to create two powers of the same sort, possessed by governments essentially equal in constitutional status. The myth grew that the Fathers had meant the central government to have untrammelled power to make laws for the peace, order, and good government of Canada and had therefore assigned the residuary power in full to the Dominion. The refusal of the Quebec conference to follow the American pattern by assigning it to the local legislatures was taken as evidence of that decision.

If Ottawa's legislative authority was as sweeping as centralists maintained, what possible need – what conceivable excuse – was there to apply any circumstantial test to its measures? Centralists had begun by citing Lord Watson's judgment in the *Prohibition Case* as a sane alternative to Lord Haldane's dottiness, but by 1939 Watson himself was under fierce attack as the source of the rot.

In 1935 the Conservative government of R.B. Bennett, desperate for re-election after half a decade's floundering in the political morass of the Great Depression, carried a bundle of measures that commentators christened Mr Bennett's New Deal.[21] One act imposed compulsory, employer-funded unemployment insurance; others established a minimum wage, regulated hours of work, and set up a national board for the marketing of natural products, with power to regulate prices. They were the sort of measures that centralists thought appropriate to the crisis, and which they thought the Fathers of Confederation had meant Ottawa to be able to take in such a crisis. Not only that, but the minimum-wage law and the statutes regulating hours of work conformed to a convention of the International Labour Organization (ILO) that Canada had ratified. Section 132 of the BNA Act empowered Ottawa to legislate as needed to perform Canada's obligations under treaties concluded between the British empire and foreign governments. Even if section 132 did not apply to treaties concluded by Canada as an independent nation, surely Ottawa's residuary power authorized Parliament to make the laws that such treaties required. The Privy Council itself had suggested this in a judgment of 1932.[22]

When it came to Bennett's New Deal, however, the Judicial Committee thought otherwise. Lord Atkin presented its reasons with tedious verbosity, but it all boiled down to one basic proposition. The division of legislative powers was the most essential condition of the interprovincial compact to which the BNA Act gave effect – it was the cornerstone of provincial autonomy. That principle precluded Parliament from making laws, no matter how desirable, that affected civil rights in the provinces, and Ottawa could not acquire the power to make such laws simply by agreeing with a foreign country to enact them. When

Canada's treaty obligations entailed law-making within the provincial ambit, Ottawa would have to rely on provincial cooperation.[23]

The *Labour Conventions Case* riled centralists as much as Haldane's rejection of the Lemieux Act a decade earlier. In their minds, the idea that Ottawa might conclude treaties with foreign powers in order to make laws outside its ordinary sphere was a case of judicial dementia to rival Haldane's.[24] But in effect Ottawa had done just that: Bennett's government had ratified the ILO convention precisely in order to boost Parliament's claim to enact the New Deal laws, fearing that they might not otherwise pass muster.[25] The whole affair seemed to justify Ontario premier Howard Ferguson's fears of what might follow from Ottawa's acquisition of extraterritorial authority. (It is ironic that the culprit was R.B. Bennett, to whom he had appealed in 1930 for protection against such wrongs.) But of course centralists had never sympathized with Ferguson. They thought that Parliament should be able to pass such laws in the ordinary exercise of its power to legislate for the peace, order, and good government of Canada. To be told that it could not do so even in the exercise of treaty obligations infuriated them.

The *Labour Conventions* decision, and two others striking down the Unemployment Insurance and the Natural Products Marketing acts, were announced in January 1937. One result was an outburst of resentment against the Privy Council; another was the launching of two government inquiries. The more famous was the so-called Rowell–Sirois Commission – officially, the Royal Commission on Dominion–Provincial Relations. In setting it up, Mackenzie King acted under the influence of Norman Rogers among others; Rogers had become minister of labour on the Liberals' return to power in 1935, and his office gave him a special interest in the fate of the New Deal legislation. One of the commissioners was J.W. Dafoe, Rogers's ally in the fight against the compact theory of Confederation, which Lord Atkin had so annoyingly endorsed in the *Labour Conventions Case*. With Dafoe on the board, a historical approach to the problem of dominion–provincial relations was assured. One of the special studies ordered by the commissioners was a treatise on the origins of Confederation by a newly prominent Toronto historian, Donald Creighton.[26]

But with a Québécois co-chairman, the royal commission had to hedge on matters of historical interpretation (F.R. Scott would rebuke it for conceding that there might be honest differences of opinion as to the intentions of the Fathers of Confederation).[27] The other inquiry suffered under no such constraints. Its sole commissioner was W.F. O'Connor, charged by the Senate with inquiring into the enactment of the BNA Act and 'any lack of consonance between its terms and judicial construction of them.' O'Connor's other great contribution to Canadian constitutionalism was his drafting in 1914 of the War Measures Act, a measure so sweeping that the federal government had seriously doubted whether it could pass muster even in wartime. Shortly afterwards he had become an enthusiastic and activist member of the Board of Commerce, a wartime instrument of price control, which Lord Haldane had struck down in the first of his three leading decisions on the federal residuary power. A partisan of central power, O'Connor was far from happy that Ottawa's power to make laws for the peace, order, and good government of Canada should be confined to such emergencies as war, famine, and pestilence.[28]

O'Connor's argument, spread over hundreds of pages of appendices, was the fullest statement yet of the centralist case. He repeated and elaborated Rogers's legalistic account of the process of Confederation in order to discredit the compact theory once and for all. Even more than Rogers, he set the fashion for insisting that Confederation could not be traced back to any so-called treaty of 1864: only the London resolutions of 1866, which no legislature had ever ratified, could be regarded as the true progenitors of the BNA Act. But he devoted even more space and energy to documenting the distortions that he believed the Privy Council had wrought on the division of legislative power. His terms of reference were obviously a licence to go after the Judicial Committee, and he acted on it gladly.

We have seen how Creighton in 1944 would mock Lord Haldane for presuming to interpret the BNA Act without any historical research. But O'Connor had little interest in historical research beyond the years 1864–7. Lawyer-fashion, he confined his pursuit of the Privy Council to an analysis of its judgments; but he examined these much more closely than any predecessor and soon traced to a single source Atkin's concern for provincial autonomy and Haldane's insistence that the power to make laws for the peace, order, and good government of Canada must be subject to a test. The villain was Lord Watson – the first judge to ordain, in the *Prohibition Case*, that Parliament's power must be limited for the sake of provincial autonomy.

Watson had had his reasons, of course, and we know what they were. We know that he was trying to resolve a conundrum set by Mowat: the problem posed by the apparent contradiction between *Russell* and the *McCarthy Act Case*. But O'Connor could not know that. He looked only at the Privy Council judgments, and the *McCarthy Act Case* had not yielded a written judgment. 'I dislike Lord Watson's assumption of the guardianship of the autonomy of the provinces,' he sneered. 'His proper function was merely that of an interpreter of the meaning of the words of a statute. When the London Conference framed its terms and the Imperial Parliament enacted them the true guardians of the autonomy of the provinces had done, in their way, what Lord Watson was presuming, without the necessary equipment, to do in his way.'[29]

What had the 'true guardians' actually done (and perhaps we may include the members of the Quebec conference, who thrashed the matter out)? We know that they had based Canada's constitution on a model that seemed to them to guarantee local autonomy: the constitution of the British empire. We know that they had divided the residuary power, thereby signalling the constitutional equality of the central and local governments. But the centralist revolutionaries of the 1930s were deaf to their words and blind to their intentions. 'If the provinces had wished to "preserve their autonomy,"' wrote F.R. Scott in jeering reference to the *Labour Conventions* judgment, 'they would never have entered Confederation at all.'[30]

A striking feature of the centralist revolt was its appeal to the authority of history. As Donald Creighton was to put it in 1966, even 'quiet' revolutionaries need to make up their mind about history. The centralists of the 1920s and 1930s were of one mind from the start. They found ample authority for their beliefs in the words of the founders of Canada, and they looked back to the early years of Confederation as a golden age of federal pre-eminence. To Herbert Smith, Haldane's judgment on the Lemieux Act epitomized the folly of the doctrine that barred judges from using historical evidence to interpret statutes. W.P.M. Kennedy, himself a historian by training, praised *Russell v. The Queen* as a decision that 'favoured the historical facts,' and he faulted later Privy Council decisions for failing to do so.[31] Norman Rogers and J.W. Dafoe went back in time in order to discredit the compact theory.

This was history to a purpose. These centralist revolutionaries cited neither past nor contemporary historians, either to commend or condemn them. The opinions of scholars, however congenial, were not grist to their mill; what they wanted was testimony. They summoned the Fathers of Confederation to bear witness to their intentions; they summoned opponents of Confederation to grumble about the obvious irrelevance of provincial autonomy to those intentions. This testimony they found in the records of the time: in the proceedings and discussions of the Quebec conference, as taken down by John A. Macdonald's chief aide and future brother-in-law, Hewitt Bernard, and published with supporting documents by the great man's long-time private secretary, Joseph Pope; in the verbatim record of the debates in the parliament of United Canada, where the Dorion brothers and other anti-confederationists eloquently proclaimed the impossibility of provincial autonomy under the Quebec resolutions; and in the terse minutes of the legislatures of Nova Scotia and New Brunswick, documenting those bodies' distaste for the Quebec agreement and grudging consent to take part in the London conference. These they augmented with one or two cheerleading accounts of the great events by contemporaries, replete with speeches extolling the grand new nation that was to be. They made little effort to expand the inquiry beyond the three or four most obvious sources and none at all to imagine what words might have meant in the mouths of men of the time (except when inconvenient allusions to a *treaty* needed explaining away). The same set of quotations popped up time after time.

This tunnel vision served them well enough. Had they delved as far back in time as the Grit convention of 1859, and heard Toronto's St Lawrence Hall resounding with paeans to the new transcontinental nationality that a federated Canada might bring to life, they might have had to admit that such rhetoric did not necessarily entail the centralist ardour that they imagined. You could be a nationalist without being a centralist.[32] Had they pushed ahead into the era of the provincial-rights controversy, they might have had to confront the views of Oliver Mowat and others who were intimate with the events of Confederation but did not share Macdonald's view of them.

But to these centralist revolutionaries the history that counted began only in 1864 and ended in 1867. When Norman Rogers glanced briefly at 'the genesis of provincial rights,' less than half of his fifteen pages dealt with events after 1867, and his inquiry stopped short with Mowat's appointment as premier in 1872.[33] In 1931 F.R. Scott got wind of a proposal to include a session on Macdonald's great gerrymander of 1882 in the program of the annual meeting of the Canadian Political Science Association. He protested against wasting time on such stuff when the economic and social crisis produced by the Great Depression cried out for attention.[34] This was the very meeting at which Rogers demolished the compact theory and Scott himself presented his first sketch of the travails of Canadian federalism under the baneful aegis of the Privy

Council.[35] To study history with such ulterior ends in view was laudable; all else was froth.

Those who probe the past from ulterior motives rarely fail to find what they seek. Centralists did not have to dig far to unearth expressions of nationalist ardour, and of a determination to improve on the American example by creating a powerful central government. From there it was but a small step to find the effects of that zeal in aspects of the Confederation settlement that had no counterpart in the constitution of the United States: in Ottawa's power to disallow provincial legislation; the power of lieutenant-governors appointed by Ottawa to veto or reserve it; Parliament's authority to levy any tax, direct or indirect, appoint all judges above the rank of magistrate, and impose a uniform code of criminal law and procedure; and the Dominion's general power to make laws for the peace, order, and good government of Canada. All together, such provisions lent support to the idea that the founders had meant the Dominion government to possess a predominance beyond that of its American counterpart. And to some extent the founders had; but not necessarily the degree of supremacy that Rogers, Scott, and others so eagerly read into their words.

For this misreading there was one preponderant cause: in making their appeal to the past, our centralist revolutionaries treated the founding of Canada in a profoundly unhistorical manner. They seized on facts that supported their ideal, and they ignored any that pointed the other way. We saw in the last chapter how Norman Rogers, in demolishing the compact theory, ignored both the origin of Confederation as an agreement to federalize United Canada and the way in which responsible government had transformed the constitution of the empire.[36] Writer after writer cited Ottawa's quasi-imperial powers as evidence of the founders' intention to create a dominant central government. None stopped to think that by the 1860s those powers had become subject to unwritten but powerful constitutional constraints and that the founders had meant to import those constraints into the Canadian constitution.

Constitutional constraints on Ottawa's use of its veto were quite consistent with an intention to create a more powerful central government than the American. So was the splitting of the residuary legislative power. In each case the Fathers gave the federal government real powers that its American counterpart lacked. To be sure, those powers were not as sweeping as centralists such as Rogers, Scott, and Creighton imagined; their effect was not to make the central power dominant over the provinces but rather to make it first among equals. But British Americans had perceived the U.S. government as constitutionally *inferior* to the state governments.[37] From this standpoint, a central government that was first among equals was indeed stronger than its American counterpart. Twentieth-century centralists, however, never stopped to ask what the Fathers actually meant by rejecting the American division of powers.

They might have done so, however, if only they had heeded the remarkable critique of the O'Connor Report by V. Evan Gray, a constitutional lawyer who had represented Ontario before the Privy Council in the *Insurance References* of 1922 and 1931. In 1951, when Scott chided the Rowell–Sirois Commission for temporizing on the centralist intent of Confederation, Gray's was the only substantial English-Canadian dissent from centralist orthodoxy that he could find to set against dozens of affirmations.[38] There is no more eloquent testimony to the intellectual ascendancy of centralism at mid-century than the rarity and neglect of Gray's review; for in the process of exposing O'Connor's prejudice and illogicality, it managed to piece together a story that would otherwise remain untold until 1986.[39] To a generation that would or could not hear, Gray revealed the crucial importance of the *McCarthy Act Reference*, its bearing on the *Prohibition Reference*, Lord Haldane's participation in both cases as counsel for Ontario, and Oliver Mowat's crucial role in these disputes and the *Insurance Case*.

Gray's discussion highlights by comparison the flaws in his contemporaries' approach. He willingly looked beyond the years 1864–7 for clues to the meaning of Confederation, and he rebuked O'Connor for ignoring earlier writers on the constitution. He himself relied on one book in particular: a biography of Oliver Mowat by the premier's son-in-law.[40] This enabled him to see Confederation from a vantage denied to Scott, O'Connor, and other centralists – one from which Lord Watson's concern to protect provincial autonomy seemed neither novel nor unjustified but simply an attempt to codify the unwritten *McCarthy Act* decision and so keep Ottawa's legislative power within the bounds envisaged by the Fathers of Confederation. In making that attempt, Gray noted, the Privy Council had done nothing to which it had not been urged by Canadian statesmen, acting with the support of Canadian voters. For the most part it had upheld the decisions of Canadian courts, though not necessarily the Supreme Court, and it had got far closer to the truth of Confederation, as expressed in the BNA Act, than O'Connor had. 'All this talk about distortion of the framework of Confederation

and defeat of national purposes by judicial authority is silly and puer-
ile,' he concluded. 'Our constitution is what our forefathers made it and
as we have applied it – not what British judges gave us.'[41]

No English Canadian matched Gray's scorn for centralist orthodoxy,
but another sceptic was the political economist Harold Innis, one of the
great original thinkers of twentieth-century Canada. Appointed in 1934
to a royal commission on the economy of Nova Scotia, he submitted a
personal report that impeached Ottawa's inept handling of the economy
in general and of the fishing industry in particular. Canada's vast extent
rendered detailed centralized control of the economy ineffective if not
impossible, he declared. In investigating the fishery, he was 'forcibly
struck by the callousness, lack of sympathy, and general disregard of
broad policy, which has characterized federal supervision.'[42]

Innis's remarks evoked several critical letters, one of which in particular showed that the bureaucrats were not uniquely callous. 'I certainly
do not like the present tendency towards localism,' wrote the historian
Arthur Lower. 'If ever we are going to create a nation here, we have got
to get away from that and I for one would be prepared to say, in last
resort, that whatever N.S.'s hard fate, she must look forward to continued submission of her will and interests to those of the Dominion at
large. I am not a "states rights" man.' Innis replied, mildly enough, that
he probably agreed with Lower on provincial rights in general, but he
doubted Ottawa's omniscience and deprecated the evils of 'dominance
and remote control.' 'While a federalist and a nationalist,' he declared, 'I
am extremely reluctant to support measures which injure regions or
groups and which set up causes of irritation within the nation.'[43] To
Innis, provincialism was an inevitable consequence of Canada's nature
as an aggregate of regions, economically distinct and varying widely in
wealth and population. It was regrettable when regions hit hard by
depression talked in terms of secession, but the real problem was that
such talk was the only weapon by which disadvantaged regions had
been able to obtain 'a reasonable distribution of the burdens of Canadian nationalism.'[44]

Innis's words suggest the same thing as the paeans to nationality at
the Reform convention of 1859 – that Canadian nationalism need not be
centralist. Indeed, Innis was openly sceptical of centralist constitutionalism and its exponents' efforts to ground it in history. 'The British North
America Act has produced its own group of idolators and much has
been done to interpret the views and sayings of the fathers of Confederation in a substantial body of patristic literature,' he wrote with his typi-

cal ironic detachment. Critics of the Privy Council might grumble about inconsistencies in its judgments, but at least inconsistency implied flexibility, offsetting the danger of rigidity inherent in written constitutions.[45]

Gray the lawyer wrote as a critic of centralist constitutionalism. Innis the economic historian thought in terms less of provinces than of regions and considered the division of powers less from a constitutional than from an administrative standpoint. What he disliked about the centralization of political power in Ottawa was its inhumanity and inefficiency. Yet the two shared an antipathy to centralism that marked them out among English-Canadian writers of the 1930s. It can hardly be a coincidence that they were closest among English-speaking intellectuals to the populist roots of the nineteenth-century Reform tradition. Both men came from Oxford County, where in 1807 the inhabitants had alarmed a local official by celebrating the Fourth of July; which thirty years later had been a hotbed of insurrection; and whose sturdy support for Reform Mowat had extolled at Woodstock at the outset of his premiership in 1872. Mowat was still premier twenty-two years later, when Innis was born, the son of a farmer and leading local Reformer. Gray, born four years earlier in the same rebel reaches of south Oxford, attended the same high school as Innis, Woodstock Collegiate Institute, and the same university, Baptist-founded McMaster.[46]

Through the eyes of Innis and Gray, we can see the biases and omissions in the new centralist orthodoxy. These biases are also revealed by comparison of the new centralism and the old – that of men who had taken part in Confederation or closely observed it. One such person was John Wellington Gwynne, from his appointment in January 1879 to his death in office, twenty-three years later, the most fervent centralist on the Supreme Court. Another was William McDougall, the sometime Clear Grit. If O'Connor and company had been right about Confederation, their understanding of the BNA Act should have agreed with that of Gwynne and McDougall. Actually, it was quite different.

Gwynne was an old friend of John A. Macdonald's, and in the 1840s and 1850s he had been an ardent railway promoter. When Macdonald had to resign in 1873 because of the Pacific Railway scandal, Gwynne denounced the prime minister's critics as hypocrites, who had treasonously sacrificed 'all our hopes of nationality' and 'our iron zone' (presumably the Sault Ste Marie region, which he feared must fall into American hands in the absence of a rail link to central Canada). He spoke of quitting the bench to fight once more for 'Canadian railway progress.' Oliver Mowat had recently left the bench to become first minister of Ontario. Gwynne declared a preference for the office 'not of a *first* but of the *last minister* of the crown – I mean the Doomsman or Headsman or Hangman.'[47]

Clearly Gwynne did not conform to anyone's ideal of a dispassionate, apolitical judge; and Macdonald undoubtedly knew of his commitment to 'railway progress' and a powerful central government when, soon after returning to office in 1878, he named him to the Supreme Court. Gwynne did not fail him. His judgments derided provincial pretensions to constitutional equality with the Dominion. When Mowat achieved his first breakthrough with the Supreme Court's decision in the *Insurance Case*, Gwynne at once warned Macdonald that the case should be appealed to the Privy Council. 'To my mind the thin end of the wedge to bring about Provincial Sovereignty ... is inserted,' he wrote. When the Privy Council proved to be less centralist than he, he derided its members as 'dispensers of the prerogative ... of dispensing with the BNA Act.' 'Old as I am,' he told a friend in 1889, 'I fully expect that both you and I shall be present as mourners at the funeral of Confederation cruelly murdered in the house of its friends.'[48]

Where Gwynne diverged from twentieth-century centralism was in his approach to the division of legislative power. Both approaches strongly favoured the Dominion, but they differed significantly in focus. You can see the discrepancy in Gwynne's attitude towards the *Prohibition Reference*, which I discussed at the beginning of the chapter. To him the main point of the case was not Ottawa's residuary power as treated in *Russell v. The Queen* but the broad conception of its itemized powers as laid down in *City of Fredericton v. The Queen*. As an observer of Canada's founding, he understood that, whatever *Russell* might seem to say, the Canadian Parliament could not be allowed to legislate as it liked on matters reserved to the provinces. Accordingly, ardent nationalist though he was, he rejected the McCarthy Act as an offence against provincial autonomy.[49]

Gwynne knew that the Fathers had set out to create legislative spheres that were mutually exclusive and that they had done so by dividing the leading functions of government into two bundles, one federal and the other provincial. Although they had rounded off each list with a residuary category, he did not worry much about what might fall into those categories. He valued Parliament's residuary power less as a substantive grant of authority than as a symbol of national unity and what he called the Dominion's supreme national sovereignty.[50] When it came to working out the division of powers in detail, what mattered was what that sovereignty meant for Ottawa's itemized powers and their relation to the provincial powers listed in section 92. As a fan of big business, a devotee of Canadian railway progress, and a believer in Macdonald's goal of centrally directed transcontinental expansion, he thought that federal powers should be defined broadly and provincial powers narrowly, as the Supreme Court had done in *Fredericton*.

Mowat won that argument too, of course, and forty years later a centralist could no longer hope to argue, as Gwynne once had, that Ottawa's legislative power enjoyed a pre-eminence based on supreme national sovereignty. All hope of an expansive federal role in economic regulation, and in handling the social problems which industrialization and the Great Depression had made so urgent, now seemed to depend on the courts' readiness to accept such legislation as a valid exercise of Parliament's power to make laws for the peace, order, and good government of Canada. O'Connor's strained reading of the division of powers was born of the traumatic disappointment of that hope.

The difference between the ways in which nineteenth-and twentieth-century centralists understood the division of powers mirrored a difference in their understanding of Canada's founding. Gwynne knew perfectly well that Confederation was the work of an interprovincial compact: his judgment in the *Prohibition Case* called it 'a treaty of union.' A colleague, Joseph Sedgewick, who shared his view of that case, called the BNA Act 'in effect a constitutional agreement or compact, or treaty,' much as William and Robert Baldwin about seventy years earlier had called the Constitutional Act 'in fact a treaty.'[51] Gwynne and Sedgewick recognized the founding compact as a historical reality and would have found Norman Rogers's efforts to deny that reality absurd.

This attitude is the more striking because the idea of the Confederation compact had been challenged on legalistic grounds as early as 1881. Confronting the Québécois jurist T.-J.-J. Loranger in the *Escheats Case* before the Supreme Court of Canada, William McDougall portrayed Confederation as an act of absolute imperial power. Unlike Norman Rogers fifty years later, however, McDougall made it quite clear that he was presenting a strictly doctrinal argument, not a historical one. 'No one can doubt the power of the Imperial Parliament to have deprived Canada (*so far as an Act of Parliament could do it*) of representative government altogether,' he declared. 'It might have converted, or reconverted, our provinces into Crown colonies, with some new experimental form of colonial government. Probably it would not have been well received ... but *as a matter of law – as a matter of argument before a court of law* – I contend that the whole subject was completely within the control of the Imperial Parliament.'[52] McDougall had to use such language because he had taken part in all three conferences of 1864–7 and, speaking as a minister of the Crown, had himself described the Quebec resolutions as a treaty to the legislature of United Canada.[53] He knew – and so did his audience, which included Gwynne – that it would have been politically impossible for Westminster to pass the BNA Act, or impose any such change, without the consent of the elected colonial authorities.

The problem that confronts us in this book is to explain how Rogers could say otherwise. Every Canadian nationalist of his generation was preoccupied with the limits of imperial authority over Canada. They knew as well as McDougall and Gwynne that responsible government posed limits to imperial control over Canada – that the imperial Parliament, for instance, could not amend the BNA Act except at the demand of the proper Canadian authorities. But something prevented them from understanding what that implied about Confederation. The next two chapters explain how that obstacle to understanding arose and how it caused a rift between English and French Canadians.

12

Continentalism, Imperialism, Nationalism

A good starting-point is those early quarrels on the subject of amending the constitution, which I reviewed in chapter 10. Looking back on them as Norman Rogers and other centralists did in the late 1920s, the Confederation compact may have appeared to have been doomed from the start. Like the principles of responsible government, in Britain as well as in the colonies, its terms were not inscribed in any official document. They were an unwritten gloss on the BNA Act, just as the principles of responsible government were an unwritten gloss on English constitutional law. Inevitably they were somewhat vague and disputable; inevitably they were left to be shaped by the cut and thrust of political debate, just like the principles of responsible government in eighteenth- and early-nineteenth-century Britain. As a result, although politicians agreed that Confederation was the work of an interprovincial compact, they quarrelled over what that meant in practice. They adapted the theory to the exigencies of the moment, tarnishing it by their opportunism and muddying the waters of memory.

For an unwritten accord to survive the generations, there must subsist a strong common memory of its origins and purpose. How could a lasting agreement be achieved that was both unwritten and uncertain? And that is just the point. Those early quarrels about the compact did not prevent Canadians from acknowledging its historical reality: in the 1890s both provincialists and centralists did so, as we have seen. They argued about what it meant, not whether it had happened, and in the process they worked towards a consensus as to its meaning. By 1930, however, all that had changed. Not only had the consensus broken down, but centralists, with Dafoe and Rogers at their head, rejected its basis in history. They chanted incessantly that the emperor had no clothes, and provincialists – especially English-speaking ones – could not say why they were wrong. Even those who denied that the emperor was naked could not say exactly what he was wearing.

Some rupture of memory must have occurred before Rogers and company could cite the early ambiguities surrounding the compact as evidence that the theory itself was fictitious. But when and how did that happen? And why did Canadians suddenly begin to notice the emperor's nakedness only in the 1920s? The answer lies partly in the profound changes in Canadian life between 1880 and 1930 and partly in the passage of time itself.

The compact theory was more than an opportunistic coinage of John A. Macdonald's political opponents: as we have seen, it was embedded in the political thought of both French and English Canada. But it was not the first thing most Canadians thought of when they woke up in the morning: it was something of which they had to be reminded when nec-essary by politicians anxious to persuade them that it entailed this, that, or the other consequence. As the nineteenth century gave way to the twentieth, the compact remained a matter of urgent concern to French-Canadian politicians. But there came a time when it ceased to matter much to English Canadians. Oliver Mowat had won his constitutional battles; Wilfrid Laurier was entrenched in office on Parliament Hill. Pol-iticians and intellectuals stopped worrying about Dominion–provincial relations and began to fret instead about Canada's place in North Amer-ica, the British empire, and the world at large.

In this respect, Mowat's and Laurier's victories were themselves preg-nant with defeat: the defeat – indeed, the demise – of the Upper Cana-dian Reform tradition. They fostered a shift in political perspective that deprived the Reform movement of intellectual as well as political lead-ership. The movement had always been an army of agrarian populists led by urban liberals. Different as they were, the Baldwins, William Lyon Mackenzie, and George Brown – and, after Confederation, Mowat, Edward Blake, and David Mills – were all men who harnessed the pop-ulist desire for local autonomy to great liberal ideas of the nineteenth century. The campaign for responsible government was a fight for polit-ical liberty and its indispensable corollary, the rule of law. The battle against the Family Compact, and later against commercial vested inter-ests such as the big railways, was a fight against monopoly and class privilege; the struggle for the separation of church and state was a fight for freedom of thought.[1] By the end of the century, those ideals were either secure or no longer compelling. The Canadian intelligentsia moved on to other projects, spurning provincial autonomy as the petty concern of party hacks.

The very word *provincial* signified small-mindedness and rusticity. For decades Canadians had attended to business, happy enough for the most part to leave their external affairs in the hands of the mother country, the greatest naval power in the world. But now the world had entered upon an era of national integration and global political rivalries. The birth of Canada had coincided more or less with Italian and German national union and the eclipse of states' rights after the American Civil War. The new century brought Australian and South African union, and an assortment of nationalist movements threatened the multinational empires of Europe. The great European powers, Britain included, were in an unprecedented state of global confrontation. In Canada, commentators such as Goldwin Smith, George Parkin, and John Ewart occupied themselves with the merits of continental union, imperial federation, and Canadian independence.

But the fate of the Reform tradition was not just a matter of competing ideologies. Constantly exposed to the flood-tide of British immigration – an unceasing influx of newcomers indifferent to its history of struggle and often to its sentiments – the Reform movement had survived by a mixture of adaptability and sheer luck. Schooled in the arts of appealing to British politicians, Reformers prospered by identifying their cause with that liberal trend which for much of the century was a leading feature of British politics. From the 1850s on they also gained from the anti-French bias of their politics. As we saw in chapter 9, this tendency harmonized nicely with the anti-Catholicism and Francophobia so deeply engrained in the British political culture and with the broader anti-clericalism that animated religious dissenters such as the Free Church Scots. The cry of Home Rule for Ontario helped to bring even Irish Catholics into the fold. At last, in the 1880s, the Reform coalition embraced the French-speaking Catholics of eastern Ontario.[2]

What single word could comprise this dizzying diversity? In the liberal vocabulary of Reform politics, it was the People – the People armed for liberty against the oppressions of Aristocracy, Privilege, Monopoly. But this parlance masked a contradiction that was steadily intensifying. Reformers imagined the People as a virtuous agrarian antithesis to urban corruption, but farmers formed only one element of the coalition and a dwindling proportion of Ontario's population. By the 1890s the National Policy, Macdonald's hated protective tariff of 1879, was rapidly industrializing and urbanizing the province. This trend coincided with a crisis in Ontario agriculture, itself the result of large-scale western grain production in the United States, and – thanks to Macdonald's Pacific railway – on Canada's own newly acquired prairie. Economic hardship weakened Reform's electoral infantry even as urban growth was eroding its preponderance within the provincial electorate.

As long as Reform politicians could credibly claim to be resisting an external oppressor, they managed to contain this contradiction. By the 1890s, however, Mowat had taken the struggle for provincial rights about as far as it could go. The great fight for responsible government – Ontario's battle against the Quebec Tories – could no longer outweigh the great issues that tended to divide the Reform coalition. The grievance of separate schools – monuments to Lower Canadian domination – still rankled in many minds, but separate schools were entrenched in the BNA Act. Prohibition also appealed to many, but it was less popular in the towns. So was that great Reform principle, free trade. To Reform orators of the 1880s the National Policy was the latest embodiment of Monopoly and Privilege, but to city-dwellers it was increasingly a source of prosperity.

In 1896 the Reform party embraced the National Policy in order to carry Laurier to national victory. It was a turning-point in Ontario politics. For more than half a century the party had figured in Reform rhetoric as the vanguard of the People, a People conceived in the image of the province's agrarian smallholders. Now the party symbolically rejected agrarian populism and embraced a more pluralistic notion of the People. From now on, members of the Canadian Manufacturers' Association were 'people' too, and farmers an interest like any other. Increasingly since Confederation Reform politicians had been calling themselves Liberals. Now there would be only Liberals. The Reform era had passed.[3]

Something like it had happened before. Twice Reform leaders had declared victory in the great fight for responsible government, and the rank and file had dissented. In 1854 the Baldwinite leadership had deserted the movement *en masse*; in 1867 John Sandfield Macdonald, William McDougall, and William Howland had done likewise. But in 1854 George Brown had been there to rally the headless army of Reform, and in 1867 the Brownite leadership had remained largely intact. This time there was no one.

At the Ontario election of 1894, many rural voters deserted Reformers and Conservatives alike in favour of a new populist movement of American origin called the Patrons of Industry. The Reformers also lost votes to the Protestant Protective Association, an anti-Catholic nativist organization that resented Mowat's policy of accommodation with the church on matters such as French-language education in eastern Ontario. His party won no more than half the seats, and only Tory foolishness helped it regain its majority. The Conservative leader, who had lost four times to Mowat and now saw his party finish third, gladly quit to become a judge. His successor was a type of leader the party would not favour again for ninety years: a small businessman from northern Ontario. The party chose George Marter, hoping that his anti-Catholicism and prohibitionism would induce the Patrons to accept a political alliance. But the retiring leader had sat for London, a longtime Tory stronghold but also the site of Labatt's brewery. The Liberal candidate won the by-election in a landslide, and Mowat had his majority again. Soon the Patrons were voting as a steady auxiliary of Reform; for the first time in Ontario's history, agrarian populism was a dead duck. The sight must have encouraged the province's Liberal leaders to opt for the National Policy in 1896.[4]

By embracing the tariff, Liberals gained twice over. To many voters the National Policy was the source of their present and hope of their future prosperity; to many, opposition to the National Policy was proof of disloyalty, especially when combined with hopes for a trade agreement with the United States. Such hopes had not always been seen as a badge of disaffection. Canadian conservatives had happily accepted free trade with the United States in natural products in 1854 and had tried to renew the agreement a decade later. In 1871 Macdonald had made another bid for a trade agreement. But Tories could get away with things that Liberals could not. Liberal opposition to the National Policy was of a piece with Liberal indifference to the Pacific railway and Liberal hostility to Ottawa. It was disloyal.

But then, Liberal trade policy in the late 1880s went much further than Tories had ever done. Blaming the protracted depression on the high tariff barriers between Canada and the United States, Liberals sought relief in a policy called commercial union. This entailed more than free trade with the United States; it meant joining the republic behind its high tariff wall against European imports, including those from Britain. With commercial union achieved, how distant could political union be? The question took its point from the existence of a Liberal fringe that openly advocated political union as a cure for the colony's ills. The county attorney for (of all places) the Orange stronghold of Dufferin turned out to be one such zealot. Mowat fired his injudicious underling, and in 1892 his forthright stand against annexationism earned his appointment as Knight Grand Cross of the Order of St Michael and St George. The Liberal party forsook commercial union for the less drastic policy of unrestricted reciprocity – free trade with the United States, but without the common tariff barrier. Still, as long as the party opposed the National Policy, the taint remained.[5]

Ironically, the foremost annexationist in 1890 was no Liberal but an independent, whose contempt for Liberals was even greater, if possible, than his contempt for Conservatives. Goldwin Smith had once been Regius Professor of History at Oxford. He wrote little history but specialized in brilliant political essays of a sharply radical tone. During the American Civil War, he was one of the few voices of the British establishment to speak up for the Union. In 1864 he visited the United States as a spokesman of those in Britain who supported the North. Four years later he returned to teach at the new university founded by Ezra Cornell on the heights above Ithaca, New York. After a few years he moved on to Toronto, leaving his name to grace a rather large building on Cornell's Arts Quad. In 1875 he married the widow of William Henry Boulton, a scion of the Family Compact and sometime Tory MPP and mayor of Toronto. Along with a wife he acquired a rather large building of his own, the Boulton mansion on Dundas Street – The Grange, it was called. Smith lived there for thirty-five years and left it on his death to house an art museum, the future Art Gallery of Ontario. While in residence he supported with his wealth and pen an assortment of unconventional enterprises and causes. His enterprises included a clutch of literary and political journals and a radical farmers' newspaper.[6]

Back in 1861, in a short book on the British empire, Smith had predicted alternative futures for the North American dependencies: either national independence or annexation to the United States. A dozen years later, newly installed in the Grange, he discerned hope for national independence in the Canada First movement and its favourite politician, Edward Blake. In 1874 Blake piqued political Canada with a speech in which he described his fellow Canadians as 'four millions of Britons who are not free.' Blake's distaste for Canada's continuing subordination to Britain in external affairs veered dramatically from the traditional Reform line, with its celebration of responsible government as the acme of colonial freedom, but it sounded well to an old-established anti-imperialist like Smith.

In fact, though, what Blake contemplated was not quite anti-imperialism. Along with other nationally minded Canadians, he hoped that Confederation would exalt Canada's status within the empire rather than preface its departure. What he and the Canada Firsters had in mind was imperial federation: the representation of Canada and the other self-governing colonies in the imperial Parliament at Westminster. George Brown's *Globe* sharply called the young lion to order (a toothless beast, he proved to be) and condemned Canada First as a treasonous organization. A harmless coterie of idealistic young patriots, it soon faded away.[7] Three years later, in 1877, Smith published the obituary of Canadian nationalism in a British periodical.

His essay was entitled 'The Political Destiny of Canada,'[8] but he began by insisting on the impermanence of the empire as a whole. India, Malta, Gibraltar, Australia, South Africa, Mauritius – could they possibly share a common future? Could the slender filament that bound each of them to Downing Street be the thread of a common destiny? What then of Canada? The first thing to remember – although official optimism was apt to forget it – was the million and more French-speakers lying in solid and unyielding mass between the British of Atlantic Canada and the British of Ontario. For their ancestral homeland they had something of a patriotic feeling, for England none whatever. They had fought off American invaders in 1776 and 1812, but that was a reflex of their ancient enmity towards New England. It would be foolish to count on that now, in an era when French Canadians readily sought work in the factories of New England.

Smith recalled Lord Elgin's remark that it would be easier to make French Canadians into Americans than make them English. As for making them Canadian: they had accepted Confederation as an act of divorce from English Canada, not as a measure of wider union. The two races had a history of unabated antagonism towards each other, a mutual hostility lately epitomized by Protestant Ontario's hatred for the Métis leader Louis Riel. So far the conservatism of the French priests and the ambitions of politicians such as Cartier and Macdonald had held that hostility in check, but this could not be counted on to continue. A truer guide to the future, Smith prophesied, was New Brunswick's recent defunding of Catholic schools. One could bank on education as a cause of future strife.

The French were one problem. There were also 400,000 patriotic Irish, whose feelings towards England differed in no way from those at home. And there was a considerable German settlement in Ontario, whose unimpaired nationality in the heart of a British population bore witness to the weakness of assimilating forces in Canada compared to those in the United States. Confederation had done nothing so far to fuse the races, or even the provinces. Members of Parliament from the smaller provinces acted as blocs, for whose support the Ontario-based political parties were constantly vying with offers of 'better terms.' Whether in composing a cabinet or assembling a rifle team, sectionalism was the rule.

Canada's separation from the empire was inevitable. The mere fact of distance made imperial federation a non-starter. Apart from that, there was a basic divergence between Canadian and British interests. Canadians cared nothing about Britain's European and Oriental diplomacy; Britain had no incentive to stand up for Canada's interests against the United States. Canadian manufacturers saw their British counterparts as rivals. Even now they were rallying to a protectionist movement led, oddly enough, by the same 'Conservative' politicians who were loudest in professing loyalty to Great Britain. But even more fundamental was a divergence of political character. English-Canadian society was more American than British. It was essentially democratic. Aristocracy had never taken root there; neither had the Church of England managed to establish itself as an arm of the state. Equality was the rule.

These impulses to separation were fundamental. At the moment a variety of forces held them in check, but those were secondary and transient. Smith listed, among others, the reactionary tendencies of the French priesthood; the sentimental appeal of United Empire Loyalism in Ontario; the influence of British immigrants (himself excluded, obviously); the continuing strength of Orangism; and a lingering anti-Americanism. None of these would last. Nor could Canada count on any tangible benefits from a continuing link with the United Kingdom. British monarchical forms did not make Canadian politics any less democratic than American politics. The British connection produced neither greater immigration nor more investment. What Canada needed was continental free trade.

If separation was inevitable, what then was Canada's political destiny? Certainly not nationhood: the time had passed for that. Canada might have become a nation had it bid for independence at the moment of Confederation. It would have required a swift transition from federalism to legislative union in order to quell the Dominion's endemic sectionalism, and that would not have sat well with Quebec; but Quebec could have been made to swallow it. Now it was too late. Canadian politics had set in the demoralizing mould of faction, corruption, and sectional bickering. Canadian nationalism was a lost cause, and union with the United States, sooner or later, a moral certainty. Nothing was left for Canadian patriotism but to ensure that it should be a true union and not an annexation.

So wrote Smith in 1877, and so he wrote at greater length in *Canada and the Canadian Question* (1891). Little had happened meanwhile to prove him wrong. Industrial protection had swiftly become a reality with Macdonald's return to office in 1878, but the Canadian economy languished in the doldrums. The flow of immigration was sluggish. The Liberal party spanned the gamut of continentalist policies from free trade to annexation, but the engrained loyalism of Anglo-Canadian voters kept it from power. The 1880s had been years of rampant sectionalism, with rabble-rousing discord between Grit Ontario and Tory Ottawa and the resurgence of separatism in impoverished Nova Scotia. Louis Riel's hanging and the advance of a militant Catholicism in Quebec had embittered relations between French and English Canada. The accession of a Liberal government to power in Winnipeg had produced in Manitoba the predicted school controversy to match the New Brunswick dispute of the 1870s.[9] Times were changing, but not obviously for the better.

Smith presented his analysis neither as a lament for the defeat of Canadian nationalism nor as a challenge to Canadians to prove him wrong. His stance was always that of the detached intellectual; for years he wrote a column for a Toronto periodical under the nom-de-plume 'Bystander.' But he certainly saw nothing to regret in what he regarded as inevitable. Political union would be the best thing all round. Canada and the United States would both derive an economic advantage from continental free trade. Canadians would no longer have to worry about military defence and would enjoy the moral benefit of following their natural democratic bent rather than shoehorning themselves into ill-fitting clogs of deference to monarchy and aristocracy. Britain would gain by the addition of a large anglophile element to American political counsels.

Meanwhile, though, the empire stood at the summit of hope and glory, and an influential group of Canadians was far from ready to concede the inevitability of annexation or the impossibility of imperial federation. Indeed, the movement owed its emergence in 1887 as a political force in Canada to the anxiety of George Taylor Denison, a Canada First veteran, to articulate a credible alternative to the new fad of commercial union. Quite a few federationists bore the royal and patriotic name of George. As well as Denison himself, a soldier whose treatise on cavalry warfare earned him a gold medal from Tsar Nicholas II, there was George Monro Grant, principal of Queen's University, and Sir George Ross, premier of Ontario from 1899 to 1905 and later a senator. There was Sir John George Bourinot (of 'Bourinot's Rules'), chief clerk of the House of Commons, and Sir Charles George Douglas Roberts, poet, story-teller, and historian. And there was Sir George Parkin, headmaster of Upper Canada College and first secretary of the Rhodes Scholarship Trust.[10]

In 1892 Parkin replied to Smith in a book called *Imperial Federation: The Problem of National Unity.*[11] It was a piquant title, for the nation in question was not Canada but Britain. The problem as Parkin saw it was not to achieve British national unity, for unity already existed; it was to preserve it. This meant eradicating what he called gross inequalities in the conditions of citizenship throughout the empire. On the one hand, many British subjects had no say in the governance of the empire; on the other, the 'British nation at home' bore an unfair share of the burden of imperial defence. These inequities might seem to be mutually compensating, but they were not. No immunity from taxation could compensate Canadians for the loss of a share in the higher life of the British nation and the higher dignity of full citizenship. Britannia's colonial subjects must be raised to full political equality with residents of the mother country.[12]

Parkin was a United Empire Loyalist of the New Brunswick strain, and his starting point was the confrontation between North American loyalism and the anti-imperialism of mid-Victorian Englishmen such as Smith. He hearkened back to 1866, when *The Times* of London had asserted that Canada's separation from the empire was inevitable. He wrote of the great shock these words had administered to Canadian sentiment, built as it was on a century of fidelity to the idea of a United Empire. Certainly Canadians were not about to betray a history of sacrifice and loyalty by abandoning a British for an American destiny. Remaining independent of the United States was for them the touchstone of national honour, wrote Parkin. The mere suspicion of disloyalty on the part of a few of its members had kept the Liberal party out of power in Ottawa for a period almost unprecedented in British lands.[13]

Imperial federation was the negation of Smith's defeatist vision and a positive answer to Canada's present dilemma. A few months earlier Oliver Mowat, campaigning against annexationism, had confronted

Canadians with a choice. As a people they were not yet ready for national independence: they must follow the British route or the American.[14] Parkin rejected Mowat's assumption that adherence to the empire was inconsistent with independence. On the contrary, for British colonies imperial federation was the highest form of independence: that of full and equal participation in a greater whole. 'Our admiration is not given to the independence of the American state, or the Canadian or Australian province when holding aloof from union, where we feel that a spirit of petty provincialism is at work ... We reserve our admiration for the reasoned and secured independence of a state whose members have abandoned the petty side of their individuality, and displayed that political self-restraint, sagacity, and largeness of view which is implied in wide organization for the attainment of great ends.'[15] In urging Canadians to reject the pettiness of colonial nationality in favour of full citizenship in the great British nation, Parkin spurned the mercenary terms in which Smith had cast his analysis. No noble public life could be founded on the principles of the counting-house. Commercial values might be strong, but nationality possessed a spiritual force that was stronger. Spiritualizing the National Policy, Parkin asserted that the struggle to compensate for U.S. protectionism had brought Canada a moral gain that far outweighed any material loss.

This argument met the federationist ideal of offering a compelling alternative to continentalist economic policies; but Parkin did not stop there. Like any good polemicist, he turned his enemy's own weapons back on him, rebutting Smith's contention that Canada's natural trade links were with the United States. The republic itself produced all the natural products that Canada could supply. Canada's market was the great British industrial economy, whose strengths were complementary to its own. Parkin's argument foreshadowed the policy with which a Liberal prime minister would shortly attempt to reconcile the British loyalism of some Canadians with others' resentment of the protective tariff. This was the policy of tariff preference for British imports, somewhat grudgingly embraced by Laurier in 1897 in order to put the best face on his conversion to the National Policy.[16]

So far, so good; but what about the problem that Goldwin Smith identified as the greatest obstacle to Canadian unity? Parkin recognized the French Canadian's parochialism and rooted antipathy to assimilation, but he dismissed them as irrelevant. The population of the yet unsettled North-West would be English-speaking. Quebec might persist as a backwater, but the inertia of its people could never inhibit Canadian development. Nor did he give much credence to Smith's notion that the

French might one day develop an affinity for the United States. The French-Canadian emigrant to New England displayed the same resistance to assimilation as his people at home. He could be counted on to defend his Canadian homeland against all comers, and in the event of war between Britain and France his loyalty to the empire was assured.

The French-Canadian problem declined in magnitude when considered from the viewpoint of British rather than Canadian national unity, and Parkin ingeniously turned it to his advantage by quoting John A. Macdonald. The year was 1889, a moment when anti-French fervour was at a peak in Manitoba and Ontario and when certain Québécois politicians, including members of Macdonald's own cabinet, were declaiming against the idea of imperial federation. The veteran statesman had told Parkin not to worry: French-Canadian adherence to the empire was guaranteed by the imperative of cultural survival on an English-speaking continent. For that, French Canadians relied on the good faith of the British government, as pledged in the Treaty of Paris and the Quebec Act. That compact was as dear to them as Magna Carta to the English, and either annexation to the United States or Canadian independence would be fatal to it. What Goldwin Smith saw as the prime impediment to Canadian nationalism, and what might prove a fatal flaw in a Canada separated from the empire, might actually be an asset to the cause of imperial federation.[17]

Like Oliver Mowat's idea of Confederation, presented to the electors of North Oxford on a snowy November morning twenty years earlier, Parkin's dream of imperial federation rested on a vision of the past. In Parkin's case it was that of Canadians united in century-old resistance to Americanism. Reaching for the language of reverent remembrance that the Loyalist centenary of 1884 had brought to full flower,[18] he affirmed that no victory that Britain had ever won on land or sea was more worthy to be blazoned on the pages of its history than the fidelity of that great body of men and women who, refusing to abjure their ancient allegiance, had given up their homes, their professions, and all that made life comfortable and, crossing over into a forest wilderness, had built up those provinces that had since grown into a great British confederation. Their descendants had nothing to regret in their choice. The events of a century – the invasions, boundary quarrels, and fishing disputes – had imbued Canadians as a whole with that same revulsion against Americanism, founded on devotion to the unity of the empire, which had animated the Loyalist émigrés. Canada's political institutions left nothing to be desired when compared to those of the United States. Goldwin

Smith's insistence that no barriers of principle or sentiment separated the mass of Canadians from their neighbours was simply wrong.[19]

In reality the future headmaster of Upper Canada College and the sometime professor of history at Oxford were not arguing on the same ground. Where Parkin depicted the present in the light of the past, Smith viewed the future in the light of the present. Smith foresaw the decline of those historic forces – Anglo-Canadian loyalism and French-Canadian conservatism – on which Parkin relied. Smith was the more penetrating and prescient, but perhaps Parkin had one crucial advantage over him. As the historian Frank Underhill was to remark in 1950, in a radio broadcast marking the fortieth anniversary of the sage's death, Smith had spent his life in an ivory tower, insulated from Toronto and from Canada by the bookshelves of his library in the Grange. If he had got out and met a few ordinary Canadians, it would have increased his faith in Canada's capacity to survive as an independent community.[20] Perhaps so. On the other hand, perhaps Parkin needed to meet a few ordinary French Canadians. In the near future, in any case, neither imperial loyalism nor pragmatic annexationism would win the day. The twentieth century would fulfil the vision of a man who combined Parkin's appeal to the past with Smith's anti-imperialism.

John Skirving Ewart was named after his paternal grandfather, a Scottish builder. In 1833 Lieutenant-Governor Sir John Colborne appointed the elder Ewart a magistrate of the town of York, the first mere tradesman to reach that rank in the status-conscious colonial capital. Thomas Ewart, the builder's son, shed further lustre on the family name as head boy of Upper Canada College, the academy founded by Colborne at the behest of the Rev. John Strachan to educate the provincial elite in classical languages and British principles.

John Ewart the builder was a Tory, of course, but in the altered Canada of the 1840s Thomas, like other communicants of the Church of Scotland, crossed over to Reform. He was an early friend of George Brown in Canada and took a prominent part in the first general meeting of the Reform Association of Canada, founded in 1844 under the leadership of Robert Baldwin to stand up for responsible government against the reactionary Governor General Sir Charles Metcalfe.[21] His son John was born in 1849, the year in which another governor general, Lord Elgin, symbolically registered the advent of responsible government by signing the Lower Canadian Rebellion Losses Act. Eighteen months later, Thomas Ewart died of tuberculosis.

John duly followed his father into Upper Canada College but earned there a different sort of distinction. He could not abide the regime, kicked over the traces, and was expelled. This did not stop him from launching a successful career as a lawyer, aided no doubt by his late father's brother-in-law and law partner, Oliver Mowat. In 1864 Uncle Oliver had become a judge, but young Ewart apprenticed in the office of another prominent Reformer, Samuel Blake. When Mowat quit the bench to succeed Edward Blake (Samuel's brother) as premier and attorney general of Ontario, Samuel stepped into the vacant judgeship and Ewart became a partner in Uncle Oliver's law firm.

In 1881 Ewart quit Toronto for Winnipeg for the sake of his health. After a brief partnership in Winnipeg with Ebenezer Vining Bodwell, who had figured so prominently in the Toronto Reform convention of 1859,[22] he joined forces with James Fisher, president of the provincial Liberal Association and member of the Manitoba legislature. He became Winnipeg's leading lawyer and, profiting from the collapse of the Manitoba property boom in 1883, made a fortune investing in land. He also plunged into western Canada's cultural and racial controversies, first conducting Louis Riel's unsuccessful appeal in 1885 against his conviction and capital sentence for high treason and then defending Riel's legacy to the francophones of Manitoba. In 1870, when negotiating the annexation of the Red River Colony to the Dominion of Canada, Riel had insisted that French should constitute an official language in the new province and that Catholics and Protestants should receive equal treatment in public schooling. The Manitoba Act was drafted to guarantee these conditions, but in 1890 the province's newly elected Liberal government abolished public funding for its Catholic schools, which mainly served the francophone minority. Ewart represented the deprived minority in court when it challenged the provincial school act as a breach of its rights under the Manitoba Act.

In the Supreme Court of Canada Ewart won a unanimous decision – no easy feat in constitutional litigation in the era of the provincial-rights controversy – only to see the case bungled by others on appeal to the Privy Council. In a subsequent suit, however, Edward Blake and he persuaded the Judicial Committee that the Parliament of Canada could override the Manitoba measure under section 93 of the BNA Act, which guaranteed certain educational rights and empowered Parliament to pass remedial legislation if a provincial government contravened those rights. The Conservative government of Sir Charles Tupper introduced such a bill in 1896, and it became the major issue in the Dominion election when the opposition accused the government of abusing provincial rights by resorting to coercion without first trying to negotiate a compromise. Laurier promised negotiation and employed Ewart as an intermediary to secure a commitment from Oliver Mowat, if the Liberals won the election, to join his cabinet and help in the bargaining. After the Liberals' victory, Mowat duly joined Laurier in working out a compromise with the government of Manitoba.[23]

In 1904 Ewart left Winnipeg for Ottawa, a better base for his growing practice in the Supreme Court and the Privy Council. There he took on a new role, that of nationalist orator and pamphleteer. During the next quarter-century, he would write and distribute a stream of papers on the problem of Canadian nationality, supplementing these with an equally copious, and to some minds tedious, outpouring of 'op-ed' articles and letters to the editor. An unsympathetic commentator recalled in 1927 that it was 'a very obscure Canadian newspaper indeed which was not regularly deluged with contributions from his pen. He brought very forcibly to the attention of Dominion editors the value of the wastebasket.'[24]

Ewart's nationalism grew out of his exposure to Prairie politics, which imbued him with a profound concern for the problem of Canadian unity. How could French- and English-speaking Canadians – not to mention the polyglot host of continental Europeans now flooding the Prairies – be brought to feel a common citizenship? In his view, the grand obstacle was the propensity of Canadians such as George Parkin to think of themselves as British rather than Canadian. An earlier generation of British North Americans had based its loyalty to the empire on an appreciation of British political virtues: in particular, the cultivation of an orderly liberty rooted in the rule of law. The loyalism of Ewart's time, however, shared the ugly racism that marred British nationalism. One consideration that Parkin, for instance, urged against annexation to the United States was the 'amazing flood of immigration' that was 'steadily diluting the Anglo-Saxon element' there.[25] Such attitudes could hardly appeal to the eastern Europeans who were so prominent in settling the Prairies, let alone to French Canadians.

Indeed, for some Canadian imperialists French Canadianism was the main enemy. The Conservative politician D'Alton McCarthy (of McCarthy Act fame), who led the campaign to extirpate the French fact in Canada, did so as president of the Imperial Federation League and in the name of British unity. 'This is a British country,' he declared, 'and the sooner we take in hand our French Canadian fellow subjects and make them British in sentiment and teach them the English language, the less trouble we shall have to prevent.'[26] McCarthy's words were not *quite* racist, but they were not apt to make French Canadians feel a community of interest with their anglophone compatriots.

For Ewart, an essential step towards Canadian unity was to establish full independence from Britain. Throughout the nineteenth century, British American ideas of independence had been coloured by the American Revolution. The very word conjured up the overthrow of monarchy and a severing of the British connection. That idea had rarely received strong support among English Canadians, and to Conservatives in particular it was a sort of disloyalty scarcely distinguishable from annexationism. Ewart, however, presented it in another light. He reminded Canadians of John A. Macdonald's wish that the confederation established in 1867 should be called the Kingdom of Canada, and he proposed that Canada should become independent as a parliamentary monarchy under its present sovereign.

Indeed (Ewart argued), considered in this light Canada was independent already. The country's legal subordination to the British Parliament was purely theoretical. He compared it to the monarch's legal power to veto bills passed by Parliament – the very analogy (though probably he did not know it) that the *Globe* had used in 1864 to belittle the proposed federal power to veto provincial legislation. 'Really, and indubitably,' he declared, 'Canada's power of self-government is complete and indisputable. No one imagines that, constitutionally, she can, in any way, be interfered with.' He quoted leading British statesmen to the same effect, among them Joseph Chamberlain, the chief British advocate of imperial federation.

It was still desirable, however, to abolish even the fiction of colonial subordination. As long as Canada remained part of the British empire, it ran the risk of becoming involved in British quarrels. There were also psychological advantages to be gained. Where George Parkin had asserted that Canadians, as citizens of the British empire, had no reason to feel inferior to citizens of the United States, Ewart resented Canada's condition as 'squalid and ignoble.' Facing the world as citizens of a sovereign country would enhance Canadians' prestige and self-esteem. This in turn would give them a solidarity that they now lacked.[27]

Among other things, settling Canada's destiny would remove the inhibitions that made so many Canadians nervous about trade agreements with the United States. Ewart was writing on the eve of the general election of 1911. Since 1891 the Americans had become more receptive to the idea of tariff reciprocity with Canada, and Laurier, after fifteen years of magisterial leadership, believed that he had acquired enough prestige at home to achieve a limited agreement at small political cost. A pact was duly negotiated, but Ontario manufacturing interests whipped up a demagogic campaign against it, questioning the loyalty of Laurier and his supporters as they had twenty years earlier. The Liberal government went down to an unexpected but decisive defeat.[28]

This episode confirmed Ewart's belief in the importance of persuading English Canadians to consider themselves as Canadian rather than British. Accordingly, he shaped his case for independence to appeal to supporters of imperial federation. Their project was identical to his own, he asserted – it was to establish an evident and indisputable equality between the King's subjects in Canada and those who resided in the United Kingdom. But they must acknowledge that their sentimental regard for the mother country had never been reciprocated. British politicians had always looked on the colonies as possessions, to be used for the benefit of the United Kingdom. For much of the nineteenth century, most had seen the colonies as a nuisance rather than an asset and had viewed the prospect of their separation from the empire with indifference if not gladness.

British attitudes had changed now that the British empire was but one among several world powers and imperial defence appeared to require colonial assistance. Even so, Britain's discovery of its dependence on the colonies had not helped Canada in the recent Alaska boundary arbitration, when Whitehall had sacrificed Canada's interests to a more important objective: harmonious relations with the United States. It would ever be thus while Britain controlled Canada's external affairs. Imperial federation could change nothing, when Canada's population was so much smaller than the United Kingdom's.[29]

Just as George Parkin had invoked history in aid of imperial federation, so Ewart did so in support of Canadian independence. In an essay entitled 'Colonial Disloyalty,' he mused provocatively on the readiness of so many British Americans to acquiesce in Westminster's claim to rule the colonies instead of claiming equality for their own legislative assemblies as the British Parliament's colonial counterparts. From generation to generation, loyalists such as John Beverley Robinson had bewailed every advance towards colonial self-government as a step towards the abyss, denouncing as rebels and traitors their fellow-colonists who strove for self-government. Unlike Robinson, today's loyalists applauded responsible government as the very salvation of the

British connection, and if Robinson were alive he would do so too. Yet, like them, he would also deplore any further step towards Canada's independence as a fatal blow to the British connection. Like them, he would condemn as 'disloyalty' a yearning that flowed inevitably from Canadians' possession of a truly British trait: the aptitude and craving for self-government.[30]

By evoking the shade of Robinson and raising the standard of 'colonial disloyalty,' Ewart pointedly placed his advocacy of independence in the Reform tradition. Like the first campaigners for responsible government, he took his stand against imperial authority and its colonial minions. His attitude reveals the confrontation between himself and Goldwin Smith on the one side, and the imperial federationists on the other, as a projection into the twentieth century of a primary antithesis of Canadian politics since the 1820s. Like Smith, he insisted that Canada was North American before it was British and must inevitably secede from the British empire. Unlike Smith, however, he saw separation coming through independence, not through annexation to the United States.

Ewart's conception of Canada's destiny was in fact the optimistic correlative of Goldwin Smith's pessimism. The difference reflected the change in Canada's fortunes over twenty years. In the newly settled wilderness of the North-West Territories, massive immigration had given rise to two new provinces, Saskatchewan and Alberta. Canada's trade with Britain was booming, aided by technology that facilitated the transoceanic export of meat and dairy products. With a French Canadian, Laurier, presiding capably over Canada's destinies on Parliament Hill, the cultural rift between French- and English-speakers no longer seemed an insuperable barrier to the consolidation of what George Cartier, speaking in 1865, had called a political nationality.[31]

Smith, Parkin, and Ewart embodied three distinct visions of Canada that possessed English-Canadian political thinkers about the turn of the century, but one thing they shared was a contempt for provincialism. Smith of course had an all-embracing contempt for Canadian politics, but it arose from his belief that Canada was incapable of transcending provincialism to achieve genuine nationality. Parkin extolled imperial federation as a sort of nationalism that did transcend 'petty provincialism.' But what about Ewart, who had so pointedly tied his cause to the great Reform tradition? Surely Oliver Mowat's nephew, of all people, must sympathize with the provincial outlook on Canadian politics? Far from it: his hostility would reveal itself in 1930, when Howard Ferguson invoked the compact theory of Confederation against the prospective enactment of the Statute of Westminster. The altered outlook of the Canadian intelligentsia had turned him, like other liberals, into a devotee of central power.

13

English Canada Forgets

The Statute of Westminster fulfilled Ewart's vision of Canada's destiny. By then he had become mentor to a younger generation of Canadian nationalists – men forty and fifty years his junior, such as Frank Underhill and Frank Scott. Underhill wrote short studies of both Ewart and Goldwin Smith in pursuit of his lifelong quest to define Canadian Liberalism;[1] Scott and others followed Ewart in campaigning for an end to judicial appeals to the Privy Council.[2] Ewart's part in the meeting of the Canadian Political Science Association in Ottawa in 1931 symbolized his patriarchal status. He was chairman and commentator at the momentous session in which Norman Rogers demolished the compact theory of Confederation and Scott presented his first general statement on the Canadian constitution. In his commentary, he damned the compact theory as heartily as Rogers did.[3]

Ewart's encounter with the compact theory is a remarkable moment in the history of Canadian political thought. Most of the leading nationalists of the 1930s and 1940s were born between 1889 (Underhill and Arthur Lower) and 1902 (Creighton). In trying to explain their ignorance of the Reform tradition and its implications for Confederation, phrases such as 'gap in historical consciousness' or 'rupture of collective memory' come easily to mind and seem to make sense. But Ewart was born in 1849. He was Oliver Mowat's nephew and a constitutional lawyer. Not even such senior nationalists of the 1930s as J.W. Dafoe (born 1866) possessed his familiarity with the thought underlying Mowat's campaign for provincial rights and the compact theory of Confederation as articulated by Mowat and Honoré Mercier in 1887.[4] If we can fathom *his* attitude in 1930, it will help us understand the lacuna at the heart of Canadian nationalism.

Ewart had no dogmatic objection to the idea that a statute might constitute a compact. During the Manitoba school controversy of the 1890s he had published a long essay presenting the Manitoba Act as a treaty. He based his argument on a detailed reconstruction of the train of events leading from Canada's acquisition of Rupert's Land in 1869 to the implementation of the Manitoba Act a year later. The act had resulted from negotiations between Louis Riel's emissaries and the government of Canada, based on a list of demands presented by Riel's envoys. Those demands had included official status for the French language and the establishment of separate schools along the same lines as those in Ontario and Quebec, and the language of the Manitoba Act reflected Ottawa's intention to entrench those provisions in the provincial constitution. The act itself had been formally accepted by the legislature of the Red River Colony as a basis for annexation to the Dominion. These facts proved its status as a treaty between the government of Canada and the people of the colony.[5]

When, more than thirty years later, Ewart confronted the compact theory of Confederation as invoked by Howard Ferguson, he approached it empirically, just as he had the Manitoba Act. In this case, however, he concluded that the facts did not justify the theory. The negotiations between colonial leaders did not suffice – like J.W. Dafoe and Norman Rogers, and later Frank O'Connor, he dismissed the Quebec resolutions of 1864 as irrelevant and noted that the London resolutions of 1866 had not been submitted to the colonial legislatures.[6] This reasoning shows that by 1930 the octogenarian Ewart had lost sight of the *facts* that justified the idea of Confederation as an interprovincial compact. The question is how that happened.

A good starting-point for our inquiry is the estrangement of the English-speaking intelligentsia from the Reform tradition. As I said in chapter 12, for much of the nineteenth century the objectives of Reform politics had appealed to liberal intellectuals because they seemed to embody leading liberal ideas. By the end of the century this was no longer true; the cause of provincial rights had lost its lustre and become merely 'provincial.' But the rejection of provincial rights did not take the form of some noisy and principled rebellion of the mind: that did not happen for a generation. In the meantime, provincial rights simply ceased to matter.

You can hear that silence in Ewart's writing. Not only did he not write about federal–provincial relations, but he failed to do so on occasions when, had the subject been controversial, it must have come to mind. One small example is his comment in 1916 on the case of the *Bonanza Creek Gold Mining Co. v. The King*, in which the Privy Council decided that a company incorporated by a provincial legislature could operate anywhere in Canada, not just within the incorporating province. F.R. Scott would later condemn this ruling as a landmark in the extension of provincial legislative power over trade and commerce at Ottawa's expense. Ewart himself impeached it as one of the worst judgments that the Privy Council had ever delivered on the BNA Act, proof positive of its incompetence to deal with Canadian matters. But he did not even mention the division of powers: his criticism had nothing to do with federal–provincial relations.[7]

A more telling example of Ewart's indifference to the topic is a short piece on the Canadian constitution that appeared in 1908 in an American law review. This article said nothing about the division of legislative powers or any other aspect of the provinces' constitutional status. Not only that: its perspective on Confederation was quite at odds with his attack on the compact theory twenty-two years later. To illustrate the growth of colonial self-government, he contrasted Canada's current constitution with earlier ones. Those had been drafted in London with little or no colonial consultation, but the BNA Act had been drafted in Canada, agreed to by Canadians, and only then taken to London to be enacted. The fact that 'some changes had been made in Downing Street, and agreed to by the Canadian delegates there,' made no difference to its basically consensual nature.[8] In short, the Quebec agreement was what counted: a far cry from his position in 1930, when he dismissed the Quebec resolutions and belittled the role of colonial consent in general.

Ewart's silence in 1908 and 1916 illustrates the insignificance of provincial rights as a topic of political controversy during the thirty years following Laurier's accession to office in 1896. During those thirty years, Canada changed greatly, and the world even more. Industrialization and urbanization put a new set of social concerns on the Canadian political agenda. Problems of urban disease and poverty that had long occupied European governments now began to plague North America. Capitalism ceased for ever to be primarily a matter of individual entrepreneurship and became the concern of massive corporations.

Confronting these developments, liberalism itself changed – not only in Canada but in Europe and the United States as well. Liberals became less preoccupied with relations between the individual and the state and more with moderating gross inequalities of wealth within society. In the mouths of Edward Blake and David Mills, provincial and individual autonomy had been virtually synonymous; to them federal and provincial governments were antithetical, just as the state and the individual were. To twentieth-century liberals a government was a government, and the key question was which one – federal or provincial – was better suited to dealing with the problems of urban society and confronting the selfish power of large corporations. Increasingly they opted for Ottawa.[9]

Meanwhile, Ewart single-mindedly pursued the objectives of Canadian unity and independence. In the process he endured, in a very personal way, the trauma of the Great War. He watched and worried as the conscription crisis of 1917 sundered British and French Canadians as nothing had before. He watched and worried as British statesmen strove to control Canada's wealth and power for the sake of the imperial war effort. It was too much, and watching and worrying exploded into impassioned protest. At the outbreak of war he had stopped beating the drum for Canadian independence, but in August 1917 he issued, as the last of his series *The Kingdom Papers*, a short book entitled *Imperial Projects and the Republic of Canada*. In strident tones he announced his conclusion that Canada must throw off the British yoke even at the price of rejecting monarchy itself.[10]

Eventually, by sapping British power and prestige, the war brought an independent kingdom of Canada in sight. But at what cost: the slaughter of millions and the overthrow of empires – one need not admire the empires to be stunned by the manner and consequences of their passing. Ewart began to mute his professed republicanism only several years after the war, when his old ideal of an independent kingdom of Canada seemed about to be realized.[11] And it was just then that provincial politicians raised the banner of provincial rights, rousing the compact theory of Confederation from its long torpor in order to block the very act that would achieve his ideal: Westminster's formal acknowledgment of Canadian independence.

In the decades since Laurier's accession to office, provincial rights had not profited the cause of Canadian unity. In 1905 the sacred principle had been invoked against the establishment of Catholic separate schools and the French language in the new provinces of Saskatchewan and Alberta. In 1912 the Conservative government of Ontario had abruptly renounced Mowat's old policy of tolerating francophone public education in French-speaking areas. Three years later, with Canada at war and a long, bruising struggle over French-language education still raging in Ontario, the Liberals had returned to power in Manitoba committed to abolishing the school compromise of 1896, which Ewart had done so much to achieve.[12] And now, in the 1920s, provincial politicians began invoking the compact theory against a measure that he had long considered essential to the consolidation of a Canadian political nationality.

Clearly the compact theory was raised in the 1920s under circumstances that must have predisposed Ewart to reject its applicability. Does that suggest that he challenged the theory with arguments that he knew to be false? Not necessarily: quite possibly, after so many years spent advocating and justifying Canadian independence, he had simply forgotten why the arguments in favour of the theory were *not* false. The passage of thirty fraught years and the long hibernation of federal-provincial controversy: these were partly to blame for his forgetting. But there were other reasons too, relating to his personality and profession and to the influence that these exerted on his approach to history.

Ewart based his argument for Canadian independence on extensive historical research, only fragments of which ever appeared in print. The partial manuscript of a projected constitutional history of Canada in thirteen volumes rests today in the National Archives at Ottawa, and his researches were not confined to Canada. He spent years on a two-volume analysis of the causes of the Great War, published in 1925 by a leading New York house. Then he began issuing a new series of pamphlets in support of Canadian independence, including a collection of essays entitled 'British Foreign Policy and the Next War.' These documented British responsibility for a series of conflicts ranging from the Great War and the French Revolutionary War at one extreme of magnitude to the Afghan Wars and the Zulu War – bloody colonial conflicts of the 1870s and 1880s – at the other.[13]

Naturally, so politically charged an approach to history did not pass unchallenged. Even before the First World War the Toronto historian Edward Kylie, who was to die in the war, had impeached Ewart's work for its 'unhistorical temper.' Ewart was 'too ready to judge the people of every age by his modern wisdom' instead of evaluating their policies and actions with an eye to the historical context. 'Mr. Ewart is writing history, not for its own sake, but with a political purpose,' Kylie concluded. 'The result is, as in nearly all such cases, bad history, and it is to be feared bad politics.'[14] Another historian, W.L. Grant, son of George Monro Grant, the champion of imperial federation, ascribed Ewart's failings to his profession. Grant contended that lawyers were almost invariably bad historians.[15] Their object was to prove their case and win the verdict, and to this end they often imposed a tendentious simplicity on the complexity of the past. They sifted out the facts that might help their case and ignored the rest. 'In dealing with history, such a man tends to think that he has proved everything by an appropriate quotation, and as Goldwin Smith has very truly said, "Nothing can stand against a really resolute quoter."'

So Kylie and Grant said much the same about Ewart as I have said about F.R. Scott: they accused him of quarrying the past for data that would support his argument and ignoring whatever might contradict it. Ewart took these charges seriously. Like Scott, he set great store by the authority of history; and he prided himself on his historical technique. Being neither a fool nor wholly mistaken in his views, he defended himself rather effectively. Looking back, his admirer Frank Underhill was able to applaud his insight and prophetic accuracy compared with the imperialistic delusions of his academic detractors.

Yet there was more than a grain of truth in Grant's remarks. Ewart was indeed a resolute quoter – he may well have set an example in this for Scott and other centralist writers of the younger generation. More important, like nearly every British thinker of his time – the heyday of the so-called Whig interpretation of history – he saw history as a story of progressive advance towards liberty, with Britain and its self-governing colonies leading the way. For Canada, in his view, full independence was the inevitable next step along that path. Naturally he seized on facts and statements that seemed to foreshadow that outcome and overlooked the rest.[16]

Either to convince Conservative imperialists or to confound them, Ewart gladly cited the nation-building rhetoric of John A. Macdonald and other Fathers of Confederation, often with scant regard for the context in which they had spoken. This habit got him into trouble with Sir Joseph Pope, Macdonald's biographer and sometime private secretary, who resented what he saw as Ewart's abuse of the great man's memory.[17] More important in shaping Ewart's understanding of Confederation was his use of the Reform tradition. As a Grit contending for colonial independence, he naturally celebrated the tradition of 'colonial disloyalty' associated with the Baldwins – the tradition of struggle for self-rule against the British government and its local Tory enforcers such as John Beverley Robinson, whom he argumentatively identified with the imperialists of his own day; but his nationalism led him to imagine this tradition as a Canadian struggle, although Canada as he knew it had not existed then. Identifying with his predecessors' struggle against British authority, Ewart ignored its reincarnation as an Upper Canadian and Ontarian struggle against the perceived oppression of French Canada and its Tory enforcers. And so Ewart imperceptibly excised provincial rights from the Reform tradition.

These gradual transformations of thought in an ageing man's mind were emanations not merely of a 'lawyer's mentality' but of a lawyer's culture. The Baldwins, lawyers themselves, had based their campaign for responsible government not on any ideology specific to Upper Canada but on an abstract idea of the constitutional rights of British subjects living in British colonies. In the abstract, this argument applied equally to Upper Canada and United Canada, and after Confederation it was easily transferable to Canadian claims to full independence. It came naturally to Ewart, as a constitutional lawyer, to appropriate the Baldwinite argument and apply it to Canada, supposing that in doing so he was following the true Reform tradition. And in the abstract he was; but his supposition ignored the fact that, to many Reformers, the appeal of responsible government lay in its promise of autonomy for the particular community with which they identified. That community was not 'Canada,' still less some abstract colonial entity: it was Upper Canada, and later Ontario.

Other features of the intellectual climate may also have prompted Ewart to 'nationalize' the struggle for responsible government as he did. Historians had been writing of the coming of responsible government to 'Canada' ever since the publication of John Mercier McMullen's *History of Canada* in 1855, when 'Canada' meant only United Canada and the Reform struggle against 'Lower Canadian domination' had barely begun. Another possible influence was the transformation of liberalism, which obliterated its old congruence with the doctrine of provincial rights but made it no less nationalistic, especially when it came to asserting the right of nations to self-government. Obsessively urging the right of the Canadian nation to complete self-determination, assiduously applying the history of the Reform movement to that purpose alone, Ewart lost sight of the historical justification for provincial claims that seemed to oppose his ideal of Canadian nationality.

Ewart died in 1933. The Statute of Westminster had become law fifteen months earlier, and he could well feel that he had had a hand in that momentous event – Prime Minister Bennett told him so. True, Canadian legal appeals still went to Whitehall, and formal control over the Canadian constitution still reposed at Westminster; but these were details that time would surely rectify. Ewart died believing that his life's work had been crowned with success.[18] But there was a worm in the apple, one which Ewart did not live to encounter. In causing him to forget the history that justified provincial claims to constitutional equality with Ottawa, his dream of Canadian nationality had taken a self-defeating turn. French Canada had been left behind.

This turn was the more tragic because the auspices had been so promising. Ewart's championing of Franco-Manitoban rights and hostility to Canadian entanglement in imperial adventures, or even imperial defence, had engendered a long political rapport with the Quebec nationalist Henri Bourassa. His defence of the Franco-Manitobans went beyond legalities to an impassioned repudiation of the jingoistic British nationalism that animated his opponents, and his Canadian nationalism was founded on a frank acceptance of Canada's cultural duality. Bourassa was a precocious politician in his early twenties when the Manitoba school question arose. The older man's advocacy moved and influenced him.

But time would reveal that the two men's mutual sympathy rested on a fault-line of irreconcilable differences. One was their attitude towards the British connection. Ewart's commitment to Canadian independence flowed from his belief that the fondness of many Canadians for the British empire prevented Canadians of all cultures from forming a sense of common nationality. Only the experience of coexistence in an independent state could engender a Canadian national feeling. Bourassa, by contrast, epitomized that French-Canadian diffidence towards the prospect of independence on which George Parkin had quoted John A. Macdonald. Despite his dislike of British imperialism and its Canadian worshippers, Bourassa saw the British connection as a shield for French Canadianism. He was reluctant to forgo its protection until a sense of common nationality, based on a mutual acceptance of cultural differences, had become established in the Canadian political culture.

Alongside this irreconcilable clash of priorities there grew, unperceived, a gulf between the two men's conception of Canadian nationality itself. It originated in a difference in their understandings of Confederation. Despite his concern for the plight of French Canadians outside Quebec, Bourassa remained wedded to the provincial compact theory as a last line of defence against possible Anglo-Canadian efforts to undermine French Canadianism in Quebec itself. Here too, Ewart's departure from the Reform tradition as articulated by his uncle Oliver

Mowat led him in a direction that Bourassa could not follow: that of a centralist compact theory, which saw Ottawa as the protector of minority rights.[19]

If there was no interprovincial compact – if Quebec did not share with the other provinces even a limited right of veto over constitutional change – how did Confederation provide for the secure coexistence of French Canada with the majority culture? In 1881, confronting the Quebec jurist T.-J.-J. Loranger, William McDougall had raised this question in the *Escheats Case*. McDougall granted that French Canadians might have brought into Confederation some rights derived from imperial recognition of their special status, but he denied that these had anything to do with the province of Quebec. Omitting the Constitutional Act of 1791 from the genealogy of the compact theory, he declared: 'Those rights were not secured to Quebec according to her present limitary lines. They were conceded to the French population who were scattered at that time over the whole northern part of this continent ... They extended to the *people*, and not to any geographical or territorial circumscription or boundary.'[20]

If Quebec were not the protector of French-Canadian rights, what authority was? McDougall ignored the question, but two answers were possible: Britain and Ottawa. At least the first answer fitted Bourassa's idea of the British empire as a bulwark between French Canada, Christian and pastoral, and the English-speaking materialism that he called *l'américanisme saxonisante*. But how could that answer suffice in an independent Canada? Saxonizing, secularizing Americanism was not confined to the United States – it was a continental phenomenon, which had shown its baleful power since Confederation in New Brunswick, in Ontario, on the Prairies. How could British authority protect French Canada once the BNA Act was brought under Canadian control and judicial appeals no longer went to the Privy Council?

It was not Ewart who confronted this question but a man fifty years younger. In an article of 1930, Frank Scott dismissed the idea that the Privy Council had ever effectively defended minority rights in Canada. It had certainly upheld provincial rights, but what had that done for French Canadians outside Quebec? Nowadays francophones were spreading throughout Canada. Surely it was to their advantage to have power concentrated at Ottawa, where their political influence was much greater than in any province outside Quebec. Later Scott would state outright that the BNA Act made Ottawa the guardian of minority rights against the provinces. He cited Ottawa's power to veto provincial legislation and to compel the provinces to respect minority rights in education.[21]

Such arguments could do nothing to reassure French Canadians who feared the menace of saxonizing Americanism within Canada. Scott might prove to his own satisfaction that the Privy Council had done nothing for minority rights, but he could not demonstrate to their satisfaction that the Supreme Court of Canada had done any better. As for the veto, Ottawa had never used it to protect minorities, and the power itself was all but defunct. And how had Ottawa's coercive power in regard to education helped the francophones of Manitoba? Everything went to show that a sovereign province of Quebec, armed with the power to veto constitutional reform, was French Canada's only hope. French Canadians such as Bourassa could never accept an idea of Canadian nationality founded on Ottawa's dominance over the provinces, any more than Ontario Reformers could accept it in the 1880s.

If French and English Canadians could not come together on the basis of nationalism, they could still do so, like Mowat and Mercier in 1887, on that of support for provincial rights. Howard Ferguson and his Quebec counterpart, Louis-Alexandre Taschereau, demonstrated this in 1927, when the Ontarian cemented their alliance against insurgent centralism by abolishing Regulation 17, the controversial order that had curtailed French-language public education in Ontario fifteen years earlier. The demonstration was the more telling because it was Ferguson, an Orangeman from eastern Ontario, who had led the campaign for Regulation 17. Ferguson's retreat handed Taschereau a satisfying victory over Bourassa, now editor of the Montreal newspaper *Le Devoir*. Bourassa had blasted the Liberal premier for truckling to the Tories, but now Taschereau's accommodating tactics succeeded where Bourassa's confrontational approach had failed.[22]

I have ascribed English Canada's forgetting of the history that underlay the provincial compact theory to the demise of the Reform tradition, and I have used John Ewart's career to suggest how that happened. But a major question remains unanswered. Politically speaking, Howard Ferguson was Ewart's opposite. He was a Tory and an Orangeman, whose father had been elected to the House of Commons five times in a row as a supporter of John A. Macdonald. He was a dedicated imperialist, not obviously susceptible to any of the influences that induced Ewart's political amnesia.[23] Yet as the outcry against the interprovincial theory grew in English-speaking Canada, neither he nor any other Conservative managed to mount a coherent historical defence of the theory.[24] Why not?

The answer, I think, is this. Among English-speaking Canadians, it was Upper Canadians of the Reform tradition who felt the historical justification for provincial rights. For them provincial autonomy was not just a constitutional principle but the cherished prize of a historic struggle. To Conservatives such as Ferguson, provincial rights rested on a different basis. They existed because the judges said so, and history had nothing to do with it. When Ferguson invoked the compact theory in 1930, he noted the federal character of the Quebec resolutions and their description by Cartier and Macdonald as a treaty, but he relied just as much on *Hodge v. The Queen* and the *Maritime Bank Case*, the two crucial Privy Council judgments that asserted the constitutional equality of provinces and Dominion.[25]

History's irrelevance was reinforced by the legal culture of the time. Discussing Lord Haldane's rejection of the Lemieux Act in 1926, I noted that the dominant legal thought of the day shunned historical evidence as an aid to interpreting statutes. Haldane's career spanned the period when this approach was in the ascendant; in fact, his neglect of history in 1926 is oddly reminiscent of his argument as counsel for Ontario in the *Prohibition Case* nearly thirty years earlier. In a last-ditch defence of the centralist interpretation of the division of powers, John Wellington Gwynne of the Supreme Court had quoted John A. Macdonald, and the British ministers responsible for the BNA Act, in order to prove its centralist design. Haldane dismissed this argument as 'a little odd.' Gwynne's judgment contained 'a great many very edifying things like speeches from people who introduced these things into Parliament, and a number of other things which are of great historical value but not otherwise pertinent.'[26]

History was irrelevant. In interpreting statutes, judges were supposed to be guided by fundamental principles of law. On political platforms Mowat and his allies might defend provincial rights by appealing to history, but success in the law courts depended on their skill in relating those rights to the principles of British common-law constitutionalism: in particular, the ideal of the individual's autonomy vis-à-vis the state. So it was, thirty years later, in the mind of a lawyer called Howard Ferguson, that provincial rights had no basis in Canadian history but only in the words of the BNA Act as interpreted by judges. They were a set of propositions of positive law, which Ferguson valued because they upheld provincial claims against the ambitions of centralizing Liberals.

This approach helped Ferguson to fend off federal claims to regulate insurance and water-rights – matters on which the courts had laid down the law[27] – but was less useful in sustaining the theory of Confederation as an interprovincial compact. That idea was expressed neither in the BNA Act nor in any judicial decisions but was implicit in the circumstances under which Confederation had come to pass. It could not flourish if Canadians read the BNA Act and the speeches of the Fathers of Confederation without remembering the world that had brought men to write and say those words.

By 1930, however, the provincialist idea of Confederation was a vine-strangled tree, held upright by a constricting girdle of doctrine but only feebly nourished by the sap of historical recollection. And now, with the transformation of liberalism throughout the English-speaking world, a new legal paradigm emerged to challenge the old orthodoxy. It rejected the idea of law as the application of fundamental principles to particular cases. It adjured judges to interpret the law in a fashion that served modern social needs. Its American exponents called themselves legal realists.[28] Their Canadian counterparts demanded an interpretation of the BNA Act that would empower the federal government to manage an industrialized economy. Scornful of the old school's Olympian detachment, they went back to history, using Ewart's method of 'resolute quotation' to expose the travesty that they believed Haldane and company had made of the BNA Act and charging supporters of the compact theory with twisting the facts of history.[29] Now the academics were massed in the centralist camp, just as, before the First World War, they had been in the imperialist camp; but there was no provincialist Ewart to take them on. Partisans of provincial rights retreated to the shrinking high ground of legal orthodoxy, abandoning history to the foe.

Among the francophones of Quebec, by contrast, the constitutional thought of Loranger and Bourassa, and the memories in which it was embedded, remained vigorous. As late as 1956 it found authoritative expression in the report of Quebec's Royal Commission of Inquiry on Constitutional Problems, called the Tremblay Commission after its chairman, Judge Thomas Tremblay. One of the commissioners was the Jesuit historian Richard Arès. Between 1941 and 1967 Arès published several treatises documenting the character of the BNA Act as both a provincial and a national compact. The Tremblay Report asserted the same view and insisted also on Quebec's special status within Confederation. Quebec was not a province like the others, because Confederation

had made it the sole guardian of French-Canadian civilization throughout the Dominion. Any move by Ottawa to foster francophone culture,
except through the agency of the government of Quebec, was a usurpation of Quebec's special mission.[30]

The Tremblay Commission reviewed some of the same historical
sources as centralists such as Norman Rogers and F.R. Scott, but it read
them with different eyes. As Goldwin Smith had noted in 1877,[31] the
Québécois had accepted Confederation not as a nation-building venture
but as a divorce from Upper Canada. To most of their descendants,
accordingly, the BNA Act was simply the latest expression of the
original *pacte solennel*, the foundation of their national life within the
British empire. They took literally the contemporary descriptions of the
Quebec and London resolutions as a treaty and the later judicial declarations that the BNA Act was in effect a treaty too.

For English-Canadian intellectuals, however, confident in their own
nationalist understanding of Canadian history, it was easy to dismiss
this Québécois idea of Confederation as the anxious mythologizing of a
backward people. Goldwin Smith had also remarked that French Canadians were governed by the priest, with the occasional assistance of the
notary. Eighty years later this was only just ceasing to be true. Francophone Quebec was still turned in on itself, its wagons circled against the
clamorous siege of saxonizing Americanism. Priests controlled its education and its labour unions. Maurice Duplessis, the populist premier
who had set up the Tremblay Commission, may have been something of
a social and economic modernizer, but this trait was hidden from
English-Canadian eyes by his corrupt politics and repressive government. Like other nationalist Québécois, he viewed with the same jaun-
diced eye the centralist idea of Confederation, the expansion of the
federal welfare state, and the creation of the Canada Council to foster
Canadian culture.[32]

Duplessis insisted on Quebec's right to veto constitutional reform but
was sometimes a little vague as to the rights of other provinces. In 1946,
for instance, he conceded that the right of veto might be confined to the
four original provinces.[33] Such inconsistency, together with the nationalist insistence on Quebec's special role, influenced English-Canadian
attitudes towards the compact theory of Confederation. With the with-
ering of its roots in English-Canadian memory, the theory began to look
like the special pleading of a group perversely resistant to full participation in the great national adventure.

Part Four

1940–1982:
Continentalism and Nationalisms

14

The New Canadian Nationalism

On the eve of the Second World War, English-Canadian thinking was dominated by the continentalist nationalism expounded by John Ewart, which visualized Canadian society as North American rather than British. The First World War had placed this nationalism in the ascendant, but the Second, by virtue of its effects on the international order, would gravely compromise it. One sign of this change was a revival of anti-Americanism; another was a shift in historical consciousness. Writing for an international audience in 1958, one writer interpreted the one change in terms of the other under the title 'Canada Rediscovers Its History.'[1]

But a vital part of Canadian history remained undiscovered. The new Canadian nationalism was no less centralist than the old, as we will see in the response of leading anglophone intellectuals to the heightened militancy of Quebec nationalism in the 1960s. The resulting clash between the two nationalisms reached a climax in the patriation controversy of 1980 to 1982. This chapter examines the new nationalism, chapter 15 its response to the Quiet Revolution, and chapter 16 the patriation controversy.

We can detect the shift in historical consciousness in a talk given by Donald Creighton in 1947 to the Graduate History Club at the University of Toronto under the title 'John A. Macdonald and Canadian Historians.' Why, asked Creighton, had so little been published during the past thirty years on the life of Canada's first prime minister? His answer: Macdonald was a Conservative, and the historical profession was dominated by Liberals. He launched into a sarcastic account of what he called the Liberal or Grit interpretation of Canadian history: a drab saga of prophets such as Robert Baldwin, wise kings such as Lord Elgin, great moments of deliverance from bondage such as the formation of the Reform ministry in 1848, and horrid plagues and tribulations, as when Governors Metcalfe and Head were sent to smite the chosen people. To be exposed to this Liberal litany, with its unrelenting and tendentious emphasis on politics, was to undergo (said Creighton) an experience of colossal tedium.[2]

Creighton blamed the failings of Canadian historical writing on the dominance of journalism and politics in nineteenth-century intellectual life. Here he launched into a surprisingly bitter assault on the Victorian pundit Goldwin Smith. With his prestige as a former Regius Professor at Oxford, Smith might have stood up for the values of detachment, urbanity, and moderation; he might have stood up for civilization. He had had a following awaiting him: the young idealists of the Canada First party, so disillusioned with the pettiness and corruption of Canadian politics. But he had let them down and disappointed an entire generation of Canadians. True, Smith had stood ostentatiously aloof from both political parties and affected a detachment from public life; but that was just a pose. In reality he was a one-man party, the Goldwin Smith party, to which he had attached himself with all his petulant vanity and rancorous vindictiveness. He was a debater, who always fought to win.

Why this unexpected attack on the long-dead Smith? Creighton himself was not immune to the weaknesses of vanity and vindictiveness, and within the history department at Toronto they tended to focus on Frank Underhill. Creighton's senior by a dozen years, Underhill had glided through the Great Depression on a full professor's salary, while Creighton struggled as a lecturer. But during those difficult years Creighton had completed his great work *The Commercial Empire of the St. Lawrence*, and two years later he had produced *British North America at Confederation* for the Royal Commission on Dominion–Provincial Relations (the Rowell-Sirois Commission). Since then he had also published *Dominion of the North*, his general history of Canada. In all that time, Underhill had written – what? Quite a bit, actually; but there was no book, and most of Underhill's writing was not scholarship at all. It was gadfly journalism in the manner of his hero Goldwin Smith, except that Underhill sought to improve on Smith by criticizing Canadian politics according to a generous notion of social justice, not in terms of some abstract standard of liberty and political propriety.[3]

Actually, Underhill may well have relished Creighton's opening salvoes against the Liberal interpretation. They were aimed not at him but at the fuddy-duddy constitutional history favoured by their department chairman, Chester Martin, and another Toronto eminence, W.P.M. Kennedy, dean of the law school. Underhill had spent most of the 1920s in Saskatchewan, and the populist fervour of Prairie politics in those years had helped him discover the similar ferment that had sustained the Reform party of George Brown and Edward Blake half a century earlier. Ever since then he had mocked the pieties of the constitutional school, condemning it for its neglect of class conflict and its smug assumption of the superiority of Canada's British institutions to those of the United States.[4]

But even if Underhill enjoyed Creighton's opening bombardment, he may not have been surprised when the sudden thud of exploding metal around Goldwin Smith signalled a change of target. In any case, Creighton now unleashed a barrage against what he called the nationalist interpretation of Canadian history, signifying the modern trend in Grit history that followed Smith in playing down Canada's British heritage and insisting on the essentially American nature of English-speaking Canadians. He singled out the Winnipeg journalist J.W. Dafoe for the title of his book *Canada – An American Nation* and the Harvard historian W.B. Munro for his book *American Influences on Canadian Government*, but he might just as easily have named others still living or closer at hand. He might have named Arthur Lower, the Winnipeg historian whose history of Canada, *Colony to Nation*, had just entered the lists against his own *Dominion of the North*.[5] And he might have mentioned the other leading nationalist historian of the day, Frank Underhill.

As Creighton described it, nationalist history was obsessed with the twin achievements of Responsible Government and Dominion Status (the attainment of full independence under the British Crown). These it misrepresented as the fruits of a constant and bitter struggle against imperial oppression, when in fact they were the outcome of a long process of bargaining, adjustment, and reorganization, in which the British had sometimes taken the lead. The reality of Canadian nationality depended at least as much on Canada's separate existence within North America as on its autonomy within the British Empire; but nationalist history consistently ignored that fact. 'Other "imperialisms" were supposititious, and fictitious; British imperialism alone was horribly real.'[6]

Forty years earlier, such an assault might well have been aimed at Underhill's hero John Ewart, but in 1947 Creighton commended Ewart in order to condemn others. At least Ewart had shared Macdonald's ideal of a kingdom of Canada. No modern Liberal would dream of calling Canada a kingdom, although many were sick of the term Dominion, which Macdonald had had to accept as second best. But though Creighton discreetly ignored Ewart's republican phase the better to attack the crypto-republicanism of living Grits, in essence his quarrel was one that W.L. Grant and Edward Kylie had had with Ewart, and George Parkin with Goldwin Smith.[7] Had the North American environment moulded Canadians into a people that was more American than British in character? Was Canada's natural economic partner the United States rather than Britain? To both questions Creighton answered 'No.' Did Canada owe Britain a debt of gratitude for protecting it against American expansionism? Creighton thought it did.

What had happened to revive the old quarrel just then, in 1947? Nothing less than the sudden and complete collapse of the historical conditions that had made for 'the separateness of Canada in North America.' Canada had grown to political maturity guarded from American expansionism by British gunboats, its economy nourished by British financial might. But the collapse of British imperial power in 1940, followed by a long, wasting struggle on three continents, had reduced the old protector to military and economic decrepitude, leaving Canada cheek by jowl with a militarized United States.

Creighton and Underhill viewed these changes differently. Creighton eyed with foreboding the rise of the American empire. He saw the United Nations intervention in Korea in 1950 as an adventure in American imperialism and resented Canada's part in it. These apprehensions affected his politics. During the war he had approved of close military cooperation with the United States, as expressed in the permanent joint defence pact signed in 1940 at Ogdensburg, New York; but now he began to see Liberal policy since 1940 as a wholesale sell-out of Canada's political and economic independence. Oscar Skelton, one of the specific targets of his talk on Macdonald and Canadian historians, was a leading architect of this policy as undersecretary (deputy minister) for external affairs. Twenty-five years later, Creighton would angrily recall how Skelton and his political master, Liberal prime minister Mackenzie King, had worked steadily to remove Canada from a British imperial system in which it enjoyed a recognized position and considerable authority to an American one in which it had no standing or influence whatever.[8]

Underhill, in contrast, viewed what he called the revolution of 1940 with resignation if not complacency, an attitude reflected in his steadily rising esteem for King. On the prime minister's death in 1950 he praised him for doing just what Creighton was to condemn him for. Without consulting either Parliament or the people, he had moved with remarkable alacrity after 1939 to bind Canada to the United States. He had achieved this without ever arousing that anti-American fever to which Canadians were so susceptible and which had swamped the Liberals under Laurier in 1891 and 1911. Thanks to King, wrote Underhill, most Canadians had come to recognize that their fundamental interests were identical to those of the Americans and that any interests that were not were better defended from within the North Atlantic alliance than by Canada's trying to stand aloof from its powerful neighbour. Now, in 1950, only Communists and a diehard remnant of the Tories went about talking of 'American Imperialism.' No, that was not quite correct, he added as if in afterthought: there were also those academics who liked to think up nasty wisecracks on the subject even though most of their own pet projects were apt to be funded by the Rockefeller, Carnegie, or Guggenheim foundations. Underhill no more needed to name Creighton as the butt of this gibe than Creighton had to name Underhill when attacking the nationalist interpretation of Canadian history.[9]

Politics and personality charged the two men's rivalry, but the politics at least matched their divergent approaches to Canadian history. Underhill presented Canada as an essentially North American society, moulded by the frontier experience and resembling the United States rather than Britain. This was the scholarly orthodoxy of the 1940s, but it echoed a theme that went back to the democratic republicanism of the Lower Canadian Patriotes and the Upper Canadian populism of William Lyon Mackenzie and the Clear Grits. Later it had resounded in the polemics of Goldwin Smith and John Ewart.[10]

Liberal nationalists such as Underhill tended to see the boundary between Canada and the United States as a historical accident, reflecting no fundamental differences of environment or political values. Creighton's conservative nationalism reflected a different vision, which Creighton had developed together with his friend and mentor, the economic historian Harold Innis. Innis had depicted the early history of European colonization in North America as a struggle between the French fur traders on the St Lawrence River and their competitors based on two other great water routes into the continental interior: to the north the Hudson's Bay Company, and to the south the British and Dutch merchants at Albany, a settlement at the confluence of the Mohawk and Hudson rivers. The international boundary established in 1783 had sundered the primarily agricultural settlements of the thirteen seaboard col-

onies, whose great ambition was westward expansion into the fertile
Ohio Valley, from the largely infertile fur-trading domain to the north.
From this point of view Canada had emerged not in spite of geography
but because of it. In a striking phrase, Innis characterized the North
West Company, the great Montreal-based enterprise of the post-
Conquest period, which had extended the boundaries of the fur trade
northward into the Athabaska country and west to the Pacific Ocean, as
the forerunner of Confederation.[11]

Creighton's first book, *The Commercial Empire of the St. Lawrence, 1760–
1850*,[12] developed this view by recounting Canada's history from the
1760s until about 1850 in terms of a sustained effort by Montreal-based
merchants to dominate the continental interior and make the St
Lawrence its main outlet to Europe. That venture had foundered on a
succession of obstacles. American independence had inscribed a political boundary across the middle of the Montrealers' visionary empire.
Then the Constitutional Act of 1791 had carved the old province of Quebec into Upper and Lower Canada despite its geographical unity. It had
also founded legislative institutions, thus enabling the small-minded
spokesmen of agriculture to defy – and in Lower Canada frustrate – the
grand designs of commerce. In 1821 the North West Company had
abandoned fur-trading, thereby cutting Montreal's commercial ties to
the northwestern hinterland. Finally, in the 1840s, the British had opted
for free trade, abandoning the system of imperial tariff preference that
had underpinned the Laurentian commercial system.

Creighton's taste for drama required his story to end on a sombre note.
Innis may have called the North West Company the forerunner of Confederation, but in *Commercial Empire* Confederation figured in the closing
pages as distinctly second best. Canadian trade had continued to flow to
the United Kingdom, Montreal had remained the focus of an east–west
trading system, and Canadians had shortly devised a new continental
strategy. But the new strategy was less grandiose. The National Policy,
Macdonald's protective tariff of 1879, 'expressed the purpose of the
northern economy to turn in upon itself rather than to rely once more
upon the old transatlantic associations. Canada's designs in North
America were destined to be more Canadian and less international in
scope; and Canada's status in the western world had already become
less imperial and more North American in character.' The imperial
connection, 'once the homely concern of practical, hard-headed men,
threatened to become the object of the refined speculations of political
theorists and the emotional outbursts of after-dinner speakers.'[13]

Creighton's view of Canadian history made a dramatic contrast with traditional approaches. His heroes were neither the Loyalists beloved of imperialist writers nor the great men of Liberal historiography (Robert, Francis, and Wilfrid Responsible-Government, he named them in derision of its bloodless and hagiographic treatment of Baldwin, Hincks, and Laurier.)[14] From his standpoint, colonial responsible government was merely the political corollary of the demise of the Old Colonial System. Still less did he esteem William Lyon Mackenzie and the rebels of 1837, whose 'American' values earned them the sympathy of nationalists such as Underhill, Arthur Lower, and the historical sociologist S.D. Clark.[15] Creighton looked back past these pygmies to the visionaries of the commercial empire. In contrast to their continental outlook, the merely transcontinental polity so dear to Canadian nationalists represented a decline.

Soon, however, Creighton's historical perspective began to shift from imperialist anti-nationalism towards a nationalism equally hostile to the prevailing liberal creed. It was a faith that synthesized the merchants' practical imperialism with the sentimental imperialism of the Loyalists, those idols of the after-dinner speakers. From this new standpoint the commercial ambitions of the Montrealers and the political convictions of the Loyalists were in many ways simply two aspects of the same purposeful philosophy – the defence and extension of British interests in North America. The St Lawrence had inspired both. Merchants and Loyalists fused in Creighton's mind into a single entity, the 'old Tories,' or 'Canadian commercial imperialists,' whose fundamental political principles were unification and centralization. He severed the division of old Quebec in 1791 from the Loyalists' revulsion against the French system of land tenure (a dislike the merchants had shared) and blamed it on 'other people' (unnamed) who 'did not take the St. Lawrence so seriously.'

The old Tories' design had failed with the advent of the railway and the shift of British policy in the 1840s from imperial tariff preference to free trade. This and its political corollary, colonial self-government, had brought the Old Colonial System to an end. But the Tories had adjusted to the new order without relinquishing their essential commitment to unification and central control; they had replaced the old system by Confederation. The personification of this new Toryism was John A. Macdonald, who combined the political values of the old Tories with the skills of a North American political tactician and party manager. Macdonald was a better Canadian than his 'old Tory' predecessors, more truly a nationalist; and his work was essentially a great effort in political and economic nationalism. The grand pillars of his national edifice were the National Policy and the Canadian Pacific Railway; but the foundation was his alliance with George-Étienne Cartier. Macdonald above all had convinced the Tories that Canada could develop the St Lawrence as a political and commercial system without first suppressing the French. United in its political allegiance and material interests, Canada must be accepted (explained Creighton) as dual in its cultural loyalties.[16]

By the outbreak of war in 1939, Creighton's vision of Canadian history was already formed. When he mocked the wise kings and prophets of the Liberal interpretation in 1947, including the Responsible-Government clan, he was already labouring to raise Sir John A. Nationbuilder to pre-eminence in the Canadian pantheon. The postwar shift in the international balance of power, which threatened to bring his hero's great design to nothing, only made his endeavours more urgent.

In *Lament for a Nation*, published in 1965, the philosopher George Grant hailed Creighton as 'the leading contemporary theorist of the conservative view of Canadian history.'[17] Creighton had defined the conservative view of Canada to a whole generation despite the hostility of the liberal establishment. Perhaps Grant forgot that it was a leading Conservative, John Diefenbaker, who had come closest to landing Creighton in hot water. In 1954, in a broadcast talk called 'Canada and the Cold War,'[18] Creighton had chided Canadians for their unthinking support of American foreign policy and especially their perception of the Cold War as a conflict of ideologies rather than of interests. With the appearance of his first stout volume on John A. Macdonald, Creighton had begun to figure in the public mind as a 'Conservative historian.' Diefenbaker found Creighton's criticism of the Korean War, and of the recent American-inspired overthrow of democracy in Guatemala, mighty strange for a Conservative historian and said so.[19] But recalling all this a decade later would not have served Grant's purpose, which was to celebrate Diefenbaker's futile but courageous defence of Canadian sovereignty against American domineering and the glad treason of Canada's own 'Liberal establishment.'

Grant did not enlarge on the dangers that menaced a tenured, senior professor who presumed to elaborate a conservative view of Canadian history. For that matter, neither had Creighton when he himself alluded, in a lecture of 1957, to the moral courage it took to challenge the Liberal interpretation – the *authorized version*, as he called it, in sneering comparison with King James's Bible. That lecture came ten years after his first manifesto on Macdonald and Canadian historians, yet he spoke as if nothing had changed – as if, meanwhile, both volumes of his own great biography of Macdonald had not been acclaimed with that grand prize of the Canadian establishment, the Governor General's Literary Award. He ventured (he said, with a parade of diffidence) to ask Canadians to admit of the possibility of another version of history, and to begin their own reinterpretation of the great man's career.

It sounded like an invitation to collude in heresy. But soon Creighton was acknowledging (without admitting his own part) an 'extraordinary contemporary revival of interest in Macdonald and in Macdonald's design for Canada.' He linked this revival to Canada's postwar prosperity, which had prompted Canadians, like their predecessors of the 1860s, to take large views of the future. But their imaginings were vexed with a vague sense of danger, a dim perception that they had frittered away much of their patrimony and that, if they now squandered their second chance, there would not be a third. 'We were all taught – it was the basic doctrine of the Liberal interpretation – that national progress was to be identified solely with emancipation from British control. We all believed that once the great crusade against British imperialism was won, we would ascend unimpeded to the serene and spacious uplands of nationhood.' Things had not worked out that way, and a whole generation was now reaching the angry conclusion that it had been deceived.[20]

Creighton was speaking on the eve of a federal general election: one which, unlike any since 1945, offered the prospect of real change. In 1949 and 1953 the Liberals, led by Mackenzie King's successor, Louis St Laurent, had won massive majorities. The Conservatives, with forty or fifty seats, had been reduced to a virtual Ontario rump party (though comfortably outpolled by the Liberals even there). Lulled by prosperity, preferring a cold war to the real thing, most Canadians accepted enlistment in the ranks of the American-led crusade against world communism. But in 1956 two events dashed the bloom from the Liberal rose. The government showed an alarming contempt for public opinion by repeatedly using closure to carry an unpopular bill subsidizing construction of a gas pipeline to be controlled by an American-dominated company. Then came the Suez Crisis, when Ottawa seconded the United States in pressing Britain and France to withdraw from Egypt, which those countries had invaded in response to nationalization of the

Suez Canal. The pipeline affair was a classic example of Liberal arrogance; the Suez episode, a textbook illustration of the Liberal penchant for deploring British while ignoring American imperialism.[21]

In the thick of these events the Conservative party chose Diefenbaker as its leader. 'Dief' was not only a new leader but a Tory chief of a new sort. Like most, he was a lawyer; but he was a defence lawyer from a small town in northern Saskatchewan and a passionate defender of civil rights. As a Prairie populist, he also differed from the Tory establishment in his suspicious attitude towards big government and big business. But he was certainly more Tory than populist in his respect for Canada's British heritage and parliamentary institutions, and his character and beliefs made him the man of the hour to Canadians offended by Liberal nationalists' contempt for that heritage and the Liberal government's contempt for those institutions. In June 1957 the country elected its first Conservative prime minister in twenty-two years, though only as head of a minority government. Nine months later, another election returned 208 Conservatives in a house of 265. Quebecers, alive as always to the importance of being on the winning side, elected a Conservative majority to the House of Commons for the first time since the heyday of John A. Macdonald.[22]

Diefenbaker hoped to reduce Canada's growing economic and political dependence on the United States, but he could not turn back the clock. He looked to Britain as an economic counterweight just as the erstwhile mother country, a shadow of its old glory, finally turned its back on its empire and began trying to join the European Common Market (now the European Union) after standing aloof from its founding in 1956. In military affairs, his nationalism took second place to the anticommunism that had spurred him to condemn Creighton's views on the Korean War. He had hardly taken office when he committed Canada to the North American Air Defence Agreement (NORAD), which created an integrated command structure for continental air defence. This was as sweeping a commitment as the Ogdensburg Agreement of 1940, and Canada was not even at war. His reluctant abandonment of the Avro Arrow fighter-bomber was a further step towards continental integration, since it meant buying American hardware instead and resulted in the Defence Production Sharing Agreement, which allowed Canadian companies to bid for American military contracts on equal terms with American ones.

The general election of 1962 cost the government eighty-eight seats, thirty-six of them in Quebec and thirty-three in Ontario. The apparent gap between Diefenbaker's aspirations and his actions loomed large in the campaign, but the result was also affected by local concerns. The Prairie populist had little sympathy for Quebec nationalism, and Quebec's 'Quiet Revolution' was gathering momentum, suddenly marginalizing the conservative circles that had supported him most strongly in 1958. In both Quebec and Ontario, the Conservatives' popularity was weakened by the first significant falterings of the postwar boom. In the recession of the early 1960s, the 14,000 jobs lost in the Toronto area by the cancellation of the Avro Arrow were sorely missed.

Had Diefenbaker lost office in 1962 instead of becoming again the head of a minority government, he could have been written off as an ambitious demagogue: George Grant conceded that.[23] What redeemed him in Grant's eyes, and made him a figure both noble and tragic, was his conduct during the crisis that began in October 1962. Alarmed by evidence of the construction in Cuba of launching sites for intercontinental missiles, the United States sought, with no consultation and scant notice, to move NORAD to a heightened state of readiness. Diefenbaker insisted on thrashing the issue out in cabinet; but it soon transpired that the defence minister, Douglas Harkness, had pre-empted the decision by giving the requisite orders behind his colleagues' backs. His precipitancy enabled critics to dismiss Diefenbaker's insistence on due deliberation as mere dithering.

The crisis also brought to a head a controversy over equipping the armed forces with nuclear weapons. In partial substitution for the Avro Arrow, the government had purchased American-made Bomarc anti-aircraft missiles, which were designed for use with nuclear warheads. The Canadian armed forces wanted other nuclear weapons too. But the secretary of state for external affairs, Howard Green, strongly believed in nuclear disarmament and was correspondingly anxious to maintain an independent position for Canada in international diplomacy. He also resented the Americans' increasing arrogance towards their allies under John F. Kennedy. Diefenbaker himself objected neither to nuclear arms nor to the zealotry of American anti-communism but was deeply committed to preserving Canadian sovereignty. American law forbade the surrender of nuclear weapons to foreign control. If Canada acquired the arms in question, an American finger would have to be on the trigger. This Diefenbaker could not accept.

After the Cuban crisis, the United States began pressing Ottawa to accept nuclear warheads for the Bomarc as a necessary implication of Canada's commitment to NORAD. Green resisted, and Diefenbaker supported him. The Liberals had opposed Canadian nuclear armament, but now they changed their minds and favoured accepting the American warheads. The media overwhelmingly backed the Liberals, as did the Canadian armed forces, whose leaders sponsored a press conference in Ottawa by the retiring American commander-in-chief of NATO. In Washington the State Department contradicted Diefenbaker's assertion that Canada was not pledged to accept nuclear warheads; on Parliament Hill the Liberals attacked him with a motion of no confidence. In cabinet Harkness demanded Diefenbaker's resignation and, when their colleagues demurred in the interest of party solidarity, resigned himself. Next day the government was defeated in the Commons, and the ensuing general election restored the Liberals to office, though not with a majority. For the next five years the prime minister was Lester B. Pearson, whose efforts in 1956 to smooth the French and British exodus from Egypt had won him the Nobel Peace Prize.

To his enemies, Diefenbaker was indecisive, incompetent, and unprincipled – the vainglorious architect of his own defeat. His enemies – *Lament for a Nation* began by sketching the remarkable breadth of the alliance that had brought him down, an alliance that united Frank Underhill, socialist MPs, and the Conservative *Globe and Mail* under the same banner. Grant saw Diefenbaker's victory in 1957 as the last gasp of Canadian nationalism and his defeat as its defeat. He did not mean the anti-British nationalism that Creighton derided: the nationalism of Frank Underhill and the liberal left. That, he believed, had been proved phoney by the rush of most of its proponents towards continentalism after the Second World War. Grant's nationalism was the true Canadianism of his father, the historian W.L. Grant, who had duelled with John Ewart, and of the grandfathers whose names were fused in his own: George Parkin, who had crossed swords with Goldwin Smith, and George M. Grant of Queen's University. It was the creed (so Grant believed) of their Loyalist ancestors: a faith at once British and North American, grounded in the wisdom of John A. Macdonald, who had seen clearly that the only threat to Canada lurked in the south, not across the Atlantic. Its grand project was to build, along with the French, a more ordered and stable society than the liberal experiment in the United States.[24]

This nationalism was also the creed of Diefenbaker and Howard Green. Children of the nineteenth century, they believed that Canada's membership in the Commonwealth still stood for something. They saw

Canada as an independent country, whose special role in international affairs was to mediate between the United States and Europe, particularly Britain. Grant's own imperialist forebears of the 1890s had helped to form that vision. But in the modern world, with both Canada and western Europe bound to the United States by the vassalage of the North Atlantic alliance, there was no need for such mediation. British statesmen, sunk in post-imperial dependence on their 'special relationship' with the United States, took the lead in reproving Diefenbaker's Canada as a 'bad ally.'[25]

It was easy to mock Diefenbaker and Green for their quixotic folly. Grant preferred to sympathize with these men of deep loyalty, who found themselves impotent in the face of their disappearing past. He did not blame Diefenbaker for his failure, though he recognized the flaws of character that had rendered him ineffective in office.[26] The defeat of Canadian nationalism was lamentable, but it was also inevitable. The United States had become too wealthy and powerful, and most English-speaking Canadians too American in culture and ideals to value, even if they remembered, the differences for which their predecessors had been willing to die. They had voted for Diefenbaker as a protest against Liberal arrogance, not Liberal principles, and by 1963 were ready to return to their true allegiance.

What were Liberal principles, if not an oxymoron? As Grant told it, the Liberals presented themselves as more effective, because more realistic, defenders of Canada's national interests. They recognized the inevitability of economic and political subordination to the United States and worked to maximize Canada's prosperity and freedom of action within the American empire. They were willing to eradicate the surviving symbols of Canada's British past if that was necessary to reconcile its francophone citizens. In Grant's eyes, though, these policies had been as futile as Diefenbaker's. Eradicating a nation's past, and integrating its economy with that of a much larger neighbour, simply did not constitute a basis for nation-building. Economic fusion could only lead to cultural fusion.[27]

The Liberals' fatal flaw was their refusal to stand up against big business. Capitalism was a way of life based on the principle that the most important activity is profit-making. When everything was made relative to profit-making, all traditions of virtue were dissolved, including that aspect of virtue known as love of country. In dominant countries such as the United States, the loyalty of the capitalist class was assured, for their interests were tied to the strength and vigour of the empire. But no small country could depend on the loyalty of its capitalists, since international interests might require them to sacrifice the lesser loyalty of patriotism.

The economic self-seekers had never cared about Canada. As long as trade with Britain was a leading source of Canadian wealth, big business had been happy to foster and celebrate the British connection: most conspicuously, during the jingoistic campaign against unrestricted tariff reciprocity with the United States in 1911. Even during the heyday of the empire, however, the traditionally Tory merchants of Montreal had exposed the self-serving nature of this business patriotism by responding in 1849 to Britain's abandonment of the Old Colonial system with a call for Canada's annexation to the United States. The flood of British capital investment that began after 1850 had restored their loyalty, but not for ever. After 1940, Canadian businessmen had reached eagerly for the profits to be made as agents of American capitalism. They were happy to look south for their final authority in both politics and culture. 'Canadian nationalism! How old-fashioned can you get?' – so E.P. Taylor, the great businessman and racehorse owner, was reported to have exclaimed at the height of the defence crisis.[28]

After 1940, wrote Grant, Canadian nationalism needed to go hand in hand with some measure of socialism – at the very least the sort of strong government practised in France under Charles de Gaulle, with effective controls on foreign investment and the firm implementation of a national will to limit French participation in the North Atlantic alliance. In Canada, this sort of policy had traditionally belonged to Conservative governments: Grant instanced John A. Macdonald's National Policy, the Ontario Tories' nationalization of hydroelectric power production in 1910, and the establishment of Canadian National Railways in 1919. Mackenzie King's alliance with big business precluded such policies, and after the Second World War the government relaxed its regulation of the economy.[29]

The internationalism of the liberal intelligentsia differed little from that of the Department of External Affairs: 'Even the finest talk about internationalism opens markets for the powerful.' At first, Canadian officials had supported NATO as a multilateral forum, which might serve to mediate Canada's bilateral relations with the United States. By the 1960s, however, NATO was simply the military instrument of the strongest empire on earth; but meanwhile the officials of External Affairs had come to see themselves as members of an international rather than a national bureaucracy. When Diefenbaker and Green broke ranks during the defence crisis, the officials' instinct was to undermine rather than support them.[30]

Such was Grant's story. As history, it had flaws. He hailed Crown corporations of Conservative origin, such as Ontario Hydro and the CNR, as feats of constructive nationalism, while dismissing Liberal ones such as Trans-Canada Airlines (later Air Canada), a creation of 1937 that he did not mention by name, as expedients to meet 'certain complementary needs' of the corporate capitalist economy.[31] He mocked Mackenzie King for esteeming Franklin Roosevelt as an anti-imperialist but not Diefenbaker for valuing him as a populist. More fundamentally, since he conceded that certain Liberals were sincere nationalists, though sadly misguided, he could have portrayed them as tragic failures almost on the scale of Diefenbaker and Green, though obviously less heroic.

The reason he did not is that his ultimate goal was not political but philosophical. He mourned Diefenbaker as the carrier of the last residues of an 'organic' conservatism dating back to classical antiquity, a selfless communitarianism destined to fail before a progressive scientific materialism that had found its highest, irresistible expression in American corporate capitalism. Organic conservatism had fled to Canada with the Loyalists, but flight had only postponed its doom, which was inscribed in the progress of science and technology. 'The impossibility of conservatism in our era is the impossibility of Canada. As Canadians we attempted a ridiculous task in trying to build a conservative nation in the age of progress, on a continent we share with the most dynamic nation on earth. The current of modern history was against us.' The great contribution of the Liberals was to reconcile most Canadians to the inevitable. So well had they wrought that the formal end of Canada might well be prefaced by a period during which the United States had to resist the strong desire of English-speaking Canadians to be annexed.[32]

Despite its pessimism, *Lament for a Nation* became almost at once an inspiration for a new sort of Canadian nationalism: one that was anti-American but left-wing. The new creed did not specially value the vanishing symbols of Canada's British and Loyalist heritage, but it embraced the old ideal of creating a more civilized society than that of the United States. Now, however, the standard of excellence was social as well as political; the criterion of welfare joined that of orderliness. The distinguishing badge of Canadian superiority was not just the absence of that discord which began in the 1960s to burn large holes in the centre of American cities; it was also the completeness of the Canadian welfare state. Yet though the new nationalism differed from the old, it was rooted in the old. For this Grant bore a special responsibility.

Grant had hailed Creighton for his exposition of the conservative view of Canada, but his perspective differed from Creighton's in being anti-capitalist. In 1965 Creighton had still published little on the twentieth century, and what he had written contained little of the bite and bile of his attack on Grit history. As a result, his history of Canada remained above all a story of the construction of a commercial empire – a story in which capitalists were heroes. He had even managed to excuse the Montreal annexationists of 1849, blaming Britain's abandonment of imperial tariff preference for unhinging them.[33] Grant's anti-capitalism, his denigration of big business in the modern era as the glad handmaid of American imperialism, his trenchant analysis of the corrosive effect of consumer capitalism on local culture – all these features of his argument endeared him to the left-wing intelligentsia that flowered as the baby-boom generation began to fill the universities. In marrying politics and philosophy, Grant had contrived to create a literary masterpiece, concise yet epic, idiomatic yet poetic, ironic yet poignant. His writing had the power to move.

There was one problem. Grant respected socialism, because, like conservatism, it aimed to restrain individual greed in the common interest; but he doubted that, in Canada at any rate, it possessed the moral stringency to counteract the corrosive force of consumer capitalism.[34] His idea of a confrontation between Canadian conservatism and American liberalism could not serve as a fighting creed for the new left-wing nationalism unless it was given a more hopeful twist. That would be the work of Gad Horowitz, a young political scientist who admired Grant while rejecting his fatalism.

Horowitz performed this feat by adapting the ideas of an alienated American thinker, Louis Hartz. Hartz wanted to understand why liberalism had become so completely dominant in the United States as to eradicate socialism as a political force. With a team of collaborators, he approached this question by examining several colonies of European settlement. He posited that such settlements had not been complete replicas of the parent society, but homogeneous fragments struck off from the parent. Thus New France had not reproduced the society of seventeenth-century France in all its complexity, with its mixture of Catholics and Protestants, of nobility, peasantry, and commercial bourgeoisie. The colony had been a 'feudal fragment' of the parent state, deliberately isolated from Protestant and bourgeois contamination. Nor had Australia reproduced the social complexity of nineteenth-century Britain. In every case, though, the homogeneity of the founding fragment had produced a uniformity of culture that precluded the dialectical interplay of ideas. Even where subsequent immigration had introduced individuals steeped in different ideas, those ideas could have no impact on the political culture once it had 'congealed.' French Canada had stayed feudal. Similarly, American liberalism was an inevitable consequence of the puritan individualism of the original English settlers.[35]

As history, Hartz's 'fragment thesis' was a gross simplification. As a sweeping idea, powerfully expressed, it appealed strongly to ideologically susceptible minds at a time when the young were about to rediscover the allure of ideology. It was also well adapted to imparting a hopeful spin to Grant's gloomy account of the encounter between American liberalism and Canadian conservatism, though this was not immediately obvious.

Hartz saw English Canada through the eyes of the liberal-nationalist historians, still influential despite Creighton. This school celebrated the similarities between Canada and the United States, which it ascribed to the effects of the North American environment. To Arthur Lower, for instance, the American Tories were seekers of power and privilege, who 'did not have the same chance of becoming Americans as the ordinary people' because their position in colonial society insulated them from the full stress of the environment. They 'could not rise to spiritual concept which is America,' but remained mere 'provincials.' Similarly, he rejected the sentimental conception of the Loyalists as 'chosen spirits, resolved to die rather than submit to a political philosophy of which they disapproved.' Some were 'courtiers,' committed to the colonial regime by their self-interest; others were ordinary folk who, trying to keep out of trouble, had had the bad luck to end up on the wrong side.[36]

Regarding the Loyalists – the founding fragment of English Canada – from this standpoint, Hartz and his Canadian collaborator, Kenneth McRae, saw little difference between their ideas and the 'American' liberalism of the colonies they had fled. Loyalism had a 'Tory touch,' but vestigial and insignificant – hence the cultural resemblances between the United States and English Canada, including the weakness of socialism in both countries. Horowitz did not reject this view outright, but he ingeniously neutralized its implications by focusing on what distinguished Canada from the United States. Thereby he contrived to legitimize

Canadian socialism rather than dismissing it as Hartz and McRae had.[37]

His key move was to postulate that the Loyalist 'Tory touch,' though it may have counted for nothing in colonial America, had acquired potency in the Loyalist diaspora. It had determined not only the less egalitarian character of Canadian society but also the greater willing-ness of English-Canadian elites to use the power of the state in order to develop and control the economy. Another 'un-American' feature of Canadian conservatism was its concern for social welfare. The Canadian New Deal, nipped in the bud by the Privy Council in 1937, had been the work of R.B. Bennett's Conservative government, and Diefenbaker too had strongly supported the welfare state. These observations led Horowitz to identify a most un-American phenomenon, which he called the 'red tory.' Red toryism was visible in the tendency of many Conser-vatives and socialists to prefer each other to the Liberals and, at a higher level, in the fact that the Conservative historian W.L. Morton and the socialist labour activist Eugene Forsey could be devoted to monarchy and welfare state alike. Horowitz identified George Grant too as a red tory.[38]

How did this reasoning help to legitimize Canadian socialism? Social-ism was an ideology that combined 'the corporate-organic-collectivist' ideas of Toryism with the 'rationalist-egalitarian' ideas of liberalism. Horowitz argued that the Loyalist synthesis of American liberalism with a 'Tory touch' had set off a dialectic that had produced Canadian socialism. Socialism was weaker in North America than elsewhere, but what counted was its strength in Canada as compared to the United States. The Co-operative Commonwealth Federation (renamed the New Democratic Party in 1961) had governed Saskatchewan from 1944 to 1964 and become a powerful force in British Columbia. Unlike Ameri-can socialist parties, it had ties with the country's trade unions. It was not a major presence in Ottawa but was more prominent than before the Second World War. It might not be 'going anywhere' at the national level, but it was not about to disappear.[39]

If Canadian socialism was not about to disappear, neither presumably was Canada. Horowitz did not propose to leave this to chance, though. His overtly political writing, in the Marxist periodical *Canadian Dimen-sion*, proclaimed the need for action. Canadians must work to preserve English-Canadian distinctiveness: they must be ready 'to pay "the price of being Canadian."' Socialists must resist the temptation to compro-mise with English Canada's dominant liberalism for the sake of political expediency, and they must also become wholehearted nationalists:

socialism and nationalism needed each other in all small nations. As nationalists, socialists must strive to build a society that was different from, and better than, that of the United States; it need not be unique as long as it met those two criteria. To achieve those objectives, Canadians must take control of their economy and must subsidize Canadian 'cultural production' on a very much larger scale than anything currently contemplated.[40]

'English Canada is not worth preserving unless it can be different from the United States. Our British past provides the foundations for building on the northern half of this continent a social democratic order (let Grant call it conservative if he wishes) *better* than the liberal society of the United States. A tory past contains the seeds of a socialist future.' With these words, Horowitz sealed the connection between the old anti-American nationalism and the new. The goal he set for the new nationalism was the same as had inspired the old: building something better than the United States. So was the source of inspiration: those aspects of Canadian society that were not American because they were British. ('What is un-American about English Canada can be summed up in one word: British.')[41]

Horowitz's words marked a historic moment. For the first time ever, the left wing of British North American politics was anti-American rather than anti-British. For the first time, instead of invoking the force of the North American environment against that of the British inheritance, it was doing the opposite. Paradoxically, it was doing so even as the red maple leaf replaced the red ensign as the emblem of the Canadian state.

The decade from the mid-1960s to the mid-1970s was a golden age of Canadian nationalism. Barely liberated from the toils of their costive British heritage, Canadians flaunted their liberation from the political hegemony of American-led resistance to world communism. As the United States floundered in the mire of the Vietnam War, Canada became a haven for draft-evaders. As race war reduced American inner cities to rubble and ash, Canadian cities held expressways at bay and sprouted pedestrian malls. The Canadian dollar, which Diefenbaker's government, to its embarrassment, had had to devalue below the American, briefly traded at a premium. The Canadian Labour Congress became more and more Canadian as its member unions freed themselves from the tutelage of their American founders and mentors.

Left-wing and nationalist ideas became fashionable. Grant and

234 1940–1982: Continentalism and Nationalisms

Horowitz co-hosted a series of television programs.[42] The New Democratic Party gained power for the first time in Manitoba and British
Columbia and regained it in Saskatchewan. Even from Ottawa, where
the Liberals governed continuously from 1963 to 1979, there issued left-
wing and nationalist policies. Once Saskatchewan had blazed the trail,
Ottawa promoted the establishment of universal health insurance
throughout Canada. It set up a Foreign Investment Review Agency to
monitor the growth of foreign (i.e., American) economic control. A
National Energy Policy, augmented by the creation of a national energy
company (Petro-Canada), sheltered Canadians from the oil shortages of
the mid-1970s. Public funding of culture abounded, and stronger 'Canadian content' regulations were imposed on radio and television. Canadian magazines were protected against unfair competition from the
United States. Cable TV companies imposed their own slant on cultural
nationalism by carrying American shows but patching in Canadian
commercials. In foreign policy, the country scaled down its commitment
to NATO and scrapped the nuclear capacity that Lester Pearson's government had accepted in 1963. In 1970, impatient of the power-political
gamesmanship that still excluded Communist China from the United
Nations, Canada became only the second NATO country to extend diplomatic recognition to Peking. (Gaullist France had led the way.)

Bliss was it in that dawn to be alive, but to be young was very heaven.
Two men who were not young, however, observed with misgivings the
quiet revolution in Canadian political values. In 1970 George Grant
revisited the terrain of *Lament for a Nation* in an introduction to the
paperback edition. He conceded that Canadians were less enamoured of
continentalism than before: that was hardly surprising, since Nixon's
America was less alluring than Kennedy's, and it took little intelligence
or patriotism to be glad that one's sons were not being drafted for the
Vietnam War. The young, moreover, had acquired a realistic suspicion
of 'corporation capitalism.' Grant grudgingly acknowledged in the policies of Pierre Trudeau's government 'traces of care about Canada' that
had been lacking in those of King, St Laurent, and Pearson. But Canada
was still Washington's partner in crime. Canadians were making money
out of the Vietnam War, and many were as devoted as ever to con-
sumerism. Grant viewed sceptically the notion that the new nationalism
could succeed where the old had failed and make a better America
north of the U.S. border.

In 1970, too, Donald Creighton published his first book dealing
mainly with twentieth-century Canada. It was, in the words of fellow-

historian W.L. Morton, a full orchestration of *Lament for a Nation*, and it rehearsed in detail the tragedy by which Canada's rise to material prosperity had destroyed its moral purpose. For half a century after Confederation, Britain had continued to provide markets, capital, immigrants, and diplomatic protection; but after the First World War, Canada's economy had been reoriented from east to south. The shift had weakened the historic Anglo–Canadian alliance, and the damage had been compounded by the policy of Mackenzie King, the archetypal continentalist, who had broken up the Britannic union and gladly thrown Canada into the arms of the United States.[43]

Since 1940 Canada had stood alone, its independence exposed to the penetrative power of American economic and military imperialism, its identity subject to the continual hammering of the American mass media. Its citizens were sadly ill-equipped to deal with this predicament. 'Continentalism had divorced Canadians from their history, crippled their creative capacity, and left them without the power to fashion a new future for themselves.'[44] Only through a great collective effort, in which both English and French Canadians participated fully, could the nation have escaped from the mental vassalage into which it had sunk. But the vital effort – the united push for national regeneration – was not forthcoming. Cultural conflict had destroyed national unity just when unity was most needed.

15

Canadian Nationalists and the Quiet Revolution

The conservative nationalism of George Grant and Donald Creighton was defined by anti-Americanism, centralism, and esteem for the country's traditional political values and institutions. This left plenty of room for dissension, and nothing caused more of that than the Quiet Revolution in Quebec. Liberals and socialists also differed among themselves on how to respond, but with conservatives in particular the disagreement took on the aspect of a quarrel about history. The two leading historians of the day were prominent conservatives, and they disagreed. When Creighton set out to shed 'the hard light of history' on certain 'revolutionary' myths that had begun to be propagated, one of his targets was his fellow-conservative W.L. Morton.

The quarrel reflected differences in the origins and nature of their conservatism. Creighton was the bard of British imperial power in North America and of the transcontinental extension of central Canadian power under the British shield. His Laurentian interpretation of Canadian history viewed the country from Montreal and Ottawa, the financial and political headquarters from which its unification had been planned and executed. Growing up in the Tory Toronto of the early twentieth century, he saw Canada as his hero John A. Macdonald had seen it: a vast domain to be brought – by force if necessary – under Ottawa's control for the benefit of central Canada. French Canada could make only a modest contribution to this enterprise: that of hewing wood and drawing water, and perhaps toting a loyal musket when required; but, above all, that of not making trouble.

Morton's conservatism was a more complex creed. He yielded nothing to Creighton in anti-Americanism, in centralism, in loathing for Mackenzie King and Oscar Skelton, or in the fierceness of his opposition to special status for Quebec. He accepted the centralist thesis that Confederation was less a federal than an imperial union. As a Manitoban, however, steeped in his youth in a vigorous tradition of western protest against the political and economic hegemony of central Canada, he viewed the imperialism of the centre through victim's eyes. The Prairies had been annexed to imperial Canada as a colony to be exploited. Both the National Policy and the Canadian Pacific Railway monopoly had penalized western consumers and enterprise for the sake of British, American, and central Canadian capital. The Prairie provinces had not been provinces like the others, for until 1930 Ottawa had retained control of their natural resources. In sum, Confederation had been carried out to augment the wealth of central Canada. Until that original purpose was altered, 'Confederation must remain an instrument of injustice.'[1]

Morton's sense of sectional injustice extended to the Métis. To Creighton, Louis Riel was a troublemaker and ultimately a traitor, like the Lower Canadian Patriotes before him. He was to blame for all the later trouble over bicultural institutions on the Prairies, because they should not have been set up in the first place and would not have been but for him.[2] Morton, by contrast, sympathized with the doomed efforts of the Métis, under Riel's leadership, to defend their way of life and institutions against the pending invasion of English-speaking settlers from Ontario. He saw the abolition of cultural duality on the Prairies as a blow against the rights of a cultural minority.

The two men's disagreement over history found expression in their responses to the upsurge of francophone militancy in the 1960s. Creighton perceived the issue of national unity as a dangerous distraction from that of national independence. Once more, as in the conscription controversies of both world wars, francophone troublemakers were breaking ranks with the rest of Canada in the face of an external threat, this time emanating from the United States. Morton, in contrast, admitted the legitimacy of francophone grievances. As early as 1946 he had recognized French Canada, along with the west, as a victim of the Laurentian perspective. In the 1960s he acknowledged that a fair settlement of the national unity question was vital to the preservation of Canadian independence. So the two men quarrelled over Canadian history and its relevance to a burning question of the present. But they remained conservatives, nationalists, and centralists.

When the Quiet Revolution began, in 1960, French-Canadian nationalism had been in a defensive posture ever since the final defeat of the

Lower Canadian rebellion in 1838. French Canada's leaders had set out
to cooperate with the imperial power and its North American surrogate
in the hope of preserving their society and culture within the ancestral
homeland. At first, within United Canada, they had collaborated with
the most accommodating of the Upper Canadian political factions; from
the mid-1850s on, this was John A. Macdonald's Liberal-Conservatives.
Soon the growing disparity between the two language groups had
required a supplementary strategy, and the *bleus* had come round to
George Brown's policy – *rouge* in origin – of federalizing United Canada,
if necessary within a larger British American union. The result was Confederation, which Quebec's francophone elite saw as a compact of sovereign polities joined in federal union for certain common purposes.
That compact was dual in nature: it was that of a province with other
provinces, and it was the latest in the series of compacts that had
regulated relations between themselves and the English ever since the
Conquest.[3]

This conception of Canada as a compact between a sovereign Quebec
and a number of English-speaking provinces dominated Québécois
political thought until the 1950s, when it received a full airing in the
Tremblay Report. It was based on the idea of the division of powers
between provinces and Dominion that had triumphed in the 1880s and
1890s and become entrenched during Wilfrid Laurier's long tenure as
prime minister. By charging provincial governments with the regulation
of provincial society, the constitution seemed to give the government of
Quebec the power it needed to ensure, in cooperation with the Catholic
church, the survival of francophone Quebec as a distinct society.

In the 1930s, however, the balance of power had begun to tilt alarm-
ingly towards Ottawa. The Great Depression had convinced many
Canadians that modern industrial society required government on a
scale that the provinces could not provide. The Second World War, and
then the Cold War, had lifted Ottawa to an ascendancy over the provinces that the leaders of francophone Quebec found especially disturbing. Then, in 1949, the Parliament of Canada abolished judicial appeals
to the Privy Council, which had been so attentive to the principle of provincial rights.[4] From 1897 to 1944, Liberal governments had ruled Quebec for all but three years; but from 1936 on the centralism of the Liberal
government at Ottawa turned francophone voters more and more
towards the Union nationale of Maurice Duplessis, just as in 1886 they
had flocked to the Parti national of Honoré Mercier.

Since the late nineteenth century, the Québécois elite had developed a system of government designed to stabilize francophone society and culture. A tax and labour regime favourable to big business enticed capital to exploit the province's natural resources and reserves of cheap labour. This arrangement created industrial jobs for the surplus rural population and reduced francophone emigration. In order to maintain a docile labour force, the elite ceded to the Catholic church a leading role in education, social welfare, and even labour organization. In collaborating with big business, it turned French Canadians into what one writer would hyperbolically call 'white niggers of America.'[5]

Duplessis continued these policies in the face of growing postwar labour unrest, siding with English-speaking capital against his own people, playing on traditional francophone fears to hold the restive minority in check. In his zeal to keep his province at arm's length from the rest of Canada, he followed his Liberal predecessor, Louis-Alexandre Taschereau, in refusing to take part in 'shared-cost' (federally subsidized) social programs initiated by Ottawa. A blatant bias against the cities in the distribution of legislative seats helped to keep him in power from 1944 until his death in 1959. But the stability of Quebec society – essentially a rural society with industrial ghettos – was breaking down under the pressure of industrialization and urban growth. The sudden death of Duplessis's successor in 1960 plunged the Union nationale into a general election unready and divided. Led by a former federal cabinet minister, Jean Lesage, the Liberals won an unexpected victory.

A feeling of liberation swept through a repressed people, and the Quiet Revolution commenced. It was quiet because it was constitutional, but a revolution because it entailed the overthrow of a corrupt and oppressive political and social order. The church was stripped of its privileges as the traditional guardian of French culture. Committed to modernizing Quebec, the new government was inspired by the mood of the moment to more and more radical measures. In 1963 it nationalized the hydroelectric industry and directly confronted Ottawa. The expansion of both federal and provincial governments since 1940 had heightened the competition for revenue. Quebec's ambitious plans created an especially urgent need for new fiscal resources. Profiting from the political instability at Ottawa after the fall of Diefenbaker's government, and the dependence of the Liberals in particular on Quebec votes, Lesage demanded a wholesale redistribution of responsibilities and resources from the federal government to the provinces – his own in particular. By the end of 1964, Ottawa had conceded a larger share of personal income tax and the right to opt out of shared-cost programs with compensation.

Quebec also won the right to set up its own contributory old-age pension scheme instead of Ottawa's proposed Canada Pension Plan.

The nationalist tenor of these policies was undisguised; it was in fact a principal selling-point to the Quebec electorate. Hydroelectricity, immense in its economic potential, was vital to the development of the provincial economy. The pension scheme promised to amass a huge fund under provincial control to be used for economic development and social improvement. Together with 'opting out' from shared-cost programs, it had another effect: in Quebec the welfare state would be French-speaking, and Quebecers beholden for its benefits to the provincial, not to the federal government. Finally, these policies created a plethora of jobs for the new francophone managerial middle class, the chief supporters of the Quiet Revolution. The bureaucracies of corporate capitalism tended to be English-speaking, especially in their middle and upper reaches. Those of the francophone state were French-speaking to the very top.[6]

The Quiet Revolution sprang from changes outside Quebec as well. Francophones had deferred to British imperial power, and cooperated with its surrogates in North America, for protection against what Henri Bourassa called 'l'américanisme saxonisant.' But now a revolution in world affairs had demolished the British empire, reducing its forces to a regiment in the American world empire. British power could no longer safeguard Quebec against American imperialism; but was that protection even necessary? The same revolution in international affairs had turned the American empire from an enemy of French Canada into its protector against a greater peril: the threat of world communism.

Either way, the old strategy of collaboration with the English had lost its point, and the crisis of morale that beset English-speaking Canada during the early 1960s only underlined the fact. For two centuries a leading feature of French Canada's survival strategy in the face of assimilative pressures had been the 'revenge of the cradle.' The term referred to the breathtaking fecundity that had kept the francophone population at about 30 per cent of the Canadian total ever since Confederation, despite transcontinental expansion and the great increase of English-speaking numbers by immigration. Now the Québécois gratefully abandoned the revenge of the cradle for less strenuous revenges: the revenge of the ballot box and the conference table. They discovered the pleasures of voting for the nationalist option. In 1966 the Union nationale regained office partly by outdoing Lesage's Liberals in nationalist zeal. A year later René Lévesque, leader of the Liberal left ('English

Canada needs a Lévesque,' wrote Gad Horowitz in 1965[7]) broke away to found the 'sovereigntist' movement that became the Parti Québécois.

Even under Lesage, however, an incessant barrage of demands on Ottawa and the rest of Canada evoked the question: What exactly does Quebec want? To which Lesage pithily replied: What exactly do you want Quebec *not* to want? Lesage's evasion prompted Donald Creighton to a wry comment on the premier's precarious position atop the nationalist tiger: a Canadian from the other nine provinces, he said, might well have as little relish for specifying what he did *not* want Quebec to want as Lesage evidently did for specifying what Quebec *did* want.[8]

Militancy in francophone Quebec, confusion in the rest of Canada: these were the circumstances that drove Creighton in 1965 to speak out on domestic politics as he had on external affairs. He had spent a quarter-century documenting the greatness of John A. Macdonald and the transcontinental empire that was Macdonald's masterwork. He had just capped the biography with a book describing in detail how and why, a century earlier, Confederation had come to pass.[9] Starting out a true believer in the myth of the Fathers' centralist intent, he had become its most intransigent advocate. He had brought the centralist idea of Confederation to its peak and become in the process English Canada's leading historian.

And yet, to a pessimist, both that history and Creighton's career might seem the stuff of tragedy. He had begun by recounting the failure of the commercial empire in its competition with the United States. He had embarked on the story of its successor state, the Dominion of Canada, believing that one of the pillars of that state, its centralism, had already been gravely, if not fatally, damaged by judicial misconstruction. Almost at once another pillar, British power, was shattered by military defeat. Now the very foundation seemed to be crumbling. Just when a common front was desperately needed against American economic and cultural penetration, Quebec had chosen to challenge the deal struck by Macdonald and Cartier regarding French Canada's place in Confederation.

Worse still, Ottawa seemed all too ready to give in. Soon after taking office, Pearson set up a royal commission of inquiry into bilingualism and biculturalism in Canada, with authority to recommend measures 'to develop the Canadian Confederation on the basis of an equal partnership between the two founding races.' Equal partnership, founding races: the very words invited the commission to propose radical changes in the structure of Confederation. The appointment as co-chairman of André Laurendeau, editor-in-chief of *Le Devoir* (Henri Bourassa's old paper) and a pioneer of the new secular Quebec nationalism, seemed to guarantee such proposals (although in fact the commission would wind up several years later, after Laurendeau's death, without tackling constitutional problems).[10] Then, in 1964, the devolution of power and resources to Quebec further threatened the status quo. Nominally, Ottawa's concessions were available to any province that chose to take them; but only Quebec wanted them. The result was to establish a special status for the province of Quebec within Confederation, weakening Canada (thought Creighton) without satisfying Quebec nationalism.

Beyond Ottawa's faint-heartedness Creighton detected a widespread public readiness to question and discard Canada's historic institutions in the interest of national renewal. The inclination came naturally, he opined, to city dwellers in their cramped but modern high-rises. They had been taught by journalists, television personalities, and advertisers that anything older than ten years was positively medieval. Sharing this prejudice or hoping to exploit it, would-be renovators could be heard scorning the BNA Act as 'a battered old hulk,' 'a relic of the horse and buggy days,' and, worst of all, 'a piece of antiquated mid-Victorian plumbing' – in affluent North America, no stigma could be more humiliating than that. Then there were those other revolutionaries who wanted not simply to dismiss the past but to rewrite it to suit their agenda. How could Canadians, in general so ignorant of history, be expected to see through all these politically inspired distortions? Creighton set out to remind his fellow-citizens of the framers' intentions and to shed the 'hard light of history' on some of the shiny new myths.[11]

His chief target figured in the title of a controversial article in *Saturday Night*: 'The Myth of Biculturalism, or the Great French-Canadian Sales Campaign.'[12] The 'myth' was the idea that Confederation was founded on a compact between two founding cultures, anglophone and francophone, whereby the two would coexist on equal terms throughout Canada. Far from it: the Fathers of Confederation had provided for the use of both French and English in the federal courts and legislature and in those of Quebec. They had also guaranteed the continuance of Quebec's distinctive civil law and the educational rights of religious minorities wherever those rights were established by law. That was all: they had done nothing more.

Actually, wrote Creighton, the myth of biculturalism was so utterly unsupported by any contemporary document that its propagators were reduced to representing the supposed compact as an 'extra-legal,' 'implicit,' or 'tacit' agreement – an 'unspoken moral commitment.'[13] They deduced it from the federal laws passed to set up government on the Prairies once Rupert's Land, the old fur-trading domain of the Hudson's Bay Company, was incorporated into the Dominion in 1870. The Manitoba Act had set up that province on the same lines as Quebec, with similar provisions as to schools and official languages. The North-West Territories Act of 1875, as amended in 1877, had followed suit. Biculturalists insisted that the abolition of these arrangements between 1890 and 1905 constituted a breach of Canada's founding compact. Creighton disagreed. He denied that either statute reflected a commitment to Dominion-wide biculturalism by the Fathers of Confederation. The relevant provisions of the Manitoba Act had been forced on Ottawa by the resistance of the Red River Colony – or, rather, of Louis Riel's upstart 'provisional government' – to incorporation into Canada; the federal government had chosen to bargain rather than fight. Those of the North-West Territories Act had been imposed on the federal government by exigencies of a different and less dramatic sort but were no more binding.

It had been unwise, thought Creighton, to make the Prairie territories into replicas of Quebec before they had had time to develop their true, anglophone character. They had thrown off the yoke of biculturalism as soon as they could, in a controversy as prolonged and bitter as anything in Canadian history. Any bid to placate French Canadians at the present day by trying to reimpose biculturalism on western Canada was likely to cause the same backlash as the first attempt in the 1870s. Creighton deplored the prospect as divisive at a juncture when united resistance to American power was imperative. Besides, on an English-speaking continent, one did francophones no favour by trying to cocoon them in a culture that must condemn them to isolation and backwardness.[14]

Creighton developed these arguments, historical and political, in a series of talks and articles and in *Canada's First Century*. In 1971 he summarized them in a brief to a special joint committee of both houses of Parliament on the Canadian constitution.[15] Naturally, such frankness on so sensitive a subject provoked an emphatic response. Creighton must have expected hostility from Quebec, but he was taken aback by the reaction of some of his own colleagues and former students. One whom he singled out for tart notice was the historian Ramsay Cook, whose essay on 'The Meaning of Confederation' was cited against him by Claude Ryan, Laurendeau's successor as editor of *Le Devoir*. Also painful was the public repudiation by W.L. Morton, who charged Creighton with 'cultural continentalism' (of all things) for invoking the predominantly English-speaking nature of North America against the national aspirations of French Canada. Morton and Creighton were joint editors of the Canadian Centenary Series, an ambitious multi-volume history of Canada, and Morton delivered his rebuke in an introduction to the English version of a French-Canadian nationalist tract.[16] This was taking sides with a vengeance!

Another bruising episode was the rebuttal of Creighton's arguments by one of his former students in the *Canadian Historical Review*. When it appeared, Ralph Heintzman was still only a graduate student – though no ordinary student, being also associate editor of the *Journal of Canadian Studies*. He had been urged to submit his paper for publication by the editor of the *Review*, R. Craig Brown, a former protégé of Creighton's and a member of the department from which Creighton had just retired. Consulted by Heintzman before publication, Creighton replied supportively, but perhaps he had no choice, and he may have expected voices to rise in his defence. When one such statement, which he knew about, did not appear in the *Review*, he accused the editor of suppressing it, only to be told that no 'acceptable' manuscript had been received on the subject. The article in question appeared only three years later, not in the *Review* but under Heintzman's aegis in the *Journal*.[17]

In 1960 Creighton had stood among English-speaking Canadians as the ranking expert on Canadian history and on the origins of Confederation in particular. Now, scarcely a decade later, his own colleagues and students seemed all but unanimously determined to reject his authority on these matters. Even among his contemporaries, only Senator Eugene Forsey, the veteran constitutionalist, stood beside him.[18]

The quarrel over the bicultural compact went to the heart of the Confederation settlement.[19] For the peoples of United Canada, of course, placing cultural matters under local control had been a primary object of Confederation. However, each of the four original provinces contained cultural minorities. The BNA Act protected these not on any uniform basis, but according to their numbers and power. The act made English an official language in Quebec, but it did not make French an official language in the other three provinces, although New Brunswick in particular contained a large francophone minority.

Another important cultural issue was education. Nothing had done more to turn Upper Canadians against the union of 1841 than the government's reliance on Lower Canadian votes to impose Roman Catholic schools on Upper Canada against the wishes of the local majority. Upper Canadians supported Confederation largely to prevent such abuses in future, and Lower Canadians – especially French Canadians – supported it largely to preclude reprisals. But this security for the majority in each section came only at the price of entrenching the existing privileges of the minority – Catholic in Ontario, Protestant in Quebec – in the BNA Act. Section 93 of the act empowered the provinces to make laws on education, provided that they did not impair 'any right or privilege with respect to denominational schools which any class of persons have by law in the province at the union' (that is, at the moment when the province joined Confederation) or was established subsequently by provincial law. An aggrieved minority could appeal to Ottawa for protection, as the Franco-Manitobans had in the 1890s.

The meaning of section 93 was central to both the New Brunswick school question of the 1870s and the Manitoba school question. In 1871 the New Brunswick legislature had replaced the province's denominational schools with secular ones. The measure had become a federal issue when John A. Macdonald was asked to disallow it and refused to do so. Later the Judicial Committee of the Privy Council had decided that there was no room for federal remedial legislation because the denominational system had existed by *custom*, not by *law*. Perhaps in recognition of this flaw in section 93, the Manitoba Act of 1870 had authorized Parliament, for that province only, to pass remedial legislation to restore rights existing by custom as well as by law.

The defunding of Catholic schools had not hurt only francophones, but in both New Brunswick and Manitoba it had affected them above all. In both provinces the francophone community was entirely Catholic and supplied the great majority of pupils in the Catholic schools. In the case of the Manitoba Act, moreover, the school provisions had been included at the behest of Louis Riel and his supporters in return for their consent to Canada's takeover of the Red River Colony. For this reason the constitutional status of Catholic schools in both provinces was understood, then and subsequently, to form part of the deal between French- and English-speaking Canadians that underpinned Confederation.

The historical disagreement between Creighton and his opponents concerned the terms of the deal. Had the Fathers of Confederation meant to protect Catholic educational privileges in New Brunswick, only to be thwarted by those two little words 'by law,' or had those words been inserted into the BNA Act precisely to preclude such protection? And what about the west? In both Manitoba and the North-West Territories, the Parliament of Canada had established Catholic educational privileges. Had it acted in the belief that 'the spirit of Confederation' required it or for reasons that made those provisions less sacrosanct? If those provisions did indeed manifest 'the spirit of Confederation,' what might that spirit imply for the three remaining provinces: British Columbia, Prince Edward Island, and Newfoundland? And might not the spirit of Confederation reach beyond the matter of denominational or non-denominational schooling to establish minority-language rights, including the language of instruction?

In the absence of any express commitment, it is difficult to conclude that Confederation entailed some broad agreement to set the two founding cultures on an equal footing throughout Canada. The BNA Act established French and English as official languages in Quebec and in federal institutions, but in general the founders treated culture as a local issue – indeed doing so was, for Canadians, a primary object of Confederation. Accordingly, the act included various provisions regarding schools, some relating only to Quebec and Ontario, others protecting minority privileges that might exist elsewhere. It laid down no general principle regarding biculturalism in Canada as a whole; neither did it provide specifically for Rupert's Land, though the annexation of that territory was a major object of Confederation.

But these omissions do not justify Creighton's contention that the bicultural provisions of the Manitoba Act and the North-West Territories Act were just temporary expedients, lacking the force of a compact. In Manitoba they had such force for the reasons that John Ewart had stated in the 1890s: they were the outcome of negotiations between the government of Canada and the de facto government of the Red River Colony. Riel's government, moreover, had demanded those cultural safeguards precisely because the French-speaking inhabitants feared that annexation to Canada would occasion a swamping influx of anglophone settlement, and the federal government had conceded those provisions in the same expectation. For these reasons, the idea that the predominantly anglophone character of Manitoba in 1890 justified the abolition of bicultural institutions without the consent of the minority is groundless. If ever John A. Macdonald should have vetoed a provincial statute, it was the Manitoba School Act of 1890.

The North-West Territories Act was also in essence a compact, because it was a constitution – a fundamental law. I explained in chapter 9 why the Constitutional Act of 1791 could be interpreted as a treaty even though it was not the result of negotiations.[20] Creighton tried to belittle the bicultural provisions of the North-West Territories Act by minimizing the deliberation with which they were adopted. It happens, though, that the school provisions were included very deliberately. They were added to the bill at the suggestion of Edward Blake, who in 1875 stood second only to Prime Minister Alexander Mackenzie in the Liberal hierarchy, although he had temporarily withdrawn from the government. Blake noted that the measure's object was that of 'determining in advance of settlement what the character of the institutions of the country should be in which we invite people to settle.'[21] Clearly he saw his educational provisions as fundamental features of the territorial constitution.

I explained in chapter 9 that a statute that was also a compact, such as the Constitutional Act and the North-West Territories Act, relied for its force as a compact on two related features of British constitutionalism: respect for the rule of law and a culture or habit of restraint in the exercise of political power. The distinction between what was legal and what was constitutional; the importance of avoiding unconstitutional legislation – these ideas formed the basis for the defence of minority rights in Manitoba and the North-West Territories in the 1890s. The Conservative imperialist D'Alton McCarthy proposed to extinguish those rights on the ground that Canada was a British country and the sooner French Canadians were turned into British ones the better. McCarthy's chief opponents – Edward Blake, David Mills, Wilfrid Laurier – condemned the very idea as un-British. For Mills, the state existed to defend the rights of individuals, not to express some national essence and impose it on every individual within its reach. He denied its right 'to undertake to destroy the mental vision of one section of a population with a design to creating it anew.' Laurier condemned McCarthy's proposal as the antithesis of all traditions of British government in North America.[22]

Blake, Mills, and Laurier were Liberals. But the ideology of the rule of law was not exclusively Liberal: it was British, and that eminent Conservative John A. Macdonald, who also deplored McCarthy's proposal, had summed it up pithily in the Confederation Debates of 1865. 'In all countries the rights of the majority take care of themselves,' he said, 'but it is only in countries like England, enjoying constitutional liberty, and safe from the tyranny of a single despot or of an unbridled democracy, that the rights of minorities are regarded.' To Ramsay Cook, a century later, these words expressed 'the essential spirit of Confederation.' In his essay 'The Meaning of Confederation,' which Claude Ryan cited against Donald Creighton in *Le Devoir*, Cook quoted Creighton's hero in order to explain why the Winnipeg journalist J.W. Dafoe had been wrong, back in 1915, to suppose that the extinction of minority rights in Manitoba was justified just because it was legal and favoured by public opinion. Dafoe was mistaken both in his legalism and in his appeal to the tyranny of the majority. Macdonald's words showed that Canada was not meant to be that sort of place.[23]

Cook was no Conservative, but W.L. Morton was, and Morton's support for biculturalism fitted his preference for 'constitutional liberty' over 'unbridled democracy.' His historical studies persuaded him that Canada's existence had a moral purpose and that its traditions formed part of that purpose, which was to cultivate a distinct and superior society, resisting all pressure or temptation to assimilate to the American model. The Liberal governments of the 1940s and 1950s ('the unprincipled régime of today, which rots Canadian political life as fungus rots a log'[24]) seemed to him the very antithesis of that purpose. Like Creighton and George Grant, he was disgusted by their eagerness to cast off Canada's British traditions in favour of a subservient intimacy with Washington. By 1960, this son and grandson of Liberal and Progressive farmer-politicians had become an adherent of the Progressive Conservative party.

Morton's historical vision blended the Laurentian thesis of Creighton and Harold Innis with the focus of those Grit historians whom Creighton had derided for their devotion to 'Robert, Francis and Wilfrid Responsible-Government.' Morton rejected, however, the continentalism of the liberal-nationalist historians who had been Creighton's chief targets. He excused Dafoe's sketch of Canada as 'an American nation' (which so vexed Creighton) as a valid reaction to earlier overemphasis on its Britishness, but he resented depictions of Canada as a second-rate United States, robbed by historical accident of its birthright of frontier democracy. As he saw it, the country formed a distinct society with distinct origins, distinctive northern resources, and distinctive values and institutions sprung from a sparse economy and confrontation with the harsh northern habitat.[25]

Location and habitat aside, Canadian society and institutions had been shaped chiefly by cultural diversity. With French and English,

Gaelic and English-speaking Scots, and two mutually antagonistic sorts of Irish, plus German-speaking communities in Upper Canada and Nova Scotia, British North America had needed political institutions that could combine these elements in concord – needed, in Macdonald's terms, 'constitutional liberty' rather than 'unbridled democracy.' That was why responsible government was so important. The one political value that most British Americans shared was the habit of loyalty to a monarch – an absentee monarch. Responsible government used this habit to control frontier democracy, combining popular representation with royal power in a strong government moderated by two unwritten conventions of governance: executive accountability to the elective legislature and a commitment to the rule of law. In 'whiggish' language that might have been used by John Ewart and a score of other voices from his youth, W.P.M. Kennedy and Chester Martin among them, Morton declared responsible government to be Canada's 'single but significant contribution to the slow elaboration of human freedom.'[26]

Canadian constitutionalism was less individualist in its philosophical basis than American democracy, but Morton believed that it offered greater scope for cultural diversity. In the republic, the supposed sovereignty of the people emboldened society to demand of individual citizens far greater conformity than was required of them in Canada. Because Canada was founded on allegiance to a monarch rather than to a sovereign people, there was no pressure to conform to some 'Canadian way of life.' Morton summed up the difference in another chestnut of Canadian political thought. 'Not life, liberty, and the pursuit of happiness, but peace, order, and good government are what the national government of Canada guarantees. Under these, it is assumed, life, liberty, and happiness may be achieved, but by each according to his taste. For the society of allegiance admits of a diversity the society of compact does not, and one of the blessings of Canadian life is that there is no Canadian way of life, much less two, but a unity under the Crown admitting of a thousand diversities.'[27]

It was that unity, carried over into Confederation, which made the union of 1867 imperial rather than federal in character. Here Morton cited features of the BNA Act that centralists had been emphasizing for decades: the supposed allocation of the residuary legislative power to Ottawa; the limited powers of legislation assigned to the provinces; the federal power to disallow provincial legislation; the naming of the Parliament of Canada as the final guardian of minority rights in education. To these he added 'the maintenance of the Crown and common allegiance, with the legislative sovereignty of Parliament and the rule of law rather than popular will.'[28]

So Morton shared John A. Macdonald's taste for 'constitutional liberty' rather than 'unbridled democracy' and esteemed Canada's monarchical institutions for providing it. But was there more to this than the smugness that had sustained conservative British Americans ever since the days of John Beverley Robinson – the complacency that Goldwin Smith had challenged in dismissing Canadian monarchy as a fig-leaf for a politics that was really more democratic than that of the United States?[29] After all, when Morton delivered the paean to Canadian liberty quoted above, Quebec was still under the rule of the Union nationale and much of the rest of Canada groaned under the Presbyterian Sabbath. Quite apart from that, there was the New Brunswick schools question, the abolition of bicultural institutions on the Prairies, and the elimination of French-language public education in Ontario. Where had Ottawa, vaunted guardian of constitutional liberty, minority rights, and the rule of law, been then?

Before convicting Morton of smugness, we must remember two things: he was comparing Canada with the United States of McCarthyism and racial segregation, and he was only too aware of the limits of constitutional liberty in Canada. To him, unlike most twentieth-century centralists, the triumph of provincial rights was tragic less for its supposed erosion of Ottawa's legislative power than for its destruction of Ottawa's capacity to protect the rights of francophone minorities against the tyranny of provincial majorities. He called the story of Ottawa's failure 'The End of the Macdonaldian Constitution and the Return to Duality' and placed it in the very period that had evoked Goldwin Smith's scepticism. The 'Macdonaldian constitution' was the supposedly centralist settlement of 1867 – a constitution preponderantly national in powers and interest, in which the national interests were safeguarded by disallowance, and minority educational rights by the national power of remedial action under section 93 of the BNA Act. Duality meant 'political action by English Canada and French Canada as groups, or blocs': that is, the reflection in politics of the country's cultural duality.[30] Morton saw the breakdown of the 'Macdonaldian constitution' as the origin of the unity crisis of his own day.

Cultural duality was, to Morton, the fundamental fact of Canadian history. It had existed since the Conquest and been recognized in law ever since the Quebec Act of 1774, never acknowledged as a matter of principle but accommodated piecemeal, as circumstances required, in a series of legal instruments beginning with the Treaty of Paris. But some of those instruments had established a corresponding political duality, and this he regretted. The first was the Constitutional Act of 1791, which had divided the old province of Quebec into Upper and Lower Canada in order to satisfy the Loyalists. In 1840 the Act of Union had preserved that duality, even within United Canada, by allotting Upper and Lower Canada equal representation in the Legislative Assembly. The executive had recognized it in practice by appointing equal numbers from each section to the legislative council.

The temper of Canada in the 1960s strongly reminded Morton of United Canada a century earlier, when the sectional tensions of political duality within a legislative union had produced separatist movements in both Canada East and West. The modern demand for special status for Quebec reminded him of the 'small federation' of the *rouges* and Grits: the proposal for loose federal association between the two sections that had been mooted by Antoine-Aimé Dorion and adopted by the Upper Canadian Reform convention of 1859. It was now forgotten, he remarked, that the 'small federation' had remained a real alternative to Confederation until only a few months before the passage of the BNA Act.[31]

Morton valued the 'Macdonaldian constitution' so highly because he saw it as something more than just the 'small federation' framed in a larger association. With its concentration of power in the federal government, it meant to him a rejection of the notion that cultural duality must entail political duality. The spirit of Confederation had consisted in charging the federal government with the protection of minorities throughout Canada rather than leaving each province's minority at the mercy of the local majority. Unfortunately, the structure was shoddy and collapsed under strain. The Privy Council was partly to blame, through its recognition of provincial sovereignty and diminution of Ottawa's power to legislate for the peace, order, and good government of Canada. By increasing the power and prestige of the provincial governments, ignorant British judges had sapped the political and legal power of the Dominion to protect minority rights, for the provincial governments were the strongholds of local democracy, and majoritarian local democracy was the great enemy of minority rights. Even before that, though, Macdonald himself had shown an inexplicable failure of will in refusing to veto the New Brunswick School Act of 1871, although that measure contravened the spirit of Confederation if not the letter of the BNA Act.

But the triumph of provincial rights had done its worst damage in the west. Together with the upsurge of English–French animosity, as manifest in the career of Louis Riel and the enactment of the Manitoba Schools Act, it had demolished cultural duality there. The decisive moment had come in 1896, when Laurier had thwarted the Conservative government's intention to coerce Manitoba and then won the ensuing general election. Significantly, Laurier won his majority in Quebec – evidence that racial tension had driven French Quebec to take refuge in the bunker of provincial rights. What Morton called the 'Laurierian constitution' had lasted until 1926, and Quebec's continuing political isolation had culminated in the present crisis.[32]

To Morton then, as to every mid-century centralist, Canada's constitutional history was a story of declension from a pristine ideal, and salvation lay in a return to that ideal. Morton believed that the only hope for national unity lay in reviving Ottawa's guardianship of minorities and adapting it to the modern world. Cultural duality should be established throughout Canada in every department of public life under the aegis of a reinvigorated federal government. To this end, individual and group rights should be entrenched in a written charter of fundamental law and a process devised for amending the constitution without recourse to the British Parliament. Morton also favoured establishing a special judicial panel as the final court of appeal in civil-law matters originating in Quebec. This would answer a longstanding grievance of Quebec nationalists: the common-law bias that they accused the Supreme Court of Canada and the Privy Council of imposing on Quebec's civil code.

English Canada's historic rejection of cultural duality, and Ottawa's failure to defend minority rights, gave Morton every sympathy for Quebec nationalism. He acknowledged an imperative need to respond to French-Canadian discontents. But he emphatically denounced any move towards special status for Quebec: 'I cannot avoid a wry surprise when I hear my French compatriots urge that Quebec must be further freed from federal controls ... To me it seems that the provinces, except in a relatively few matters, can, and in fact do, do exactly what they please.' Quebec must remain a province like the others, and any attempt to secede must be resisted by force if necessary.[33] Those English-Canadian intellectuals who sympathized with the demand for special status he disparaged as showing 'that extraordinary capacity of the English Canadian liberal to be convinced of the justice of any cause except his own.' He named Ramsay Cook in particular; but Cook himself would shortly break with the New Democratic Party over its commitment to special status.[34]

Creighton and Morton both believed that the national unity crisis threatened Canada's survival, that an accurate appreciation of Canadian history was necessary for solving the crisis, and that Canadians, in their anxious search for a solution, were rejecting the lessons of history. However, they quite disagreed as to what those lessons were. Both men were conservatives, both centralists, and both nationalists, but when it came to national unity they saw Canadian history and its implications for the current crisis quite differently.

What was the nature and the source of their disagreement? I suggested at the start of this chapter that it concerned the nature of the relationship between French- and English-speaking Canadians. Morton saw the two peoples as historic equals, their equality arising from Canada's fundamental cultural duality. He was willing therefore to entrench that equality in the constitution, though only in ways that seemed to him likely to heal rather than harm the Canadian political nationality. Creighton saw French Canadians as fundamentally marginal to the life of an English-speaking continent. He gladly granted their equality as individual fellow-citizens but thought it could only weaken Canada to grant them equality as a group.

This divergence of opinion on national unity flowed partly from differences of temperament. Morton's thought was more diffuse than Creighton's; he was a historian of vision and insight but lacked the Ontarian's logical consistency and single-mindedness. Creighton, sure in his Laurentian vision, could confidently make statements for which he could have no jot of proof but which followed from his assumptions as the night the day. *Most Canadians* would have preferred legislative union in 1867; *of course* the Fathers of Confederation had based their design on the Old Colonial System; the London conference had rejected the proposal to call the head of the provincial executive superintendent rather than lieutenant-governor *perhaps with some regret.*[35] Creighton could write such things because he believed them implicitly. Morton *wanted* to believe them but could not attain the same degree of certitude. Take their treatment of the New Brunswick Schools Act. Creighton simply ignored the problem, both in his biography of Macdonald and in *Canada's First Century,* but Morton agonized over it: Macdonald's refusal to disallow the act all but undermined Morton's belief in the centralist design of Confederation. Having followed the collapse of the

254   1940–1982: Continentalism and Nationalisms

'Macdonaldian constitution' to its glum dénouement, he concluded: 'Such was the curious outcome of the Macdonaldian attempt to use the constitution of the Empire for national ends. It is even difficult now, particularly in the light of his own stand on the New Brunswick Schools Act, to see how he could have hoped that it might succeed.'[36]

The temperamental difference between Morton and Creighton appears clearly in the confessional tone of a talk that Morton gave in 1964. He spoke as one who had been raised to think of himself as British and the better for being so, but who had suddenly and belatedly realized that now all that counted for nothing.[37] Creighton, bred in the same beliefs, seems never to have doubted the continuing value of his native tradition, even while he lamented its abandonment and destruction by the liberal intelligentsia of his time.

Having distanced himself from 'the British illusion,' as he put it, Morton found himself able to contemplate what he called revolutionary solutions to the national unity crisis even before Creighton began throwing the term around. Despite his esteem for Canadian-style parliamentary government, he was able to consider such 'American' ideas as a charter of rights, an elected senate, even a constitutional convention. His personal epiphany, moreover, had a counterpart in his insistence that the Quiet Revolution was above all a revolt of French Canadians against French Canadians – 'only a small part ... against "the English," and still less against Canada.'[38] Together, the two observations implied this conclusion: that if 'the English' had lost the prestige and arrogance of empire, and French Canadians had cast off their subservience to Rome, each had cast off those characteristics that had traditionally repelled the other, and there was no further obstacle to their association as equal individuals rather than mutually antagonistic groups.

This assumption led Morton to hope against hope that Canadians could now abandon political duality for ever and cooperate to ensure Canada's survival, which he believed vital to the endurance of both French- and English-Canadian culture. However essential cultural duality might be to the Canadian political nationality, political duality must be avoided at all costs. For one thing, modern Canada was too diverse, in its regional and ethnic plurality, to tolerate it. For another, history taught Morton that a strong central government was essential to Canada's survival, and he refused to take his personal revolution to the point of rejecting history. Finally, political duality was a negation of what he saw as Canada's moral purpose. The chief importance of 'the Canadian experiment' in the modern world was to show that cultural plurality could be combined with political unity without recourse to repression.[39]

Morton's propensity to recognize French- and English-speaking Canadians as equal partners in a joint enterprise was reinforced by his Manitoban perspective on Canadian history. Although he came to value the constitution of 1867 for its centralism, that did not mean that he was reconciled to the economic and political hegemony of central Canada. He took up the idea of an elective Senate because it would redress the balance of political power between the populous centre and the rest of Canada.[40] History taught him, though, that central Canada's hegemony was not only a matter of parliamentary votes and financial dealings in Montreal, Ottawa, and Toronto; it was also present in the political culture of his own province. His term for the political and demographic trend that had led to the extinction of cultural duality in Manitoba was 'the triumph of Ontario democracy.'[41]

He came to this perception perhaps because, though he was a farmer by background and proud of it, he was not of the Ontario farming stock that had settled his province after the annexation of the North-West. His British antecedents and Anglican faith set him apart from the predominant Presbyterianism and Methodism of the Ontarian settlement. At any rate, though born into Manitoba's Liberal-Progressive tradition, in manhood he turned away from the majoritarian liberalism of J.W. Dafoe and the *Manitoba Free Press* to the 'national' liberalism of that great upholder of the rule of law, John Ewart. He recognized Ewart as the founder of a nationalist tradition in Manitoba that Dafoe had continued, and he borrowed the title of Ewart's nationalist manifesto, 'The Kingdom of Canada,' for his own general history. But he also admired Ewart for his championship of Franco-Manitoban rights, and his own assessment of the events leading to the annexation of the Red River Colony in 1870 had much in common with Ewart's, published seventy years earlier.[42]

His bicultural ideal of Canada was very much in the tradition of Ewart, for nationalism led them both to a centralism to which they were not born. Morton's feeling for the wrongs inflicted on French Canadians outside Quebec revealed to him, in the education and language provisions of the BNA Act, the Manitoba Act, and the North-West Territories Act, the outline of the compact that was implicit in Ewart's thought and somewhat more articulate in F.R. Scott's: a centralist compact, in which the federal government stood as guarantor of the rights of French- and English-speaking minorities throughout Canada.[43] That compact had not originated in any explicit agreement among the Fathers of Confederation – Morton denounced that idea as vigorously as Dafoe and Ewart had impeached the provincial-compact theory – as emphatically as even Creighton could wish. 'The claim that Confederation was in any way a treaty or compact, political or cultural, is the purest mythology, without a shred of historical evidence to support it.'[44] Historically, the compact had arisen out of pragmatic responses to the pressure of circumstances. Still, it was a historical reality, and the fruits of its repudiation were proving bitter. The time had come to establish French–English equality throughout Canada as a matter of principle – or was it already too late?

Ewart, Scott, Morton: three English Canadians featured in the last five chapters who combined constitutional centralism with a desire to establish French- and English-speaking Canadians as equal partners in a shared political nationality, a common Canadianism. One was a lifelong Liberal, one a lifelong social democrat and founder of the Co-operative Commonwealth Federation, and one a convert to conservatism from his native liberalism. What did they share? One thing was a close encounter with cultural duality: a lived encounter in the cases of Ewart the Winnipegger of the 1880s and 1890s and Scott, a Montrealer; a historical encounter in Morton's case. Another element perhaps was Anglicanism. Except for Irish Anglicans such as D'Alton McCarthy, it was Methodists and voluntarist Presbyterians – adherents of the two religious traditions that shaped 'Ontario democracy' – who were most deeply hostile to French Canadianism. Ewart forsook his native Presbyterianism in a Manitoba in which 'Ontario democracy' was on the rampage; Morton's Anglicanism helped to distance him from the spirit of that transplanted populism; Scott's father was an Anglican cleric.[45]

The one prominent English-Canadian historian of his time to uphold the provincial-compact theory was also an Anglican and a westerner. This was George Stanley, who published two books on Louis Riel: a study of the North-West Rebellion and a biography. In *A Short History of the Canadian Constitution*, published in 1969, Stanley declared: 'When I first began teaching, my attitude reflected the period in which I lived as well as the ideas of John S. Ewart. However, during the years which have followed, I have modified my views and today I believe that the constitution of 1867 was just what the writers and politicians of the nineteenth century called it, a compact.'[46] Canadians had accepted it as such for more than half a century, until the stresses of the First World War and the Great Depression had led to a rewriting of history and the denunciation of the compact theory. Now it was time to rewrite the constitution in the interest of national unity.

In 1956, Stanley had made the compact theory the theme of his presidential address to the Canadian Historical Association. That year the annual meeting was in Montreal, and Stanley's talk was basically a précis of the arguments of the Tremblay Commission – a fact he advertised by borrowing his title from Father Arès, the commission's constitutional expert. This may explain what happened during his talk.

While Stanley was speaking, the door opened and a man in his mid-thirties entered the room, attended by a group of what might be called his acolytes. They made their way to the front of the room and sat there for a while, making no secret of their dissent from the speaker's views. Then they demonstratively walked out. Their leader was a law professor at the Université de Montréal and co-founder of the iconoclastic political magazine *Cité libre*, by name Pierre Trudeau.[47] Twelve years later, Trudeau would become prime minister of a government committed to implementing the centralist compact of Ewart, Scott, and Morton.

16

A Historic Blunder:
Trudeau and Patriation

Pierre Elliott Trudeau was the federal Liberals' answer to the Quiet Revolution. Alarmed at the advance of separatist nationalism in Quebec, wary of the charisma of René Lévesque, the Liberals in 1965 recruited three leading Québécois federalists into the Ottawa caucus. Jean Marchand was a trade union leader, a close collaborator with the Lesage government, and a member of the Royal Commission on Bilingualism and Biculturalism. Gérard Pelletier, also of working-class origins, had been editor of the Montreal daily *La Presse* until 1964, when he was fired for his radicalism. Trudeau, the son of a successful businessman, shared his colleagues' egalitarian values. Influenced by his English-speaking mother and a cosmopolitan education, including courses at Harvard and the London School of Economics, he scorned the parochialism of Quebec nationalism even in its secular, progressive form. In the intellectual circles of postwar Montreal he was drawn to F.R. Scott, with whom he shared a commitment to social democracy and civil liberties. Not being a Quebec nationalist, he had no instinctive dislike of Scott's centralism, although he did reject the dogmatic centralism of the Canadian left as self-defeating.[1]

Though a lawyer by profession, Trudeau was that quintessence of twentieth-century liberalism, the social scientist. His intellectual make-up contained a strong technocratic tincture. Having rejected the victim-history of Quebec nationalism, he was not strongly moved by any other version of the past: he was more interested in making history than in fulfilling its promise. The rescue of that beleaguered enterprise, the Canadian political nationality, was an irresistible challenge to his abilities and ambition. An English Canada bereft of its old British identity but resisting the imposition of an American one, a French Canada self-emancipated from bondage to clericalism but still in thrall to a petty ethnic nationalism, the whole fertilized by massive immigration from many lands: here were the ingredients of crisis, but also perhaps the raw materials of something new and grand. Trudeau came to the prime ministership in April 1968 as the potential Father of Reconfederation. A year later, Parliament passed the Official Languages Act, cornerstone of a new centralist compact.

Trudeau's first effort at constitution-making began in February 1968, when he was still minister of justice. It took place in the shadow of a spectacular failure a few years earlier. Between 1961 and 1964 the federal and provincial governments had worked out a procedure for constitutional amendment that could remove the embarrassing necessity of recourse to Westminster. The so-called Fulton–Favreau principles (named after the federal ministers of justice, Conservative and Liberal, respectively, who had presided over the negotiations) required unanimous consent to changes in the division of powers or the provisions governing the use of the English and French languages. Most other amendments were subject to the '7/50' formula: they required the support of the federal government and of seven provinces comprising at least half of the Canadian population.

The formula met Quebec's traditional insistence on a veto over any amendment affecting its powers under the BNA Act. Prime Minister Pearson declared victory, but too soon. Having agreed to the proposal, the Lesage government (including René Lévesque) found its position in Quebec undercut by a tide of nationalist protest. Objectors feared that, once the constitution was patriated, the province would lose its leverage in bargaining for the extra powers they thought it needed to consummate the Quiet Revolution. Outplayed in nationalist militancy by the Union nationale, Lesage had to withdraw his government's support for the formula after a long and divisive quarrel that contributed to his party's defeat in the 1966 election.

When the quest for patriation resumed in 1968, with the Union nationale in power in Quebec, it was clear that negotiations must embrace the substance of the constitution, not just an amending procedure. But Trudeau, as a centralist hostile to Quebec nationalism, wished to avoid further concessions to the French-speaking particularism ascendant in his native province. His ideas challenged that outlook by proposing a constitutional charter of rights, which would afford security to French Canadians as individuals throughout the land by enabling them to learn and, as far as possible, live in their mother tongue wherever they might reside.

It was the full centralist compact, of which the Official Languages Act afforded a first instalment by providing for bilingual service to the public in all federal offices and institutions. There was to be no recognition of the notion of Canada as the creature of two founding nations. In Québécois minds that idea was tied to the claim that the government of Quebec, as the voice of one nation, was equal to the government of Canada as the voice of the other; but in Trudeau's political lexicon the federal government represented all Canadians, whatever their mother tongue. His government set out to smother biculturalism by fostering multiculturalism, the concept of Canada as a congeries of many cultures and many tongues.

Unfortunately for Trudeau's aspirations, the usages of Canadian politics required him to pursue his goals through the medium of the federal–provincial conference. Here he met not only the hostility of Quebec's Union nationale government but the indifference of other provincial governments. As usual, they were interested less in civil rights and liberties, and the other baubles of the constitution-maker, than in practical matters such as the distribution of taxing and spending powers. At last, when the swing of the political pendulum returned the Liberals to power in Quebec, Trudeau decided to cut his losses.

At Victoria in June 1971, the first ministers agreed to a modest charter of rights and a constitutional amending procedure that gave a veto to Quebec, Ontario, and any other province that might in future make up 25 per cent of the population of Canada. Other proposals aimed to alleviate provincial misgivings about the Supreme Court of Canada by giving the provinces a role in the appointment of justices, and the suspicions of Quebec in particular by guaranteeing that three of the nine justices should come from that province, those three forming a majority of any panel appointed to hear cases originating in Quebec's civil law. However, the proposed language rights were a ludicrous hotchpotch – a monument to the indifference of many Canadian politicians (and presumably of the voters to whom they were responsible) to the ideal of a Canadian political nationality. The three westernmost provinces refused to authorized the use of French in the legislature. They, plus Manitoba and Nova Scotia, refused to grant the right to communicate in French with the head office of their various departments and agencies. Minority education rights were ignored.

After all that, the process failed; and for the same reason as the Fulton–Favreau proposals: Quebec demurred. At least Jean Lesage had got his ministers to accept the earlier deal; Robert Bourassa, Liberal premier of Quebec since April 1970, could not manage even that. But that difference paled by comparison with what was not different: the retreat of a federalist provincial government before a public opinion primed to accept nationalist arguments, however irrational.[2]

Canadian unity suffered further setbacks during the 1970s. One was the continued advance of Quebec nationalism, driven partly by a slight fall in the proportion of native francophones in the province's population and partly by the hostility of some English-speaking Canadians to the extension of bilingualism. Bourassa's government tried to relieve the demographic fear by promoting the use of French in business and prohibiting children whose mother tongue was not English from attending English-language public schools. It also made French the province's sole official language except as provided by the BNA Act. This brought Quebec into line with the other provinces, none of which was officially bilingual. By offending non-francophone Quebecers, the government's measures split the federalist vote in the provincial election of 1976 and helped René Lévesque's separatist Parti Québécois to win a majority in the legislature. The new government set about making the environment much less friendly to non-francophones, in particular by restricting English-language public education to native Quebecers of anglophone descent – historically a fast-diminishing group – and banning the use of English in commercial signs, even in English-speaking areas of the province.

Another blow to Canadian unity was the petroleum shortage engineered by the Organization of Petroleum Exporting Countries (OPEC) after the Arab–Israeli War of October 1973. Canada's large petroleum reserves enabled Ottawa to mitigate the inflationary effects of the shortage and ensure that the Canadian public benefited from the rise in the value of the resource, but only at the cost of increasing in western alienation. The reserves lay in western Canada, especially Alberta, and the west had its own victim-history. The Albertan economy was thriving as never before, but Ottawa's actions inflamed a western chauvinism already piqued by the promotion of bilingualism. The western provinces became interested in reforming the constitution to weaken Ottawa's power to regulate the trade in natural resources.

The rise of the Parti Québécois may or may not have made constitutional reform more urgent, but at least in the short run it made it more difficult. Lévesque's government was committed to presenting its own proposals to the voters of Quebec in a referendum. Those proposals were unlikely to be acceptable to most Canadians outside Quebec, and the Quebec government could hardly agree to anything else in the meantime. Inflation also hurt the prospects for reform, producing economic difficulties that weakened the popularity and authority of Trudeau's government. After a nasty shock in 1972, when the Conservatives came within two seats of recapturing office in Ottawa, the Liberals had regained their majority two years later. For most of the next five years, however, they ran far behind the Conservatives in public esteem, although the Conservative leader from 1976 on, Joe Clark, did not command public confidence. Although Trudeau made some concessions to western aspirations, the new round of constitutional discussions that Ottawa initiated in 1978 merely crystallized the divisions between the various provincial governments and between them and Ottawa.[3]

In 1980, however, two events transformed the state of politics: the Canadian general election in February and Quebec's constitutional referendum three months later. In 1979 a general election had brought Joe Clark to office at the head of a minority government; but the new ministry could not capture the public imagination as Diefenbaker's had in 1957, and its unpopularity emboldened the opposition to defeat it in the House of Commons after only six months. The ensuing election returned the Liberals to power with a parliamentary majority. Trudeau had announced his resignation as leader of the Liberal party, but the parliamentary caucus, caught leaderless by the impending election, invited him to stay on. His return to office in March 1980 was a resurrection as remarkable as John A. Macdonald's in 1878, and it galvanized him in a comparable manner.

Trudeau's resurrection was doubly the gift of the voters of Quebec. Even in 1979 the Liberals had won 62 per cent of the Quebec vote and sixty-seven of the province's seventy-five seats in the House of Commons. This success had offset massive losses elsewhere and helped to deprive the Conservatives of a majority. In 1980 the Liberals won 68 per cent of the Quebec vote and seventy-four seats. In terms of votes, the party had never done so well, except in the wartime elections of 1917 and 1940 and in that of 1921, which was influenced by the conscription crisis. In terms of seats it had done better only in 1921, when it won all sixty-five Quebec seats. Three months later, when the Quebec government's proposals for 'sovereignty-association' gained only 40 per cent of the vote in the referendum, Trudeau could believe that he had finally gained the upper hand in his long struggle with Quebec nationalism.

His proposals for constitutional reform, published just after the referendum, reflected this presumption. They made no concession to the idea that Quebec had a special position in Confederation; they recognized instead 'a distinct French-speaking society centred in though not confined to Quebec.' Neither did they offer any concessions to provincial aspirations for a devolution of legislative power, such as the Liberals had toyed with before the election of 1979. They included a charter of individual rights and an amending formula that incorporated a veto for Quebec and Ontario, and they entrenched in the constitution the federal equalization payments to poorer provinces that had become a feature of Canadian political practice since 1957.

Negotiations ensued. They culminated, in September 1980, in a first ministers' conference, which was sabotaged in advance by the leaking of a federal official's advice that Ottawa should act alone if the ministers could not agree on a plan. The leaked memorandum suggested that Ottawa could justify unilateral action by blaming either the intransigence of the provincial governments or (a little more tactfully) the impossibly cumbersome nature of the consensual process. When the provinces, thus goaded, failed to deliver acceptable counter-proposals, Trudeau presented resolutions to Parliament authorizing a request to the British Parliament for one last amendment to the British North America Act. The proposed amendment did not disturb the existing division of powers between Ottawa and the provinces, but it added two important new elements to the country's written constitution: a charter of individual rights and liberties and a procedure for amending the constitution within Canada.[4]

It was a critical moment in Canadian history. In chapter 10 I described the controversies that had arisen over the proper procedure for amending the BNA Act. No one seriously supposed that the British Parliament would amend the Act in substance without an authoritative Canadian request, or that it would deny such a request, any more than it had refused the request of the provinces to be federally united in the first place. But what constituted an authoritative request? Normally the Dominion government took the initiative in launching the process and the Canadian Parliament requested the amendment by petitioning the Crown; but what were the limits, if any, to Ottawa's freedom to act?

According to the compact theory of Confederation, as articulated in 1930 by Howard Ferguson, the federal government should consult the provinces and obtain their consent before Parliament took action; yet Ferguson himself admitted that Ottawa had habitually flouted this requirement. Centralists such as Norman Rogers and F.R. Scott had dismissed the compact theory, maintaining that the Canadian constitution was as much imperial as federal, if not more so. Scott went so far as to suggest that the Parliament of Canada was legally competent to amend the constitution in its entirety and that custom alone obliged it to request British aid. In 1935 he proposed that the two Canadian houses of Parliament should vote on such requests in joint session, with no obligation to consult the provinces before or after doing so.[5]

One leading participant in the debate, Louis St Laurent, developed a position between those of Ferguson and Scott. In 1931, as president of the Canadian Bar Association, he declared that Ottawa must have the consent of the provinces before initiating any constitutional amendment that might curtail their rights and powers. Subsequently, as federal minister of justice and then as prime minister, he reiterated this position. He differed from Ferguson, however, by distinguishing those parts of the BNA Act that defined provincial rights and powers from those concerning the federal government alone, which Ottawa had frequently altered without consulting the provinces. In 1949, on the basis of this distinction, he secured an amendment to the BNA Act empowering the Parliament of Canada to amend the constitution in almost every respect except those pertaining to the rights and powers of the provinces and the rights of minorities.[6]

Several premiers resented St Laurent's reform, Maurice Duplessis of Quebec and Ernest Manning of Alberta being the most outspoken, but his underlying distinction between changes affecting provincial rights and powers and those affecting the federal government alone differed little, if at all, from that of Senator Sir George Ross in 1914. Ross had declared that the BNA Act could not, technically speaking, be amended in any respect without provincial consent, but the provinces could not reasonably object to Ottawa's acting alone on amendments that did not prejudice any provincial rights or privileges. Considered in this light, the threat to provincial autonomy from Ottawa's new legislative powers paled beside that which was latent in the other major constitutional reform of 1949, the abolition of judicial appeals to the Privy Council.[7]

In 1949 then, despite two decades of centralist stridency, Ottawa in the august person of Louis St Laurent still deferred to Ross's dictum that constitutional reform affecting provincial rights and powers needed the consent of all the provinces. But something important had changed. Although St Laurent held to the old principle, he had found it necessary to make a significant change in its theoretical basis, a change which reflected the vanishing of the Reform tradition and the discrediting of the provincial compact theory.

Ross, a leading Reformer since the 1880s, had taken the theory for granted. In 1930 Howard Ferguson had also invoked it, although he relied also on *Hodge v. The Queen* (1883) and the *Maritime Bank Case* (1892), leading Privy Council decisions that had established the provinces' constitutional equality to the Dominion. A year later, obviously prompted by the attacks of leading centralists, St Laurent ditched the compact theory and relied solely on 'the constitutional documents themselves' – that is, on the BNA Act as explained by *Hodge* in particular. Declining to comment on the theory 'either as an abstract proposition of law or as a disputable assertion of fact,' he suggested that the constitutional equality of the federal and provincial legislatures, as confirmed by *Hodge*, itself sufficed to preclude the Parliament of Canada from interfering with the provincial legislative power. As long as both the Dominion and the provinces remained legally subordinate to the British Parliament, the latter had perhaps retained a theoretical capacity to alter the distribution of legislative power between them. Now Canadian independence had relieved the provinces from this last vestige of colonial subordination, and the provincial jurisdiction must henceforth be as free from Westminster's interference as from Ottawa's.

In 1950 a young Québécois constitutional lawyer, Paul Gérin-Lajoie, enshrined St Laurent's position in the most systematic treatment of the question so far. In the 1960s, under Jean Lesage, Gérin-Lajoie would play a leading part in the Quiet Revolution as Quebec's first-ever minister of education. He was also a friend and former fellow-student of Pierre Trudeau's, whose government he would serve from 1970 to 1977 as president of the Canadian International Development Agency. As a Rhodes Scholar at Oxford he had written his doctoral thesis under the supervision of K.C. Wheare, a British political scientist whose writing was cited by F.R. Scott, among others, to illustrate what Scott called 'the special nature of Canadian federalism': the view that the Canadian constitution was 'quasi-federal' rather than genuinely federal. Despite these influences, he presented an analysis of the constitutional-amendment conundrum that was quite at odds with the dogmatic centralism of most English-speaking authorities.[8]

On the controversy over the compact theory, Gérin-Lajoie was quietly scathing. Opposite conclusions had been drawn from the same historical facts, and general theories built on single instances or special cases. Some contributions came close to wishful thinking (here he cited F.R.

Scott's belief that the constitution could be amended in any respect 'whenever a mere majority of our Senate and House of Commons demand it'). To Gérin-Lajoie, as to St Laurent, both law and convention dictated a different conclusion, and the compact theory was irrelevant. The last word on the matter was *Hodge*, which placed the requirement for provincial consent on a much stronger foundation than any reliance on 'assumed historical grounds, or on the "intentions" of the Fathers of Confederation, or on any notion of compact, or even on precedents as such.'[9]

To this Gérin-Lajoie added four precedents that, though not essential in his view, seemed to him to constitute a convention consistent with the law. In three of these cases, amendment had occurred with the consent of all the provinces. These included the Statute of Westminster and an amendment of 1940, which had remedied the Privy Council's decision in one of the 'Bennett New Deal' cases by empowering the Canadian Parliament to legislate on unemployment insurance; the third was an amendment of 1907 altering the minimum scale of federal subsidies to the provinces. To these he added an amendment that affected only the Prairie provinces and had been enacted after consultation with, and with the consent of, those provinces alone. This was the amendment of 1930 transferring control of those provinces' natural resources from Ottawa to the provincial governments.

During the next twenty years or so, further precedents accrued in support of the Ross–St Laurent line. In 1951 and 1964 the BNA Act was amended to empower the Parliament of Canada to legislate on old age pensions and related issues. Both changes received the prior consent of all the provinces, as did an amendment of 1960 establishing a compulsory retirement age for judges. Two other precedents were provided by the failure of the Fulton–Favreau formula and the Victoria Charter, both of which were sunk by the opposition of a single province. In 1965, reviewing developments to that date, a federal White Paper recognized a 'general principle' whereby the Canadian Parliament would not request an amendment directly affecting federal–provincial relationships without prior consultation and agreement with the provinces. Since 1907, and particularly since 1930, this principle had gained increasing recognition and acceptance. The White Paper added, however, that the nature and degree of provincial participation in the amending process had not lent themselves to easy definition.[10]

Such was the state of play in 1980, when Trudeau decided to go it alone on patriation and the charter of rights and freedoms. From the standpoint of St Laurent and Gérin-Lajoie, it might seem that his initiative was doomed to failure. But that standpoint did not command universal acceptance. Gérin-Lajoie himself admitted that readers of his manuscript prior to publication, who included Scott and Trudeau, had not accepted his contention that Scott's position was mere wishful thinking. Distinguishing constitution-making and constitution-amending powers from mere legislative capacity, they had denied that the provinces' legislative supremacy exempted their powers from federal interference. Another factor was the capacity for extraterritorial action that Ottawa had acquired by the Statute of Westminster. In an influential statement of 1960, Judge Ivan Rand, recently retired from the Supreme Court, distinguished this too, as a mark of sovereignty, from that 'mere finality or definitiveness of legislative power which, in a federal organization, is found distributed between component units.'[11]

These were ominous words for provincial rights. In the days when the BNA Act was written, constitutional lawyers had equated sovereignty with the power to make laws. Oliver Mowat had based his campaign for coordinate sovereignty on both *Hodge* and the compact theory. So, fifty years later, had Howard Ferguson. St Laurent had found it expedient to abandon the disputed ground of the compact theory and rely solely on the division of legislative powers as explained by *Hodge*. But legislative power, this sole remaining prop of provincial sovereignty, had become devalued by overuse, sometimes in disregard of the limits traditionally imposed by the principle of the rule of law. Legislative and constituent power had become conceptually separated, and centralist constitutionalism had hit on other ways of defining sovereignty.

Under the Statute of Westminster, the legal capacity to amend the BNA Act remained with the British Parliament. That body had never refused an amendment requested by the Parliament of Canada, and there was no certain limit, either legal or conventional, to the capacity of the Parliament of Canada to request such amendments. St Laurent had maintained that Canadian independence precluded Westminster's interference with the provinces without their consent, even at the behest of the Parliament of Canada; but this assumed that legislative equality implied constitutional equality. That was no longer certain.

There were, of course, the precedents I have mentioned; but they were part of a cake that could be cut in different ways. Why should amendments adding to provincial powers be lumped with those detracting from them? Why should an amendment relating to the Prairie provinces alone be lumped with those affecting every province? Why should an amendment concerning the retirement of judges be grouped with any of these? Why should Ottawa's caution in obtaining unanimous provincial consent to certain amendments, and in refusing to act without such consent on other occasions, be considered as anything more than so many examples of political prudence? And how convincing was a requirement for provincial participation of a nature and degree that had not 'lent themselves to easy definition'? By 1980 the British Parliament had substantively amended the BNA Act twenty-one times since Confederation. In the *Patriation* cases, some judges would boil the number of precedents in favour of the requirement for provincial consent down to just one.

It was the patriation controversy that brought the question of constitutional amendment to a courtroom showdown. Trudeau's initiative was challenged in the highest courts of Manitoba, Quebec, and Newfoundland and ultimately in the Supreme Court of Canada, since 1949 the country's court of final appeal. The hearings in Manitoba and Quebec produced split decisions in favour of Ottawa's right to act on its own, but the Newfoundland bench issued a unanimous judgment declaring that the proposed amendment needed unanimous provincial consent. In the Supreme Court, which pondered both sets of questions, seven judges out of nine found no legal barrier to the federal initiative, but four of that majority agreed with the minority that there existed a constitutional convention requiring at least substantial provincial consent to such initiatives.

With one exception, the judges who favoured a legal requirement for unanimous provincial consent followed the line mapped out by St Laurent and Gérin-Lajoie. In the Supreme Court, for instance, they began by discussing the BNA Act – in particular the preamble, with its declaration that the provinces desired to be 'federally united,' and the division of legislative power in sections 91 and 92. Then they considered *Hodge* and the *Maritime Bank Case* before concluding that federalism was 'the dominant principle of Canadian constitutional law' and that neither order of government could be allowed to encroach on the other's domain, directly or indirectly.[12] The Canadian Parliament could curtail the provinces' legislative power against their will neither by legislating itself nor by petitioning the British Parliament to do so.

The majority countered this position with a highly legalistic argument, which rested heavily on what F.R. Scott had called the 'special nature of Canadian federalism.' It granted that the provinces of 1867 had asked to be federally united but noted that the scheme of union was not *classically* federal. Admittedly the unitary features of the constitution had little *practical* importance and did not *substantially* modify the provinces' legislative supremacy; still, those features raised a doubt as to whether federalism was the *dominant* principle of Canadian constitutional law. This doubt was enough to undermine St Laurent's contention that the British Parliament could not amend provincial powers without the provinces' consent. *Legally speaking,* the one constant in the process of constitutional amendment since 1867 was the authority of the British Parliament to amend the BNA Act. By convention, Westminster exercised that authority only in response to a request from the Parliament of Canada. The law knew nothing of any requirement of provincial consent, 'either to a resolution of the federal Houses or as a condition of the exercise of United Kingdom legislative power.'[13]

For the most part, the judges on both sides reasoned without historical insight; some even scorned it. Of the eight who found a legal requirement for provincial consent, only two endorsed the compact theory of Confederation. A third followed St Laurent and Gérin-Lajoie in disclaiming any reliance on the theory; the rest ignored it.[14] As for the centralist judges, they had to notice the theory because counsel for the provinces had raised it in argument, but they gave it short shrift. Citing the conclusion of the Rowell–Sirois Report, back in 1940, that the arguments from history did not lead to any single view of the founders' intentions, the Supreme Court's majority judgment on the law dismissed appeals to history as futile. 'Compact theories' in particular were useless, because they operated only in the realm of politics and political science and did not engage the law.[15]

If their reasoning on the law revealed most of the judges as reluctant historians, their treatment of convention exposed them as bad ones. The case for a convention was basically that stated in the White Paper of 1965, which fortified Gérin-Lajoie's precedents with three later instances of provincial consent in 1951, 1960, and 1964. The half-dozen positive precedents were rather a jumble, since only three concerned amendments that curtailed the provincial legislative domain. Two others were the Statute of Westminster and the amendment of 1960, which established a retirement age for judges. To this was added the amendment giving the Prairie provinces control of the natural resources within their boundaries in implementation of an agreement between those provinces and Ottawa. The argument built on these precedents was so problematic that, when first considered in the Manitoba Court of Appeal, it was dismissed even by the two judges who found that provincial consent was required in law.[16] It had been beefed up by the time it reached the Supreme Court but even so was convincingly criticized by the centralist minority there.

The centralist judges, however, had their own foibles. Take their treatment of the amendment empowering Ottawa to legislate on unemployment insurance. Mackenzie King had said in the House of Commons that the question as to whether such amendments required unanimous or merely substantial provincial consent was a difficult one. Some judges took King's words to mean that there was no requirement whatever for provincial consent, and Chief Justice Freedman of Manitoba went even further. Ernest Lapointe, the minister of justice, had noted that neither he nor King had admitted that the amendment in question required provincial consent. Freedman read this as meaning that Lapointe and King believed provincial consent to be unnecessary![17]

Disposing of the 1951 and 1964 precedents was harder, but the centralist judges minimized them by reasoning that, since the first amendment concerned old age pensions and the second supplementary retirement benefits, they both dealt with the same matter and so constituted only one precedent. As for the White Paper of 1965, with its recognition of a requirement for provincial consent that 'since 1907, and particularly since 1930,' had gained increasing recognition and acceptance, this posed no problem. The document's qualifying remark – that the nature and degree of provincial participation had not lent themselves to easy definition – permitted Freedman of Manitoba and the Supreme Court centralists to argue that a convention surrounded by such uncertainty was no convention at all.[18]

The most impressive breach of historical rationality, however, was the centralists' treatment of the Statute of Westminster. This was an event of obvious and crucial relevance to the process of constitutional amendment, since the provinces had forestalled its enactment without their consent and had secured alterations designed to preserve the existing practice. Not only did it constitute an example of provincial participation in the process, but it demonstrated a prevailing disbelief in Ottawa's right to proceed unilaterally (why else would the provinces have wanted to preserve the status quo?). Yet the Supreme Court centralists rejected it as a precedent on the ground that the statute did not affect the provincial legislative power. The mere fact that it did not do so because the provincial governments had banded together to prevent its doing so was immaterial.[19]

The majority judgment on convention – the judgment that was to determine the course of events – skewered these errors of reasoning and noted that uncertainty as to the requisite degree of provincial consent was hardly grounds for rejecting any such requirement. To the few positive precedents of action with prior provincial consent, it added those negative precedents – the abortive agreements of 1966 and 1974 – where the lack of unanimous consent had deterred Ottawa from acting. So far, so good; but then it shot itself – and Canada – in the foot. Having amassed several precedents that favoured a requirement for *unanimous* consent, and none at all that favoured a requirement for merely *substantial* consent, it concluded that the precedents favoured a requirement for substantial, not unanimous consent![20]

Under the circumstances prevailing in 1981, the very idea of substantial consent was unhistorical. It had arisen about 1930 in connection with the quarrel over the provincial-compact theory. The terms of that quarrel permitted only an all-or-nothing solution: either the consent of all the provinces was necessary, or Ottawa could act alone. The idea of substantial consent, by contrast, represented Norman Rogers's notion of what might be a *reasonable* amending formula on the example of other federations, such as the United States and Australia.[21] As a solution to the patriation conundrum, it had a grave flaw: it confused the problem of defining a reasonable amending formula with that of defining the procedure that must be followed, under the existing constitutional order, to bring that new formula into effect.

The judges' confusion mirrored that of the influential jurist William R. Lederman. In 1966 he had argued that, no matter how badly the current amending procedure needed revision, it must be followed in making the revision if the change were to be legitimate rather than revolutionary. At that time he assumed that the current procedure required unanimous provincial consent, but later he came to favour substantial consent. He reasoned that the current procedure consisted of rules 'made directly by custom, precedent and practice over significantly long periods.' Those rules derived their authority from popular acceptance and could therefore evolve in accordance with popular expectation. On this basis he suggested that the opposition of one or two of the smaller provinces might not impair the legitimacy of an amendment.[22]

Lederman's views were cited in the *Patriation* hearings, where the government of Saskatchewan urged the idea of substantial consent in preference to the unanimous consent demanded by Ottawa's other challengers. Since he stated plainly that the opposition of any of the four largest provinces should suffice to prevent such a change, he cannot be blamed for a judgment that enabled patriation to proceed over the objections of Quebec. I call him confused, however, because the very idea of substantial provincial consent reflected the ascendancy of the centralist idea of Confederation.

Constitutional amendment is a fundamental act of sovereignty, and the essence of federalism is divided sovereignty. Without express provision to the contrary, as in the U.S. constitution, divided sovereignty must mean that the terms of union can be fundamentally altered only with the consent of each sovereign member. Lacking such provision, it was reasonable to suppose that Canadians had taken a 'significantly long period' to work out which of the terms of Confederation required such consent and which did not. To suppose, however, that something so amorphous as the evolution of public expectation could justify dispensing with the requirement for unanimous consent to *fundamental* change was quite unjustified. Apart from anything else, it ignored the question: which public? If Canada was a genuine federation, eleven publics had a say.

Lederman and the Supreme Court majority failed to see this because English Canadians had forgotten what it was about Confederation that made Canada genuinely rather than 'quasi' federal. In exalting the nation-building aspect of Confederation at the expense of its federal aspect, and nationalizing responsible government into a 'Canadian' achievement, largely complete by 1850, centralist story-tellers had lost sight of the relation between responsible government and provincial autonomy. They forgot that the founders, in basing Confederation on the imperial constitution, had meant to duplicate within Canada the relations of coordinate sovereignty that had developed between Britain and its North American colonies. In the 'imperial' features of the constitution – the Dominion's power to appoint lieutenant-governors, veto provincial legislation, and so on – they saw only 'the special nature of Canadian federalism': proof that the constitution was not really federal at all but a unitary structure with federal modifications. In the absence of an explicit amending procedure, why should the constitution's federal trimmings, rather than its unitary essence, be the guide to the proper course of action?

Given the state of historical understanding at the time, this outcome was no doubt inevitable; but one remarkable contribution to the debate shows that it was still possible to infer the link between responsible government and provincial autonomy from the known facts of Canadian history. This was the judgment of Joseph F. O'Sullivan of the Manitoba Court of Appeal, papal knight and former president of the Liberal party of Manitoba. I don't know the source of his unique insight – perhaps his Jesuit education helped – but of all the judges who found a requirement for provincial consent, he alone realized that neither the division of legislative powers nor the grab-bag of available precedents could supply a convincing rationale for it. He understood that it must rest on an anterior sovereignty in the provinces, which would make the constitution genuinely federal; and he saw responsible government as the source of that condition. 'Responsible government is a fundamental principle of our Constitution,' he declared. 'It has been recognized over and over by Canadian Courts. Our whole history does not make sense unless responsible government is a keystone of our constitutional system. If the Queen can act for Canada on the advice of her British ministers, then we have no fully responsible government.'[23]

Just so in 1823 had William Baldwin protested that, if the British government could amend the Constitutional Act without Canadian consent, then Upper and Lower Canada had no constitution. In 1981 the point needed making because counsel for the dominion had attempted to justify the patriation initiative by arguing that the British Parliament remained legally sovereign over Canada, though bound by convention to exercise its sovereign power only as the Canadian Parliament requested. O'Sullivan rejected that idea, for he believed that the constitutional convention that limited British sovereignty was binding in law as well. 'If the Courts could not take account of constitutional convention and practice,' he scoffed, 'we would still be enforcing the Divine Right of Kings as understood by the Stuarts.'[24]

But the courts *could* do so, for the constitutional convention known as responsible government entailed legal as well as political sovereignty. Responsible government meant that the Queen of Canada could constitutionally act for Canada only on the advice of her Canadian ministers. If the British Parliament were to legislate for Canada except at the request of the competent Canadian authorities, and the Queen assented to that legislation on the advice of her British ministers, Canadian courts would refuse to enforce that legislation. To say otherwise was to belie the very meaning of responsible government; if the Queen could act for Canada on the advice of her British ministers, then Canada indeed had no fully responsible government. But Canada did have such a government, and Canadian courts had a duty to uphold its responsibility.

Of course, the Canadian government favoured patriation; but to legit-imize the process something more was needed, for Canada had not one responsible government but eleven. Just as it would be unconstitutional for the Queen to act in a Canadian matter on the advice of her British ministers, so it would be unconstitutional for her to act in a provincial matter on the advice of her Dominion ministers. This principle bore on the question before the court because the Queen received a petition from the Parliament of Canada, such as the proposed patriation petition, as Queen of Canada and acted on it on the advice of her Canadian minis-ters. If that petition affected provincial matters, as the patriation resolu-tions did, it would be unconstitutional for the Queen to act on it against the advice of her provincial ministers.

The Queen, in short, was not only Queen of the United Kingdom, of Canada, and of certain other Commonwealth countries; she was also Queen of each of the Canadian provinces. 'She is the same Queen over all, but she acts in different rights; she acts in executive matters on the advice of responsible ministers and in legislative matters on the advice of responsible Parliaments.' The courts themselves recognized this whenever they had to decide disputes between Ottawa and one or more provinces. In such cases they habitually distinguished 'the Queen in right of Canada' from the Queen in right of the various provinces. This division of *executive* authority, as signified by the monarch's many crowns, formed the basis of the provinces' sovereignty as it did of the Dominion's. Canada's sovereignty did not flow from the Statute of Westminster; 'it was not conferred by the British Parliament but by the Queen's acceptance of the constitutional principles which have become part and parcel of our fundamental law.' Those principles entailed provincial sovereignty too, and the courts had the same duty to uphold the sovereignty of the provinces as of the Dominion.[25]

O'Sullivan understood the patriation question so differently from his colleagues because he adopted the historical standpoint that they shunned. Perplexed by the modern controversy as to the founders' intentions, his colleagues chose to consider Confederation as a special case of a general problem in political science and constitutional law – a problem called 'Federalism.' O'Sullivan's approach freed him from these perplexities by placing him, so to speak, in the founders' frame of mind. To him the patriation question had its antecedents not in the 1860s but in the 1680s; the relevant history did not commence with Con-federation but went back to the beginnings of modern parliamentary government (hence his allusion to divine right). This long view enabled him to see Confederation as nineteenth-century Canadians had – that is, from the perspective of Baldwinite constitutionalism – and to perceive Canadian independence, like responsible government before it, as the product not of legislation but of concession by the British Crown. Canadian independence was in fact an extension of the sovereignty inherent in responsible government – a sovereignty that appertained to the provinces as well as to the Dominion.

To O'Sullivan, as to the Baldwinites, the sovereignty that went with responsible government was a negative sovereignty, a sovereignty of veto. In picturing the Constitutional Act as a treaty between Upper Canadians and the mother country, the Baldwinites had claimed not that the British Parliament must amend it at the colonists' behest, but only that Parliament could not properly amend it against the colonists' will. The Canadian sovereignty that O'Sullivan thought enforceable in the courts was similarly a sovereignty of veto. Clearly he did not suppose that the courts could force the British Parliament to amend the BNA Act in any particular fashion but thought merely that they could nullify any change made without due Canadian authority. The sovereignty that he claimed for the provinces was similar, and, just as the Baldwinites had tied their claim to a compact theory of the Constitutional Act, so O'Sullivan tied his to the idea that the Canadian constitution was a compact of provinces.[26]

Despite his lucidity and eloquence, O'Sullivan could not cut through the din in his colleagues' ears – the clamour of decades of centralist dogmatizing and invective. By 1981 this had rendered the argument in favour of provincial consent so problematic that even sympathetic judges could not all agree on their reasons, or on whether unanimous or merely substantial consent was required. Only one other judge, Bisson of Quebec, invoked the compact theory of Confederation in support of his decision, but his appeal was to the national, not the provincial compact.[27] As we have seen, a majority of the Supreme Court manufactured a convention that required substantial but not unanimous provincial consent to the patriation proposal. Shortly after its delivery, one authority hailed this judgment as an act of bold statecraft based on questionable jurisprudence. On a longer view it looks like a classic case of throwing out the baby and saving the bathwater.[28]

The Supreme Court's decision drove Ottawa and the provinces back to the bargaining table. The new talks yielded an agreement between all the parties save Quebec. As in 1867, the British Parliament acted quickly on this agreement; the result was the Constitution Act, 1982. Meanwhile, Quebec went back to court in an attempt to verify that it at least had a right to veto the proposed reform, since Quebec formed 'a distinct society within the Canadian federation.' Having rejected the idea of Confederation as a compact of provinces, however, the courts showed no more sympathy for the notion that it was a compact of nations or cultures. In the eyes of the law, a province was a province and Quebec a province like the others.[29] Patriation was achieved without the sanction of the government of Quebec and to the chagrin of many Québécois. Two years later, the Liberal party of Canada suffered an electoral defeat of unprecedented magnitude in the country at large. In Quebec it won just seventeen seats, eight fewer even than in the rout of 1958.

There is no need to describe here the document that defines Canada's current constitution, but one provision is noteworthy for the way in which it mirrors the unhistorical nature of that document and the technocratic genius of its inventor, Pierre Trudeau. I mean the attempt to censor historical memory by providing that the British North America Act, 1867, should henceforth be known as the Constitution Act, 1867, a name for which there was no historical warrant. Donald Creighton would have recognized this as one more effort by liberal nationalists to bury traces of Canada's British heritage. But government fiat alone will not suffice to censor historical memory. In this book Canada's founding charter figures as the British North America Act, and Canada itself as what the British North America Act called it: a Dominion.

17

Conclusion:
Getting It Wrong, Putting It Right

I have now explained how it is that biased history and its application to politics have contributed to Canada's endemic disunity. I began with some forgotten history – with Upper Canadians quarrelling over the meaning of their identity as British North Americans – and described how that clash between 'loyalism' and 'patriotism' animated a successful movement for autonomy within the British empire, one based on a federal conception of the empire and a belief in the inalienable right of British subjects to self-government. In the 1860s, feeling that their province's incorporation in United Canada deprived it of the substance of self-government, Upper Canadian Reformers brought that idea of the empire to bear on the problem of federalizing United Canada and incorporating other British territory into what George-Étienne Cartier boldly termed a political nationality. Later in the nineteenth century, now Ontarians, they invoked the analogy between the imperial and Canadian constitutions to justify the provinces' claim to autonomy within the Canadian Confederation.

This commitment to provincial autonomy, and the corresponding idea of the federal and provincial governments as coordinate sovereigns, fitted well with the French-Canadian idea of Confederation. As time passed, though, anglophone intellectuals came to identify with the Canadian state and to scorn both provincial identities and the persisting fidelity of many Canadians to the British empire – two loyalties connected by the Privy Council's support for provincial rights. I have explained how Canadian nationalism sapped English-Canadian awareness of the historical basis for coordinate sovereignty, leaving French Canadians isolated in their adherence to the old understanding of Confederation. After the Second World War the old British loyalties resurged in the form of anti-American nationalism, but the new ideology was no less hostile to 'provincialism' than the old anti-British nationalism. In the end all Canadians – French- or English-speaking, centralist or provincialist – lost sight of the full dimensions of the bargain they called Confederation. The upshot was the patriation bungle, when (with one notable exception) even Canadians opposed to Ottawa's unilateral action lacked the historical knowledge to reason correctly on the question.

Perhaps, if the information in this book had been available twenty years ago, it might have deterred the Canadian government from proceeding unilaterally or emboldened the majority of the Supreme Court to insist on provincial unanimity. That thought prompts the question: why was it *not* available? I have explained how English Canadians lost sight of the historical rationale for the compact theory of Confederation, and I have traced into the 1970s the centralist nationalisms that arose in its absence. But the 1960s and 1970s saw a huge growth in research and writing on Canadian history. Why did that collective endeavour fail to unearth the seminal facts about Canada's founding that are presented here? And how might those facts help Canadians working today on remedies for the country's perennial constitutional quandary? These questions are the subject of this concluding chapter.

At the heart of the matter is the rise of an account of Confederation that exaggerated its centralism. This story stressed the founders' determination to create a more centralized union than the United States by modelling it on the constitution of the British empire. It recounted how they had reversed the American scheme of union by giving the residue of legislative power to Ottawa instead of the provinces. It equated nation-building with centralism, and centralism with the federal ascendancy that John A. Macdonald had tried to impose in the 1870s and 1880s.

The centralist narrative emphasized the elements that had brought British North Americans together in the 1860s rather than those which had forced Canadians apart. Although it acknowledged the sectional tensions that plagued the province of Canada, it discounted what they implied about Confederation: as W.L. Morton remarked, people forgot that the union of 1867 had originated in the desire of many Canadians to dissolve or federalize United Canada and that that scheme had remained a real alternative to the larger union until the adherence of New Brunswick and Nova Scotia was assured. Centralist story-tellers had to acknowledge French-Canadian national feeling in order to explain why the new constitution was federal rather than unitary, but they presented Confederation as the transcendence of national animosities. Arthur Lower called it a miracle: 'The Miracle of Union.'[1]

This idea of Confederation depended on minimizing the historical force of Upper Canadian identity and the ideal of Upper Canadian autonomy. Centralists depicted responsible government as a 'Canadian' accomplishment, complete by 1850. They took for granted that responsible government for United Canada meant responsible government for Upper Canada, and they dismissed Upper Canadian discontent with the outcome as an unsavoury blend of rural localism and religious intolerance. Then they treated Confederation the same way, identifying it with Macdonald's centralism and belittling the Ontario campaign for provincial rights as the repudiation of a solemn bargain. By prematurely converting Upper Canadians into Canadians, centralist story-tellers prevented themselves from seeing Confederation as Oliver Mowat had seen it: as the belated achievement of autonomy under monarchical institutions – that is, of responsible government – by Upper Canada. They saw the 'imperial' powers in the Canadian constitution purely as instruments of central dominance over subordinate governments, unmindful of the constitutional conventions that restricted their use in relation to colonies enjoying responsible government.

Indeed, the whole centralist edifice rested on a misunderstanding of what responsible government had meant to the Upper Canadian Reformers. I have traced this misconception to the strategy of the Baldwinites, who deftly adapted the British constitutionalism of responsible government to the colonial milieu, muting (though never repudiating) their original appeal to the inalienable rights of British subjects. The spirit of that first assertion of right lived on in later campaigns for Upper Canadian autonomy until the end of the century, when economic and demographic changes and the desertion of the liberal intelligentsia brought the Reform tradition to an end; but the roots of the first campaign in a colonial constitutionalism that denied British legislative sovereignty over the colonies was lost to hindsight. Not even John Ewart or W.P.M. Kennedy, its deepest investigators, seem to have recognized it, although both were familiar with the American colonists' ideas on the subject.[2]

Once buried, the character of Reform constitutionalism stayed buried. Britain's ready embrace of colonial self-rule in the 1840s made it easy for Canadians, looking back, to interpret self-government as a natural outgrowth of British liberty: they needed no other explanation and did not look for one. In the 1920s, when Aileen Dunham unearthed the Letter on Responsible Government, she noted only its advocacy of responsible government and ignored the underlying federal idea of the imperial constitution, with its coordinate sovereignties, compact theory of the Constitutional Act, and division of powers between the imperial and colonial legislatures. A few years later the Baldwins' responsible government resolutions of 1828, with their similar conception of the Constitutional Act, appeared in a collection of documents on Canadian constitutional history, but no one made anything of that – not even W.L. Morton, who was familiar with eighteenth-century ideas of colonial sovereignty and brought that knowledge to bear on the Letter.[3]

So it was that Canadian historical consciousness was diverted from the link between responsible government and provincial rights. When historians came to consider the genealogy of Confederation, they overlooked the Reform tradition and gave Canada's founding a mainly conservative pedigree adorned with the motto 'Peace, Order and Good Government' – a pedigree descending from mid-eighteenth-century schemes of British North American union, via the Loyalists, to the conservative coalition of the late 1850s. The Letter on Responsible Government had quite as much to say about Confederation as any of those unrealized schemes, but it was a proposal for cabinet government in Upper Canada, not for the union of British North America, and no one noticed.[4]

Between 1930 and 1970, the centralism of most leading theorists of Canadian history dominated English-Canadian understandings of Confederation. Donald Creighton argued fiercely about history with the liberals Frank Underhill and Arthur Lower and with his fellow-conservative Morton, but on the centralizing intent of the framers there was no quarrel: even Lower, who had some insight into the provincial patriotism of late-nineteenth-century Ontarians, disparaged Oliver Mowat and his campaign for provincial rights, though limiting his indictment to smallmindedness while Creighton alleged actual perfidy.[5] Harold Innis was not a dogmatic centralist, but he impartially condemned the follies of centralism and provincialism, and his historical writing made a vital contribution to the centralist conception of Canada.

By 1970 the nationalist bias of the English-Canadian canon was quite apparent to the discerning; but recognition did not result in significant revision. Perplexed perhaps by the intractable problems of Canadian sovereignty and unity, historians forsook Canadian political history in order to explore the presumably less problematic 'limited identities' of region, ethnicity, and class.[6] This shift in part mirrored a general trend in the English-speaking world to dismiss political history in favour of a social history that aspired to reconstruct the lives and thought of common people. Canadians, however, went further than others. The Marxist tenor of the new social history invested it with the glamour of anti-Americanism. This had wide appeal throughout the American empire but above all in Canada, where a new left-wing nationalism flourished under the auspices of *Lament for a Nation*.

Fortified if anything by the quarrels of the 1950s and 1960s, the centralist master-narrative easily weathered this revolution in historical thought and practice. Centralism was one thing that liberal and conservative nationalism had shared, and it was one thing that the new nationalism shared with the old. In the face of this unanimity, the decline of interest in political history simply served to petrify the centralist consensus of the previous generation. These years saw the consolidation of the idea of Canadian history as a confrontation between a centralizing conservative tradition, nationalist in its anti-Americanism, and a liberal tradition that was anti-centralist in the nineteenth century and continentalist in the twentieth. 'Peace, order and good government,' the words that enshrined the Dominion legislative power, were mythologized into an emblem of that centralizing conservatism.[7]

The waning of interest in political history was one obstacle to rediscovering the lost English-Canadian perspective on Confederation. Another was the lack of historically informed knowledge of Canadian constitutional law. Political scientists and constitutional lawyers could hardly have developed this without the help of historians, but nationalist historians had no incentive to question the constitutional history that flowed from these sources. They happily joined in the outcry against the Privy Council, and the few who went into detail only exposed their own incompetence. Arthur Lower, for instance, hypothesized that the Judicial Committee had been misled by Judah Benjamin, sometime attorney general of the American Confederacy and doughty advocate of states' rights, who had emigrated to Britain after the defeat of the Confederacy and been called to the bar. On the contrary: far from influencing the committee, it was Benjamin who botched the attack on the Scott Act in *Russell v. The Queen*.[8] Lower misstated the nature of the *Escheats Case* and wrongly reported that Mowat had lost in every Canadian court, only to be handed the victory by the Privy Council. Actually, Mowat had won in two Canadian courts out of three.[9]

This second error was an instance of the myth that the Privy Council had repeatedly overruled 'Canadian' decisions that were centralist in thrust, when in most cases (as Evan Gray had observed) it had merely restored Canadian decisions that the Supreme Court had reversed. But even when historians avoided such howlers, they still sported centralist blinkers. The standard account of Ontario's relations with Ottawa, published in the Ontario Historical Studies Series in 1982, the very year of patriation, offered an account of the provincial-rights controversy unabashedly based on an MA thesis by a student of Donald Creighton's in the 1940s.[10]

Historians' treatment of the compact theory of Confederation reflected these defects of historical knowledge. Even George Stanley had no idea of its Upper Canadian antecedents. Ramsay Cook, in his study for the Royal Commission on Bilingualism and Biculturalism, treated it as an opportunistic fabrication, which had originated as a weapon of political controversy and may as such have been most valuable for its imprecision. Cook, the leading authority of the time on Canadian political culture, conveyed no hint of the theory's diverse pre-Confederation roots and no awareness that its ambiguities might reflect that diversity.[11] In an otherwise illuminating book on *The French-Canadian Idea of Confederation, 1864–1900*, published in the year of patriation, Arthur Silver ignored the compact theory's French-Canadian antecedents and its first elaborator, Judge Loranger.

By robbing the theory of its pedigree, the centralist master-narrative undermined its authority. The idea of provincial rights, and the notion that unanimous provincial consent was requisite for certain sorts of constitutional amendment, had deep roots in the Upper Canadian Reform tradition, with its compact theory of the Constitutional Act and federalist theory of the imperial constitution. By Canadianizing the achievement of responsible government, and so obscuring the continuity between the initial Upper Canadian campaign and later movements for Upper Canadian autonomy within United Canada and Confederation, the centralist narrative undermined provincial claims to equality with the Dominion government and to a veto over constitutional amendment.

In the 1960s and 1970s, the ascendancy of the centralist master-narrative seriously handicapped thinkers who aspired to develop a genuinely federalist constitutionalism. Political scientists justified the Privy Council's treatment of the BNA Act by arguing that it suited Canadian realities better than the founders' centralism, but they did not challenge the centralist orthodoxy regarding Confederation itself.[12] As to the actual mechanism for constitutional reform, we have seen the difficulties that plagued the thinking of constitutional lawyers from St Laurent to Lederman.

Donald Smiley, a political scientist of 'red tory' leanings, typifies the quandary of those who sought to accommodate the Quiet Revolution by reshaping Confederation to do justice to regional interests and sentiments. In his essay *The Canadian Political Nationality*, he asked: 'Was Confederation a compact? – or does it matter?' He thought it did matter – 'The problems which occur without some such formulation seem to me to be insurmountable' – but found it impossible to make historical sense of the theory. It was clearly not a contract or treaty in the technical sense in which lawyers used those terms, but George Stanley's idea of Confederation as a moral compact was too vague. Which was *the* bargain? The agreement among the Canadian leaders to federalize United Canada? The settlement between the Canadian and Maritime politicians? Or the whole complex of settlements both establishing the original Dominion and bringing the subsequent provinces into it? If there was a French–English agreement among the Canadian leaders, in what ways were provinces other than Quebec and Ontario bound by its cultural aspects? What was the 'spirit of Confederation'?[13]

Smiley's confusion vividly illustrates the gap that the ascendancy of centralism left in the repertory of Canadian constitutionalism. His reasons for doubting the compact theory were the now standard arguments of Norman Rogers; he also cited Donald Creighton, Eugene Forsey, and Ramsay Cook. Such sources left him totally ignorant of the historical process by which the distinct Upper Canadian and French-Canadian compact theories of the Constitutional Act had fed into Confederation, and of the historical significance of responsible government as a convention that overbore the legal defects of the provincial compact theory. Thus bereft, he concluded that the compact theory in any version was a myth; but he saw it as a 'necessary myth' because it asserted a standard of constitutional equity that transcended the temporary or permanent dominance of particular interests (i.e., the tyranny of the majority).

For this reason, Smiley found it especially disturbing that Canadians in the 1960s had ceased to invoke the theory in constitutional debate. English-speaking Canadians had scorned it for decades of course, but now the trend had spread to Quebec. Surveying the decade, he found only two compact-based analyses of the constitution from a Québécois perspective, and one of those was by the separatist Raymond Barbeau, who declared in effect that the Confederation compact (if there was one) had been so comprehensively broken by Ottawa and the other nine provinces as to be null and void.[14] Another Quebecer quoted by Smiley, the constitutional lawyer Pierre Carignan, summed up his people's frustration in words that might serve as a motto for this book. 'It seems,' he wrote, 'that the majority of French-speaking Quebecers are prepared to reject the constitution in its present form. Unable to convince their fellow-countrymen that the constitution is a compact, they have lost faith in it themselves; as a result, they no longer feel bound by it and regard nothing as settled.'

Carignan's words, like those of Barbeau, point to the centralist narrative, with its denial of coordinate federalism and the compact theory, as a source of this constitutional malaise, and both men indicated the logical consequence of that denial: the necessity of annulling the understandings of 1867. This could mean conceding that the spirit of 1867 was a centralizing one and insisting that Quebec needed more power in order to realize its destiny. Or it could mean, as with Barbeau, separation.

Smiley's solicitude for the compact theory earned no more respect than George Stanley's a decade earlier: Ramsay Cook dismissed his book as 'bordering on the tedious.'[15] Yet thirty years later, Carignan notwithstanding, the theory remains important in Québécois political thought. The words of the Allaire Report of 1991 show this; so do those of the 'somewhat sovereigntist' political scientist Guy Laforest, who invokes the compact theory in order to condemn patriation as a historic betrayal (a verdict in which Smiley preceded him by a decade) and, in terms that the Baldwins would have appreciated, a Lockean 'dissolution of government.'[16] Recently in Quebec City I met a senior civil servant who quite spontaneously invoked the idea of the Confederation 'contract.' Another Quebecer, who had voted 'Yes' in 1980 and 1995 but was not sure about the next time, confided that it would strongly influence his thinking if Ottawa admitted that patriation had been a mistake and undertook to adhere more scrupulously to the division of powers as he conceived it.

Patriation is in fact the chief contemporary focus, though not of course the source, of Québécois discontent with Confederation. The Meech Lake and Charlottetown imbroglios both originated in efforts to placate Quebecers aggrieved by that earlier affront. Many 'Yes' votes in the sovereignty referendum of 1995 were cast less in support of separation than in protest against not being taken seriously. I have tried to explain why patriation was a blunder if not a betrayal, an offence against the rule of law if not a dissolution of government. It was a breach of the Confederation compact as I find it illustrated in history; and not the first, if you count the breach of the supplementary compacts constituted by the Manitoba Act and the North-West Territories Act.

I should add, however, that it was not to my mind so heinous a breach as to justify in itself the secession of Quebec. For one thing, the new constitution, though not instituted by due process, preserved – and in some ways reinforced – the federal nature of the Canadian state. With certain restrictions, it enabled provincial legislatures to override most of the rights conferred by the Charter of Rights and Freedoms and to opt out of subsequent amendments to the Constitution Act. Secondly, it was adopted at the urging of Pierre Trudeau, whom English Canadians had good reason to accept as a representative of French Canada. Lise Bissonette, editor of *Le Devoir*, has said that when Quebecers voted for Trudeau they were playing tribal politics, voting for one of their own;[17] but tribal politics is a dangerous game, and those who choose to play it cannot complain if they get hurt. In this case, however, no one got hurt.

Perhaps I should summarize here my understanding of the compact so harmlessly, if tactlessly, breached in 1982. What I find in Canadian history is a compact both of nations and of provinces. The *provincial* compact consisted in the equality of the provinces and their individual possession of a right of veto over fundamental changes in the terms of association. The *national* compact was more complex. In part it consisted in establishing Quebec as one of several sovereign provinces, each of them constitutionally equal to the federal government; in part, in making the federal government the protector of Quebec's anglophone minority and of francophone minorities elsewhere. It did not establish the government of Quebec as protector of francophone minorities; nor did it establish equality between the governments of Quebec and Canada as the political organs of two 'founding peoples,' although two founding peoples there undoubtedly were. The Fathers of Confederation saw the government of Quebec as the government of all Quebecers, not just francophones, and they saw the government of Canada as the government of all Canadians.

What does all this imply about the relationship between the francophones of Quebec and other Canadians? I intend to discuss this in terms of 'equality of the provinces,' 'distinct society,' and 'Canadian unity.' But I do not suppose that history should dictate policy. I have discussed various examples of Canadians invoking history – sometimes very biased history – in support of their political goals. To my mind the political value of history lies in its contribution to collective self-awareness. False self-awareness is no better a guide to collective than to individual action, and we owe it to ourselves to achieve the fullest possible understanding of our common past. But while self-knowledge may point us in one direction rather than another, the past cannot be allowed to constrain us from taking new paths. For instance, the historical reality of two 'founding peoples' no more impairs the claims of the Aboriginal peoples to appropriate recognition of their own distinct societies than it impairs the Canadian state's claim to the loyalty of all Canadians.

That being said, I would suggest that, while the provincial compact mandates the equality of the provinces, that equality need not be defined so as to hamper the government of Quebec in preserving the 'distinct' or 'unique' character of Quebec society. History and politics have combined to bless Canada with a clutch of distinct provincial societies, but clearly language and culture help to make Quebec 'uniquely distinct,' so to speak, and a leading object of Confederation as a national compact was to create a provincial government empowered to protect that uniqueness. To that end it may be necessary for the government of Quebec to execute for that province certain functions that the federal government may better perform for the rest of Canada.

Luckily, the equality of the provinces does not pose an insuperable obstacle to that. We need only apply the distinction between power and status that George Brown's *Globe* posited in 1864 in discussing the problem of sovereignty.[18] The *Globe* argued that the formal sovereignty of the central government need not imply its dominance over the local governments, because what really counted was the division of powers. This distinction between power and constitutional status enables us to acknowledge the *constitutional* equality of the provinces without implying that they must all possess the same powers. Since this argument is based on the *national* compact, it affords no reason for provinces other than Quebec to claim special powers.[19]

In what might the constitutional equality of the provinces practically consist? For a start, in their participation in the federal–provincial conferences and other processes that constitute what is called cooperative federalism. It might also consist in each province's possession of a veto over fundamental constitutional change, as provided by the provincial compact. The Constitution Act of 1982 introduced a different arrangement, of course, and some might contend that the prior consent of the nine provinces other than Quebec to that arrangement vitiates their claim to a veto now. However, those provinces surrendered their claim in the expectation that Quebec's would lapse too, and arguably that surrender is not binding under the present circumstances. In any case, the four largest provinces still have a veto in some form or other, and it might not be injudicious to extend it to the six smaller provinces, whose size and circumstances tend to make them less egotistical. (I say this recognizing that it was Manitoba and Newfoundland that torpedoed the Meech Lake Agreement in 1990.)

As I said, the principle of provincial equality need not preclude a certain asymmetry in the division of powers in order to enable the government of Quebec to protect that province's distinct society. What must set limits to that asymmetry is the principle of Canadian unity. In one sense this is a tautology: membership of the federation by definition entails limits on Quebec's sovereignty that secession would terminate. But I have something more in mind. Even 'sovereignty-association' means maintaining a single Canadian economy, and to some degree a single economy must impose a single society – that, after all, is one reason that so many Canadians opposed free trade with the United States in 1988. Canadian unity is meaningless without a basic equality in living conditions throughout the land, and a federal government is meaningless if it lacks the power and resources to maintain such equality.

Apart from that, too great a functional imbalance between Quebec and the other provinces could only weaken further the increasingly tenuous ties between French-speaking Quebecers and the rest of Canada. How could Quebec MPs expect to play a full role at Ottawa if the government of Quebec were responsible within its borders for a wide range of matters administered for other Canadians by Ottawa? What sort of commitment to the public interest could either induce or entitle Quebecers to play a leading role in a federal government that was, in a significant sense, not their own? Too great an asymmetry between Quebec and the other provinces can only be a halfway house for secession.[20]

Much has been written on these aspects of federalism, and I have little to add to the discussion; but just as important, if not more so, is the matter on which I quoted Archbishop Desmond Tutu at the outset: 'If you don't have some accepted history the chances are you will not gel as a community.' After attending my course on Canadian political thought and culture, a young Québécois said that he had found the course very interesting, because 'in Quebec we learn Quebec history, we learn French history, and we learn American history – but we don't learn

Canadian history.' To my mind, the rest of Canada can give the Québécois everything they say they need to preserve their distinct society and
it will still do nothing for Canadian unity unless English and French
Canadians start acknowledging the same history.

As I noted at the start, French-speaking Quebecers have traditionally
learned a history designed to inspire loyalty to the French-Canadian
national homeland. Much of that history projects an attitude of aggrieved defiance towards the people with whom history has obliged
French Canadians to share the territory once known as New France and
then as British North America. That attitude is justified up to a point,
but it often goes to extremes. Michael Ignatieff quotes a Quebec nationalist as lamenting that her six million francophone compatriots would
have been twelve million by now if impoverishment and emigration
had not made half of them Americans instead. She automatically blames
the Conquest, not stopping to think that, but for the maintenance of British and later Canadian sovereignty, all twelve million might have been
English-speaking citizens of the United States. Again: a brief historical
sketch circulated by the Quebec government belittles the representative
institutions set up by the Constitutional Act of 1791. No doubt the
Lower Canadian constitution had many shortcomings; but there were
no representative institutions at all under the French regime, and those
introduced by the British incontestably allowed the *Canadiens* a significant amount of political power.[21]

These are examples of the tendency of Québécois historical thinking
to harp on the negative. Another trait is to misread 'the negative' as
uniquely anti-French in tendency. The Québécois who attended my
course was very surprised to read Oliver Mowat's complaints to the
Reform convention of 1859 about the baneful domination of Lower Canada. We talk like that about the English, he said; I never knew they
talked like that about us. He also expressed the common French-
Canadian perception of the campaign for representation by population:
when 'they' (Upper Canadians) were a minority, they insisted on equal
representation for Upper and Lower Canada, but when they became a
majority they began demanding 'rep by pop.' I explained that there was
no 'they,' in the sense of a group of Anglos united against French Canadians. The British had introduced sectional equality into the Act of
Union at the behest of Upper Canadian conservatives such as John Beverley Robinson, who feared that Upper Canadian Reformers would
combine with French Canadians to control the Legislative Assembly.
Once responsible government was achieved, and the *bleus* had com-

bined with the English-Canadian conservatives, sectional equality gave the conservatives of both sections an advantage over the liberals.[22] Culture had nothing to do with it, except in deterring French-Canadian liberals from accepting representation by population instead.

For much of the twentieth century, English Canadians cultivated a nationalist historiography that could only alienate French Canadians. Neither the centralism nor the glorying in transcontinental expansion could gratify those who identified with beleaguered francophone communities on the Prairies or found themselves treated as second-class citizens at home. But that nationalism was made the more objectionable by the historical distortions that sustained it, and none of these was more pernicious than the biased argumentation that underpinned the attack on the compact theory of Confederation. In this book I have revealed a lost English-Canadian perspective on Confederation that conformed closely to French-Canadian ideas. Perhaps this disclosure can inspire a broader reconciliation of historical traditions and so help to nurture a more wholesome and inclusive sense of what it means to be Canadian.

But goodwill is needed on both sides. Control of education remains in the provincial domain, where it was placed to enable Upper and Lower Canadians to maintain their distinct societies. A revised history cannot of itself cure past injuries: separatists can still harp on the ill will that led both sides to agree to the softer separation entailed in Confederation, and which yet found such ample expression within Confederation. The story told here will mean nothing to such persons. It will appeal to that different spirit, newly celebrated by John Ralston Saul, which disdains nationalism as egoism and relishes the Canadian adventure as a disciplined exercise in cooperation based on respect for differences;[23] the spirit that esteems the idealism which impelled John Willson and William Baldwin to resist the Union Bill as an injustice to French Canadians, spurred John Ewart to resist British imperialism for the same reason, and stirred W.L. Morton to hope that, now that English Canadians had lost the British identity that offended francophones and Quebec had cast off the clericalism that alienated anglophones, the two peoples could get on with the business of being Canadian.

It is becoming fashionable for governments to express contrition for their forerunners' misdeeds as a means to reconciliation with historically aggrieved or injured peoples. Recently the British prime minister acknowledged the British government's errors during the Irish potato famine of the 1840s. The Canadian government has apologized for the barbarities once inflicted on the Aboriginal peoples. It has been suggested that the president of the United States should apologize for slavery; and so on. Is there any place for some similar act of contrition as a means to reconciliation between Québécois and other Canadians?

In a recent newspaper article on the subject, Monique Jérôme-Forget identifies the Acadian deportations, the Conquest of New France, the quelling of the Rebellions of 1837–8, the assimilation policy of Lord Durham, the exodus of francophones to the United States, the hanging of Louis Riel, the conscription controversies, and the historical domination of the Quebec economy by the English as leading sources of Québécois angst.[24] Of these, it seems to me that the execution of Riel is the only reasonable matter for contrition. Among the events listed, only the Acadian deportations and Riel's execution are even remotely commensurate with American slavery, the historic British mistreatment of Ireland, or Canadian abuse of the Aboriginals. The deportations are a matter that concern the Acadians, however, not the Québécois, and they happened too long ago in any case. Louisiana Cajuns have recently demanded an apology from the British government, but it would be pointless to expect formal contrition by Canadians for an act perpetrated by British authorities nearly a quarter of a millennium ago.[25]

Chronology aside, there are several reasons why the Conquest and its consequences are inappropriate matters for contrition. Firstly, no one outside the French empire can be blamed for the fact that Louis XV's government preferred, at the end of the Seven Years' War, to retain Martinique rather than New France. Secondly, in retrospect, one can argue that the British conquest of New France aided the survival of francophone culture in North America: it is that matter of the six million and the twelve million again. As for the rebellions and Durham's policy, neither was a matter between the French- and English-speaking inhabitants of British North America. English Canadians also rebelled and suffered repression, and some united with francophones to ensure that Durham's policy was abandoned almost before it was implemented. Some English Canadians opposed conscription too, especially during the First World War.

Riel's execution falls into a different category because it epitomizes the culture war that some – though by no means all – English Canadians waged against their francophone compatriots, during the first fifty years of Confederation, in repeated breach of the national compact. Curiously enough, Jérôme-Forget does not include the breach or denial of the compact in her list of historic grievances, but this seems to me to be a topic on which English-Canadian self-criticism can usefully focus. To my mind, the best way to do that is simply to get the story right at last; but this must be a two-sided commitment.

English Canadians are no longer the British North Americans of old, and French Canadians no longer the clericalist conservatives they once were. If the former will make amends for the dogmatic nationalism of the twentieth century, with its ill-disguised contempt for the historic Québécois wish to remain a distinct society, the latter must be ready to teach and learn Canadian history as their own, giving due credit to the positive aspects of the historic relationship between the founding peoples. If Archbishop Tutu is right, nothing less will work.

Notes

Chapter 1. Introduction: 'The Hard Light of History'

1 On the cultural significance of Québécois historiography, see Ramsay Cook, *Canada and the French-Canadian Question* (1966; repr. Toronto, 1986), 119–42, and Cook, *The Maple Leaf Forever: Essays on Nationalism and Politics in Canada,* 2nd ed. (1977; repr. Toronto, 1986), 81–122.

2 Quoted in Guy Laforest, *Trudeau and the End of a Canadian Dream* (Montreal, 1995), 46. Laforest is a leading exponent of the idea of Canadian nationalism as a source of peril to the Québécois nation.

3 See below, 138.

4 Pierre Carignan, quoted in Donald Smiley, *The Canadian Political Nationality* (Toronto, 1968), 29.

5 *Manchester Guardian Weekly*, 4 Jan. 1998, 5.

6 *Journal of Canadian Studies* 1, no. 1 (May 1966).

7 Donald Creighton, *Canada's First Century, 1867–1967* (New York, 1970), 46.

8 Quoted in Carl Berger, *The Writing of Canadian History: Aspects of English-Canadian Historical Writing, 1900 to 1970,* 2nd ed. (Toronto, 1986), 225.

9 F.H. Armstrong, 'William Lyon Mackenzie, First Mayor of Toronto: A Study of a Critic in Power,' *Canadian Historical Review* 48 (1967).

10 Aileen Dunham, *Political Unrest in Upper Canada, 1815–1836* (1927; repr. Toronto, 1963), 18; Gerald M. Craig, *Upper Canada: The Formative Years, 1784–1841* (Toronto, 1963), 241–2.

11 Colin Read and Ronald J. Stagg, ed., *The Rebellion of 1837 in Upper Canada: A Collection of Documents* (Toronto, 1985), xcviii–xcix.

12 C.P. Stacey, *A Very Double Life: The Private World of Mackenzie King* (Toronto, 1976); Joy Esberey, *Knight of the Holy Spirit: A Study of W.L. Mackenzie King* (Toronto, 1980).

13 Creighton, *Canada's First Century*, 268.

14 Arthur R.M. Lower, *Colony to Nation: A History of Canada* (1946; 5th ed., Toronto, 1977), 331–6; Berger, *Writing of Canadian History*, 131–6.

15 See below, 282–3.

16 Lower, *Colony to Nation*, 381–5.

17 Iris Chang, *The Rape of Nanking: A Forgotten Holocaust of World War II* (New York, 1997).

18 Creighton, 'Confederation,' 5.

19 This interpretation of Canadian history is brilliantly stated in George Grant's jeremiad *Lament for a Nation: The Defeat of Canadian Nationalism* (Toronto, 1965).

Chapter 2. Reform versus Loyalism: Two Canadian Myths

1 On Mowat, see *Dictionary of Canadian Biography* (*DCB*), XIII, 724–42, and A. Margaret Evans, *Sir Oliver Mowat* (Toronto, 1992); on McKellar, see *DCB*, XII, 643–5.

2 Joseph Schull, *Edward Blake: The Man of the Other Way, 1833–1881* (Toronto, 1975), 56, 60, 66–8; Evans, *Sir Oliver Mowat*, 62–4.

3 The by-election, and Mowat's speech, were reported in the *Globe* (Toronto), 30 Nov. 1872.

4 On Hincks, see *DCB*, XI, 406–16, and William G. Ormsby, 'Sir Francis Hincks,' in J.M.S. Careless, ed., *The Pre-Confederation Premiers: Ontario Government Leaders, 1841–1867* (Toronto, 1980); on McDougall, see *DCB*, XIII, 632–6; on Brown, see J.M.S. Careless, *Brown of the Globe*, 2 vols. (Toronto, 1959–63).

5 On J.S. Macdonald, see Bruce W. Hodgins, *John Sandfield Macdonald, 1812–1872* (Toronto, 1971), and Hodgins, 'John Sandfield Macdonald,' in Careless, ed., *Pre-Confederation Premiers*.

6 S.F. Wise, *God's Peculiar Peoples: Essays on Political Culture in Nineteenth-Century Canada*, ed. A.B. McKillop and Paul Romney (Ottawa, 1993), 217–18; Evans, *Sir Oliver Mowat*, 348.

7 John Charles Dent, *The Canadian Portrait Gallery*, vol. II (Toronto, 1880), 88; Sir George W. Ross, *Getting into Parliament and After* (Toronto, 1913), 192.

8 On Baldwin, see *DCB*, VIII, 45–59, and J.M.S. Careless, 'Robert Baldwin,' in Careless, ed., *Pre-Confederation Premiers*.

9 See above, 7–8.

10 Jo-Ann Fellows, 'The Loyalist Myth in Canada,' in Canadian Historical Association, *Historical Papers* (1971); Murray Barkley, 'The Loyalist Tradition in New Brunswick,' *Acadiensis* 4 (1974–5); Barkley, 'Prelude to Tradition: The

Loyalist Revival in the Canadas, 1849–1867,' in S.F. Wise et al., *'None Was Ever Better ... ': The Loyalist Settlement of Ontario* ([Cornwall, Ont.], 1984).

11 See above, 14.

Chapter 3. Strangers in Their Own Land

1 Both quoted in David Mills, *The Idea of Loyalty in Upper Canada, 1784–1850* (Montreal, 1988), 23–4. On Rogers, see *DCB*, VI, 655–7.

2 This chapter is based on Paul Romney, *Mr. Attorney: The Attorney General for Ontario in Court, Cabinet and Legislature, 1791–1899* (Toronto, 1986), 83–104, and Romney, 'Re-inventing Upper Canada: American Immigrants, Upper Canadian History, English Law, and the Alien Question,' in Roger Hall et al., ed., *Patterns of the Past: Interpreting Ontario's History* (Toronto, 1988).

3 *DCB*, IX, 668–78; Patrick Brode, *Sir John Beverley Robinson: Bone and Sinew of the Compact* (Toronto, 1984).

4 Francis Collins, *An Abridged View of the Alien Question Unmasked* (York, UC, 1826), 3.

5 *Kingston Chronicle*, 21 Feb. 1823 (Charles Jones).

6 *Report of the Honourable Legislative Council on the Civil Rights of Certain Inhabitants* (York, UC, 1825), 54.

7 E.A. Cruikshank, ed., *The Correspondence of Lieut.-Governor John Graves Simcoe*, 5 vols. (Toronto, 1923–31), vol. I, 108–9, 151–4. See also S.R. Mealing, 'The Enthusiasms of John Graves Simcoe,' in J.K. Johnson, ed., *Historical Essays on Upper Canada* (Toronto, 1975), 312.

8 *Report of the Honourable Legislative Council*, 57; Cruikshank, ed., *Correspondence*, III, 172–3, 237. See also *Kingston Chronicle*, 22 Feb. 1822 (Robinson). Collins, *Abridged View*, 13, credibly names Robinson as having a hand in the legislative council report too.

9 *Kingston Chronicle*, 9 May 1823. On Willson, see *DCB*, VIII, 945–7.

10 *Colonial Advocate* (Toronto), 15 Dec. 1825 (John Clark).

11 'Catharus,' reprinted in ibid., 5 Jan. 1826.

12 *Kingston Chronicle*, 29 March 1822.

13 *Report of the Honourable Legislative Council*, 80.

14 *Kingston Chronicle*, 22 Feb. 1822. On Hagerman, see *DCB*, VII, 365–72, and Wise, *God's Peculiar Peoples*, caps. 4 and 6. Collins, *Abridged View*, 4, accused Hagerman of being 'Catharus,' quoted above (see reference to 'Catharus the political daggerman').

15 Arthur G. Doughty and Norah Storey, ed., *Documents Relating to the Constitutional History of Canada, 1819–1828* (Ottawa, 1935), 7.

16 Craig, *Upper Canada*, 128–9.

17 Doughty and Storey, ed., *Documents*, 303–5.

Chapter 4. A Federal Constitution: Reformers and the Empire

1 On Fothergill, see *DCB*, VII, 317–21; on Matthews, ibid., 496–9.
2 Paul Romney, 'From the Types Riot to the Rebellion: Elite Ideology, Anti-legal Sentiment, Political Violence, and the Rule of Law in Upper Canada,' *Ontario History* 79 (1987).
3 Romney, *Mr. Attorney*, 109–15.
4 Ibid., 121–53; Romney, 'Upper Canada in the 1820s: Criminal Prosecution and the Case of Francis Collins,' in Murray Greenwood and Barry Wright, ed., *Canadian State Trials: Law, Politics and Security Measures, 1608–1837* (Toronto, 1996).
5 Doughty and Storey, ed., *Documents*, 466–77.
6 *Canadian Freeman* (Toronto), 10 July 1828.
7 H.A. Tulloch, 'Changing British Attitudes towards the United States in the 1880s,' *Historical Journal* 20 (1977).
8 Goldwin Smith, *Canada and the Canadian Question* (1891; repr., with intro. by Carl Berger, Toronto, 1971), 129–34, 143, 149; Paul Romney, 'From the Rule of Law to Responsible Government: Ontario Political Culture and the Origins of Canadian Statism,' Canadian Historical Association *Historical Papers* (1988), 113–14; and see below, 188.
9 Helen Taft Manning, *The Revolt of French Canada, 1800–1835* (Toronto, 1962), 151–70; Doughty and Storey, *Documents*, 123–31.
10 Donald Creighton, *The Empire of the St. Lawrence* (Toronto, 1953), 217; Craig, *Upper Canada*, 101–3.
11 *Kingston Chronicle*, 7 and 14 March 1823.
12 Doughty and Storey, *Documents*, 479 (emphasis added).
13 See below, 276.
14 2 vols. (London, 1822), I, 189 (emphasis added). On Gourlay, see *DCB*, IX, 330–6.
15 *DCB*, VI, 54–9; J.E. Rea, 'Barnabas Bidwell: A Note on the American Years,' *Ontario History* 60 (1968); William Renwick Riddell, 'Robert (Fleming) Gourlay,' Ontario Historical Society *Papers and Records* 14 (1916), 34.
16 It is reprinted, with an introduction, in K.D. McRae, 'An Upper Canada Letter of 1829 on Responsible Government,' *Canadian Historical Review* 31 (1950).
17 Dunham, *Political Unrest in Upper Canada*, 154–9.
18 Graeme Patterson, 'Whiggery, Nationality, and the Upper Canadian Reform Tradition,' *Canadian Historical Review* 56 (1975), 35–44.

19 Neil Longley York, *Neither Kingdom nor Nation: The Irish Quest for Constitutional Rights, 1698–1800* (Washington, DC, 1994); Vincent Todd Harlow, *The Founding of the Second British Empire, 1763–1793*, vol. I (London, 1952), 527–57.

20 Jack P. Greene, 'From the Perspective of Law: Context and Legitimacy in the Origins of the American Revolution,' *South Atlantic Quarterly* 85 (1986).

21 *Kingston Chronicle*, 14 March 1823 (supplement), 26 March 1823 (supplement).

22 Canada, Bureau of Archives, *Report on Canadian Archives* (1892), 122.

23 Dunham, *Political Unrest in Upper Canada*, 159; McRae, 'Upper Canada Letter,' 290; W.L. Morton, 'The Local Executive in the British Empire, 1763–1828,' *English Historical Review* 78 (1963), 446. One writer concluded that Bidwell was X on the perversely ingenious ground that Bidwell, as a republican, must have deplored Canadiensis's monarchical prescription and that X's disparaging remarks on the treatise were sincere: see *DCB*, VII, 57, and Patterson, 'Whiggery,' 35–41. More probably Bidwell approved of the treatise, and X's comments (see next chapter) were satirical.

24 McRae, 'Upper Canada Letter,' 293; and see below, 65–6.

Chapter 5. Myths of Responsible Government

1 The fullest account of British policy is Phillip A. Buckner, *The Transition to Responsible Government: British Policy in British North America, 1815–1850* (Westport, Conn., 1986).

2 Romney, *Mr. Attorney*, 105, 139–41, 155.

3 Archibald S. Foord, *His Majesty's Opposition, 1714–1830* (Oxford, 1964), 1; Paul Romney, 'A Conservative Reformer in Upper Canada: Charles Fothergill, Responsible Government and the "British Party," 1824–1840,' Canadian Historical Association *Historical Papers* (1984), 47–8; Doughty and Storey, ed., *Documents*, 481–3.

4 Craig, *Upper Canada*, 14–15; Paul Romney, 'Upper Canada (Ontario): The Administration of Justice, 1784–1900,' in Dale Gibson and W. Wesley Pue, ed., *Canada's Legal Inheritances* (Winnipeg, forthcoming); this essay appears also in *Manitoba Law Journal* 23 (1996), but mistitled. See also Ann Gorman Condon, *The Envy of the American States: The Loyalist Dream for New Brunswick* (Fredericton, 1984), 43–59.

5 Craig, *Upper Canada*, 194–5. On Boulton and Hagerman, see Romney, *Mr. Attorney*, passim, and Robert L. Fraser, ed., *Provincial Justice: Upper Canadian Legal Portraits from the Dictionary of Canadian Biography* (Toronto, 1992), 43–50, 85–99, and passim.

6 McRae, 'Upper Canada Letter,' 291–2 (emphasis added).

7 Metropolitan Toronto Reference Library, William Warren Baldwin Papers, L11 B105, Rolph to Baldwin, 5 May 1829.
8 Craig, *Upper Canada*, 232–40.
9 *DCB*, X, 344.
10 Buckner, *Transition to Responsible Government*, 251–74.
11 Romney, 'Conservative Reformer in Upper Canada,' 58–61.
12 Careless, 'Robert Baldwin,' 89–92; Michael S. Cross and Robert L. Fraser, '"The Waste That Lies Before Me": The Public and Private Worlds of Robert Baldwin,' Canadian Historical Association, *Historical Papers* (1983).
13 Canada, National Archives (hereafter NA), *Report* (1923), 329–37.
14 Ibid., 326–8.
15 Buckner, *Transition to Responsible Government*, 261.
16 Elizabeth Nish, ed., *Debates of the Legislative Assembly of United Canada*, vol. I (Montreal, 1970), 790 (3 Sept. 1841); J.M.S. Careless, *The Union of the Canadas: The Growth of Canadian Institutions, 1841–1857* (Toronto, 1967), 58–126; Careless, 'Robert Baldwin,' 120; Buckner, *Transition to Responsible Government*, 265–74.
17 Nish, ed., *Debates*, 790.
18 *Globe* (Toronto), 25 Sept. 1844.
19 On Sullivan, see *DCB*, VIII, 845–50, and Romney, *Mr. Attorney*, 178–9.
20 Careless, 'Robert Baldwin,' 118–24.
21 Legion (R.B. Sullivan), *Letters on Responsible Government* (Toronto, 1844), 84.
22 *Globe*, 25 Sept. 1844 (emphasis added).
23 Legion, *Letters*, 130.
24 Archives of Ontario (hereafter AO), RG4 A-1, box 4, 10.

Chapter 6. 'One Great Confederation'

1 Careless, *Brown of the Globe*, I, 176–237.
2 John Beverley Robinson, *Canada, and the Canada Bill* (London, 1839), 107–10.
3 Hodgins, *John Sandfield Macdonald*, 36–7.
4 Careless, *Brown of the Globe*, I, 238–80.
5 Ibid. 281–322; see also George W. Brown, 'The Grit Party and the Great Reform Convention of 1859,' *Canadian Historical Review* 16 (1935); Elwood H. Jones, 'Ephemeral Compromise: The Great Reform Convention Revisited,' *Journal of Canadian Studies* 3 (1968). The *Globe* published the proceedings in six numbers: 10–16 Nov. 1859.
6 *Globe*, 14 Nov. (McDougall), 15 Nov. (McBain, Nickerson), 16 Nov. (Brown).
7 Ibid., 11 Nov.
8 Quoted in Brown, 'Grit Party,' 245.

9 *Globe*, 15 Nov. On Lesslie, see *DCB*, XI, 516–19.

10 *Globe*, 15 Nov.

11 Careless, *Brown of the Globe*, I, 313; *The National Cyclopaedia of American Biography*, XIII, 109–10.

12 For Brown in particular, see *Globe*, 11 and 16 Nov.

13 Ibid., 11 and 12 Nov.

14 Ibid., 12 Nov. (Foley), 14 Nov. (Wylie, Johnston), 15 Nov. (D.A. Macdonald, McBain), 16 Nov. (Brown).

15 Ibid., 14 Nov.

16 Careless, *Brown of the Globe*, I, 322–5; Jones, 'Ephemeral Compromise,' 25–7.

17 *Globe*, 16 Nov.

18 Careless, *Brown of the Globe*, I, 257, 283–5. On Galt, see *DCB*, XII, 348–56.

19 *Globe*, 11 Nov. (Wilkes, Sheppard), 12 Nov. (McNaughton).

20 Ibid., 14 Nov. (Christie), 15 Nov. (Connor), 16 Nov. (Brown).

21 L.F.S. Upton, 'The Idea of Confederation, 1754–1858,' in W.L. Morton, ed., *The Shield of Achilles: Aspects of Canada in the Victorian Age* (Toronto, 1968); J.L.H. Henderson, ed. *John Strachan: Documents and Opinions* (Toronto, 1969), 165–70; Peter J. Smith, 'The Ideological Origins of Canadian Confederation,' *Canadian Journal of Political Science* 20 (1987), 17–25; Romney, 'Conservative Reformer in Upper Canada,' 55.

22 On Christie and Connor, see *DCB*, X, 168–71, and IX, 151; on Wilkes, see *Globe*, 11 Nov., and Brown, 'Grit Party,' 254, 265.

Chapter 7. Confederation: The Untold Story

1 I recount the rise of the centralist interpretation in chapter 11.

2 All quoted in F.R. Scott, *Essays on the Constitution: Aspects of Canadian Law and Politics* (Toronto, 1977), 5–7.

3 Coles quoted in ibid., 22; *Parliamentary Debates on the Subject of the Confederation of the British North American Provinces* (Quebec, 1865), 176 (Olivier); 250 (Dorion); 1002 (Macdonald).

4 *Globe*, 1 Aug., 8 Aug., 17 Sept., and 4 Oct. 1864.

5 G.P. Browne, ed., *Documents on the Confederation of British North America* (Toronto, 1969), 113–15. See also Careless, *Brown of the Globe*, II, 167–9.

6 J.C. Morrison, 'Sir Oliver Mowat and the Development of Provincial Rights in Ontario,' in *Three History Theses* (Toronto, 1961), 6; and see above, 9.

7 *Globe*, 15 Nov. 1859 (emphasis added). See also ibid., 11 Nov. (Burr).

8 Careless, *Brown of the Globe*, I, 257, 283–5; II, 61–135; Hodgins, *John Sandfield Macdonald*, 45–74; Ged Martin, *Britain and the Origins of Canadian Confederation, 1837–1867* (Basingstoke, 1995), 47–55.

9   Ibid., 1 Aug. 1864.

10 Ibid., 30 Aug. 1864; see also 3 Sept., 16 Sept., and 21 Sept. 1864.

11 Ibid., 4 Oct. 1864.

12 See, among others, the speeches of Antoine and Eric Dorion, Louis-August Olivier, Henri Joly, and Joseph Perrault.

13 Legion, *Letters on Responsible Government*, 128; Careless, *Union of the Canadas*, 82, 123–6.

14 *Globe*, 4 July 1887; Christopher Armstrong, *The Politics of Federalism: Ontario's Relations with the Federal Government, 1867–1942* (Toronto, 1981), 25–30.

15 *Debates on ... Confederation*, 258.

16 Donald Creighton, *Dominion of the North: A History of Canada* (1944; rev. ed., Toronto, 1957), 253–62, 306.

17 *Globe*, 17 Sept. 1864.

18 Browne, ed., *Documents*, 123.

19 *Globe*, 10 and 25 Nov. 1864.

20 Browne, *Documents*, 120.

21 Ibid., 42, 81–3, 122–5; John Hamilton Gray, *Confederation; or, the Political and Parliamentary History of Canada, from the Conference at Quebec, in October, 1864, to the Admission of British Columbia, in July, 1871*, vol. I (Toronto, 1872), 44–5, 55–7.

22 Creighton, *Dominion of the North*, 311.

23 Browne, *Documents*, 157–61 (emphasis added).

24 *Debates on ... Confederation*, 33, 41; *Debates and Proceedings of the House of Assembly, ... of the Province of Nova Scotia, 1865* (Halifax, NS, 1865), 207.

25 *Debates on ... Confederation*, 404 (Rose), 807 (Walsh).

26 Ibid., 221–4, 237–41, 256–60.

27 Donald Creighton, *The Road to Confederation: The Emergence of Canada, 1863–1867* (Boston, 1965), 418–19; Andrée Desilets, *Hector Louis Langevin: un père de la confédération canadienne (1826–1906)* (Quebec, 1969), 164–7. See also Alfred D. DeCelles, 'Sir Georges Étienne Cartier,' in DeCelles, *Papineau, Cartier*, rev. by W.L. Grant, The Makers of Canada Series, vol. 5 (London, 1926), 102–3.

28 Browne, *Documents*, 275, 293, 326; W.P.M. Kennedy, *The Constitution of Canada: An Introduction to Its Development and Law* (Oxford, 1922), 437–9.

29 *Report Pursuant to Resolution of the Senate ... Relating to the Enactment of the British North America Act, 1867* (Ottawa, 1939) (hereafter O'Connor Report), annex 1, 47; Scott, *Essays on the Constitution*, 35–48.

30 This is certainly what Brown, for one, had in mind: Browne, ed., *Documents*, 123.

31 *Globe*, 28 June 1867.

32 Careless, *Brown of the Globe*, II, 187–239.

33 Ibid., 239–47; on Patrick, see *DCB*, XI, 676–7.

34 *Globe*, 28 June 1867; on Morrison, see *DCB*, VIII, 642–4.

35 *Globe*, 28 June 1867 (Circular of invitation, Brown [2nd and 3rd speeches], Blake, Irving); ibid., 29 June (Crooks, Pardee).

36 Ibid., 28 June (Brown [3rd speech]).

37 Ibid.; Careless, *Brown of the Globe*, II, 199–203. On Belleau, see *DCB*, XII, 86–7.

38 *Globe*, 28 June (Brown [3rd and 4th speeches], A. Mackenzie, Spohn, Gillespie, Gordon).

39 Ibid.

40 Ibid. (Brown [4th speech], A. Mackenzie).

Chapter 8. *Je me souviens*: The Great Fight for Responsible Government, Part III

1 On Mowat as premier, see Evans, *Sir Oliver Mowat*, and *DCB*, XIII, 724–42.

2 D.G. Creighton, *John A. Macdonald: The Old Chieftain* (Toronto, 1955), 129–79.

3 On Mackenzie as prime minister, see Dale C. Thomson, *Alexander Mackenzie, Clear Grit* (Toronto, 1960), and *DCB*, XII, 647–59.

4 Sir Richard Cartwright, *Reminiscences* (Toronto, 1912), 169.

5 Paul Romney, 'The Nature and Scope of Political Autonomy: Oliver Mowat, the Quebec Resolutions, and the Construction of the British North America Act,' *Canadian Journal of Political Science* 25 (1992), 17–28.

6 John T. Saywell, *The Office of Lieutenant-Governor: A Study in Canadian Government and Politics* (Toronto, 1957), 3–18.

7 Romney, *Mr. Attorney*, 274–81.

8 *Globe*, 4 July 1887, 4.

9 W.E. Hodgins, comp., *Correspondence, Reports of the Ministers of Justice, and Orders in Council upon the Subject of Dominion and Provincial Legislation, 1867–1895* (Ottawa, 1896), 171–7; Jamie Benedickson, 'Private Rights and Public Purposes in the Lakes, Rivers and Streams of Ontario, 1870–1930,' in David H. Flaherty, ed., *Essays in the History of Canadian Law*, vol. II (Toronto, 1983), 371–4.

10 Romney, *Mr. Attorney*, 274–8; Romney, 'Nature and Scope of Provincial Autonomy,' 17–18, 21–2.

11 Peter B. Waite, *Canada 1874–1896: Arduous Destiny* (Toronto, 1971), 7, 40–2; Robert C. Vipond, *Liberty and Community: Canadian Federalism and the Failure of the Constitution* (Albany, NY, 1991), 119–23.

12 Hodgins, *Correspondence*, 179–85; Alpheus Todd, *Parliamentary Government in the British Colonies* (Boston, 1880), 359; and see *Globe*, 17–31 Jan. 1882, for commentary on the controversy and reports of the legislative debate. On Todd see *DCB*, XI, 883–5.

13 *Globe*, 28 Jan. 1882, 8; ibid., 16 Dec. 1882, 13.

14 Armstrong, *Politics of Federalism*, 14–21.
15 *Globe*, 28 Jan. 1882, 15.
16 Ibid., 31 Jan. 1882, 4.
17 *Reform Government in Ontario: The Benefits It Has Conferred upon the People. Two Speeches by the Hon. Oliver Mowat* (Toronto, 1879), 5, 48.
18 *Ontario Elections, 1883. Pamphlet No. 1: Legislative and Territorial Rights* (Toronto, 1883), 16.
19 *Globe*, 4 Jan. 1883, 9.
20 *Toronto Mail*, 3 Jan, 1883, 4.
21 *Ontario Elections, 1883. Pamphlet No. 1*, 1. This pamphlet included, in addition to editorial matter, long excerpts from the leading speeches at the convention. These were reported in full in *Globe*, 4 and 5 Jan., 1883.
22 Evans, *Sir Oliver Mowat*, 162–3; R. MacGregor Dawson, 'The Gerrymander of 1882,' *Canadian Journal of Economics and Political Science* 1 (1935).
23 *Globe*, 27 Jan. 1882, 5. On Ross, see *DCB*, XIV, 888–95.
24 *Globe*, 4 Jan. 1883, 9.
25 Ibid., 1, 10.
26 *Ontario Elections, 1883. Pamphlet No. 1*, 8–9.
27 Ross, *Getting into Parliament and After*, 188; NA, MG 26A (Sir John A. Macdonald Papers), vol. 395, 189744–7 (Robinson to Macdonald, 22 Aug. 1883).
28 *Globe*, 10 March 1883, 8.
29 Evans, *Sir Oliver Mowat*, 169–73, 179–80.
30 AO, Archibald Campbell Papers, Macdonald to Campbell, 18 Dec. 1888.
31 *Globe*, 16 Sept. 1884, 8.
32 Ibid., 17 Sept. 1884, 9–11. I describe the proceedings as far as possible in the *Globe*'s language, including the long series of headlines to its report.

Chapter 9. Peoples and Pacts

1 Quoted in Fred Landon, *Western Ontario and the American Frontier* (1941; repr. Toronto, 1967), 232.
2 John Kenneth Galbraith, *The Scotch* (Toronto, 1964), 68.
3 James Bryce, *Modern Democracies*, 2 vols. (London, 1921), I, 528; Smith, *Canada and the Canadian Question*, 140. Bryce based his remarks on Canada on personal observations made before 1914.
4 There is an excellent account of Ontario Reform ideology in B.P.N. Beaven, 'A Last Hurrah: Studies in Liberal Party Development and Ideology in Ontario, 1878–1893' (PhD thesis, University of Toronto, 1981).
5 Mills, *Idea of Loyalty in Upper Canada*.

6 Ibid., 132–9.
7 See also Gordon Stewart, 'John A. Macdonald's Greatest Triumph,' *Canadian Historical Review* 63 (1982), 21.
8 *Brockville Recorder*, 23 June 1864.
9 *Globe*, 17 Jan. 1882, 5.
10 Ibid., 27 Jan. 1882, 5; Careless, *Brown of the Globe*, I, 43.
11 *Globe*, 4 Jan. 1883, 9–10.
12 Careless, *Union of the Canadas*, 127–31.
13 John Charles Dent, *The Story of the Upper Canadian Rebellion*, 2 vols. (Toronto, 1885), I, 249; and see above, 58.
14 Beaven, 'Last Hurrah,' 353, 361.
15 *Evening Journal* (St Catharines), 22 Oct. 1864; ibid., 21 Jan. 1865.
16 See above, 80, 86.
17 *Toronto Mail*, 10 March 1885, 8.
18 *Globe*, 17 Sept. 1884, 10; *DCB*, XIII, 726.
19 *Toronto Mail*, 10 March 1885, 8, 11 March 1885, 4; *Globe*, 10 March 1885, 3, 11 March 1885, 4.
20 See above, 23.
21 *Parliamentary Guide, 1885*, 199–200.
22 See above, 63.
23 See above, 71.
24 'Fifty Years Ago Today' (1st part), *Globe*, 3 Dec. 1887, 9; (2nd part), 10 Dec. 1887, 9.
25 The story was serialized on successive Saturdays, 10 December 1887 to 14 January 1888. Riddell appears as a surgeon in the Toronto city directories for 1859–60 and 1861–2; in the two preceding ones, dating from 1856 and 1850, there appears a printer called A.A. (Archibald Alexander) Riddell. Riddell is not mentioned in the *Literary History of Canada*.
26 Toronto was so called in the *Porcupine*, a satirical broadsheet published there in 1836: Paul Romney, 'A Struggle for Authority: Toronto Society and Politics in 1834,' in Victor L. Russell, ed., *Forging a Consensus: Historical Essays on Toronto* (Toronto, 1984), 17–18.
27 *DCB*, XIII, 724–42; Evans, *Sir Oliver Mowat*; Margaret A. Banks, *Edward Blake, Irish Nationalist: A Canadian Statesman in Irish Politics, 1892–1907* (Toronto, 1957). On Home Rule, see Vipond, *Liberty and Community*, 83–107.
28 On Norquay, see *DCB*, XI, 642–7; on Mercier, see *DCB*, XIII, 719–28.
29 A.I. Silver, *The French-Canadian Idea of Confederation, 1864–1900* (Toronto, 1982), 67–87, 153–79. On Riel, see especially *DCB*, XI, 736–51, and Douglas Owram, 'The Myth of Louis Riel,' *Canadian Historical Review* 63 (1982).
30 Armstrong, *Politics of Federalism*, 27–30.

31 Silver, *French-Canadian Idea of Confederation*, 119–21; Romney, *Mr. Attorney*, 252–4.
32 T.J.J. Loranger, *Letters upon the Interpretation of the Federal Constitution Known as the British North America Act, 1867. First Letter* (Quebec, 1884), *Second and Third Letters* (Montreal, 1885). On Loranger, see *DCB*, XI, 529–31.
33 Cook, *Canada and the French-Canadian Question*, 48–9, 194–5.
34 Silver, *French-Canadian Idea of Confederation*, 38.
35 Loranger, *Letters*, 7–9; Paul Romney, 'Why Lord Watson Was Right,' in Janet Ajzenstat, ed., *Canadian Constitutionalism, 1791–1991* (Ottawa, 1993), 185–7.
36 Canada, Bureau of Archives, *Report on Canadian Archives* (1897), Note A, 24–7; W.P.M. Kennedy, ed., *Documents of the Canadian Constitution, 1759–1915* (Toronto, 1918), 332–3.
37 Kennedy, *Documents*, 378 (resolution no. 53).
38 Richard Risk and Robert C. Vipond, 'Rights Talk in Canada in the Late Nineteenth Century: "The Good Sense and Right Feeling of the People,"' *Law and History Review* 14 (1996), 5–11.
39 McRae, 'Upper Canada Letter,' 294; and see above, 50–1.
40 Loranger, *Letters*, 40–1 (emphasis added).
41 Ramsay Cook, *Provincial Autonomy, Minority Rights and the Compact Theory* (Ottawa, 1969), 30; Cook, *Canada and the French-Canadian Question*, 49; and see above, 48–9.
42 See below, 172.

Chapter 10. Amending the Constitution

1 See above, 121.
2 Ferguson's letter and memorandum were published in the *Globe* on 20 November 1930. They are reprinted in Robert MacGregor Dawson, ed., *Constitutional Issues in Canada, 1900–1931* (London, 1933), 28–34. On the background, see Paul Gérin-Lajoie, *Constitutional Amendment in Canada* (Toronto, 1950), 96–9.
3 Dawson, *Constitutional Issues in Canada*, 14–22.
4 Ibid., 15.
5 Saywell, *Office of Lieutenant-Governor*, 9–19; Romney, 'Nature and Scope of Provincial Autonomy,' 3–4.
6 Gérin-Lajoie, *Constitutional Amendment in Canada*, 50–60, 74–6, 139–41; Dawson, *Constitutional Issues in Canada*, 10–14.
7 See above, 121.
8 Romney, *Mr. Attorney*, 248–59; James G. Snell and Frederick Vaughan, *The Supreme Court of Canada: History of the Institution* (Toronto, 1985), 11–16.

9 Romney, 'Nature and Scope of Provincial Autonomy,' 23–5; Romney, *Mr. Attorney*, 264–74, 278; and see below, 178–9.

10 Sir George Ross, *The Senate of Canada: Its Constitution, Powers and Duties Historically Considered* (Toronto, 1914), 109–19.

11 Peter Oliver, *G. Howard Ferguson: Ontario Tory* (Toronto, 1977), 170–89, 292–307, 352–6; Armstrong, *Politics of Federalism*, 100–11, 128–32, 160–77.

12 See below, 170–1, 182–3.

13 Dawson, *Constitutional Issues in Canada*, 14–22.

14 *Manitoba Free Press* (Winnipeg), 5 Jan. 1927, 11; Ramsay Cook, *The Politics of John W. Dafoe and the Free Press* (Toronto, 1963), 214–23; Doug Owram, *The Government Generation: Canadian Intellectuals and the State, 1900–1945* (Toronto, 1986), 182; Armstrong, *Politics of Federalism*, 143.

15 N. McL. Rogers, 'The Compact Theory of Confederation,' *Papers and Proceedings of the Annual Meeting of the Canadian Political Science Association* 3 (1931), 208–9.

16 Ibid., 220–1.

17 Ibid., 216–17.

18 See above, 87–8, 98.

19 Silver, *French-Canadian Idea of Confederation*, 33–50; see especially 44–6.

20 *Canadian Bar Review* 9 (1931); Dawson, *Constitutional Issues in Canada*, 34–45; O'Connor Report, annex 4, 139–48.

21 See the works cited in Gérin-Lajoie, *Constitutional Amendment in Canada*, 205–6.

Chapter 11. Centralist Revolution

1 A helpful general survey is Alan C. Cairns, 'The Judicial Committee and Its Critics,' *Canadian Journal of Political Science* 4 (1971).

2 Romney, 'Why Lord Watson Was Right,' 185–9.

3 See above, 121.

4 Romney, *Mr. Attorney*, 259–74.

5 24 *Supreme Court Reports*, 229.

6 Paul Craven, *'An Impartial Umpire': Industrial Relations and the Canadian State, 1900–1911* (Toronto, 1980), 271–88; R. MacGregor Dawson, *William Lyon Mackenzie King: A Political Biography, 1874–1923* (Toronto, 1958), 133–5.

7 Haldane's judgment is printed in *Decisions of the Judicial Committee of the Privy Council Relating to the British North America Act, 1867, and the Canadian Constitution, 1867–1954*, 3 vols. (Ottawa, 1954), II, 394–412.

8 Creighton, *Dominion of the North*, 467. See also W.P.M. Kennedy, 'Law and Custom in the Canadian Constitution,' *Round Table* 20 (1929–30), 151;

Kennedy, 'The British North America Act: Past and Future,' *Canadian Bar Review* 15 (1937), 398–9; Scott, *Essays on the Constitution*, 263, 342–3; Bora Laskin, '"Peace, Order and Good Government" Re-Examined,' *Canadian Bar Review* 25 (1947); Cook, *Politics of John W. Dafoe*, 217–18.

9 H.A. Smith, 'The Residue of Power in Canada,' *Canadian Bar Review* 4 (1926).

10 Craven, *Impartial Umpire*, 264–70; Dawson, *William Lyon Mackenzie King*, 133–5.

11 On this last point see Peter H. Russell, ed., *Leading Constitutional Decisions: Cases on the British North America Act* (Toronto, 1965), 38.

12 Scott, *Essays on the Constitution*, 35.

13 Kennedy contributed a 'Historical Introduction' to Lefroy's *A Short Treatise on Canadian Constitutional Law* (Toronto, 1918); and see Kennedy, *Constitution of Canada*, x. On Lefroy see R.C.B. Risk, 'Constitutional Scholarship in the Late Nineteenth Century: Making Federalism Work,' *University of Toronto Law Journal* 46 (1996). Risk kindly let me read his work-in-progress on Kennedy.

14 Kennedy, *Constitution of Canada*, 422; Kennedy, 'Law and Custom in the Canadian Constitution,' 145–53; and see A.R.M. Lower, 'Theories of Canadian Federalism – Yesterday and Today,' in Lower et al., *Evolving Canadian Federalism* (Durham, NC, 1958), 39. Kennedy's centralism reaches a climax in his 'The Interpretation of the British North America Act,' *Cambridge Law Journal* 8 (1943). Scott's growing centralism can be traced in his *Essays on the Constitution*, a compilation of his writings.

15 See above, 100–1.

16 A.H.F. Lefroy, 'The Federal Constitution,' in Adam Shortt and Arthur G. Doughty, ed., *Canada and Its Provinces*, vol. VI (Toronto, 1914), 229, 232; Lefroy, 'A Century of Constitutional Development upon the North American Continent,' *Canada Law Journal* 42 (1906), 467; Lefroy, *Short Treatise on Canadian Constitutional Law*, 74–5.

17 *The Federation of Canada* (Toronto, 1917), 24, 89–90; Romney, *Mr. Attorney*, 252, 254.

18 Kennedy, *Constitution of Canada*, 439.

19 Smith, 'Residue of Power in Canada'; Kennedy, 'Law and Custom in the Canadian Constitution,' 146–7.

20 'The Development of Canadian Federalism,' in Scott, *Essays on the Constitution*, 35–41; see also 24–5, 98, 187–8. A rare brush with error occurs in an article of 1951, in which he says: 'The residue of unallocated subjects is centralized by the opening words of section 91, thus contrasting sharply with the principle underlying the American constitution': ibid., 256.

21 Scott, *Essays on the Constitution*, 90.

22 Ibid., 268–70. The case was *In re Regulation and Control of Radio Communication in Canada.*

23 *Decisions of the Judicial Committee,* 180–206.

24 Scott, *Essays on the Constitution,* 90–101, 183–5; Kennedy, 'British North America Act: Past and Future,' 397; Kennedy, 'Interpretation of the British North America Act,' 157–9; Creighton, *Dominion of the North,* 497–9; Cairns, 'Judicial Committee and Its Critics,' 311.

25 Larry A. Glassford, *Reaction and Reform: The Politics of the Conservative Party under R.B. Bennett, 1927–1938* (Toronto, 1992), 160–1.

26 Owram, *Government Generation,* 221–42; Cook, *Politics of John W. Dafoe,* 223–9; Donald Creighton, *British North America at Confederation: A Study Prepared for the Royal Commission on Dominion–Provincial Relations* (Ottawa, 1939).

27 Canada, Royal Commission on Dominion–Provincial Relations, *Report,* book I: *Canada: 1867–1939* (n.p., n.d.), 31–6; Scott, *Essays on the Constitution,* 264; see also Cook, *Politics of John W. Dafoe,* 227.

28 Robert Craig Brown and Ramsay Cook, *Canada, 1896–1921: A Nation Transformed* (Toronto, 1974), 213–14, 324; F. Murray Greenwood, 'The Drafting and Passage of the War Measures Act in 1914 and 1927: Object Lessons in the Need for Vigilance,' in W. Wesley Pue and Barry Wright, ed., *Canadian Perspectives on Law and Society: Issues in Legal History* (Ottawa, 1988), 293–4.

29 O'Connor Report, Annex 1, 39–50 (quotation at 47).

30 Scott, *Essays on the Constitution,* 185; see also ibid., 25.

31 Kennedy, 'Law and Custom in the Canadian Constitution,' 150.

32 See above, 85–6.

33 Norman McL. Rogers, 'The Genesis of Provincial Rights,' *Canadian Historical Review* 14 (1933).

34 Owram, *Government Generation,* 150. Presumably this was R.M. Dawson's paper, cited above, 302 n. 22.

35 Rogers and Scott presented their papers at a session on federal–provincial relations.

36 See above, 157–60.

37 Vipond, *Liberty and Community,* 29–30.

38 V. Evan Gray, '"The O'Connor Report" on the British North America Act, 1867,' *Canadian Bar Review* 17 (1939).

39 When I presented it in *Mr. Attorney.*

40 C.R.W. Biggar's book, *Sir Oliver Mowat, Q.C., LL.D., G.C.M.G., P.C.: A Biographical Sketch,* 2 vols. (Toronto, 1905), is cited on 325, 326, 334, and 335 of Gray's review.

41 Gray, '"The O'Connor Report,"' 333–4.

42 Nova Scotia, *Report of the Royal Commission Provincial Economic Inquiry* (Halifax, 1934), 156, 225.

43 University of Toronto Archives, Department of Political Economy Papers, accession no. A76–0025, box 5, Lower to Innis, 26 Jan. 1935; Queen's University Archives, Lower Papers, box 7, Innis to Lower, 2 Feb. 1935.

44 Harold A. Innis, *Staples, Markets, and Cultural Change: Selected Essays*, ed. Daniel Drache (Toronto, 1995), 443–4.

45 Ibid., 280–1.

46 Donald Creighton, *Harold Adams Innis: Portrait of a Scholar* (Toronto, 1957); *Who's Who in Canada* (1949–50), 436. I am grateful to the Archives of the Law Society of Upper Canada for supplying the latter reference.

47 NA, James R. Gowan Papers (MG27, I E17 A1), Gwynne to Gowan, 21 Dec. 1873. On Gwynne, see Paul Romney, 'From Railway Construction to Constitutional Construction: John Wellington Gwynne's National Dream,' *Manitoba Law Journal* 20 (1991), and *DCB*, XIII, 426–9. The following pages are based on those articles and Romney, 'Why Lord Watson Was Right.'

48 Gowan Papers, Gwynne to Gowan, 24 Dec. 1889.

49 Romney, 'Nature and Scope of Provincial Autonomy,' 24.

50 4 *Supreme Court Reports*, 346.

51 Richard Arès, *Dossier sur le Pacte fédératif de 1867. La Confédération: pacte ou loi?* (Montreal, 1967), 31–2.

52 5 *Supreme Court Reports*, 566 (emphasis added).

53 Arès, *Dossier sur le Pacte fédératif*, 22.

Chapter 12. Continentalism, Imperialism, Nationalism

1 On Blake and Mills, see R.C.B. Risk, 'Blake and Liberty,' in Ajzenstat, *Canadian Constitutionalism*, and Vipond, *Liberty and Community*.

2 See above, 134–5.

3 *DCB*, XIII, 737–41; Evans, *Sir Oliver Mowat*, 327–35; Carman Miller, 'Mowat, Laurier, and the Federal Liberal Party, 1887–1897,' in Donald Swainson, ed., *Oliver Mowat's Ontario* (Toronto, 1972); Robert Craig Brown, *Canada's National Policy, 1883–1900: A Study in Canadian–American Relations* (Princeton, NJ, 1964), 249–80.

4 Evans, *Sir Oliver Mowat*, 296–326; S.E.D. Shortt, 'Social Change and Political Crisis in Rural Ontario: The Patrons of Industry, 1889–1896,' in Swainson, *Oliver Mowat's Ontario*; James T. Watt, 'Anti-Catholicism in Ontario Politics: The Role of the Protestant Protective Association,' *Canadian Historical Review* 49 (1967); Janet B. Kerr, 'Sir Oliver Mowat and the Campaign of 1894,' *Ontario History* 55 (1963).

5 Ben Forster, *A Conjunction of Interests: Business, Politics, and Tariffs, 1825–1879* (Toronto, 1986), 33–80; Brown, *Canada's National Policy,* 125–249; Evans, *Sir Oliver Mowat,* 289–92.

6 Frank H. Underhill, *In Search of Canadian Liberalism* (Toronto, 1960), 85–103; Elisabeth Wallace, *Goldwin Smith, Victorian Liberal* (Toronto, 1958); *DCB,* XIII, 968–74.

7 Carl Berger, *The Sense of Power: Studies in the Ideas of Canadian Imperialism, 1867–1914* (Toronto, 1970), 49–77.

8 It appeared in the *Fortnightly Review,* no. 124 (1 April, 1877).

9 J.R. Miller, *Equal Rights: The Jesuits' Estates Act Controversy* (Montreal, 1979); Silver, *French-Canadian Idea of Confederation,* 150–217.

10 Berger, *Sense of Power*; Robert J.D. Page, 'Canada and the Imperial Idea in the Boer War Years,' *Journal of Canadian Studies,* 5 (1970); Allan Smith, *Canada – An American Nation? Essays on Continentalism, Identity, and the Canadian Frame of Mind* (Montreal, 1994), 359–89.

11 (London and New York, 1892).

12 Ibid., 15–18.

13 Ibid., 7–9, 124–6.

14 Biggar, *Sir Oliver Mowat,* II, 586–628.

15 Parkin, *Imperial Federation,* 29.

16 Ibid., 139–46; James A. Colvin, 'Sir Wilfrid Laurier and the British Preferential Tariff System,' Canadian Historical Association, *Report* (1955).

17 Parkin, *Imperial Federation,* 153–62.

18 Fellows, 'Loyalist Myth in Canada'; Barkley, 'Loyalist Tradition in New Brunswick'; Barkley, 'Prelude to Tradition.'

19 Parkin, *Imperial Federation,* 127–33.

20 Underhill, *In Search of Canadian Liberalism,* 103.

21 The fullest and most valuable study of Ewart's life and thought is Douglas Lowell Cole, 'The Better Patriot: John S. Ewart and the Canadian Nation,' PhD thesis, University of Washington, 1968. See also D.M.L. Farr, 'John S. Ewart,' in Robert L. McDougall, ed., *Our Living Tradition,* 2nd and 3rd series (Toronto, 1959), and Careless, *Brown of the Globe,* I, 56, 68.

22 J.K. Johnson, ed., *The Canadian Directory of Parliament, 1867–1967* (Ottawa, 1968), 53; Richard A. Willie, *'These Legal Gentlemen': Lawyers in Manitoba, 1839–1900* ([Winnipeg] 1994), 157; and see above, 80–1.

23 Paul Crunican, *Priests and Politicians: Manitoba Schools and the Election of 1896* (Toronto, 1974); W.L. Morton, *Manitoba: A History,* 2nd ed. (Toronto, 1967), 121–272; Cole, 'Better Patriot,' 43–97.

24 Quoted in Cole, 'Better Patriot,' 339.

25 Parkin, *Imperial Federation,* 134–5.

26 Cole, 'Better Patriot,' 138–9; Carl Berger, *Sense of Power*, 147–51; Page, 'Canada and the Imperial Idea,' 38–9. On McCarthy, see also *DCB*, XII, 578–87.

27 John S. Ewart, *The Kingdom Papers*, 2 vols. (Ottawa, 1912–17), I, 1–22 (quotations, 3 and 22).

28 Brown and Cook, *Canada 1896–1921*, 162–87.

29 Ewart, *Kingdom Papers*, I, 1–11, 32–48, 61–92; John S. Ewart, *The Kingdom of Canada, Imperial Federation, The Colonial Conferences, The Alaska Boundary, and Other Essays* (Toronto, 1908), 299–347.

30 Ewart, *Kingdom of Canada*, 115–35.

31 *Debates on ... Confederation*, 50.

Chapter 13. English Canada Forgets

1 Frank H. Underhill, 'The Political Ideas of John S. Ewart,' Canadian Historical Association *Report* (1933); Underhill, *In Search of Canadian Liberalism*, 85–103. On Ewart's influence on Underhill, see R. Douglas Francis, *Frank H. Underhill: Intellectual Provocateur* (Toronto, 1986), 58. One of Underhill's students, Prof. David Spring of the Johns Hopkins University, recalls Underhill's esteem for Ewart (pers. comm.).

2 Ewart, *Kingdom of Canada*, 225–46; Ewart, *An Imperial Court of Appeal or the Abolition of All Overseas Appeals* (Ottawa, 1919); Ewart, 'Judicial Appeals to the Privy Council: The Case for Discontinuing Appeals,' *Queen's Quarterly* 37 (1930); F.R. Scott, 'The Privy Council and Minority Rights,' ibid.

3 Canadian Political Science Association, *Papers and Proceedings*, 3 (1931), 205–58.

4 See above, 137.

5 John S. Ewart, *The Manitoba School Question* (Toronto, 1894), 311–91; Ewart, *The Manitoba School Question: A Reply to Mr. Wade* (Winnipeg, 1895).

6 John S. Ewart, 'Some Further Comments on Dominion–Provincial Relations,' Canadian Political Science Association *Papers and Proceedings* 3 (1931) 252; John S. Ewart, *The Independence Papers*, 2 vols. (Ottawa, 1925–32), II, 174; and see above, 157–60, 171.

7 John S. Ewart, 'The Judicial Committee: The Bonanza Creek Gold Mining Company v. the King,' *Canadian Law Times* 36 (1916), 679–98, 769–76; Ewart, 'Some Further Comments on Dominion–Provincial Relations,' 254–6; Scott, *Essays on the Constitution*, 267.

8 John S. Ewart, 'The Canadian Constitution,' *Columbia Law Review* 8 (1908), 27–36 (quotation on 28).

9 Vipond, *Liberty and Community*; Barry Ferguson, *Remaking Liberalism: The Intellectual Legacy of Adam Shortt, O.D. Skelton, W.C. Clark, and W.A. Mackintosh, 1890–1925* (Montreal, 1993); Owram, *Government Generation*.

10 Cole, 'Better Patriot,' 218–70.

11 Ibid., 306–7.

12 Charles W. Humphries, *'Honest Enough to Be Bold': The Life and Times of Sir James Pliny Whitney* (Toronto, 1985), 183–90, 201–4; Morton, *Manitoba* 351–4.

13 Cole, 'Better Patriot,' 291–6; Farr, 'John S. Ewart,' 190–1, 201; John S. Ewart, *The Roots and Causes of the Wars (1914–1918)*, 2 vols. (New York, 1925); Ewart, *Independence Papers*, vol. I.

14 *Review of Historical Publications Relating to Canada* 18 (1913), 1–10; Robert Bothwell, *Laying the Foundation: A Century of History at the University of Toronto* (Toronto, 1991), 56–7.

15 W.L. Grant, 'Mr. J.S. Ewart's View of Canadian History,' *Queen's Quarterly* 21 (1913–14), 473–85 (quotation, 475).

16 Cole, 'Better Patriot,' 159–64; John S. Ewart, 'Professor Grant's View of John S. Ewart,' *Queen's Quarterly* 21 (1913–14); Underhill, 'Political Ideas of John S. Ewart,' 23–4.

17 Cole, 'Better Patriot,' 347–8.

18 Ibid., 326, 330, 353–4.

19 Ibid., 231–8; Silver, *French-Canadian Idea of Confederation*, 191–4; and see above, 192, 195. Bourassa's thought is extensively treated in Mason Wade, *The French Canadians, 1760–1967*, rev. ed., 2 vols. (Toronto, 1968).

20 5 *Supreme Court Reports*, 567.

21 Scott, 'Privy Council and Minority Rights'; Scott, *Essays on the Constitution*, 14–17.

22 Oliver, *G. Howard Ferguson*, 39–50, 283–5.

23 Ibid., 3–7.

24 Arès, *Dossier sur le Pacte fédératif*, 49–122.

25 See above, 147–8.

26 *The Liquor Prohibition Appeal, 1895. An Appeal from the Supreme Court of Canada to Her Majesty the Queen in Council* (London, 1895), 160; R.C.B. Risk, 'Canadian Courts under the Influence,' *University of Toronto Law Journal* 40 (1987), 733; and see above, 166–7, 178–9.

27 See above, 156.

28 Morton J. Horwitz, *The Transformation of American Law, 1870–1960: The Crisis of Legal Orthodoxy* (New York, 1992).

29 Arès, *Dossier sur le Pacte fédératif*, 99 n. 22.

30 The report was published in both French and English. A convenient abridgment with a useful introduction is *The Tremblay Report: Report of the Royal Commission of Inquiry on Constitutional Problems*, ed. David Kwavnick (Toronto, 1973).
31 See above, 187.
32 Duplessis has been written about at even greater length than John A. Macdonald. See Robert Rumilly, *Maurice Duplessis et son temps*, 2 vols. (Montreal, 1973), and Conrad Black, *Duplessis* (Toronto, 1977).
33 Arès, *Dossier sur le Pacte fédératif*, 107.

Chapter 14. The New Canadian Nationalism

1 Article by Michael Barkway in *Foreign Affairs* 36 (1957–8).
2 *Canadian Historical Review* 29 (1948); reprinted in Donald Creighton, *Towards the Discovery of Canada: Selected Essays* (Toronto, 1972).
3 Bothwell, *Laying the Foundation*, 89, 102–3, 120–1, 133–5; Francis, *Frank H. Underhill*, 160 and passim.
4 Berger, *Writing of Canadian History*, 32–7, 41–2, 59–67.
5 On Creighton's attitude to Lower, see Charles Taylor, *Radical Tories: The Conservative Tradition in Canada* (Toronto, 1982), 24, and Donald A. Wright, 'Donald Creighton and the French Fact,' *Journal of the Canadian Historical Association* n.s. 6 (1996), 246, n. 9.
6 Creighton, *Towards the Discovery of Canada*, 204–9 (quotation, 205).
7 Grant had quarrelled with Underhill too on the subject: Francis, *Frank H. Underhill*, 93.
8 Creighton, *Towards the Discovery of Canada*, 7, 201; Taylor, *Radical Tories*, 33–4.
9 Underhill, *In Search of Canadian Liberalism*, 135–6, 222–6, 257.
10 Francis, *Frank H. Underhill*; Berger, *Writing of Canadian History*, 61–7.
11 Harold A. Innis, *The Fur Trade in Canada: An Introduction to Canadian Economic History* (1930; American edn. New Haven, Conn., 1962), 386–92; Berger, *Writing of Canadian History*, 94–8.
12 (Toronto, 1937); Berger, *Writing of Canadian History*, 211–14.
13 Ibid., 383–4.
14 Creighton, *Towards the Discovery of Canada*, 199.
15 Berger, *Writing of Canadian History*, 117–24, 163–8.
16 D.G. Creighton, 'Conservatism and National Unity,' in R. Flenley, ed., *Essays in Canadian History* (Toronto, 1939), 157.
17 Grant, *Lament for a Nation*, 24.
18 Creighton, *Towards the Discovery of Canada*, 243–55.
19 Ibid., 4, 8–9.

20 D.G. Creighton, 'Sir John A. Macdonald,' in Claude T. Bissell, ed., *Our Living Tradition: Seven Canadians* (Toronto, 1957).
21 Robert Bothwell, Ian Drummond, and John English, *Canada since 1945: Power, Politics, and Provincialism*, rev. ed. (Toronto, 1989), 37–145 passim.
22 See Bothwell et al., *Canada since 1945*, and J.L. Granatstein, *Canada, 1957–1967: The Years of Uncertainty and Innovation* (Toronto, 1986). On Diefenbaker in particular, see Denis Smith, *Rogue Tory: The Life and Legend of John G. Diefenbaker* (Toronto, 1995).
23 Grant, *Lament for a Nation*, 25.
24 Ibid., 3–5, 23; William Christian, *George Grant: A Biography* (Toronto, 1993).
25 Grant, *Lament for a Nation*, 25–36.
26 Ibid., 33; see also 12–24.
27 Ibid., 37–52.
28 Ibid., 9–10, 33–4, 41–2, 47, 69–70.
29 Ibid., 14, 46, 71.
30 Ibid., 47–52 (quotation, 47).
31 Ibid., 38; Terry Cook, 'The Canadian Conservative Tradition: An Historical Perspective,' *Journal of Canadian Studies* 8, no. 4 (1973).
32 Grant, *Lament for a Nation*, 53–87 (quotation, 68).
33 Creighton, *Commercial Empire of the St. Lawrence*, 364–5.
34 Grant, *Lament for a Nation*, 58–9.
35 Louis Hartz et al., *The Founding of New Societies: Studies in the History of the United States, Latin America, South Africa, Canada, and Australia* (New York, 1964).
36 Lower, *Colony to Nation*, 115–19.
37 Gad Horowitz, 'Conservatism, Liberalism, and Socialism in Canada: An Interpretation,' *Canadian Journal of Economics and Political Science* 32 (1966), 144–50.
38 Horowitz, 'Conservatism, Liberalism, and Socialism in Canada,' 147–50, 156–9.
39 Ibid., 144, 171.
40 Gad Horowitz, 'Tories, Socialists and the Decline of Canada,' *Canadian Dimension* (May–June 1965), and 'On the Fear of Nationalism,' ibid. (May–June 1967), both reprinted in H.D. Forbes, ed., *Canadian Political Thought* (Toronto, 1985).
41 Forbes, ed., *Canadian Political Thought*, 359, 352.
42 Christian, *George Grant*, 259.
43 Creighton, *Canada's First Century*, 350–6; Berger, *Writing of Canadian History*, 235–7.
44 Creighton, *Canada's First Century*, 355.

Chapter 15. Canadian Nationalists and the Quiet Revolution

1 W.L. Morton, *Contexts of Canada's Past: Selected Essays of W.L. Morton*, ed. A.B. McKillop (Toronto, 1980), 103–12. On Morton generally, see Berger, *Writing of Canadian History*, 238–58, and Taylor, *Radical Tories*, 49–76.

2 Creighton, *Towards the Discovery of Canada*, 240–2, 264; Creighton, *John A. Macdonald: The Old Chieftain*, 534.

3 Jean-C. Falardeau, 'Les Canadiens français et leur idéologie,' in Mason Wade, ed., *Canadian Dualism: Studies of French-English Relations* (Toronto, 1960), 25–6.

4 Jean Beetz, 'Les attitudes changeantes du Québec à l'endroit de la Constitution de 1867,' in P.-A. Crépeau and C.B. Macpherson, ed., *The Future of Canadian Federalism* (Toronto, 1965), 120; Peter H. Russell, *The Supreme Court of Canada as a Bilingual and Bicultural Institution* (Ottawa, 1969), 37–8.

5 Pierre Vallières, *White Niggers of America: The Precocious Autobiography of a Quebec 'Terrorist'* (New York, 1971). The French title is *Nègres blancs d'Amérique*.

6 Granatstein, *Canada, 1957–1967*, 243–70.

7 Horowitz, 'Tories, Socialists, and the Demise of Canada,' 359.

8 Creighton, *Towards the Discovery of Canada*, 65.

9 Creighton, *Road to Confederation*.

10 Kenneth McRoberts, *Misconceiving Canada: The Struggle for National Unity* (Toronto, 1997), 40; Granatstein, *Canada, 1957–1967*, 255; Creighton, *Towards the Discovery of Canada*, 11–12, 82, 241.

11 Creighton, *Towards the Discovery of Canada*, 65–83, 294–5.

12 Reprinted in ibid., 256–70.

13 Ibid., 263–4.

14 Ibid., 82, 229–42, 268–70.

15 Ibid., 293–305.

16 Cook, *Canada and the French-Canadian Question*, 168–89; Solange Chaput Rolland, *My Country, Canada or Quebec?* foreword by W.L. Morton (Toronto, 1966), xi; Creighton, *Towards the Discovery of Canada*, 12, 14; Wright, 'Donald Creighton and the French Fact,' 259–63.

17 Ralph Heintzman, 'The Spirit of Confederation: Professor Creighton, Biculturalism, and the Use of History,' *Canadian Historical Review* 52 (1971); D.J. Hall, '"The Spirit of Confederation": Ralph Heintzman, Professor Creighton, and the Bicultural Compact Theory,' *Journal of Canadian Studies* 9, no. 4 (1974); Wright, 'Donald Creighton and the French Fact,' 263–5. I am grateful to Don Wright for sharing his research with me.

18 Wright, 'Donald Creighton and the French Fact,' 266; Creighton, *Towards the Discovery of Canada*, 293.

19 See, generally, Creighton, *Towards the Discovery of Canada*, 229–42; Morton, *Contexts of Canada's Past*, 208–28; Heintzman, 'Spirit of Confederation'; Hall, 'Spirit of Confederation.'

20 See above, 140–3.

21 Quoted in Heintzman, 'Spirit of Confederation,' 263.

22 Ibid., 264–7 (quotation, 267); Vipond, *Liberty and Community*, 93–6.

23 Cook, *Canada and the French-Canadian Question*, 185.

24 Book review, *Canadian Historical Review* 37 (1956), 367.

25 W.L. Morton, *The Canadian Identity* (1961; 2nd ed., Toronto, 1971), is his fullest statement of the meaning of Canadian history. On Dafoe see 72 and 127.

26 Ibid., 40.

27 Ibid., 111; see also 106.

28 W.L. Morton, 'The Conservative Principle in Confederation,' *Queen's Quarterly* 71 (1964–5), 536; Morton, *Contexts of Canada's Past*, 208–10.

29 See above, 46–7.

30 W.L. Morton, 'Confederation, 1870–1896: The End of the Macdonaldian Constitution and the Return to Duality,' *Journal of Canadian Studies* 1, no. 1 (1966), 11, 23 n. 1.

31 W.L. Morton, 'Quebec – Federation or Association?' *Centennial Review* 10 (1966), 469 and passim.

32 Morton, 'Confederation, 1870–1896.'

33 Morton, *Contexts of Canada's Past*, 263–4; Morton, 'Conservative Principle in Confederation,' 528; Taylor, *Radical Tories*, 69.

34 Morton, 'Quebec – Federation or Association?' (quotation, 470); Desmond Morton, *NDP: The Dream of Power* (Toronto, 1974), 78.

35 See above, 14, 96, 101.

36 Morton, 'Confederation, 1870–1896,' 22.

37 Morton, *Contexts of Canada's Past*, 254–65.

38 Morton, 'Quebec – Federation or Association?' 463; see also Morton, *Canadian Identity*, 117.

39 Morton, *Contexts of Canada's Past*, 254–65; Morton, 'Quebec – Federation or Association?' 474–6; Morton, *Canadian Identity*, 146.

40 Taylor, *Radical Tories*, 69.

41 Morton, *Manitoba: A History*, title of chapter 9.

42 Ibid., 247, 420; W.L. Morton, *The Kingdom of Canada: A General History from Earliest Times* (Toronto, 1963), 399; W.L. Morton, ed., *Alexander Begg's Red River Journal and Other Papers Relative to the Red River Resistance of 1869–1870* (Toronto, 1956).

43 See above, 207–9.
44 W.L. Morton, 'The West and the Nation, 1870–1970,' in A.W. Rasporich and H.C. Klassen, ed., *Prairie Perspectives 2: Selected Papers of the Western Canadian Studies Conferences, 1970, 1971* (Toronto, 1973), 9.
45 Sandra Djwa, *The Politics of the Imagination: A Life of F.R. Scott* (Toronto, 1987), 22–4.
46 (Toronto, 1969), vii–viii.
47 G.F.G. Stanley, 'Act or Pact? Another Look at Confederation,' Canadian Historical Association, *Report* (1956); reprinted in *Confederation*, intro. Ramsay Cook (Toronto, 1967). On Arès and the Tremblay Report, see above, 211–12. The story is told by S.F. Wise, who was present.

Chapter 16. A Historic Blunder: Trudeau and Patriation

1 'Marchand, Jean,' and 'Pelletier, Gérard,' *Canadian Encyclopedia*, 2nd ed.; Pierre Elliott Trudeau, *Federalism and the French Canadians* (New York, 1968), 124–50; Djwa, *Politics of the Imagination*, 236, 318–37. On Trudeau, see in particular Stephen Clarkson and Christina McCall, *Trudeau and Our Times*, vol. I (Toronto, 1990), and Laforest, *Trudeau and the End of a Canadian Dream*.
2 McRoberts, *Misconceiving Canada*, 78–146; Peter H. Russell, *Constitutional Odyssey: Can Canadians Become a Sovereign People?*, 2nd ed. (Toronto, 1993), 72–91; *The Amendment of the Constitution of Canada* (Ottawa, 1965), vii–viii.
3 Bothwell et al., *Canada since 1945*, 359–87; Russell, *Constitutional Odyssey*, 92–106.
4 Russell, *Constitutional Odyssey*, 107–12.
5 Gérin-Lajoie, *Constitutional Amendment in Canada*, 242; see above, 147–60.
6 Ibid., xiii–xxi, 155–9; L. St Laurent, 'Presidential Address,' *Canadian Bar Review* 9 (1931). The amendment also excepted those provisions of the BNA Act that called for an annual sitting of Parliament and limited the life of a Parliament to five years.
7 See above, 155.
8 Gérin-Lajoie, *Constitutional Amendment in Canada*, vii, ix–x, 212–17; Scott, *Essays on the Constitution*, 178–80; 'Gérin-Lajoie, Paul,' in *Canadian Encyclopedia*, 2nd ed.
9 Ibid., 167.
10 *Amendment of the Constitution of Canada*, 1–18.
11 Gérin-Lajoie, *Constitutional Amendment in Canada*, vii, 212–13; Ivan C. Rand, 'Some Aspects of Canadian Constitutionalism,' *Canadian Bar Review* 38 (1960), 144.
12 *Dominion Law Reports* 125, 3rd series (hereafter DLR), 54–8 (quotation 58).
13 Ibid., 43–7 (quotation, 47); see also ibid., 126.

14 The first two were O'Sullivan (Manitoba) and Bisson (Quebec); the third, Huband (Manitoba); the others were Martland and Ritchie (Supreme Court of Canada) and the bench of the Newfoundland Court of Appeal.
15 Ibid., 44–5.
16 DLR 117, 55, 70.
17 Ibid., 18–19; DLR 125, 120–1.
18 DLR 117, 19–21; DLR 125, 122–5.
19 DLR 125, 120.
20 Ibid., 79–107.
21 Norman McL. Rogers, 'Mr. Ferguson and the Constitution,' *Canadian Forum* 11 (Nov. 1930), 47–9.
22 W.R. Lederman, *Continuing Canadian Constitutional Dilemmas* (Toronto, 1981), 81–106 (quotation, 99).
23 DLR 117, 51.
24 Ibid., 48.
25 Ibid., 50–4 (quotations, 53–4).
26 Ibid., 56–63.
27 DLR 120, 455–62.
28 Peter H. Russell, 'The Supreme Court Decision: Bold Statescraft [*sic*] Based on Questionable Jurisprudence,' in Russell et al., *The Courts and the Constitution: Comments on the Supreme Court Reference on Constitutional Amendment* (Kingston, Ont., 1982).
29 DLR 140, 385–404 (quotation, 386); Russell, *Constitutional Odyssey*, 107–26.

Chapter 17. Conclusion: Getting It Wrong, Putting It Right

1 Lower, *Colony to Nation* (title of chapter 23); and see above, 251.
2 Ewart, *Kingdom of Canada,* 115–20; W.P.M. Kennedy, 'Theories of Law and the Constitutional Law of the British Empire,' in Kennedy, *Some Aspects of the Theories and Workings of Constitutional Law.*
3 Dunham, *Political Unrest in Upper Canada,* 157–9; Doughty and Storey, ed., *Documents,* 479; Morton, 'Colonial Executive in the British Empire.' Morton had studied at Oxford under Vincent Harlow, a leading historian of the British empire: Berger, *Writing of Canadian History,* 239.
4 See, for example, Upton, 'Idea of Confederation, 1754–1858.'
5 Arthur Lower, 'Ontario – Does It Exist?' *Ontario History* 60 (1968), 66–7; Lower, *Colony to Nation,* 381–5; Creighton, *Canada's First Century,* 46–9.
6 J.M.S. Careless, '"Limited Identities" in Canada,' *Canadian Historical Review* 50 (1969); Ramsay Cook, 'Canadian Centennial Cerebrations,' *International Journal* 22 (1967), 663; Cook, *Maple Leaf Forever,* 123–47, 188–205.
7 'Editors' Introduction,' in Wise, *God's Peculiar Peoples,* xii–xviii; Stephen

Eggleston, 'The Myth and Mystery of POgG,' *Journal of Canadian Studies* 31 (1996) On the historical trend in question, see Michael Bliss, 'Privatizing the Mind: The Sundering of Canadian History, the Sundering of Canada,' ibid., 26 (1991–2), and Berger, *Writing of Canadian History*, 259–320.

8 Lower, *Colony to Nation*, 383; R.C.B. Risk, 'Canadian Courts Under the Influence,' *University of Toronto Law Journal* 40 (1990), 719.

9 Lower, *Colony to Nation*, 382; Romney, *Mr. Attorney*, 248–50, 252; Romney, 'Nature and Scope of Provincial Autonomy,' 21.

10 Armstrong, *Politics of Federalism*, 241, 243 n. 1. The thesis was J.C. Morrison's 'Oliver Mowat and the Development of Provincial Rights in Ontario.'

11 Cook, *Provincial Autonomy, Minority Rights and the Compact Theory*, 1–4.

12 Peter H. Russell, ed., *Leading Constitutional Decisions*, 3rd ed. (Ottawa, 1982), 8, 12–13; Cairns, 'Judicial Committee and its Critics,' 319, 323; Romney, 'Nature and Scope of Provincial Autonomy,' 4–6.

13 (Toronto, 1968), 22–6.

14 Ibid., 28–31; Raymond Barbeau, *J'ai choisi l'Indépendance* (Montreal, 1961), 81–2.

15 Cook, 'Canadian Centennial Cerebrations,' 661.

16 Laforest, *Trudeau and the End of a Canadian Dream*, 15–55; Donald Smiley, 'A Dangerous Deed: The Constitution Act, 1982,' in Keith Banting and Richard Simeon, ed., *And No One Cheered: Federalism, Democracy and the Constitution Act* (Toronto, 1983), 76; and see above, 4. Laforest described himself as 'somewhat sovereigntist' in a talk at the School of Advanced International Studies in Washington, DC, in October 1997.

17 Bissonette said so in a talk at the School of Advanced International Studies, Washington, DC, October 1995.

18 See above, 93–4.

19 On the possibilities and problems of asymmetrical federalism, see David Milne, 'Equality or Asymmetry: Why Choose?' in Ronald L. Watts and Douglas M. Brown, ed., *Options for a New Canada* (Toronto, 1991).

20 Alan C. Cairns, 'Constitutional Change and the Three Equalities,' in ibid.; Smiley, *Canadian Political Nationality*, 102–4.

21 Michael Ignatieff, *Blood and Belonging: Journeys into the New Nationalism* (New York, 1994), 157; Marc Chevrier, *Canadian Federalism and the Autonomy of Quebec: A Historical Viewpoint* (Quebec, 1996), 7.

22 See above, 76, 80.

23 John Ralston Saul, *Reflections of a Siamese Twin: Canada at the End of the Twentieth Century* (Toronto, 1997).

24 'Looking to the Past for National Unity Solutions,' *Financial Post*, 13 Sept. 1997.

25 *Manchester Guardian Weekly*, 15 Feb. 1998, 7.

Index

on, 258. *See also* Creighton; Ewart;
Lower; Macdonald, John A.;
Morton
Charlottetown agreement (1992), 284
Charlottetown conference (1864), 87,
90, 94, 99
Charlton, John, 119
charter of rights: favoured by Morton,
252, 254; Trudeau and, 259, 260–1,
263, 266, 285
Christie, David, 85–6
Clark, S.D., 221
Clear Grits, 85–6, 219
Coles, George, 89–90
Collins, Francis, 44, 58
Colonial Laws Validity Act, 147
compact: idea of, 49
compact theory of Confederation,
4–6, 125, 137–43, 147–60, 169, 238,
275, 276, 278, 285–7, 290; ambiguity
of, 4, 150–3, 157–8, 181–2, 212, 283;
antecedents of, 4, 6 (*see also* Constitutional Act: compact theory of);
centralist version of, 208, 255–6,
257, 259–60 (*see also* Confederation:
centralist idea of); first statement
of, 152; in *Patriation References*, 269,
275
– advocates of: Richard Arès, 211;
Howard Ferguson, 147–50, 156,
157, 158, 209–11, 263–4; T.-J.-J. Loranger, 137, 142–3, 179, 208, 211,
282; George Ross, 155, 156, 264;
Donald Smiley, 282–4; George
Stanley, 256–7, 282
– critics of: Raymond Barbeau, 283–4;
Pierre Carignan, 284; Ramsay
Cook, 282, 283; Donald Creighton,
7, 242–8, 283; J.W. Dafoe, 157, 172,
181; J.S. Ewart, 201, 203, 204, 207–8;

Eugene Forsey, 283; Paul Gérin-
Lajoie, 265–6; William McDougall,
179–80, 208; W.L. Morton, 255–6;
W.F. O'Connor, 171, 201; Norman
Rogers, 157–60, 161, 172, 174, 179,
181–2, 200, 201, 263–4, 283; Louis St
Laurent, 264–5
Confederation: centralist idea of,
11–12, 17, 136, 157–81, 241, 265–72,
278–9 (*see also* compact theory: centralist version of); French Canadians and, 11, 137, 238, 277, 278, 289
(*see also* Cartier; duality, cultural;
Loranger); historical treatment
of, 11–12, 88, 90, 157–60, 168–9,
172–80, 181–2, 278–82 (*see also*
Creighton; Morton); John A. Macdonald and, 24, 87, 93, 148, 157,
210; as means to provincial autonomy, 42, 57, 93, 98, 102, 104–5, 114,
136, 137, 138, 147–8, 172, 173, 267,
268–72, 279 (*see also* Union of 1841:
Confederation as partial dissolution of; Union of 1841: federaliza-
tion of); Mowat on, 24–5, 28, 30, 87,
97, 127; nation-building conception
of, 15, 89, 221–2; Reformers and,
90–8, 102–8, 109, 159, 275, 279. *See
also* constitution, imperial: as model for Confederation
Connor, Skeffington, 86
conscription: as political issue, 136,
203, 237, 290
Conservative party: origin of, 29; in
Quebec, 135, 136
Conservative tradition: historical
treatment of, 15–17, 231–2, 281. *See
also* loyalism; Loyalists
Conservatives: and provincial rights,
209–11

centralist, 176–7; on Canadian history, 219–20
Insurance Case, 113, 154, 162, 164, 175, 178
Interprovincial Conference (1887), 135, 155

Jérôme-Forget, Monique, 290–1
Judicial Committee of the Privy Council. *See* Privy Council

Kennedy, W.P.M., 217, 249, 279; on residuary power, 167, 168, 172
King, W.L. Mackenzie, 157, 164, 170, 236; on constitutional amendment, 270; Creighton on, 11, 218, 235; George Grant on, 228, 229, 234; historical treatment of, 11, 12, 15, 16; Underhill on, 218–19
King's College (Toronto), 39, 40, 47
Kylie, Edward, 204, 205, 218

Labour Conventions Case, 169–70
LaFontaine, Louis-Hippolyte, 26, 62, 65, 75
Laforest, Guy, 284, 293 n. 1; 318 n. 16
Langevin, Hector-Louis, 101
Lapointe, Ernest, 150, 156, 270
Lash, Zebulon, 168
Laurendeau, André, 242
Laurier, Wilfrid, 155, 182, 195, 198, 219, 221, 247; Morton on, 252; and tariff policy, 184, 191, 196–7
lawyers and history. *See* history
Lederman, William R., 271–2, 283
Lefroy, A.H.F., 167, 168
legal realism, 211
legislative powers, division of, 156, 286–7; in British empire, 55, 66; in Confederation, 55–6, 100–2, 162–7;

169–70, 263; discussed at 1859 convention, 82–4; in provincial rights controversy, 111, 121, 154, 162–4, 178–9. *See also* residuary legislative power
legislative supremacy, British: denied by Baldwins, 49, 53–5, 65, 68; evaded by Robert Baldwin, 63–5; invoked by centralists, 157–8, 159, 269, 273; as obstacle to responsible government, 47, 57, 60; recognized by Mowat, 25. *See also* sovereignty, colonial
– Canadian: invoked by centralists, 250, 264, 267
– provincial: as basis of provincial autonomy, 265–7. *See also Hodge v. The Queen*
Lemieux Act (Industrial Disputes Investigation Act), 164–7, 210
Lesage, Jean, 239–41, 259, 260
Lesslie, James, 81, 82, 84–5
Letter on Responsible Government. *See* Responsible Government, Letter on (1829)
Lévesque, René, 240–1, 258, 259, 261
Liberal party: origin of, 29; in Quebec, 238, 239, 262, 276
Liberal Conservative party, 86; origin of, 27, 76
Liberal tradition. *See* Reform (Liberal) tradition
liberalism, transformation of, 202–3, 206, 211
London Resolutions, 162, 172, 173, 202; and compact theory, 157–9, 171, 201, 212; and residuary power, 100, 101, 165, 167
Loranger, T.-J.-J., 137, 142–3, 179, 208, 211, 282

Rogers, Norman, 170, 171, 212, 271; on compact theory, 157–60, 161, 179, 181–2, 200, 201, 263–4, 283; as historian, 158–9, 172, 173, 174

Rolph, John, 27, 43, 44, 59, 60–1, 63

Ross, George, 118, 124, 129; on compact theory, 155, 156, 264, 265, 266; on Mowat, 25, 120

rouges, 77, 78, 79, 92, 107, 138

Rowell–Sirois Commission, 170, 175, 216, 269

rule of law: as basis of compact theory, 140–1, 246–8; as constitutional principle, 134, 182, 195, 250, 267, 285; in Upper Canada, 43–4

Russell, Lord John, 62, 64, 67

Russell v. The Queen, 121, 154, 163–4, 165, 171, 281; as centralist ideal, 166, 168, 172, 178

Ryan, Claude, 244, 248

Ryan, Peter, 127

Ryerson, Egerton, 67

Rymal, Joseph, 118, 119

St Laurent, Louis, 223, 234, 264–5; on constitutional amendment, 264–5, 266, 267, 268, 269, 283

Saul, John Ralston, 289

schools, as political issue: in Ontario, 77, 184, 203, 209, 246; in Quebec, 246, 261. *See also* Manitoba: school question in; New Brunswick: school question in

Scott, Frank R., 200, 212, 256, 257, 268; and Canadian history, 173, 174, 205; on constitutional amendment, 263–4, 265–6, 267; on division of powers, 167, 168, 202; influence of, on Pierre Trudeau, 258; on protection of minorities, 208–9, 255; on

provincial autonomy, 172; on Rowell–Sirois Commission, 170, 175

Scott Act (Canada Temperance Act), 110, 121. *See also Prohibition Reference*; *Russell v. The Queen*

Sedgewick, Joseph, 179

Sheppard, George, 79, 82–4, 85

Sicotte, Louis-Victor, 92

Silver, Arthur, 282

Simcoe, John Graves, 33, 34, 36, 37, 59

Skelton, Oscar, 218, 236

Smiley, Donald, 282–4

Smith, Goldwin, 79, 132, 183, 190, 198, 200, 212; on Canadian nationality, 186–9; Creighton on, 216; Parkin on, 191–2, 192–3, 218; quoted, 124, 205; Underhill on, 193, 200; on U.S. and Canadian constitutions, 46–7, 188

Smith, Herbert, 165–7, 168, 172

socialism in Canada, 230, 232, 234

sovereignty: colonial, 157–8, 159, 180; colonial, Baldwins' insistence on, 48, 49, 50, 51, 273; implicit in responsible government, 47–8, 159, 273–5; shift in meaning of, 267; symbols of, 90, 93–4, 98, 111. *See also* legislative supremacy; provinces, status of

special status: of French Canadians, 4, 208, 262–3. *See also* Quebec: constitutional status of

Stanley, George, 256–7, 282, 283

Statute of Westminster, 149, 199, 200, 203, 206, 267, 274; as constitutional precedent, 266, 270

Strachan, John, 86, 193

Sullivan, Robert Baldwin, 66–8, 95, 104

Supreme Court of Canada, 194, 195,